Conflict and Cooperation in Sino-US Relations

Numerous crosswinds are buffeting the more than 40-year-old People's Republic of China–American relationship, yet only once since Nixon's historic trip to China in 1972 has a major conflagration seemed a real possibility. Anchoring the relationship throughout multiple storms are the two countries' broad areas of collaboration such as deep links in culture, economics, and education. However, for some observers, the conflictual aspects of the relationship seem to be gaining prominence.

Conflict and Cooperation in Sino-US Relations offers a timely and current look at one of the world's weightiest bilateral relationships. It goes beyond detailing the conflict and cooperation that have been integral facets of China–US interactions since 1972, to gauging the relationship's evolution and future trends, examining its nuances regarding diverse issues such as the Asia-Pacific leadership structure, the South China Sea, and the Korean peninsula. The book further delves into the causes of conflict and cooperation, offers diverse solutions for tempering frictions between Beijing and Washington, and considers the efficacy of some of the mechanisms (e.g., military-to-military exchanges) that China and the US currently employ to manage their relationship. The chapters suggest that extreme anxieties about China–US relations may be misplaced, but that there nonetheless are some worrisome signs even in areas like economics and the environment that are perceived as naturally cooperative. While the book does not offer any silver bullets, various contributors contend that successful management of Sino-American relations may require greater American accommodation of China's interests.

This book will be of great interest to students and scholars of Chinese politics, American politics, international relations, and Asian studies, as well as to policy-makers working in the field.

Jean-Marc F. Blanchard is Assistant Dean and Professor, School of International and Public Affairs, Shanghai Jiaotong University, China, and Executive Director, the Mr. & Mrs. S.H. Wong Center for the Study of Multinational Corporations, USA.

Simon Shen is Associate Professor and Director of Global Studies Programme in the Chinese University of Hong Kong.

Routledge contemporary China series

1 **Nationalism, Democracy and National Integration in China**
   Leong Liew and Wang Shaoguang

2 **Hong Kong's Tortuous Democratization**
   A comparative analysis
   Ming Sing

3 **China's Business Reforms**
   Institutional challenges in a globalised economy
   Edited by Russell Smyth, On Kit Tam, Malcolm Warner and Cherrie Zhu

4 **Challenges for China's Development**
   An enterprise perspective
   Edited by David H. Brown and Alasdair MacBean

5 **New Crime in China**
   Public order and human rights
   Ron Keith and Zhiqiu Lin

6 **Non-Governmental Organizations in Contemporary China**
   Paving the way to civil society?
   Qiusha Ma

7 **Globalization and the Chinese City**
   Fulong Wu

8 **The Politics of China's Accession to the World Trade Organization**
   The dragon goes global
   Hui Feng

9 **Narrating China**
   Jia Pingwa and his fictional world
   Yiyan Wang

10 **Sex, Science and Morality in China**
    Joanne McMillan

11 **Politics in China Since 1949**
    Legitimizing authoritarian rule
    Robert Weatherley

12 **International Human Resource Management in Chinese Multinationals**
    Jie Shen and Vincent Edwards

13 **Unemployment in China**
    Economy, human resources and labour markets
    Edited by Grace Lee and Malcolm Warner

14 **China and Africa**
Engagement and compromise
Ian Taylor

15 **Gender and Education in China**
Gender discourses and women's schooling in the early twentieth century
Paul J. Bailey

16 **SARS**
Reception and interpretation in three Chinese cities
Edited by Deborah Davis and Helen Siu

17 **Human Security and the Chinese State**
Historical transformations and the modern quest for sovereignty
Robert E. Bedeski

18 **Gender and Work in Urban China**
Women workers of the unlucky generation
Liu Jieyu

19 **China's State Enterprise Reform**
From Marx to the market
John Hassard, Jackie Sheehan, Meixiang Zhou, Jane Terpstra-Tong and Jonathan Morris

20 **Cultural Heritage Management in China**
Preserving the cities of the Pearl River Delta
Edited by Hilary du Cros and Yok-shiu F. Lee

21 **Paying for Progress**
Public finance, human welfare and inequality in China
Edited by Vivienne Shue and Christine Wong

22 **China's Foreign Trade Policy**
The new constituencies
Edited by Ka Zeng

23 **Hong Kong, China**
Learning to belong to a nation
Gordon Mathews, Tai-lok Lui, and Eric Kit-wai Ma

24 **China Turns to Multilateralism**
Foreign policy and regional security
Edited by Guoguang Wu and Helen Lansdowne

25 **Tourism and Tibetan Culture in Transition**
A place called Shangrila
Åshild Kolås

26 **China's Emerging Cities**
The making of new urbanism
Edited by Fulong Wu

27 **China–US Relations Transformed**
Perceptions and strategic interactions
Edited by Suisheng Zhao

28 **The Chinese Party-State in the 21st Century**
Adaptation and the reinvention of legitimacy
Edited by André Laliberté and Marc Lanteigne

29 **Political Change in Macao**
Sonny Shiu-Hing Lo

30 **China's Energy Geopolitics**
The Shanghai Cooperation Organization and Central Asia
Thrassy N. Marketos

31 **Regime Legitimacy in Contemporary China**
Institutional change and stability
Edited by Thomas Heberer and Gunter Schubert

32 **US–China Relations**
China policy on Capitol Hill
Tao Xie

33 **Chinese Kinship**
Contemporary anthropological perspectives
Edited by Susanne Brandtstädter and Gonçalo D. Santos

34 **Politics and Government in Hong Kong**
Crisis under Chinese sovereignty
Edited by Ming Sing

35 **Rethinking Chinese Popular Culture**
Cannibalizations of the canon
Edited by Carlos Rojas and Eileen Cheng-yin Chow

36 **Institutional Balancing in the Asia Pacific**
Economic interdependence and China's rise
Kai He

37 **Rent Seeking in China**
Edited by Tak-Wing Ngo and Yongping Wu

38 **China, Xinjiang and Central Asia**
History, transition and crossborder interaction into the 21st century
Edited by Colin Mackerras and Michael Clarke

39 **Intellectual Property Rights in China**
Politics of piracy, trade and protection
Gordon Cheung

40 **Developing China**
Land, politics and social conditions
George C.S. Lin

41 **State and Society Responses to Social Welfare Needs in China**
Serving the people
Edited by Jonathan Schwartz and Shawn Shieh

42 **Gay and Lesbian Subculture in Urban China**
Loretta Wing Wah Ho

43 **The Politics of Heritage Tourism in China**
A view from Lijiang
Xiaobo Su and Peggy Teo

44 **Suicide and Justice**
A Chinese perspective
Wu Fei

45 **Management Training and Development in China**
Educating managers in a globalized economy
Edited by Malcolm Warner and Keith Goodall

46 **Patron–Client Politics and Elections in Hong Kong**
Bruce Kam-kwan Kwong

47 **Chinese Family Business and the Equal Inheritance System**
Unravelling the myth
Victor Zheng

48 **Reconciling State, Market and Civil Society in China**
The long march towards prosperity
Paolo Urio

49 **Innovation in China**
The Chinese software industry
Shang-Ling Jui

50 **Mobility, Migration and the Chinese Scientific Research System**
Koen Jonkers

51 **Chinese Film Stars**
Edited by Mary Farquhar and Yingjin Zhang

52 **Chinese Male Homosexualities**
Memba, *Tongzhi* and Golden Boy
Travis S.K. Kong

53 **Industrialisation and Rural Livelihoods in China**
Agricultural processing in Sichuan
Susanne Lingohr-Wolf

54 **Law, Policy and Practice on China's Periphery**
Selective adaptation and institutional capacity
Pitman B. Potter

55 **China–Africa Development Relations**
Edited by Christopher M. Dent

56 **Neoliberalism and Culture in China and Hong Kong**
The countdown of time
Hai Ren

57 **China's Higher Education Reform and Internationalisation**
Edited by Janette Ryan

58 **Law, Wealth and Power in China**
Commercial law reforms in context
Edited by John Garrick

59 **Religion in Contemporary China**
Revitalization and innovation
Edited by Adam Yuet Chau

60 **Consumer-Citizens of China**
The role of foreign brands in the imagined future china
Kelly Tian and Lily Dong

61 **The Chinese Communist Party and China's Capitalist Revolution**
The political impact of the market
Lance L.P. Gore

62 **China's Homeless Generation**
Voices from the veterans of the Chinese civil war, 1940s–1990s
Joshua Fan

63 **In Search of China's Development Model**
Beyond the Beijing consensus
Edited by S. Philip Hsu, Suisheng Zhao and Yu-Shan Wu

64 **Xinjiang and China's Rise in Central Asia, 1949–2009**
A history
Michael E. Clarke

65 **Trade Unions in China**
The challenge of labour unrest
Tim Pringle

66 **China's Changing Workplace**
Dynamism, diversity and disparity
Edited by Peter Sheldon, Sunghoon Kim, Yiqiong Li and Malcolm Warner

67 **Leisure and Power in Urban China**
Everyday life in a medium-sized Chinese city
Unn Målfrid H. Rolandsen

68 **China, Oil and Global Politics**
Philip Andrews-Speed and Roland Dannreuther

69 **Education Reform in China**
Edited by Janette Ryan

70 **Social Policy and Migration in China**
Lida Fan

71 **China's One Child Policy and Multiple Caregiving**
Raising little Suns in Xiamen
Esther C.L. Goh

72 **Politics and Markets in Rural China**
Edited by Björn Alpermann

73 **China's New Underclass**
Paid domestic labour
Xinying Hu

74 **Poverty and Development in China**
Alternative approaches to poverty assessment
Lu Caizhen

75 **International Governance and Regimes**
A Chinese perspective
Peter Kien-Hong Yu

76 **HIV/AIDS in China – The Economic and Social Determinants**
Dylan Sutherland and Jennifer Y.J. Hsu

77 **Looking for Work in Post-Socialist China**
Governance, active job seekers and the new Chinese labor market
Feng Xu

78 **Sino-Latin American Relations**
Edited by K.C. Fung and Alicia Garcia-Herrero

79 **Mao's China and the Sino-Soviet Split**
Ideological dilemma
Mingjiang Li

80 **Law and Policy for China's Market Socialism**
Edited by John Garrick

81 **China–Taiwan Relations in a Global Context**
Taiwan's foreign policy and relations
Edited by C.X. George Wei

82 **The Chinese Transformation of Corporate Culture**
Colin S.C. Hawes

83 **Mapping Media in China**
Region, province, locality
Edited by Wanning Sun and Jenny Chio

84 **China, the West and the Myth of New Public Management**
Neoliberalism and its discontents
Paolo Urio

85 **The Lahu Minority in Southwest China**
A response to ethnic marginalization on the frontier
Jianxiong Ma

86 **Social Capital and Institutional Constraints**
A comparative analysis of China, Taiwan and the US
Joonmo Son

87 **Southern China**
Industry, development and industrial policy
Marco R. Di Tommaso, Lauretta Rubini and Elisa Barbieri

88 **State–Market Interactions in China's Reform Era**
Local state competition and global market building in the tobacco industry
Junmin Wang

89 **The Reception and Rendition of Freud in China**
China's Freudian slip
Edited by Tao Jiang and Philip J. Ivanhoe

90 **Sinologism**
An alternative to Orientalism and Postcolonialism
Ming Dong Gu

91 **The Middle Class in Neoliberal China**
Governing risk, life-building, and themed spaces
Hai Ren

92 **The Chinese Corporatist State**
Adaption, survival and resistance
Edited by Jennifer Y.J. Hsu and Reza Hasmath

93 **Law and Fair Work in China**
Sean Cooney, Sarah Biddulph and Ying Zhu

94 **Guangdong and Chinese Diaspora**
The changing landscape of Qiaoxiang
Yow Cheun Hoe

95 **The Shanghai Alleyway House**
A vanishing urban vernacular
Gregory Bracken

96 **Chinese Globalization**
A profile of people-based global connections in China
Jiaming Sun and Scott Lancaster

97 **Disruptive Innovation in Chinese and Indian Businesses**
The strategic implications for local entrepreneurs and global incumbents
Peter Ping Li

98 **Corporate Governance and Banking in China**
Michael Tan

99 **Gender, Modernity and Male Migrant Workers in China**
Becoming a 'modern' man
Xiaodong Lin

100 **Emissions, Pollutants and Environmental Policy in China**
Designing a national emissions trading system
Bo Miao

101 **Sustainable Development in China**
Edited by Curtis Andressen, Mubarak A.R. and Xiaoyi Wang

102 **Islam and China's Hong Kong**
Ethnic identity, Muslim networks and the new Silk Road
Wai-Yip Ho

103 **International Regimes in China**
Domestic implementation of the international fisheries agreements
Gianluca Ferraro

104 **Rural Migrants in Urban China**
Enclaves and transient urbanism
Fulong Wu, Fangzhu Zhang and Chris Webster

105 **State-Led Privatization in China**
The politics of economic reform
Jin Zeng

106 **China's Supreme Court**
Ronald C. Keith, Zhiqiu Lin and Shumei Hou

107 **Queer Sinophone Cultures**
Howard Chiang and Ari Larissa Heinrich

108 **New Confucianism in Twenty-First Century China**
The construction of a discourse
Jesús Solé-Farràs

109 **Christian Values in Communist China**
Gerda Wielander

110 **China and Global Trade Governance**
China's first decade in the World Trade Organization
Edited by Ka Zeng and Wei Liang

111 **The China Model and Global Political Economy**
Comparison, impact, and interaction
Ming Wan

112 **Chinese Middle Classes**
China, Taiwan, Macao and Hong Kong
Edited by Hsin-Huang Michael Hsiao

113 **Economy Hotels in China**
A glocalized innovative hospitality sector
Songshan Sam Huang and Xuhua Michael Sun

114 **The Uyghur Lobby**
Global networks, coalitions and strategies of the World Uyghur Congress
Yu-Wen Chen

115 **Housing Inequality in Chinese Cities**
Edited by Youqin Huang and Si-ming Li

116 **Transforming Chinese Cities**
Edited by Mark Y. Wang, Pookong Kee and Jia Gao

117 **Popular Media, Social Emotion and Public Discourse in Contemporary China**
Shuyu Kong

118 **Globalization and Public Sector Reform in China**
Kjeld Erik Brødsgaard

119 **Religion and Ecological Sustainability in China**
Edited by James Miller, Dan Smyer Yu and Peter van der Veer

120 **Comparatizing Taiwan**
Edited by Shu-mei Shih and Ping-hui Liao

121 **Entertaining the Nation**
Chinese television in the twenty-first century
Edited by Ruoyun Bai and Geng Song

122 **Local Governance Innovation in China**
Experimentation, diffusion, and defiance
Edited by Jessica C. Teets and William Hurst

123 **Footbinding and Women's Labor in Sichuan**
Hill Gates

124 **Incentives for Innovation in China**
Building an innovative economy
Xuedong Ding and Jun Li

125 **Conflict and Cooperation in Sino-US Relations**
Change and continuity, causes and cures
Edited by Jean-Marc F. Blanchard and Simon Shen

Conflict and Cooperation in Sino-US Relations

Change and continuity, causes and cures

Edited by Jean-Marc F. Blanchard and Simon Shen

LONDON AND NEW YORK

First published 2015
by Routledge
2 Park Square, Milton Park, Abingdon, Oxon OX14 4RN

and by Routledge
711 Third Avenue, New York, NY 10017

Routledge is an imprint of the Taylor & Francis Group, an informa business

© 2015 Jean-Marc F. Blanchard and Simon Shen

The right of the editors to be identified as the authors of the editorial matter, and of the authors for their individual chapters, has been asserted in accordance with sections 77 and 78 of the Copyright, Designs and Patents Act 1988.

All rights reserved. No part of this book may be reprinted or reproduced or utilized in any form or by any electronic, mechanical, or other means, now known or hereafter invented, including photocopying and recording, or in any information storage or retrieval system, without permission in writing from the publishers.

Trademark notice: Product or corporate names may be trademarks or registered trademarks, and are used only for identification and explanation without intent to infringe.

British Library Cataloguing in Publication Data
A catalogue record for this book is available from the British Library

Library of Congress Cataloging in Publication Data
A catalog record for this book has been requested

ISBN: 978-1-138-78564-9 (hbk)
ISBN: 978-1-315-76771-0 (ebk)

Typeset in Times New Roman
by Wearset Ltd, Boldon, Tyne and Wear

Printed and bound in the United States of America by Publishers Graphics, LLC on sustainably sourced paper.

Jean-Marc would like to dedicate the book to his daughter Isabelle whose sense of perspective and good humor always brighten his day.

Simon would like to dedicate the book to his wife Bonnie who supported his continuous work on the book even during wedding preparations!

Contents

List of illustrations — xvii
Notes on contributors — xviii
Acknowledgments — xx
List of abbreviations — xxii

1 **Taking the temperature of China–US conflict and cooperation: an introduction** — 1
   JEAN-MARC F. BLANCHARD AND SIMON SHEN

2 **A primer on China–US relations, 1949–2008: a friend in need is a friend indeed** — 25
   JEAN-MARC F. BLANCHARD

3 **China, the US, and the transition of power: a dual leadership structure in the Asia-Pacific** — 45
   QUANSHENG ZHAO

4 **China and America: showdown in the Asia-Pacific?** — 68
   SUISHENG ZHAO

5 **Friend or foe: Washington, Beijing, and the dispute over US security ties to Taiwan** — 89
   DENNIS V. HICKEY AND KELAN (LILLY) LU

6 **China's North Korea dilemma and Sino-US cooperation** — 112
   JINGDONG YUAN

7 **Tough love: US–China economic relations between competition and interdependence** — 136
   WEI LIANG

xvi Contents

8 US–China relations in Asia-Pacific energy regime complexes: cooperative, complementary, and competitive   157
GAYE CHRISTOFFERSEN

9 Dialogues and their implications in Sino-American relations   181
ROBERT G. SUTTER

10 Continuity and change in Sino-US military-to-military relations   204
CHRISTOPHER D. YUNG

11 From the EP-3 incident to the USS *Kitty Hawk*–*Song* class submarine encounter: the evolution of Sino-US crisis management communication mechanisms   225
SIMON SHEN AND RYAN KAMINSKI

12 Conclusion   248
STANLEY ROSEN

Index   270

Illustrations

Figure

3.1 Americans' perceptions of world economic powers 46

Tables

3.1 Top 10 world economies by GDP (2012) 50
3.2 Top Asia-Pacific holders of US Treasury securities 51
3.3 Official reserve assets and other foreign currency assets in Asia-Pacific 52
3.4 Major partners in international trade, ranked (2011) 53
3.5 FDI inflows in Asia-Pacific 54
3.6 FDI outflow by country/region across Asia-Pacific 54
3.7 US v. China across categories 55
3.8 Global military expenditures (top 10) 55
3.9 US military relationships in the Asia-Pacific 56
5.1 Major US arms sales to Taiwan as notified to Congress 2010–11 91

Contributors

Jean-Marc F. Blanchard, PhD, is Assistant Dean and Professor, School of International and Public Affairs, Shanghai Jiaotong University, and Executive Director, Mr. & Mrs. S.H. Wong Center for the Study of Multinational Corporations. He is a co-author of one book, the editor or co-editor of and a contributor to eight edited volumes and special journal issues, and the author of more than 40 articles and book chapters.

Gaye Christoffersen is Resident Professor of International Politics at Johns Hopkins University, Nanjing Center, where she teaches a course on Asian energy security. Her recent publications include work on Sino-Russian and Sino-American energy relations, and the human security implications of China's foreign energy relations.

Dennis V. Hickey is Distinguished Professor and Director of the Graduate Program in Global Studies in the Department of Political Science at Missouri State University. He is the author of numerous books, scholarly journal articles, and editorials about Taiwan and the Chinese mainland.

Ryan Kaminski obtained his master's of international affairs from Columbia University and his bachelor's from the University of Chicago. He is a 2009–2011 US Department of Homeland Security Graduate Research Fellow and previously worked with the UN Foundation, Council on Foreign Relations, and the Hong Kong Institute of Education.

Wei Liang is Associate Professor in the School of International Policy and Management at the Middlebury Institute of International Studies, USA. Her research interests include international political economy of China, trade negotiation, and global governance.

Kelan (Lilly) Lu is an assistant professor at the Political Science Department in the University of South Carolina. Her specialization is in comparative/international political economy with an emphasis on Chinese politics. She has published in *International Studies Perspectives*, *Pacific Affairs*, and *Journal of Chinese Political Science*.

Stanley Rosen is a professor of Political Science at the University of Southern California. His most recent work has addressed the Chinese film industry, Chinese youth, and state–society relations in China.

Simon Shen, a graduate of the University of Oxford and Yale University, is one of the few international relations scholars originating from Hong Kong who has earned both international recognition and local prominence. He has published more than 70 academic articles and publications in leading SSCI journals. Invited to serve as a visiting fellow by leading global think tanks like the Brookings Institution, he has gained worldwide attention scholarship on contemporary anti-Western Chinese nationalism.

Robert G. Sutter is Professor of Practice in International Affairs, George Washington University. A Harvard University PhD, he has taught for over 40 years and has published 20 books, over 200 articles, and several hundred government reports dealing with contemporary East Asian and Pacific countries and their relations with the US. His most recent book is *Foreign Relations of the PRC* (2013). His US government service of 33 years focused on East Asia and the US.

Jingdong Yuan, PhD, is an associate professor at the Centre for International Security Studies, University of Sydney. His research interests include Chinese foreign policy, regional security, and nuclear arms control and nonproliferation. His latest publications include *A Rising Power Looks Down Under: Chinese Perspectives on Australia*.

Christopher D. Yung is a senior research fellow at National Defense University and serves as an advisor to the US government. He has authored numerous books, articles, and reports on the Chinese military. He received both his PhD and MA from the School of Advanced International Studies (SAIS), at Johns Hopkins University.

Quansheng Zhao is Professor of International Relations at American University in Washington, DC. A specialist in international relations and comparative politics focusing on East Asia, Dr Zhao is the author of *Interpreting Chinese Foreign Policy*, winner of the Best Academic Book Award by the Ministry of Culture of the Republic of Korea, and *Japanese Policymaking*, selected as "Outstanding Academic Book" by Choice.

Suisheng Zhao is Professor and Director of the Center for China–US Cooperation at Josef Korbel School of International Studies, University of Denver, and editor of the *Journal of Contemporary China*.

Acknowledgments

Relations between China and the US are a topic that animates much discussion. This makes eminent sense given the import of these global giants' relations for the two countries themselves, global affairs, and countries in regions ranging from Africa to Latin America to Southeast Asia. For now, the focus of much attention rightly is on the Asia-Pacific Region (APR) where a new order seems in the making as a result of China's growing national capabilities and the increasing dependence of APR countries on China. Moreover, China and the US have been experiencing increasing frictions in the APR due to shifting relative power positions, various territorial and maritime controversies, and domestic political factors. Recognizing the need for reflection on China–US relations, the Association of Chinese Political Studies (ACPS) and Hong Kong Institute for Education (HKIEd) brought together a distinguished body of Chinese, American, and other experts for a workshop entitled "40 Years after Sino-American Normalization: A New Dawn or A New Darkness" that was held in Hong Kong in December 2011. This edited volume represents the fruits of that timely and thought-provoking workshop.

Jean-Marc F. Blanchard would like to thank the ACPS for its backing of the workshop from which this book is an outgrowth. He also would like to express his sincere appreciation to the Mr. & Mrs. S.H. Wong Foundation and HKIEd Dean Sonny Lo and the HKIEd for the financial support they provided to make the workshop possible. He thanks the School of International and Public Affairs at Shanghai Jiaotong University, and Stanford University's Shorenstein Asia-Pacific Research Center for providing an intellectual environment conducive to bringing this book to fruition, no easy task as anyone involved in shepherding an edited book project to a conclusion knows! He also would like to thank Routledge acquisitions editor Stephanie Rogers for recognizing the importance of this project and Hannah Mack for helping us navigate the process of bringing this edited volume to production. Jean-Marc further would like to express his thanks to his co-editor, Dr Simon Shen, for being a cooperative partner on this edited book, our second! Finally, he would like to thank Aimee for her understanding while he spent hours of time in front of the computer.

Simon Shen would like to thank his research assistants Ernest Ng, Vincent Hung, Saturnia Kwok, and Lena Wong for their help during various stages of the aforementioned conference and book preparation, and Professors Kaho Mok and Sonny Lo of HKIEd for their kind support for the project. Full credit must be given to his co-editor Professor Jean-Marc F. Blanchard, whose meticulous and enthusiastic academic service is simply extraordinary.

Abbreviations

6PT	Six-Party Talks
ACFTA	ASEAN–China Free Trade Area
ADB	Asian Development Bank
ADIZ	Air Defense Identification Zone
AIT	American Institute in Taiwan
APEC	Asia-Pacific Economic Cooperation
APER	Asia Pacific Energy Regulatory
APP	Asia-Pacific Partnership
APR	Asia-Pacific Region
ASEAN	Association of Southeast Asian Nations
BRICS	Brazil, Russia, India, and China
CASM	Coalition for American Solar Manufacturing
CCP	Chinese Communist Party
CEPA	Closer Economic Partnership Arrangement
CIA	US Central Intelligence Agency
COCOM	Coordinating Committee for Multilateral Export Controls
DCT	Defense Consultative Talks
DOD	US Department of Defense
DOE	US Department of Energy
DPRK	Democratic People's Republic of North Korea
EAS	East Asian Summit
ECS	East China Sea
EEZ	exclusive economic zone
ENR	US Bureau of Energy Resources
ERI	Chinese Energy Research Institute
EU	European Union
EWR	early-warning radar
FBI	US Federal Bureau of Investigation
FDI	foreign direct investment
FTA	free trade agreements
GATT	General Agreement on Tariffs and Trade
GDP	gross domestic product
GMD	Guomindang

GNP	gross national product
GWOT	global war on terror
IAEA	International Atomic Energy Agency
IEA	International Energy Agency
IMF	International Monetary Fund
IPR	intellectual property rights
JCCT	US–China Joint Commission on Commerce and Trade
JDAM	joint direct attack munition
KMT	Kuomintang (also GMD)
LNG	liquified natural gas
MFA	PRC Ministry of Foreign Affairs
MFN	most favored nation
MMCA	Military Maritime Consultative Agreement
MMT	million metric tons
MNC	multinational corporation
MOU	Memorandum of Understanding
MTCR	Missile Technology Control Regime
NATO	North Atlantic Treaty Organization
NDAA	US National Defense Authorization Act
NDRC	PRC National Development and Reform Commission
NDU	national defense university
NEA	PRC National Energy Administration
NGO	non-governmental organization
NOC	national oil company
NPT	non-proliferation treaty
NSA	US National Security Agency
OGIF	Oil and Gas Industry Forum
OPEC	Organization of Petroleum Exporting Countries
PLA	PRC People's Liberation Army
PLAN	PRC People's Liberation Army Navy
PNTR	permanent normal trade relations
PRC	People's Republic of China
RIMPAC	Rim of the Pacific Exercise
RMB	renminbi (Chinese currency)
ROC	Republic of China
ROK	Republic of Korea
S&ED	US–China Strategic and Economic Dialogue
SCS	South China Sea
SLOC	sea lines of communication
SOE	state-owned enterprises
SPC	PRC State Planning Commission
SPDC	PRC State Planning and Development Commission
SPR	strategic petroleum reserve
SRO	surveillance and reconnaissance operations
TIFA	Trade and Investment Framework Agreement

TPA	Taiwan Policy Act
TPP	Trans-Pacific Partnership
TRA	US Taiwan Relations Act
TRIMS	Trade-Related Investment Measures Agreement
TYF	Ten Year Framework
UGTEP	Unconventional Gas Technical Engagement Program
UN	United Nations
UNCLOS	United Nations Convention on the Law of the Sea
UNSC	United Nations Security Council
US	United States
USACEP	US–Asia Pacific Comprehensive Energy Partnership
USAID	US Agency for International Development
USSR	Union of Soviet Socialist Republics
USTR	US Trade Representative
WHO	World Health Organization
WMD	weapons of mass destruction
WTO	World Trade Organization

1 Taking the temperature of China–US conflict and cooperation
An introduction[1]

Jean-Marc F. Blanchard and Simon Shen

Introduction

As the latest news and the contributors to this edited volume show, numerous crosswinds are buffeting the more than forty-year-old Sino-American relationship. These include the two countries' shifting power relations, territorial and maritime controversies in the South China Sea (SCS), problems linked to the Democratic People's Republic of North Korea (DPRK) aggressiveness, cybersecurity, and multiple economic frictions. Yet only once since Nixon's historic trip to China in 1972 – the 1995/1996 Taiwan Strait Crisis – has a major conflagration seemed a real possibility. Anchoring the relationship throughout multiple storms are the two countries' broad areas of collaboration. These include deep links in culture, economics, and education. For some observers, however, the conflictual aspects of the relationship seem to be gaining prominence.[2] The intensification of Chinese nationalism and the growing power of China on one hand and the United States "pivot" to the Asia-Pacific Region (APR) on the other have made the future of the bilateral relationship even more uncertain.

Sino-American ties are not understudied. There are many classics covering the twists and turns of the relationship.[3] In addition, there is a large body of journal articles, books, and studies addressing narrow issues such as China–US military links, Sino-US–Southeast Asian dynamics, triangular politics where the third vertex is the Soviet Union, US–China energy relations, and US–China crisis management.[4] However, given the multifaceted nature of the relationship and its dynamism, most of the existing monographs are becoming dated. As well, many do not put the relationship into comparative perspective historically or relative to the politico-economic context. Another limitation is that many do not always contemplate, in depth, what fuels conflict and cooperation between Beijing and Washington in regard to specific issue areas. The lack of dialog among the various sub-fields of Sino-US relations makes inter-disciplinary understanding on this complicated subject methodologically difficult, too. Finally, many shy away from offering focused recommendations for dampening the prospects for conflict and increasing the likelihood of cooperation. This volume not only grapples with these issues, but also supplies timely insight into the direction of Sino-American ties.

From a policy vantage point, there is no doubt the Sino-American relationship warrants study. It is one of the world's most important political, military, and economic dyads.[5] Virtually all of the global issues of the day – terrorism, piracy, pandemics, climate change, and proliferation – can be addressed only with some degree of cooperation between Beijing and Washington. Clearly, a major tempest in the relationship would have profound implications for international and regional institutions, the world economy, APR security, and global stability. The dynamics of the relationship and its future direction are important to theorists, too. After all, realists, commercial liberals, and constructivists all believe their frameworks can illuminate where the relationship currently stands and where it might be headed.[6] Those focused on domestic politics such as the role of legislatures and public opinion have ideas, too, about the drivers of ebbs and flows in the relationship.[7] Finally, the course of Sino-American ties has salience to those studying the role that geography plays in international relations.[8] Given the increasing discussion of the concept of "G2," the Sino-American relationship is arguably the most important bilateral relationship in the international system.

The chapters in this book show that the relationship has experienced notable changes over the past decade or so.[9] These include the rise of China as the APR's economic leader, China's growing assertiveness in the APR, changes in US closeness to Taiwan and China's tolerance of this, expanding trade frictions, and the seeming emergence of a new crisis management mechanism. Yet, this work also demonstrates there are numerous continuities such as US dominance in the realms of military-security affairs, clashing views about DPRK nonproliferation policy, and the continued development of political, economic, and other dialogs. Indeed, as Stanley Rosen aptly puts it in his conclusion to this volume, for almost 20 years, "the larger issue on both sides has remained the management of the relationship between a rising power and an entrenched superpower."

This volume reveals, too, that conflict and collaboration currently are, much as they have been, endemic in the relationship. This is well known, however, to specialists and even many more casual observers of the two country's ties. More interestingly, the contributions in this volume show that conflict and collaboration vary within and among issue areas depending upon the time and specific matter at stake. They reveal that, even in areas that seem inherently cooperative – e.g., economics, environmental cooperation, and military-to-military exchanges – there can be serious tensions. The good news is that serious conflict is not omnipresent, has been eliminated in some areas, and is often managed. The bad news is that some issues (e.g., the DPRK issue) continue to manifest no substantive progress, other areas (the APR) show increasing tensions, and many conflict management techniques have limited efficacy.

Not surprisingly, the chapters in this volume indicate that the causes of conflict and cooperation generally and with regard to specific issue areas cannot be distilled to one or even a few causes. Differing national interests, domestic politics and events, random crises like the 2001 EP-3 incident, the increasing complexity of the relationship, and the ideologies and policy strategies of top political leaders, all seem relevant. Still, the shifting balance of power between China and the US, changes in each party's need for the other (to serve internal economic needs, meet external security challenges, or something else), and domestic politics seem to shed considerable light on the degree of conflict and cooperation between Beijing and Washington.[10] Still, Rosen's conclusion queries whether or not past models really can be a useful guide to interpreting the contemporary China–US relationship and its outlook.

Regarding the future course of relations, there is a diversity of views, though most contributors are cautiously optimistic. Quansheng Zhao (Chapter 3) takes comfort in the pacifying effect of bilateral economic interdependence and the absence of severe ideological conflict. While he gives greater stress to tensions in the relationship, Suisheng Zhao (Chapter 4) sees the two countries' need for each other, extensive links, and inability to dominate the other (for internal and external reasons) as preserving a modus vivendi. Jingdong Yuan (Chapter 6) sees positive trends in Sino-US management of the North Korean issue but also identifies a number of structural factors that will continue to hinder bilateral cooperation. In her chapter on Sino-US energy relations, Gaye Christoffersen (Chapter 8) argues cooperation will be the norm going forward. Analyzing US–China crisis management, Simon Shen and Ryan Kaminski (Chapter 11) find hope in the two sides' enhanced ability to cope with crises. Of note, none of these contributors anticipates major positive developments in the relationship. Ironically given she focuses on realm of economics, supposedly an intrinsically, cooperative one, Wei Liang (Chapter 7) supplies one of the more pessimistic assessments of future relations.

The chapters in this collection offer diverse suggestions for minimizing China–US conflict and increasing bilateral cooperation. Nevertheless, most call for China and the US to accommodate each other, to show leadership, and to enhance communication. In his conclusion, Rosen offers some reflections about the limits of these varied proposals and adds his own insights, which emphasize cultural variables, perceptual gaps, and mistrust, about what ails the Sino-American relationship. Nonetheless, Rosen's chapter echoes others in calling for conflict prevention and management, measures to build trust, and mutual understanding and respect for each other's "core interests" and "obligations."

The next section highlights some of the prominent tensions in the relationship, some new, some longstanding. The third section probes areas of Sino-American cooperation, though the contributors do the bulk of the heavy lifting in their chapters. The fourth section outlines the chapters in the book and highlights some of the contributors' insights regarding the main themes of the volume, a task undertaken comprehensively and critically in the conclusion. The last section offers summary remarks, discusses this volume's policy and theoretical implications, and identifies some important themes that students of Sino-American relations may wish to examine going forward.

Strains and pains, old and new

Bilateral cooperation was more prominent than conflict as the China–US relationship moved into the second decade of the twenty-first century. Still, the first decade of the new millennium did not witness a resolution of any of the major problems bedeviling the bilateral relationship. Moreover, the early part of the second decade showed a resurgence of familiar issues as well as the intensification of other problems that had previously been quiescent. This section identifies some of these problems and provides a general overview of them. It begins by examining Sino-American security issues, before turning to economic and energy issues. It then touches upon a variety of persistent "low politics" issues such as human rights and the environment.

Analysts give significant attention to the power shift occurring between the US and China.[11] While China has not yet passed the US in any of the metrics used to determine great power status, its military, economic, and political power has increased impressively and, in some areas such as economics, conventional wisdom is that China will surpass the US shortly if it has not already done so.[12] Assuming a power transition is occurring, some foresee an emboldened China behaving more aggressively towards the US while others see an anxious US responding to the China challenge by taking action to contain or preempt the latter.[13] The question of a power transition and its implications is not just a global one, but also relates to the situation in the APR where proximity and other factors (e.g., the extensiveness of China's economic links with local players) magnify the shifts in China's political, military, and economic power. Whatever the case about the actual extent of a power shift globally or regionally, the shifting positions of the US and China seem to be having a variety of adverse impacts on their bilateral relationship.[14] Readers are encouraged to peruse Quansheng Zhao and Suisheng Zhao's separate chapters, which offer contrasting perspectives on what is occurring and its implications.

In terms of individual security issues, Taiwan persists as a thorn in China–US relations despite the US severing diplomatic ties with the island in 1979, the conclusion of the China–US 1982 Arms Sales Communiqué, and the calm brought by Ma Ying-jeou's accession to the presidency in 2008. Per Dennis Hickey and Kelan (Lilly) Lu (Chapter 5), this has to do with the still vigorous US–Taiwan relationship, which involves large arm sales to Taiwan, significant defense ties, and extensive high-level political interactions between Taipei and Washington. It will be essential to observe whether the same trends survive the next election in Taiwan. Of course, China's cross-Strait military/missile buildup, punitive disruptions of military exchanges, and threats to sanction American companies involved in Taiwan arms sales worsen matters.[15] As Yuan shows in Chapter 6, the DPRK problem has not gone away with Washington wanting Beijing to twist the DPRK's arm more intensely and to reign in Pyongyang. But China has been unwilling to support the level of pressure the US desires and wants to protect the DPRK, whose collapse would present Beijing with a host of security, economic, and social headaches.[16]

Various chapters in the volume underscore another major stress in the bilateral relationship, the SCS. China disagrees with US military activities in its exclusive economic zone (EEZ) and American efforts to act as a SCS balancer/stabilizer. The US is displeased with Chinese assertiveness towards other SCS claimants and in China's SCS EEZ where China opposes US military activities.[17] Regarding the former, the US has challenged Chinese measures to advance its territorial and maritime claims, which include building structures, increased energy exploration and exploitation, and more aggressive patrolling. China contends the US is stirring up problems, asserts its activities are its sovereign prerogative, and has attacked other claimants' provocations.[18] With respect to the SCS EEZ, China's navy has "retaliated" by starting patrols in the US EEZ and continues to challenge/interfere with American military vessels operating in its SCS EEZ.[19] There also seem to be competitive dynamics between the US and China for influence in Southeast Asia. This is reflected in their stances towards specific Southeast Asian countries such as Myanmar, and Southeast Asian regional institutions or regionally led negotiations like, respectively, the East Asian Summit and the Regional Comprehensive Economic Partnership.[20]

Suisheng Zhao's chapter highlights diverse Sino-American frictions relating to the ECS. Unpacking the East China Sea, we find two issues. One is the China–Japan quarrel over the Diaoyu/Senkaku Islands ("the Islands") and the other is China's ECS Air Defense Identification Zone (ADIZ). The Islands became a major controversy in the early 1970s, heated up significantly in the mid-1990s, and became a serious flashpoint in 2010.[21] As far as Beijing and Washington are concerned, the crux of the problem is that the US has stated unequivocally that Article 5 of the US–Japan defense treaty covers the Islands and thus that it would support Japan in any military conflict over the Islands.[22] The ADIZ issue pertains to China's establishment of a zone in the ECS in November 2013, which covered a significant portion of the ECS EEZ and the Islands that Tokyo claims. The US rejects the zone and has labeled China's measure a unilateral (and unwelcome) attempt to change the status quo pertaining to the ECS and the Islands while China retorts that its ADIZ was established in accordance with international law.[23]

While energy, which is both a security and economic issue, has long been a part of Sino-American interactions, it, generally speaking, has not been a source of friction. Over the past ten years or so and especially the past five, however, it has acquired more competitive features. China is increasingly anxious about the security of the sea lines of communication over which its energy supplies travel, the sufficiency of its supplies, and American relations with Chinese energy suppliers like Myanmar and support for countries with which China has maritime quarrels that relate, in part, to energy. The US appears to be quite concerned about China's energy links with countries that have a long history of receiving US aid (e.g., African states), or bad relations with the US (e.g., Venezuela), China's gains in countries that previously seemed to be subject to extensive American influence (e.g., Iraq), and China's lack of faith in global energy markets.[24] In her chapter, Christoffersen demonstrates that even areas that should be cooperative – e.g., solar energy and regional energy cooperation initiatives – can be fraught with tensions.

In early 2013, the issue of Chinese cyber attacks began to emerge as a major problem for the China–US relationship with the US accusing China, formally and informally, of running systematic operations to steal business information and secrets from the US government and American businesses and threatening or hinting at action including sanctions, diplomatic pressure/shaming, and indictments or visa restrictions against relevant Chinese hackers. American officials also pursued negotiations with China to reduce tensions and develop some rules of the road. China's standard operating procedure was to deny or ignore such complaints and counter that it was the victim of cyber attacks.[25] Edward Snowden's revelations of massive US National Security Agency spying, coupled with reports of US cyber warfare against China, took much of the wind out of the US sails by making it look hypocritical.[26] Still, in May 2014, the US took formal action by indicting five Chinese military officers for stealing trade secrets from American entities.[27] Seemingly in retaliation, American firms, especially technology firms, have been facing an increasingly challenging time in China, confronting anti-trust investigations, bans on the usage of their products, and episodic media attacks.[28]

As far as economic issues (the focus of Liang's chapter) are concerned, the US and China are at loggerheads over China's currency policies, the adequacy of its efforts to protect intellectual property rights (IPR), China's satisfaction of its non-IPR WTO commitments such as financial and telecommunications market opening and trade-related investment measure commitments, Chinese barriers confronting American companies investing or operating in China, Chinese government procurement policies, and Chinese inflexibility regarding the cutting of technology tariffs. Chinese elites put forth a litany of complaints about American attitudes towards and obstacles to Chinese investment in the US, limits on US high-tech exports to China, anti-dumping and countervailing duties against Chinese imports, excess US trade negotiation demands, US budgetary woes, and the American-centric international monetary order.[29]

Human rights have been a bilateral problem for decades. Among other things, the US expresses concern about Chinese policies towards Xinjiang and Tibet, Chinese treatment of individual political dissidents and journalists, and Chinese restrictions on religious and civil rights. An ongoing recent issue has been the implications of Chinese economic dealings with countries like Angola, Sudan, and Zimbabwe for the human rights situation in those countries.[30] Of late, the situation in Hong Kong has become a bone of contention, too, as a result of decreased press freedom and demands by various Hong Kong residents for a directly elected Chief Executive and legislature, which Beijing has strongly rejected. Developments in Hong Kong have fueled tensions not only between the PRC and Hong Kong, but also between China and the US.[31] Not surprisingly, China is tired of US pressure and meetings between American presidents and other high-level US government officials and the Dalai Lama. It also is irritated by US criticism in the form of international human rights reports and international religious rights reports and it now ritualistically responds to every US report with its own human rights report on the US.[32] Given the fact that most of these issues are now handled by the Chinese Communist Party National Security Committee, China–US relations are likely to become part of China's internal political dynamics.

The environment *per se* is not a problem for US–China relations. The core issue is who should bear the cost of addressing the problem of global climate change. Washington argues that China should accept mandatory emissions targets and more demanding compliance schedules because it is the world's largest greenhouse gas emitter. China's position is that it deserves less-demanding obligations because it is a developing country. Moreover, it argues that developed countries should contribute significant funds and technological assistance to facilitate developing countries' efforts to reduce their emissions. When China is blamed by the US as being irresponsible environmentally, it has attempted to build countervailing alliances with other developing powers. Beyond this, there are issues relating to the environmental practices of Chinese companies overseas and Chinese industrial policies in the alternative energy sector.[33]

Plain gains, old and new

The previous section focused on conflictual aspects of the China–US relationship. However, to be balanced, we also need to give attention to cooperation, which is ubiquitous. This section first gives attention to cooperation regarding security issues such as North Korea, Iran, and counter-terrorism. It then notes Sino-American economic cooperation and various forms of collaboration, such as with respect to the environment. In this section, we do not address cooperation in the form of multi-level political meetings and dialogs, military exchanges and visits, and crisis management since Robert Sutter (Chapter 9), Christopher Yung (Chapter 10), and Simon Shen and Ryan Kaminski (Chapter 11) cover these topics thoroughly in their chapters.

Importantly, North Korea has not only been a source of Sino-American friction, but it has also been a basis for cooperation. For example, China played a critical role in the creation of the Six-Party Talks, which warmed its relationship with the US. Additionally, Beijing instituted various bilateral measures against Pyongyang, supported various UNSC endeavors to tackle North Korea's WMD programs and treaty violations, and admonished Pyongyang for its belligerent words and deeds.[34] After February 2013, Beijing became even less accepting of North Korean behaviors, ordering Chinese banks to stop dealings with North Korean ones, reportedly limiting energy exports to North Korea, and reducing high-level meetings.[35] Iran has been an area where Beijing and Washington have worked together, albeit to a limited extent. China, for example, supported UNSC resolutions imposing multilateral sanctions in 2010, has partially complied with US sanctions imposed against Iran in 2010, and has supported joint statements calling for Iran to meet its commitments. This said, China opposes strong sanctions on Iran, continues to be a major investor in and importer from Iran, and criticizes US penalties on Chinese companies doing business with Iran.[36]

Aside from these areas, there has been a modicum of cooperation on the antiterrorism front and some vague promises of additional bilateral cooperation. In any event, it is worth mentioning that China has supplied Pakistan with training, equipment, and intelligence and has been supportive of Afghanistan's stabilization and economic recovery initiatives, though this was not done to advance Sino-American relations.[37] On a related note, China and the US have worked together on some anti-piracy drills relating to boarding, search, and seizure off the coast of Somalia. The two countries also engaged in joint peacekeeping patrols in Port-au-Prince in the aftermath of Haiti's massive earthquake in 2010.[38]

The realm of economics is clearly one where there is a high degree of bilateral cooperation due to the complementary nature of the American and Chinese economies, among other factors. As of the end of 2011, Sino-US trade hit the astounding figure of $446.7 billion. Recent statistics put the cumulative amount of US investment in China at $67.6 billion. Although it was relatively trivial for many years, Chinese investment in the US has seen some noteworthy growth and reached the significant sum of $6 billion by the end of 2011.[39] China further is the world's largest holder of US government debt, owning approximately $900 billion as of late 2010.[40] China is also a major market for American agriculture, one of the fastest growing export markets for the US, and a major source of revenue for numerous American multinational corporations.[41] Sino-American trade and investment relations are so significant that some Chinese analysts described them as the ballast and engine for overall bilateral relations and a deterrent to political and security conflict.[42]

Regarding the environment, Beijing and Washington have collaborated on energy conservation, energy efficiency, carbon capture research, electric vehicles, and shale oil exploitation. For instance, in late 2009, the US and China established a $150 million US–China Clean Energy Research Center to "research and jointly develop energy efficient buildings, electric vehicles, and clean coal technologies."[43] As Chapter 8 details, China and the US also have implemented initiatives such as joint energy education programs, a Nuclear Security Center of Excellence, and an eco-cities project. At the recently concluded Strategic and Economic Dialogue that was held in Beijing in early July 2014, China and the US agreed to cooperate on, share knowledge about, and conduct exchanges pertaining to, inter alia, energy-saving technologies, unconventional energy exploration, and renewable energy.[44]

Chapter summaries

Chapter 2 (Jean-Marc F. Blanchard) surveys Sino-American relations from 1949 to 2008 to provide a foundation from which readers can appreciate the history behind and contexts shaping the issues discussed in this volume. Blanchard also aims to provide a basis for judgments about where the relationship is heading and where it currently stands. He shows that conflict and cooperation have been the norm in the relationship, but that their balance, both among and within issue areas, is much more complicated than this simple statement reveals. Chapter 2 also demonstrates that bilateral conflict has been most muted when the US and China have a shared need for each other, especially a shared security interest.

Quansheng Zhao (Chapter 3) presents the idea of a new, emerging dual leadership structure, involving China and the US, in the APR. He argues that China, as a rising economic power, is beginning to play a leadership role in economic and financial matters, while the US remains the unchallenged leader in the military and political realms. In contrast to some who expect a clash between China and the US, he argues that this emerging structure (which creates space as well as the need for cooperation), high interdependence, globalization, a lack of severe ideological conflict, and shared interests diminish the likelihood of Sino-American conflict. Furthermore, if Beijing and Washington adopt the 3-C principle of "coordination, cooperation, and compromise," which involves co-management of APR issues and accommodation of each other's core interests, then regional peace and prosperity likely will follow.

Chapter 4 (Suisheng Zhao) focuses on territorial and maritime tensions in the ECS and SCS and American strategy towards these controversies and the APR generally. He argues that the rapid growth of China's capabilities and the US's relative economic decline have encouraged China to take a more aggressive stance toward such disputes. Concurrently, under increasing pressure to show its allies and partners that it is still committed to, as well as capable of, exerting influence, the US has reoriented its strategic priorities towards the APR. Concurrently, many countries in the region are striving to work more closely with Washington. Some in the US and China interpret the US rebalance as an effort to reassert American primacy in the region, having the potential to cause a showdown with China. Chapter 3 argues that a US–China showdown is not inevitable because of shared interests and economic interdependence. Moreover, neither China nor the US has the ability to challenge the other forcefully given their own limits and the attitudes or limit of their allies.

The fifth chapter by Hickey and Lu speaks to the Taiwan issue. It argues that America's support for Taiwan not only has continued over the years, but actually has broadened and deepened, as exemplified by recent multi-billion dollar arms sales packages. This support has proved to be a constant source of tension between China and the US. Indeed, Chinese authorities describe arms sales as the "most sensitive" issue in bilateral relations. Hickey and Lu's chapter outlines Washington and Beijing's positions toward America's security relationship with Taiwan and explains why their differing perceptions hold the potential to put the two nations on a collision course. They suggest that some new thinking, perhaps a grand bargain regarding American arms sales and PRC missile deployments, may be required if Washington, Beijing, and Taipei ever hope to realize a "peaceful resolution" of the so-called Taiwan issue.

Yuan (Chapter 6) analyzes the bilateral relationship with North Korea. He shows that the North Korea issue remains an area of significant friction between

China and the US, but also, paradoxically, provides opportunities for bilateral cooperation. The core problem is that while Beijing and Washington share a common interest in seeing a nuclear-free North Korea they often differ on approaches and priorities. The Obama administration has adopted a policy of "strategic patience" that continues with its predecessor's emphasis on complete and verifiable nuclear dismantlement, though it emphasizes greater coordination with US allies. China, on the other hand, is increasingly torn between its desire to maintain peninsular stability and its inability to enforce discipline on its wayward neighbor. However, the broader strategic transformation in the region – China's rise and the US pivot to Asia – may impede Sino-US cooperation on North Korea unless and until mutual strategic trust develops. Yuan calls for China to restrain the DPRK and the US to maintain close communication with China on the North Korea problem.

Liang (Chapter 7) turns our attention to the economic realm. Over the last two decades, the once almost largely cooperative economic relationship has undergone fundamental changes and now witnesses much more competition, friction, and mistrust relating to trade deficits, WTO compliance, and the two countries' economic policies. Analyzing the factors that have produced greater bilateral economic conflict, Liang points to a changing balance of capabilities and needs, clashing economic ideologies, and Chinese and American domestic politics. She argues that a new approach is needed to more effectively manage the bilateral economic relations in the twenty-first century, beyond engaging China, integrating it into global economy, and binding it in the rule-based WTO. Specifically, the US has to do more to accommodate China's policy preferences and treat China more equally in global economic governance.

Chapter 8 (Christoffersen) expounds upon the China–US energy relationship. According to her, a pattern of cooperative energy relations has characterized the history of China–US energy relations, though cooperation was largely one-sided, entailing American technology transfers to China. More recently, a competitive pattern of energy relations has emerged in response to Chinese securitization of its energy imports and inability to control expanding domestic energy demand. There is an additional pattern of parallelism based on bilateral complementarity where the US and China move in a parallel direction, neither cooperative nor competitive, furthering an expanding awareness of common security interests. Recent tensions in China–US energy relations tie not only to the aforementioned factors, but also have something to do with China's growing energy footprint abroad and different preferences vis-à-vis the state or market. To reduce frictions, Christoffersen calls upon China and the US to cooperate in protecting sea lines of communication and the US to transfer more technology to China.

Chapter 9 by Sutter reviews the role exchanges and dialogs have played in US–China relations since 1972, and examines in more detail the process, significance and outlook of recent dialogs. His analysis reveals that dialogs are important instruments in the policy "tool kit" of each side to deal with areas of common interest and disagreement that have broadened in scope as a result of China's rising importance and the increasing salience of an ever-wider range of issues in US–Chinese relations. These policy instruments serve as shock absorbers in periods of difficulty, provide the basis for actual or potential channels of informal communication in times of crisis, and promote efforts to broaden common ground. Still, in the final analysis, while dialogs are instruments of improved relations they do not compel improvement, which at bottom is decided by policy elites in Beijing and Washington.

Yung (Chapter 10) concentrates on China–US military relations, which, he notes, are the weakest of all the aspects of bilateral relations. The basis for such a claim is the fact that, despite decades of interactions, the military relationship is fragile and vulnerable to shifts in the state of bilateral relations. Typically, when bilateral relations between the two countries are experiencing difficulties (e.g., over Taiwan arms sales) the military relationship is often the first to be disrupted. His chapter discusses the history of US–China military interactions from 1979 to the present, pointing out that while much has remained the same, China no longer seems so ready to terminate exchanges. Yung enumerates a multitude of obstacles to the development and deepening of military relations: different views about what exchanges should do and who should be involved, the subordination of military exchanges to the larger political relationship, and American legislation. Yung calls for more frequent and wider-ranging joint exercises, joint research studies, and realistic expectations.

In Chapter 11, Shen and Kaminski review progress in Sino-American crisis management mechanisms. Using the EP-3 Crisis (2001) and the USS *Kitty Hawk* encounter (2006) as case studies, they argue that, rather than presenting insurmountable roadblocks to bilateral cooperation, crises have presented significant opportunities for both states to learn from mistakes that might have inadvertently escalated a particular situation. Delving into the aforementioned crises, the different responses of both sides, and post-crisis developments in areas like military-to-military exchanges and China's national security structures, they argue that China and the US have become better equipped to weather future crises that hold the potential to seriously damage their relationship. They contend that the US and China need to continue to engage, reflect and reform, and add that the two countries should consider a crisis management mechanism for the cyber realm.

Conclusion

This chapter identifies numerous tensions bedeviling the Sino-American relationship. It further discusses diverse realms such as the North Korea issue and economics where China and the US collaborate. However, it goes beyond merely listing areas of conflict and cooperation to examining their presence over time or in sub-issue areas. This chapter further summarizes what the various contributors have to say about the main themes of this volume, such as change and continuity, the causes of conflict and cooperation, and techniques for increasing cooperation and decreasing conflict (see also Rosen's concluding chapter). While there is no unanimity of perspectives, contributors to this volume highlight a number of similar themes. For example, many attribute change in the Sino-American relationship to a shifting relative balance of capabilities, the evolving balance of needs, and ideological or policy differences. Many chapter writers also stress the importance of communication, accommodation, and shared interests as dampeners of conflict or as a route to bolstering the stability of the relationship.

Several policy implications flow from this volume. First, decision-makers and policy analysts need to recognize that many facets, trends, or causal factors that, on the surface, seem to be new are not. Indeed, as the chapters reveal, there is much continuity. Appreciating this can minimize the risk of alarmist interpretations or overreaction. Second, this book shows that relationship management mechanisms such as dialogs, high-level summitry, and military-to-military exchanges have value, though their ability to solve problems and transform relations should not be exaggerated. Third, many bilateral issues like North Korea, energy, and the APR that are sources of conflict can be sources of cooperation (and vice versa). Thus, intelligent policy-making requires decision-makers to give play to policies that will minimize conflict while increasing cooperation. Fourth, while sharing causal drivers (e.g., the Sino-American relative power balance), individual issue areas have their own unique dynamics. Decision-makers need to recognize this to craft efficacious policies. Finally, many contributors take the position that Beijing and Washington need to do more to accommodate the other, need to enhance communication and exchange, and need to address their mistrust.

This book is not theoretical in orientation. Even so, its chapters have theoretical ramifications. One is that it can be profitable to analyze a bilateral relationship through issue-oriented lenses. A second is that a single theoretical framework does not suffice to explain Sino-American ties. Approaches that take into account, for example, issue area, domestic politics, and culture and perceptions are needed to understand change and continuity as well as conflict and cooperation. Still, it seems we need to pay close attention to structural factors such as the balance of capabilities, the balance of needs, and interdependence. A third is that, despite the positions of realists and liberals, neither security nor economic issues are inherently cooperative or conflictual (see, e.g., the chapters by Yuan, Liang, and Christoffersen). It depends upon the nature of such issues, the politico-economic-military milieu, and other factors.

As with all books, space constraints preclude consideration of a number of important issues relating to Sino-American relations. Students of Sino-American ties may find it interesting to probe in depth the relationship with regard to strategic nuclear weapons, the developing world, South Asia, the Arctic, or foreign direct investment. Additionally, researchers might wish to study the relevance of a broader number of variables shaping the Sino-American relationship that were not covered in depth here, such as the role of business interests, militaries (particularly the People's Liberation Army), mass publics/nationalism, the media, and third parties such as Russia. Furthermore, analysts of the bilateral relationship might want to directly and systematically test the ability of various theoretical frameworks to illuminate diverse areas of the relationship.

Since China and the US normalized relations over 40 years ago, the relationship has experienced repeated ups and downs, with many expecting it to maintain roughly the same pattern in the era of Xi Jinping and Barack Obama's successor. The two giants have clashed in international organizations, on economic issues, and on environmental matters. They have buttressed their ability to challenge the other militarily. And they have threatened each other with sanctions over a slew of issues. It is not without reason China expert Harry Harding once labeled the China–US dyad "a fragile relationship."[45] However, while prone to (sometimes extreme) twists and turns, the relationship has evolved to the point where it is fair to speak of the two countries as "tangled titans."[46] As this volume makes clear, the US and China have innumerable interconnections and often work together. Still, the chapters demonstrate that many longstanding sources of conflict remain, that new ones are appearing, and that favored conflict management devices have serious limitations. The good news is that there are various options for decreasing conflict and increasing cooperation, provided the requisite political leadership is forthcoming and third parties do not drag China and the US into conflict with one another. The ominous sounding Sino-American "contest for supremacy" still may have a happy ending.[47]

Notes

1 The authors would like to thank Stanley Rosen, Robert Sutter, and two anonymous reviewers for their constructive feedback on this chapter. The comments in this chapter reflect the authors' positions and not any institutions with which the authors are affiliated.
2 See, e.g., David Shambaugh, "Preface and Acknowledgements," in *Tangled Titans: The United States and China*, ed. David Shambaugh (Lanham, MD: Rowman & Littlefield, 2013), xv–xvii.
3 Invaluable works include Robert Ross, *Negotiating Cooperation: The United States and China, 1969–1989* (Stanford, CA: Stanford University Press, 1995); Rosemary Foot, *The Practice of Power: US Relations with China since 1949* (New York: Oxford University Press, 1997); James Mann, *About Face: A History of America's Curious Relationship with China, from Nixon to Clinton* (New York: Vintage Books, 2000); Chen Jian, *Mao's China and the Cold War* (Chapel Hill: University of North Carolina Press, 2001); Robert L. Suettinger, *Beyond Tiananmen: The Politics of US–China Relations 1989–2000* (Washington, DC: Brookings Institution, 2003); Warren I. Cohen, *America's Response to China: A History of Sino-American Relations*, 5th edn (New York: Columbia University Press, 2010); Robert Sutter, *US–Chinese Relations: Perilous Past, Pragmatic Present* (Lanham, MD: Rowman & Littlefield, 2010); and Shambaugh, *Tangled Titans*.
4 See, respectively, Shirley A. Kan, *US–China Military Contacts: Issues for Congress*, report no. RL32496 (Washington, DC: Congressional Research Service, 2012); Ming-Te Hung and Tony Tai-Ting Liu, "Sino-US Strategic Competition in Southeast Asia: China's Rise and US Foreign Policy Transformation since 9/11," *Political Perspectives* 5, no. 3 (2011): 96–119; Michael Schaller, *The United States and China in the Twentieth Century*, 2nd edn (New York: Oxford University Press, 1990); Lowell Dittmer, "The Strategic Triangle," *World Politics* 33, no. 4 (July 1981), 485–515; and June T. Dreyer, "Sino-American Energy Cooperation," *Journal of Contemporary China* 16, no. 52 (August 2007): 461–76.

5 For a similar point, see Nancy B. Tucker, "The Evolution of US–China Relations," in *Tangled Titans*, ed. Shambaugh, 30.
6 See the analyses or reviews in Paul A. Papayoanou and Scott L. Kastner, "Sleeping with the (Potential) Enemy: Assessing the US Policy of Engagement with China," in *Power and the Purse: Economic Statecraft, Interdependence, and National Security*, ed. Jean-Marc F. Blanchard, Edward D. Mansfield, and Norrin M. Ripsman (London: Frank Cass, 2000), 157–87; John Mearsheimer, "China's Unpeaceful Rise," *Current History* 105, no. 690 (April 2006): 160–2; and Barry Buzan, "China in International Society: Is 'Peaceful Rise' Possible?" *Chinese Journal of International Politics* 3, no. 1 (Spring 2010): 5–36.
7 Mann, *About Face*; Robert Sutter, "Domestic American Influences on US–China Relations," in *Tangled Titans*, ed. Shambaugh, 103–24; and Yufan Hao, "Domestic Chinese Influences on US–China Relations," in *Tangled Titans*, ed. Shambaugh, 125–48.
8 Robert S. Ross, "The Geography of the Peace," *International Security* 23, no. 4 (Spring 1999): 81–118.
9 Whether these changes are positive or negative often depends upon the position and perspective of the analyst.
10 For an analysis which stresses the role of structural factors in shaping US–China relations during the administrations of George W. Bush and Barack Obama, see Jean-Marc F. Blanchard, "US–China Relations under Bush and Obama: Fill in the Blanks or It's the Structure, Stupid?" *Issues and Studies* 49, no. 3 (September 2013): 35–72. For a contrasting analysis that highlights the salience of cultural and perceptual factors, see Stanley Rosen's conclusion, Chapter 12 of this volume.
11 Aaron L. Friedberg, "The Future of US–China Relations: Is Conflict Inevitable?" *International Security* 30, no. 2 (Fall 2005): 7–45; Steve Chan, *China, the US, and the Power Transition Theory: A Critique* (London: Routledge, 2007); Mark Beeson, "Hegemonic Transition in East Asia? The Dynamics of Chinese and American Power," *Review of International Studies*, 35, no. 1 (January 2009): 95–112; Renee Jeffery, "Evaluating the 'China Threat': Power Transition Theory, the Successor-State Image, and Dangers of Historical Analogies," *Australian Journal of International Affairs* 63, no. 2 (2009): 309–24; and Tucker, "The Evolution of US–China Relations," 41.
12 US National Intelligence Council, *Global Trends 2030: Alternative Worlds* (Washington, DC: US National Intelligence Council, 2012), accessed February 6, 2013, www.dni.gov/files/documents/GlobalTrends_2030.pdf. Quansheng Zhao (Chapter 3) makes the case that China already is the dominant economic leader in the APR.
13 For review and critiques, see the sources in note 11 above as well as Quansheng Zhao and Guoli Liu, "China Rising: Theoretical Understanding and Global Response," in *Managing the China Challenge: Global Perspectives*, ed. Quansheng Zhao and Guoli Liu (New York: Routledge, 2009), 3–6; Min-Hua Huang and Yun-Han Chu, "Exploring Theoretical Implications of the Rise of China: A Critique on Mainstream International Relations Perspectives," in *Managing the China Challenge: Global Perspectives*, ed. Quansheng Zhao and Guoli Liu (New York: Routledge, 2009), 42–4; and Yi Feng, "Global Power Transitions and their Implications for the 21st Century," *Pacific Focus* 28, no. 2 (August 2013): 170–89.
14 Li Hongmei, "The US Hegemony Ends, the Era of Global Multipolarity Enters," *People's Daily Online*, February 24, 2009, accessed February 24, 2009, http://english.peopledaily.com.cn/90002/96417/6599374.html; Kathrin Hille, "Tough Questioning Reflects Relative Strength," *Financial Times*, June 2, 2009; and Gideon Rachman, "China and US Navigate in Risky Waters," *Financial Times*, November 12, 2012.
15 See also Susan V. Lawrence and Thomas Lum, *US–China Relations: Policy Issues*, report no. R41108 (Washington, DC: Congressional Research Service, 2011), 28–31; Baohui Zhang, "Taiwan's New Grand Strategy," *Journal of Contemporary China* 20,

no. 69 (2011): 269–85; Jean-Marc F. Blanchard and Dennis V. Hickey, "More than Two 'Sides' to Every Story: An Introduction to New Thinking about the Taiwan Issue" in *New Thinking about the Taiwan Issue: Theoretical Insights into Its Origins, Dynamics, and Prospects*, ed. Jean-Marc F. Blanchard and Dennis V. Hickey (London: Routledge, 2012), 8–12; Dennis V. Hickey, "Imbalance in the Taiwan Strait," *Parameters* 43, no. 3 (Autumn 2013): 43–45; and Robert G. Sutter, *U.S.-Chinese Relations: Perilous Past, Pragmatic Present*, 2nd edn (Lanham, MD: Rowman & Littlefield, 2013), 162–3, 234–47.

16 Also useful are Lawrence and Lum, *US–China Relations*, 3, 22–4, 27; Dick K. Nanto and Mark E. Manyin, "China–North Korea Relations," *North Korean Review* 7, no. 2 (Fall 2011): 94–101; and Susan V. Lawrence and David MacDonald, *US–China Relations: Policy Issues*, report no. R41108 (Washington, DC: Congressional Research Service, 2012), 18–19.

17 Lawrence and Lum, *US–China Relations*, 26–8; "US–China Spat over South China Sea Military Exercises," *BBC News*, July 11, 2011, accessed July 12, 2011, www.bbc.co.uk/news/world-asia-pacific-14097503; "ASEAN Talks: US and China Pledge to Co-operate on Asia," *BBC News*, July 12, 2012, accessed July 12, 2012, www.bbc.co.uk/news/world-asia-18807496; "China Warns US on South China Sea Row as Clinton Visits," *BBC News*, September 5, 2012, accessed September 5, 2012, www.bbc.co.uk/news/world-asia-china-19473141; and Leszek Buszynski, "The South China Sea: Oil, Maritime Rivalry, and US–China Strategic Rivalry," *Washington Quarterly* 35, no. 2 (2012): 139–56.

18 "US Presses Beijing over South China Sea Dispute," *BBC News*, February 5, 2014, accessed February 6, 2014, www.bbc.co.uk/news/world-asia-china-26062033; "China Refutes US Criticism of its Maritime Claims," *China Daily*, February 9, 2014, accessed February 9, 2014, http://usa.chinadaily.com.cn/2014–02/09/content_17272993.htm; Keith Bradsher, "South China Sea Tensions a Backdrop to Kerry's China Visit," *New York Times*, February 14, 2014, accessed February 14, 2014, http://sinosphere.blogs.nytimes.com/2014/02/14/south-china-sea-tensions-a-backdrop-to-kerrys-china-visit/; Chen Weihua, "Beijing Defends Philippine Action in South China Sea," *China Daily*, March 13, 2014, accessed March 13, 2014, http://usa.chinadaily.com.cn/2014–03/13/content_17345727.htm; and Jane Perlez and Keith Bradsher, "In High Seas, China Moves Unilaterally," *New York Times*, May 9, 2014, accessed May 9, 2014, www.nytimes.com/2014/05/10/world/asia/in-high-seas-china-moves-unilaterally.html.

19 Kathrin Hille, "Chinese Navy Begins US Economic Zone Patrols," *Financial Times*, June 2, 2013; Jane Perlez, "Chinese and American Ships Nearly Collide in South China Sea," *New York Times*, December 14, 2013, accessed December 14, 2013, www.nytimes.com/2013/12/15/world/asia/chinese-and-American-ships-nearly-collide-in-south-china-sea.html; and "Hagel: China Warship Action 'Irresponsible,'" *BBC News*, December 20, 2013, www.bbc.co.uk/news/world-asia-25459570.

20 Kathrin Hille, Ben Bland, and Geoff Dyer, "US and China Vie for Influence in SE Asia," *Financial Times*, November 23, 2012; Jean-Marc F. Blanchard, "Historical Analysis of Japan, East Asian Trade Regionalism and the US: Potential Implications for Japan-US TPP Negotiations," *Japan Spotlight*, May/June 2014, 24–7; and Jean-Marc F. Blanchard and Wei Liang, "The US, East Asian FTAs, and China" (mimeo).

21 For background on the disputes, their drivers, and relevant features, see Jean-Marc F. Blanchard, "The US Role in the Sino-Japanese Dispute over the Diaoyu (Senkaku) Islands, 1945–1971," *China Quarterly*, no. 161 (March 2000): 95–123; Jean-Marc F. Blanchard, "China's Peaceful Rise and Sino-Japanese Territorial and Maritime Tensions," in *China's "Peaceful Rise" in the 21st Century: Domestic and International Conditions*, ed. Sujian Guo (Burlington, VT: Ashgate, 2006), 211–36; and Linus Hagstrom, "Quiet Power: Japan's China Policy in Regard to the Pinnacle Islands," *Pacific Review* 18, no. 2 (June 2005): 159–88.

22 Bhubhindar Singh, "Obama, the Senkaku/Diaoyu Islands, and the US–Japan Security Treaty," *PacNet* 36A, May 7, 2014, http://csis.org/files/publication/Pac1436A.pdf

23 "Biden: US and China in 'Very Direct' Air Zone Talks,'" *BBC News*, December 5, 2013, accessed December 5, 2013, www.bbc.co.uk/news/world-asia-25227609; "Biden Urges Chinese to 'Challenge Government on Visit,'" *BBC News*, December 4, 2013, accessed December 5, 2013, www.bbc.co.uk/news/world-asia-25211032; and Demetri Sevastopulo, "US Says China 'Acting Professionally' in Air Defense Zone," *Financial Times*, February 5, 2014.

24 Dreyer, "Sino-American Energy Cooperation," 461–76; Suisheng Zhao, "China's Global Search for Energy Security: Cooperation and Competition in Asia-Pacific," *Journal of Contemporary China* 17, no. 55 (May 2008): 207–27; Tim Arango and Clifford Krauss, "China Is Reaping Biggest Benefits of Iraq Oil Boom," *New York Times*, June 2, 2013, accessed June 3, 2013, www.nytimes.com/2013/06/03/world/middleeast/china-reaps-biggest-benefits-of-iraq-oil-boom.html; Li Li, "No Alarm for US as China, Venezuela Cement Ties," *People's Daily Online*, July 20, 2014, accessed August 7, 2014, http://english.peopledaily.com.cn/n/2014/0720/c90883–8758117.html; and Christoffersen's chapter in this volume.

25 Jamil Anderlini, "Chinese Premier Pressed on Cyber Spying," *Financial Times*, March 20, 2013; Siobhan Gorman, "US Eyes Pushback on China Hacking," *Wall Street Journal*, April 22, 2013, http://online.wsj.com/news/articles/SB10001424127887324345804578424741315433114; Reuters, "US Defense Secretary Hagel Calls for Cyber Security Rules," *Financial Times*, May 31, 2013; David E. Sanger and Mark Landler, "US and China Agree to Hold Regular Talks on Hacking," *New York Times*, June 1, 2013, www.nytimes.com/2013/06/02/world/asia/us-and-china-to-hold-talks-on-hacking.html; and Geoff Dyer, "Cyber Theft: A Hard War to Wage," *Financial Times*, June 3, 2013. Chinese industrial espionage was an issue more generally for the US. "US Charges 3 NYU Researchers in Chinese Bribery Case," *Financial Times*, May 21, 2013.

26 David E. Sanger and Nicole Perlroth, "NSA Breached Chinese Servers Seen as a Threat," *New York Times*, March 22, 2014, accessed August 7, 2014, www.nytimes.com/2014/03/23/world/asia/nsa-breached-chinese-servers-seen-as-spy-peril.html;
David E. Sanger, "US Tries Candor to Assure China on Cyberattacks," *New York Times*, April 6, 2014, accessed August 7, 2014, www.nytimes.com/2014/04/07/world/us-tries-candor-to-assure-china-on-cyberattacks.html; Kristine Kwok and Stephen Chen, "Snowden Effect Changes US–China Dynamic on Cybersecurity," *South China Morning Post*, June 15, 2014, www.scmp.com/news/china/article/1532984/snowden-effect-changes-us-china-dynamic-cybersecurity; David E. Sanger and Nicole Perlroth, "NSA Breached Chinese Servers Seen as Security Threat," *New York Times*, March 22, 2014, accessed August 7, 2014, www.nytimes.com/2014/03/23/world/asia/nsa-breached-chinese-servers-seen-as-spy-peril.html.

27 Ellen Nakashima and William Wan, "US Announces First Charges against a Foreign Country in Connection with Cyberspying," *Washington Post*, May 19, 2014, accessed May 19, 2014, www.washingtonpost.com/world/national-security/us-to-announce-first-criminal-charges-against-foreign-country-for-cyberspying/2014/05/19/586c9992-df45–11e3–810f-764fe508b82d_story.html.

28 See, e.g., Steven Yang and Edmond Lococo, "IBM Challenger Inspur Woos China Customers Amid Dispute," *Bloomberg*, May 28, 2014, accessed May 28, 2014, http://mobile.bloomberg.com/news/2014–05–28/china-s-inspur-wooing-ibm-customers-as-hacking-dispute-escalates.html.

29 Jean-Marc F. Blanchard, "China's Grand Strategy and Money Muscle: The Potentialities and Pratfalls of China's Sovereign Wealth Fund and Renminbi Policies," *Chinese Journal of International Politics* 4, no. 1 (Spring 2011): 31–53; Wayne M. Morrison, *China–US Trade Issues*, report no. RL33536 (Washington, DC: Congressional Research Service, 2012), 14–42; Li Jiabao, "Trade Friction 'To Intensify,'" *China*

Daily, March 22, 2012, accessed March 22, 2012, http://usa.chinadaily.com.cn/business/2012-03/22/content_14886457.htm; US Department of the Treasury, "Remarks by Secretary Geithner at the Commonwealth Club of California," April 26, 2012, US Department of the Treasury, accessed April 26, 2012, www.treasury.gov/press-center/press-releases/Pages/tg1553.aspx; Alan Beattie, "US–China Economic Tiff Simmers," *Financial Times*, February 13, 2012; Lawrence and MacDonald, *US–China Relations*, 27–31; Chen Weihua and Bao Chang, "China and US Agree on Major Trade Measures," *China Daily*, December 21, 2012, accessed December 21, 2012, http://usa.chinadaily.com.cn/china/2012-12/21/content_16037377.htm; Richard McGregor, "Smithfield Bid Tests US Appetite for Chinese Investment," *Financial Times*, May 30, 2013; Simon Rabinovitch and Jamil Anderlini, "China Blocks MasterCard Processing Renminbi Transactions," *Financial Times*, June 2, 2013; Li Jiabao, "US Suspending ITA Talks Is Disappointing, Minister Says," *China Daily*, November 25, 2013, accessed November 25, 2013, www.chinadaily.com.cn/bizchina/2013-11/25/content_17129782.htm; Charles W. Freeman, III, "The Commercial and Economic Relationship," in *Tangled Titans*, ed. Shambaugh, 192–202; Sutter, *US–Chinese Relations* (2nd edn), 215–22; Jean-Marc F. Blanchard, "China, Foreign Investors, and TRIMS: Bulking up, but Not Fully Compliant," in *China and Global Trade Governance: China's First Decade in the World Trade Organization*, ed. Ka Zeng and Wei Liang (London: Routledge, 2013), 43–68; and James F. Paradise, "The New Intellectual Property Rights Environment in China: Impact of WTO Membership and China's 'Innovation Society' Makeover," *Asian Journal of Social* Science 41, nos. 3–4 (December 2013): 312–32.

30 Sutter, *US–Chinese Relations*, 253–61; "Hillary Clinton: China Crackdown 'a Fool's Errand,'" *BBC News*, May 10, 2011, accessed May 10, 2011, www.bbc.co.uk/news/world-us-canada-13353199; and Lawrence and MacDonald, *US–China Relations*, 4, 35–42.

31 Michael Gonzalez, "Why America Must Stand Up for Hong Kong's Democracy Movement," *National Interest*, July 10, 2014, accessed August 7, 2014, http://nationalinterest.org/feature/why-america-must-stand-hong-kongs-democracy-movement-10842; and "Prying Eyes," *Global Times*, July 23, 2014, accessed August 7, 2014, www.globaltimes.cn/content/872236.shtml.

32 Huang Xiangyang, "US, Stop Acting as Guardian of Human Rights," *China Daily*, March 12, 2010, accessed March 12, 2010, www.chinadaily.com.cn/opinion/2010-03/12/content_9583554.htm; "Human Rights Record of the United States in 2011," *China Daily*, May 26, 2012, accessed May 26, 2012, www.chinadaily.com.cn/cndy/2012-05/26/content_15392452.htm; "China Slams US Report on Human Rights," *China Daily*, October 11, 2012, accessed October 11, 2012, http://usa.chinadaily.com.cn/china/2012-10/11/content_15811917.htm; Mark Landler, "China Criticizes Obama over Visit by Dalai Lama," *New York Times*, February 21, 2014, accessed February 22, 2014, www.nytimes.com/2014/02/22/world/asia/us-brushes-off-chinese-rebuke-as-obama-meets-with-dalai-lama.html.

33 On this and other Sino-American energy/environmental issues, see Christoffersen's chapter in this volume. Also informative are Sutter, *US–Chinese Relations*, 213–17; Lawrence and MacDonald, *US–China Relations*, 30–4; and Rosemary Foot, "US–China Interactions in Global Governance and International Organizations," in *Tangled Titans*, ed. Shambaugh, 358–9.

34 Eric A. McVadon, "Korean Issues in US–China Relations 1990–2010," *Korean Journal of Defense Analysis* 22, no. 2 (2010): 141–62; Sutter, *US–Chinese Relations*, 175; Thomas J. Christensen, "The Advantages of an Assertive China: Responding to Beijing's Abrasive Diplomacy," *Foreign Affairs* 90, no. 2 (March/April 2011): 56; Nanto and Manyin, "China–North Korea Relations," 94–101; Lawrence and MacDonald, *US–China Relations*, 18–19; and Yuan's chapter in this volume.

35 Sanger and Landler, "US and China Agree to Hold Regular Talks on Hacking;"

Koichiro Ishida, "North Korea Getting Antsy about Growing Ties between China and South Korea," *Asahi Shimbun*, July 26, 2014, accessed August 7, 2014, http://ajw.asahi.com/article/asia/korean_peninsula/AJ201407260035; and Shin Hyon-hee, "China–NK Relations Face Bumpy Road," *Korea Herald*, July 30, 2014, accessed August 7, 2014, www.koreaherald.com/view.php?ud=20140730000967.

36 Erica Downs, *Cooperation with China on Iran*, policy brief (Washington, DC: German Marshall Fund of the United States, 2012); Lawrence and MacDonald, *US–China Relations*, 17–18; Rick Gladstone, "China: Criticims of US Move on Iran," *New York Times*, April 30, 2014, accessed August 7, 2014, www.nytimes.com/2014/05/01/world/asia/china-criticism-of-us-move-on-iran.html; "US Calls on China for Cooperation," *Al Jazeera America*, July 15, 2014, accessed August 7, 2014, http://america.aljazeera.com/articles/2014/7/15/us-china-cooperationnkorea.html; and Steve Holland, "Obama Tells China's Xi Wants 'Constructive Management of Differences,'" Reuters, July 15, 2014, accessed August 7, 2014, www.reuters.com/article/2014/07/15/us-usa-china-obama-idUSKBN0FK06G20140715.

37 Michael D. Swaine, "China and the 'AfPak' Issue," *China Leadership Monitor*, no. 31 (Winter 2010), http://carnegieendowment.org/files/CLM31MS.pdf; Shannon Tiezzi, "Can the US and China Cooperate to Fight Terrorism?" *The Diplomat*, May 3, 2014, accessed August 7, 2014, http://thediplomat.com/2014/05/can-the-u-s-and-china-cooperate-to-fight-terrorism/; and "China, US Will Cooperate on Counter-Terrorism, Military: Chinese Officials," Reuters, July 10, 2014, accessed August 7, 2014, www.reuters.com/article/2014/07/10/us-china-usa-military-idUSKBN0FF0O620140710.

38 "China, US Peacekeepers Conduct Joint Patrol in Haiti," *People's Daily Online*, January 30, 2010, accessed August 7, 2014, http://english.people.com.cn/90001/90776/90883/6883221.html; "China, US Conduct First Joint Anti-Piracy Drill," *People's Daily Online*, September 18, 2012, accessed February 8, 2013, http://english.people.com.cn/90786/7951411.html; and "US, Chinese Navies in Joint Anti-Piracy Drills off Somalia," Reuters, September 18, 2012, accessed August 7, 2014, www.reuters.com/article/2012/09/18/us-china-usa-piracy-idUSBRE88H0PY20120918.

39 Ding Qingfen, "Stronger Trade Links Vital," *China Daily*, August 29, 2012, accessed August 30, 2012, http://usa.chinadaily.com.cn/business/2012–08/29/content_15714 090.htm.

40 Lawrence and Lum, *US–China Relations*, 12.

41 Sutter, *US–Chinese Relations*, 198–9; Cui Peng, "US Gains More from Trade" *China Daily*, January 18, 2011, accessed January 18, 2011, www.chinadaily.com.cn/opinion/2011–01/18/content_11870897.htm; and Freeman, "The Commercial and Economic Relationship," 181–2.

42 "2009: A Year of Cooperation and Conflicts for China–US Trade Relations," *Sina English*, December 22, 2009, accessed December 23, 2009, http://english.sina.com/china/2009/1222/294850.html.

43 Lawrence and MacDonald, *US–China Relations*, 34.

44 Ministry of Foreign Affairs of the People's Republic of China, "China–US Strategic and Economic Dialogue Outcomes of the Strategic Track," Ministry of Foreign Affairs of the People's Republic of China, July 11, 2014, accessed August 7, 2014, www.fmprc.gov.cn/mfa_eng/zxxx_662805/t1173628.shtml.

45 Harry Harding, *A Fragile Relationship: The United States and China since 1972* (Washington, DC: Brookings Institution Press, 1992).

46 Shambaugh, *Tangled Titans*.

47 Aaron L. Friedberg, *A Contest for Supremacy: China, America, and the Struggle for Mastery in Asia* (New York: W.W. Norton, 2011).

References

"2009: A Year of Cooperation and Conflicts for China–US Trade Relations." *Sina English*. December 22, 2009. Accessed December 23, 2009. http://english.sina.com/china/2009/1222/294850.html.

Anderlini, Jamil. "Chinese Premier Pressed on Cyber Spying." *Financial Times*. March 20, 2013.

Arango, Tim, and Clifford Krauss. "China Is Reaping Biggest Benefits of Iraq Oil Boom." *New York Times*. June 2, 2013. Accessed June 3, 2013. www.nytimes.com/2013/06/03/world/middleeast/china-reaps-biggest-benefits-of-iraq-oil-boom.html?pagewanted=all.

"ASEAN Talks: US and China Pledge to Co-operate on Asia." *BBC News*. July 12, 2012. Accessed July 12, 2012. www.bbc.co.uk/news/world-asia-18807496.

Beattie, Alan. "US–China Economic Tiff Simmers." *Financial Times*. February 13, 2012.

Beeson, Mark. "Hegemonic Transition in East Asia? The Dynamics of Chinese and American Power." *Review of International Studies* 35, no. 1 (January 2009): 95–112.

"Biden Urges Chinese to 'Challenge Government' on Visit." *BBC News*. December 4, 2013. Accessed December 5, 2013. www.bbc.co.uk/news/world-asia-25211032.

"Biden: US and China in 'Very Direct' Air Zone Talks." *BBC News*. December 5, 2013. Accessed December 5, 2013. www.bbc.co.uk/news/world-asia-25227609.

Blanchard, Jean-Marc F. "China, Foreign Investors, and TRIMS: Bulking Up, but Not Fully Compliant," in *China and Global Trade Governance: China's First Decade in the World Trade Organization*, edited by Ka Zeng and Wei Liang, 43–68 (London: Routledge, 2013).

Blanchard, Jean-Marc F. "China's Grand Strategy and Money Muscle: The Potentialities and Pratfalls of China's Sovereign Wealth Fund and Renminbi Policies." *Chinese Journal of International Politics* 4, no. 1 (Spring 2011): 31–53.

Blanchard, Jean-Marc F. "China's Peaceful Rise and Sino-Japanese Territorial and Maritime Tensions," in *China's "Peaceful Rise" in the 21st Century: Domestic and International Conditions*, edited by Sujian Guo, 211–36 (Burlington, VT: Ashgate, 2006).

Blanchard, Jean-Marc F. "Historical Analysis of Japan, East Asian Trade Regionalism and the US: Potential Implications for Japan–US TPP Negotiations." *Japan Spotlight*, May/June 2014, 24–7.

Blanchard, Jean-Marc F. "The US Role in the Sino-Japanese Dispute over the Diaoyu (Senkaku) Islands, 1945–1971." *China Quarterly*, no. 161 (March 2000): 95–123.

Blanchard, Jean-Marc F. "US–China Relations under Bush and Obama: Fill in the Blanks or It's the Structure, Stupid?" *Issues and Studies* 49, no. 3 (September 2013): 35–72.

Blanchard, Jean-Marc F., and Dennis V. Hickey. *New Thinking about The Taiwan Issue: Theoretical Insights into Its Origins, Dynamics, and Prospects* (London: Routledge, 2012).

Bradsher, Keith. "South China Sea Tensions a Backdrop to Kerry's China Visit." *New York Times*. February 14, 2014. Accessed February 14, 2014. http://sinosphere.blogs.nytimes.com/2014/02/14/south-china-sea-tensions-a-backdrop-to-kerrys-china-visit/.

Buszynski, Leszek. "The South China Sea: Oil, Maritime Claims, and US–China Strategic Rivalry." *Washington Quarterly* 35, no. 2 (2012): 139–56.

Buzan, Barry. "China in International Society: Is 'Peaceful Rise' Possible?" *Chinese Journal of International Politics* 3, no. 1 (Spring 2010): 5–36.

Chan, Steve. *China, the US, and the Power Transition Theory: A Critique* (London: Routledge, 2007).

Chen, Jian. *Mao's China and the Cold War* (Chapel Hill: University of North Carolina Press, 2001).

Chen, Weihua, and Bao Chang. "China and US Agree on Major Trade Measures." *China Daily*. December 21, 2012. Accessed December 21, 2012. http://usa.chinadaily.com.cn/china/2012–12/21/content_16037377.htm.

Chen, Weihua. "Beijing Defends Philippine Action in South China Sea." *China Daily*. March 13, 2014. Accessed March 13, 2014. http://percent3Apercent2Fpercent2Fusa.chinadaily.com.cnpercent2F2014–03percent2F13 percent2Fcontent_17345727.htm.

"China Refutes US Criticism of Its Maritime Claims." *China Daily*. February 9, 2014. Accessed February 9, 2014. http://usa.chinadaily.com.cn/2014–02/09/content_17272993.htm.

"China Slams US Report on Human Rights." *China Daily*. October 11, 2012. Accessed October 11, 2012. http://usa.chinadaily.com.cn/china/2012–10/11/content_15811917.htm.

"China, US Conduct First Joint Anti-piracy Drill." *People's Daily Online*. September 18, 2012. Accessed February 8, 2013. http://english.people.com.cn/90786/7951411.html.

"China, US Peacekeepers Conduct Joint Patrol in Haiti." *People's Daily Online*. January 30, 2010. Accessed August 7, 2014. http://english.people.com.cn/90001/90776/90883/6883221.html.

"China, US Will Cooperate on Counter-terrorism, Military: Chinese Official." Reuters. July 10, 2014. Accessed August 7, 2014. www.reuters.com/article/2014/07/10/us-china-usa-military-idUSKBN0FF0O620140710.

Christensen, Thomas J. "The Advantages of an Assertive China: Responding to Beijing's Abrasive Diplomacy." *Foreign Affairs* 90, no. 2 (March/April 2011).

"Clinton Meets China Leaders amid South China Sea Tension." *BBC News*. September 5, 2012. Accessed September 5, 2012. www.bbc.co.uk/news/world-asia-china-19473141.

Cohen, Warren I. *America's Response to China: A History of Sino-American Relations*. 5th edn (New York: Columbia University Press, 2010).

Cui, Peng. "US Gains More from Trade." *China Daily*. January 18, 2011. Accessed January 18, 2011. www.chinadaily.com.cn/opinion/2011–01/18/content_11870897.htm.

Ding, Qingfen. "Stronger Trade Links Vital." *China Daily USA*. August 29, 2012. Accessed August 30, 2012. http://usa.chinadaily.com.cn/business/2012–08/29/content_15714090.htm.

Dittmer, Lowell. "The Strategic Triangle." *World Politics* 33, no. 4 (July 1981): 485–515.

Downs, Erica. *Cooperating with China on Iran*. Issue brief (Washington, DC: German Marshall Fund of the United States, 2012).

Dreyer, June T. "Sino-American Energy Cooperation." *Journal of Contemporary China* 16, no. 52 (August 2007): 461–76.

Dyer, Geoff. "Cyber Theft: A Hard War to Wage." *Financial Times*. June 3, 2013.

Feng, Yi. "Global Power Transitions and Their Implications for the 21st Century." *Pacific Focus* 28, no. 2 (August 2013): 170–89.

Foot, Rosemary. *The Practice of Power: US Relations with China since 1949* (New York: Oxford University Press, 1997).

Friedberg, Aaron L. *A Contest for Supremacy: China, America, and the Struggle for Mastery in Asia* (New York: W.W. Norton, 2011).

Friedberg, Aaron L. "The Future of US–China Relations: Is Conflict Inevitable?" *International Security* 30, no. 2 (Fall 2005): 7–45.

Gladstone, Rick. "China: Criticism of US Move on Iran." *New York Times*. April 30,

2014. Accessed August 7, 2014. www.nytimes.com/2014/05/01/world/asia/china-criticism-of-us-move-on-iran.html.

Gonzalez, Michael. "Why America Must Stand Up for Hong Kong's Democracy Movement." *National Interest*. July 10, 2014. Accessed August 7, 2014. http://nationalinterest.org/feature/why-america-must-stand-hong-kongs-democracy-movement-10842.

Gorman, Siobhan. "US Eyes Pushback on China Hacking." *Wall Street Journal*. April 22, 2013. http://online.wsj.com/news/articles/SB10001424127887324345804578424741315433114.

"Hagel: China Warship Action 'Irresponsible'" *BBC News*. December 20, 2013. www.bbc.co.uk/news/world-asia-25459570.

Hagstrom, Linus. "Quiet Power: Japan's China Policy in Regard to the Pinnacle Islands." *Pacific Review* 18, no. 2 (June 2005): 159–88.

Harding, Harry. *A Fragile Relationship: The United States and China since 1972* (Washington, DC: Brookings Institution Press, 1992).

Hickey, Dennis V. "Imbalance in the Taiwan Strait." *Parameters* 43, no. 3 (Autumn 2013): 43–53.

"Hillary Clinton: China Crackdown 'a Fool's Errand'" *BBC News*. May 10, 2011. Accessed May 10, 2011. www.bbc.co.uk/news/world-us-canada-13353199.

Hille, Kathrin. "Chinese Navy Begins US Economic Zone Patrols." *Financial Times*. June 2, 2013.

Hille, Kathrin. "Tough Questioning Reflects Relative Strength." *Financial Times*. June 2, 2009.

Hille, Kathrin, Ben Bland, and Geoff Dyer. "US and China Vie for Influence in SE Asia." *Financial Times*. November 23, 2012.

Holland, Steve. "Obama Tells China's Xi Wants 'Constructive Management of Differences'" Reuters. July 15, 2014. Accessed August 7, 2014. www.reuters.com/article/2014/07/15/us-usa-china-obama-idUSKBN0FK06G20140715.

Huang, Xiangyang. "US, Stop Acting as Guardian of Human Rights." *China Daily*. March 12, 2010. Accessed March 12, 2010. www.chinadaily.com.cn/opinion/2010–03/12/content_9583554.htm.

"Human Rights Record of United States in 2011." *China Daily*. May 26, 2012. Accessed May 26, 2012. www.chinadaily.com.cn/cndy/2012–05/26/content_15392452.htm.

Hung, Ming-Te, and Tony Tai-Ting Liu. "Sino-US Strategic Competition in Southeast Asia: China's Rise and US Foreign Policy Transformation since 9/11." *Political Perspectives* 5, no. 3 (2011): 96–119.

Ishida, Koichiro. "North Korea Getting Antsy about Growing Ties between China, South Korea." *Asahi Shimbun*. July 26, 2014. Accessed August 7, 2014. http://ajw.asahi.com/article/asia/korean_peninsula/AJ201407260035.

Jeffery, Renée. "Evaluating the 'China Threat': Power Transition Theory, the Successor-State Image, and Dangers of Historical Analogies." *Australian Journal of International Affairs* 63, no. 2 (2009): 309–24.

Kan, Shirley A. *US–China Military Contacts: Issues for Congress*. Report no. RL32496 (Washington, DC: Congressional Research Service, 2012).

Kwok, Kristine, and Stephen Chen. "Snowden Effect Changes US–China Dynamic on Cybersecurity." *South China Morning Post*. June 15, 2014. www.scmp.com/news/china/article/1532984/snowden-effect-changes-us-china-dynamic-cybersecurity.

Landler, Mark. "China Criticizes Obama Over Visit by Dalai Lama." *New York Times*. February 21, 2014. Accessed February 22, 2014. www.nytimes.com/2014/02/22/world/asia/us-brushes-off-chinese-rebuke-as-obama-meets-with-dalai-lama.html.

Lawrence, Susan V., and Thomas Lum. *US–China Relations: Policy Issues*. Report no. R41108 (Washington, DC: Congressional Research Service, 2011).

Lawrence, Susan V., and David MacDonald. *US–China Relations: Policy Issues*. Report no. R41108 (Washington, DC: Congressional Research Service, 2012).

Li, Jiabao. "Trade Friction 'to Intensify'" *China Daily* USA. March 22, 2012. Accessed March 22, 2012. http://usa.chinadaily.com.cn/business/2012–03/22/content_14886457.htm.

Li, Jiabao. "US Suspension of ITA Talks Is Disappointing, Minister Says." *China Daily*. November 25, 2013. Accessed November 25, 2013. www.chinadaily.com.cn/bizchina/2013–11/25/content_17129782.htm.

Li, Li. "No Alarm for US as China, Venezuela Cement Ties." *People's Daily Online*. July 20, 2014. Accessed August 7, 2014. http://english.peopledaily.com.cn/n/2014/0720/c90883–8758117.html.

Liu, Hongmei. "The US Hegemony Ends, the Era of Global Multipolarity Enters." *People's Daily Online*. February 24, 2009. Accessed February 24, 2009. http://english.peopledaily.com.cn/90002/96417/6599374.html.

Mann, James. *About Face: A History of America's Curious Relationship with China, From Nixon to Clinton* (New York: Vintage Books, 2000).

McGregor, Richard. "Smithfield Bid Tests US Appetite for Chinese Investment." *Financial Times*. May 30, 2013.

McVadon, Eric A. "Korean Issues in US–China Relations 1990–2010." *Korean Journal of Defense Analysis* 22, no. 2 (2010): 141–62.

Mearsheimer, John. "China's Unpeaceful Rise." *Current History* 105, no. 690 (April 2006): 160–2.

Ministry of Foreign Affairs of the People's Republic of China. "China–US Strategic and Economic Dialogue Outcomes of the Strategic Track.". July 11, 2014. Accessed August 7, 2014. www.fmprc.gov.cn/mfa_eng/zxxx_662805/t1173628.shtml.

Morrison, Wayne M. *China–US Trade Issues*. Report no. RL33536 (Washington, DC: Congressional Research Service, 2012).

Nakashima, Ellen, and William Wan. "US Announces First Charges against Foreign Country in Connection with Cyberspying." *Washington Post*. May 19, 2014. Accessed May 19, 2014. www.washingtonpost.com/world/national-security/us-to-announce-first-criminal-charges-against-foreign-country-for-cyberspying/2014/05/19/586c9992-df45–11e3–810f-764fe508b82d_story.html.

Nanto, Dick K., and Mark E. Manyin. "China–North Korea Relations." *North Korean Review* 7, no. 2 (Fall 2011): 94–101.

Papayoanou, Paul A., and Scott L. Kastner. "Sleeping with the (Potential) Enemy: Assessing the US Policy of Engagement with China," in *Power and the Purse: Economic Statecraft, Interdependence, and National Security*, eds. Jean-Marc F. Blanchard, Edward D. Mansfield, and Norrin M. Ripsman, 157–87 (London: Frank Cass, 2000).

Paradise, James F. "The New Intellectual Property Rights Environment in China: Impact of WTO Membership and China's "Innovation Society" Makeover." *Asian Journal of Social Science* 41, no. 3–4 (December 2013): 312–32.

Perlez, Jane, and Keith Bradsher. "In High Seas, China Moves Unilaterally." *New York Times*. May 9, 2014. Accessed May 9, 2014. www.nytimes.com/2014/05/10/world/asia/in-high-seas-china-moves-unilaterally.html.

Perlez, Jane. "American and Chinese Navy Ships Nearly Collided in South China Sea." *New York Times*. December 14, 2013. Accessed December 14, 2013. www.nytimes.

com/2013/12/15/world/asia/chinese-and-American-ships-nearly-collide-in-south-china-sea.html.

"Prying Eyes." *Global Times*. July 23, 2014. Accessed August 7, 2014. www.globaltimes.cn/content/872236.shtml.

Rabinovitch, Simon, and Jamil Anderlini. "China Blocks MasterCard Processing Renminbi Transactions." *Financial Times*. June 2, 2013.

Rachman, Gideon. "China and US Navigate in Risky Waters." *Financial Times*. November 12, 2012.

Ross, Robert S. "The Geography of the Peace." *International Security* 23, no. 4 (Spring 1999): 81–118.

Ross, Robert S. *Negotiating Cooperation: The United States and China, 1969–1989* (Stanford, CA: Stanford University Press, 1995).

Sanger, David E. "US Tries Candor to Assure China on Cyberattacks." *New York Times*. April 6, 2014. Accessed August 7, 2014. www.nytimes.com/2014/04/07/world/us-tries-candor-to-assure-china-on-cyberattacks.html.

Sanger, David E., and Mark Landler. "US and China Agree to Hold Regular Talks on Hacking." *New York Times*. June 1, 2013. www.nytimes.com/2013/06/02/world/asia/us-and-china-to-hold-talks-on-hacking.html?pagewanted=all.

Sanger, David E., and Nicole Perlroth. "NSA Breached Chinese Servers Seen as Security Threat." *New York Times*. March 22, 2014. Accessed August 7, 2014. www.nytimes.com/2014/03/23/world/asia/nsa-breached-chinese-servers-seen-as-spy-peril.html.

Schaller, Michael. *The United States and China in the Twentieth Century*. 2nd edn (New York: Oxford University Press, 1990).

Sevastopulo, Demetri. "US Says China 'Acting Professionally' in Air Defence Zone." *Financial Times*. February 5, 2014.

Shambaugh, David L., ed. *Tangled Titans: The United States and China* (Lanham, MD: Rowman & Littlefield, 2013).

Shin, Hyon-hee. "China–NK Relations Face Bumpy Road." *Korea Herald*. July 30, 2014. Accessed August 7, 2014. www.koreaherald.com/view.php?ud=20140730000967.

Singh, Bhubhindar. "Obama, the Senkaku/Diaoyu Islands, and the US–Japan Security Treaty." *PacNet* 36A, May 7, 2014. http://csis.org/files/publication/Pac1436A.pdf.

Suettinger, Robert L. *Beyond Tiananmen: The Politics of US–China Relations 1989–2000* (Washington, DC: Brookings Institution Press, 2003).

Sutter, Robert G. *US–Chinese Relations: Perilous Past, Pragmatic Present* (Lanham, MD: Rowman & Littlefield Publishers, 2010, 2nd edn 2013).

Swaine, Michael D. "China and the 'AfPak' Issue." *China Leadership Monitor*, no. 31 (Winter 2010). http://carnegieendowment.org/files/CLM31MS.pdf.

Tiezzi, Shannon. "Can the US and China Cooperate to Fight Terrorism?" *The Diplomat*. May 3, 2014. Accessed August 7, 2014. http://thediplomat.com/2014/05/can-the-u-s-and-china-cooperate-to-fight-terrorism/.

"US Calls on China for Cooperation." *Al Jazeera America*. July 15, 2014. Accessed August 7, 2014. http://america.aljazeera.com/articles/2014/7/15/us-china-cooperationnkorea.html.

"US Charges 3 NYU Researchers in Chinese Bribery Case." *Financial Times*. May 21, 2013.

"US, Chinese Navies in Joint Anti-piracy Drills off Somalia." Reuters. September 18, 2012. Accessed August 7, 2014. www.reuters.com/article/2012/09/18/us-china-usa-piracy-idUSBRE88H0PY20120918.

"US–China Spat over South China Sea Military Exercises." *BBC News*. July 11, 2011. Accessed July 12, 2011. www.bbc.co.uk/news/world-asia-pacific-14097503.

"US Defence Secretary Chuck Hagel Calls for Cyber Security Rules." *Financial Times.* May 31, 2013.

US Department of the Treasury. "Remarks by Secretary Geithner at the Commonwealth Club of California." News release, April 26, 2012. US Department of the Treasury. Accessed April 26, 2012. www.treasury.gov/press-center/press-releases/Pages/tg1553.aspx.

US National Intelligence Council. *Global Trends 2030: Alternative Worlds* (Washington, DC: US National Intelligence Council, 2012). Accessed February 6, 2013. www.dni.gov/files/documents/GlobalTrends_2030.pdf.

"US Presses Beijing over South China Sea Dispute." *BBC News.* February 5, 2014. Accessed February 6, 2014. www.bbc.co.uk/news/world-asia-china-26062033.

Yang, Steven, and Edmond Lococo. "IBM Challenger Inspur Woos China Customers Amid Dispute." *Bloomberg.* May 28, 2014. Accessed May 28, 2014. http://mobile.bloomberg.com/news/2014–05–28/china-s-inspur-wooing-ibm-customers-as-hacking-dispute-escalates.html.

Zhang, Baohui. "Taiwan's New Grand Strategy." *Journal of Contemporary China* 20, no. 69 (2011): 269–85.

Zhao, Quansheng, and Guoli Liu. *Managing the China Challenge: Global Perspectives* (London: Routledge, 2009).

Zhao, Suisheng. "China's Global Search for Energy Security: Cooperation and Competition in Asia-Pacific." *Journal of Contemporary China* 17, no. 55 (May 2008): 207–27.

2 A primer on China–US relations, 1949–2008

A friend in need is a friend indeed[1]

Jean-Marc F. Blanchard

Introduction

Many are familiar with the general outlines of relations between Beijing and Washington after 1949 and even more know something about the development of US–People's Republic of China (PRC) ties after President Richard M. Nixon's path-breaking journey to the PRC in 1972. Still Nixon's trip occurred more than 40 years ago and even events that remain fresh in the minds of regular observers – e.g., the 1989 Tiananmen crackdown, the 1995/96 Taiwan Strait Crisis, and the 2001 EP-3 incident – are now decades old and thus will be unfamiliar to the vast majority of non-specialists. Moreover, many features of the contemporary relationship – e.g., China's national power relative to the US and extensive Sino-American interdependence – bear little resemblance to the features of the relationship ten years ago, much less 40 years ago. A general survey of bilateral ties since 1949 thus has value, first in giving non-specialists a foundation from which to appreciate better the history behind, and, second, alerting them to the contemporary contexts shaping the various issues discussed in the chapters comprising this edited volume.

Significant changes seem to be afoot in the China–US relationship. This shows in news reports about frictions between Beijing and Washington pertaining to the Diaoyu/Senkaku Islands, the South China Sea (SCS), China's currency policies, industrial espionage, and North Korean weapons of mass destruction (WMD) programs. They pervade Chinese analyses about the relative power positions of the two countries. The overall import of these issues can be fairly judged, however, only by concurrently acknowledging multiple areas of bilateral cooperation. These include huge trade ties, high levels of foreign direct investment (FDI), broad and deep exchanges, joint anti-piracy efforts, and counterterrorism cooperation. They also need to be juxtaposed against history. When developments are put in a historical light it oftentimes becomes clear that they are less earthshaking than they initially appeared. The third objective of this chapter, then, is to enable readers to view contemporary Sino-American relations with historical lenses.

The chapter illustrates that conflict and cooperation are a constant in the PRC–US relationship, though the degree of each varies. Additionally, it shows that conflict and cooperation often exist alongside each other in multiple issue areas and even within the same issue area. Given this, one should be careful about embracing assessments that conclude that the contemporary relationship is the worst it has ever been because of increasing frictions. Even so, it is inappropriate to conclude unhesitatingly that everything is fine because even the brightest areas of cooperation contain abundant tensions. This chapter also demonstrates that cooperation is most prevalent and conflict most muted when there is a shared threat. Economic interests never have generated the kind of ties a shared threat has. Finally, the chapter shows that the context of Sino-US relations is changing in ways that are not necessarily encouraging.

It should be noted that the narrative here draws almost entirely upon secondary sources supplemented with more contemporary publications such as scholarly articles, media reports, and government statements. Unfortunately, narratives of China–US relations, including this one, tend to be US-centric because we have far more access to declassified documents, interviews of key decision-makers, and top policy-makers' memoirs on the American versus the Chinese side. This is not to say that there are no "declassified" documents, interviews, or memoirs opening a window to Chinese perceptions, interests, and policies. There are.[2] Nevertheless, it is fair to say that the richness of such materials pales in comparison to what is available on the US side.

The next section charts China–US relations from 1949 to 1972. The third focuses on interactions between Beijing and Washington between 1972 and 1989. The fourth covers 1989 to 2000. The fifth examines Sino-US links from 2000 to 2008. Sino-American relations from 2008 to the present are not surveyed here because other authors in the volume address many of the events of the period in their contributions. The sixth identifies some general themes permeating the relationship throughout the period between 1949 and 2008. The seventh summarizes the main points of this chapter, highlights areas in need of additional investigation, and offers some concluding remarks.

US–China relations, 1949 to 1972

The groundwork for tensions between the PRC, which came into being in 1949, and the US was laid early on. After Japan's surrender in 1945, Washington took numerous actions such as occupying vital Chinese ports, transporting Guomindang (GMD/KMT) troops to key cities, and providing massive amounts of arms and money to the GMD in order to ensure that it, rather than the Chinese Communist Party (CCP), dominated the Chinese mainland. Moreover, "private" US pilots flew military missions on behalf of the GMD during the Chinese civil war. On top of this, the US supported the strengthening of Japan and backed France's war in Indochina in order to contain China.[3]

The prospects for a modus vivendi between Washington and the new CCP government in Beijing, already quite poor due to the largely antagonistic nature of US–CCP relations during the Chinese civil war, quickly dissipated. This was a function of China's hostile moves against foreign business, diplomatic, political, and religious interests in China, its decision to develop an alliance with the Soviet Union as manifest most clearly by the 1950 Sino-Soviet Treaty of Friendship, Alliance, and Mutual Assistance. They were destroyed by the Korean War, which resulted in millions of casualties, engendered domestic extremism in both China and the US, fostered closer links between Beijing and Moscow as well as Beijing and Pyongyang, intensified American political, military, and economic containment of China, and rigidified the division of the Korean peninsula.[4]

Taiwan quickly became a major source of contention in the bilateral relationship, with the US interposing naval forces in the Taiwan Strait during the initial stages of the Korean War. Thereafter, the US dispatched military forces and arms to Taiwan, established full diplomatic relations with the island, and concluded a mutual defense treaty with Taiwan. In 1954, there was a major crisis after the PRC commenced attacks against Jinmen and the Dazhen Islands, both held by the GMD. The PRC onslaught was rebuffed by the US because the US threatened nuclear strikes against the PRC. Four years later, there was a more serious crisis relating to the PRC's bombardment and blockade of Jinmen and Mazu, again terminated by US nuclear threats.[5]

Other wellsprings of friction in the 1950s included US efforts to promote separatism in Tibet (Xizang), US opposition to China's admission to the United Nations Security Council (UNSC), American efforts to contain China through the formation of alliances, the application of economic sanctions, and bans on people-to-people exchanges such as scholarly and tourist visits. For its part, China contributed to bilateral animosity by collaborating with diverse liberation movements in the developing world to undermine their Western colonial masters, many of which were American allies. Beyond this, it deepened its political, military, and economic cooperation with the Soviet Union and some newly independent Third World states.[6]

In contrast to the 1950s, bilateral relations in the 1960s were relatively quiescent. However they were anything but peaceful. First, the US backed India against China during the 1962 Sino-Indian Border War, though support was limited. Second, the US and China indirectly clashed in Indochina. The initial phase saw China backing the Vietnamese Communists against the American-backed French prior to the 1954 Geneva Accord that partitioned Vietnam. The second phase saw China supporting the communist North's quest to reunify the country. For its part, the US supplied money, political support, and soldiers to keep South Vietnam out of the Communist orbit. Third, the US, like many other countries, battled Chinese radicalism in the form of support for revolutionary movements in Africa and elsewhere, violations of diplomatic norms at home, and calls for overturning the international politico-economic order.[7]

Although Beijing and Washington had been communicating since the 1950s under the auspices of talks such as the Warsaw Talks, and the US had never abandoned the notion of a better relationship with China, it was not until after the collapse of Sino-Soviet relations that Sino-American relations experienced rapid improvement. China became much more receptive to cooperating with the US to counter the growing danger from its former ally who had massively escalated its military and political pressure on China. Likewise, the US pursued better relations with China to counter the Soviet Union's rising threat to its geopolitical interests, to ease its way out of its morass in Indochina, and to gain leverage against its new economic rival, Japan.[8] In the spirit of warming relations, Washington enlarged opportunities for cultural contacts, cut assistance to Taiwan, and ended a variety of trade and tourism barriers with China.[9]

Taiwan figured prominently in the two countries' rapprochement discussions with China demanding the US break all relations with Taiwan, abrogate its 1954 defense treaty, and remove its forces from Taiwan. The US initially balked at abandoning its long-time ally. Eventually, however, it made extensive compromises ranging from embracing a one-China policy to rejecting Taiwan independence to promising to restrain Japan from moving into its former colony, Taiwan. While China gave little in return, its promises of non-intervention in the Vietnam conflict gave the US greater latitude in choosing the methods by which it would extricate itself from Indochina.[10]

US–China relations, 1972 to 1989

In February 1972, President Richard Nixon made his momentous trip to China. Meeting with paramount Chinese leader Mao Zedong in Beijing, Nixon stated: "We can find common ground, despite our differences, to build a world structure in which both can be safe to develop in our own ways on our own roads."[11] Nixon's visit to China gave the relationship a completely new aura, but the symbol of bilateral rapprochement between the US and China undoubtedly was the 1972 Shanghai Communiqué.

In the communiqué, Beijing stated that Taiwan is a province of China, adding that the government of the PRC is the sole legal government of China and that Taiwan is China's internal affair. Furthermore, it noted that Taiwan was the issue preventing a normalization of bilateral relations. The US stated it "acknowledges that all Chinese on either side of the Taiwan Strait maintain there is but one China and that Taiwan is a part of China" and that it "does not challenge that position." Moreover, it called for a peaceful settlement of the Taiwan question. Finally, it expressed its intent to reduce forces and installations on Taiwan. The communiqué also called for increased trade and expanded contacts in science, technology, and sports.[12] At the time, though, economic ties fostered no great American interest in China and there even were doubts the US could buy anything from China.[13] Nevertheless, trade increased in the wake of the communiqué. For instance, US grain sales to China hit US $900 million in 1974. However, various political and economic factors conspired to limit an expansion of ties.[14]

Reflecting the fact that the US and China were primarily bound by shared security concerns, relations assumed a heavy military-security hue in the years following the 1972 rapprochement. This meant extensive American sharing of highly classified intelligence on Soviet military deployments, US support for third-party arms sales to China, and closer Sino-American military interactions.[15]

The US, though, would not back away entirely from Taiwan or move to full diplomatic relations with the PRC. Causes include an unwillingness to break relations fully, the distractions of Watergate/domestic politics, and, later, the desires of Presidents Gerald Ford and Jimmy Carter to avoid damaging détente with the Soviet Union and, in Carter's case, a focus on other matters such as the ratification of the Panama Canal Treaties. However, China's desire to tap foreign trade and investment, to learn from US economic models, growing American interest in the China market, continued worries about the Soviet threat, and Chinese concerns about Vietnam provided both sides with a new impetus to deepen bilateral links.[16]

In late 1978, Carter announced that China and the US would establish full diplomatic relations in 1979. The "Normalization Communiqué" recognized the PRC as the official government of China. It also acknowledged that Taiwan was part of China. Furthermore, it stated the US would abrogate its defense treaty with Taiwan. Even so, it confirmed the US would maintain commercial and other unofficial links with and the right to sell arms to Taiwan. Finally, it incorporated anti-hegemony language.[17] Congressional passage of the Taiwan Relations Act (TRA) in early 1979 diluted the glow of the Normalization Communiqué. The TRA guaranteed US arms sales to Taiwan to maintain the island's self-defense capability. Second, it stated that the US would consider any military action, boycott, or embargo against Taiwan to be of grave concern to the US.[18] Beijing was livid, but the Soviet invasion of Afghanistan in December 1979, continuing Sino-Vietnamese tensions, and economic interests propelled ties to new levels including arms sales and joint intelligence-gathering.[19]

Common security interests and military cooperation constituted the core of burgeoning Sino-American ties, but the relationship also began to develop in other areas in the late 1970s. For instance, during the Carter presidency, the US issued more Chinese student visas, gave China provisional "most favored nation" (MFN) status, and increased China's access to technology and preferential loans. The US sought to broaden the basis of the relationship, to profit economically, and to bring about the liberalization of China. For its part, China sought to enrich the non-security aspects of its relationship with the US in order to reinvigorate the economy. From China's vantage point, better relations would advance this goal by bringing American capital, technology, and know-how into China and facilitating China's re-entry into the international economy and global economic institutions.[20]

The initial years of the 1980s were rough for US–China relations because of, inter alia, President Ronald Reagan's very favorable disposition towards Taiwan, disagreements over policy towards the Soviet Union, changing economic situations in both countries, and evolving bilateral perceptions among American elites. Without a doubt, the biggest issue was continuing American arms sales to Taiwan, with Beijing adamant that Washington had to reduce the quantity and quality of weapons it was selling and set a date for the termination of all sales. Chinese desires to avoid a breakdown of relations with the US and US desires to maintain China as a bulwark against the Soviet Union prevented a breakdown in relations and resulted in a deal (the 1982 "Arms Sale Communiqué") whereby the US agreed to limit the quantity and quality of arms sales to previous levels and to gradually reduce the amount of arms sold to Taiwan.[21]

Despite the ups and downs of the relationship, a thawing Sino-Soviet relationship (which gave China less incentive to work with the US), and American concerns over Chinese missile sales, the Soviet and Vietnamese threat to Chinese and American interests still proved sufficient to bind the two countries through the late 1980s. The US and China cooperated against the Soviets in Afghanistan and against Vietnam and the Vietnamese-backed government in Cambodia. In addition, the US loosened controls over high technology exports to China. As well, there were numerous US–PRC military exchanges and even some arms sales. But there was much more going on than security cooperation. First, there were numerous educational, technical, and other exchanges. Second, trade and investment linkages strengthened. Third, the US eased China into international economic organizations such as the World Bank.[22]

US–China relations, 1989 to 2000

Reagan's successor, George Bush Sr, attempted to maintain continuity in US policy toward China, but international and domestic events conspired to undermine his plans. As for international events, the collapse of the Soviet empire in Eastern Europe and the subsequent dissolution of the Soviet Union diminished the need for Washington to cooperate with Beijing. With respect to domestic events, the seminal event was the 1989 Tiananmen massacre and subsequent political repression. As observed by one journalist, the crackdown single-handedly altered "the American perceptions of a steadily reforming China." After Tiananmen, the American Congress and public started to weigh on the bilateral relationship in a way they never had before. Pressured by events and domestic factors, Bush Sr imposed a mixture of sanctions on China while also dangling various inducements in return for China implementing some reforms.[23]

The collapse of the Soviet Union removed the security bond at the core of the US–PRC relationship. Nevertheless, China became a linchpin of American efforts to deal with the proliferation of WMDs and the North Korean problem. The US recognized, too, that it needed to work with China if it wanted to achieve its environmental, trade, and diverse other non-security goals. Nevertheless, the factor, above all, that "reconciled" the US and China was Iraq's invasion of Kuwait in 1990. The US acted pragmatically to gain China's support in the UNSC while China took advantage of the opening, gaining points by acting cooperatively. Nonetheless, in the early 1990s, the relationship faced new tensions relating to Bush Sr's election-year decision to approve an F-16 sale to Taiwan, candidate Bill Clinton's assertiveness on human rights issues, and China's arms purchases and weapons sales.[24]

President Clinton initially took an assertive stance towards China, threatening to revoke its MFN status unless it changed its policies regarding human rights, the blocking of foreign broadcasts, Tibet, prison labor exports, and trade.

Beijing's intransigence coupled with Washington's embrace of engagement, business pressures, and desire for Beijing's support to deal with North Korea and other issues, ultimately led Clinton to abandon his linkage policy.[25] Aside from disagreements about human rights, during Clinton's first presidency, China and the US clashed about matters such as Chinese missile sales to Pakistan and associated US economic sanctions and Congressional opposition to China's hosting of the 2000 Summer Olympics.[26]

Increased flexibility in Clinton's China policy following his re-election and Chinese President Jiang Zemin's 1997 visit to Washington warmed the then frosty relationship, which had been strained over the persistent thorn of Taiwan (see below). At the 1997 summit, China promised to cease nuclear cooperation with Iran while the US promised it would let American companies sell nuclear-power gear and technology to China.[27] The next year, Clinton became the first US president to visit China post-1989. In Beijing, he publicly stated the "Three Noes" while the two governments struck energy and environmental deals, promoted military exchanges, and advanced cooperation in culture, education, and people-to-people exchanges.[28] In 1999, relations underwent a major downturn as a result of the American bombing of the Chinese embassy in Belgrade in May, which provoked large anti-American protests and damage to the US embassy and consulates in China. Calm was restored after both sides worked to moderate public emotions in order to prevent further escalation.[29]

Despite tensions regarding Taiwan and other issues such as the theft of intellectual property rights (IPR), the final years of Clinton's second term in office witnessed positive developments on the Sino-US economic front. In November 1999, after 13 years of negotiations, Beijing and Washington reached agreement on the terms under which China would enter the WTO. Pursuant to the deal, Beijing committed itself to slash tariffs and import restrictions on numerous industrial and agricultural products. It further agreed to open a broad swath of sectors including banking and telecommunications. Furthermore, it accepted a wide range of international IPR rules. Finally, it embraced diverse international technical standards, trade policy transparency provisions, and limits on its ability to discriminate against foreign investors.[30] Despite this success, the bilateral relationship encountered rough patches due to, inter alia, China's crackdown on Falun Gong, American plans to deploy missile defense systems in the APR and elsewhere, and Chinese missile sales.[31]

As noted, Taiwan repeatedly emerged as a source of tension during Clinton's tenure in office. Tensions were tied to pro-independence Taiwanese President Lee Teng-Hui's effort to visit the US in 1994, Congressional efforts to upgrade the status of Taiwan and US–Taiwan relations, and Lee's visit to his alma mater, Cornell University, coupled with provocative statements during his visit.[32] These developments were followed by the dangerous 1995/96 Taiwan Strait Missile Crisis which involved large-scale Chinese military exercises, live fire drills, and threats of nuclear escalation. The US responded by deploying significant naval forces in the Taiwan Strait, reiterating the Three Noes, and moving to enhance its security relationship with Japan. In July 1999, Lee described Taiwan and the mainland as having "a special state-to-state relationship," which provoked a harsh PRC response. The US moved quickly to defuse this crisis by distancing itself from Lee's formulation, delaying some defense missions to Taipei, and reiterating its "one China" policy. However, it also cautioned Beijing to act with restraint.[33]

The end of the Cold War and the Tiananmen crackdown transformed the universe of actors attempting to shape American policy towards China. While Congress long had a role in shaping post-1949 US China policy, it generally played a peripheral part, with the notable exception of US Taiwan policy. Post-1989, it gained newfound prominence, partly as a consequence of the greater role of the American public and special interests. In addition, US bureaucracies like the US trade representative (USTR) became more salient. Beyond new actors, non-security issues such as economics and religious rights gained greater status.[34] Many highlight the US business lobby as exerting particularly heavy influence on Washington's China policies during the Clinton years.[35] At the same time, the influence of the realists, the hawks, and the Taiwan lobby seemed to be declining. As for China, the key drivers of its policy-making remained unchanged, with top Chinese leaders making the big decisions pertaining to grand strategy, major power relations, and foreign economic policy. Still, some argued that there was a broadening of foreign policy inputs.[36]

US–China relations, 2000 to 2008

There was much pessimism about the future of Sino-American relations after George W. Bush became president. After all, Bush Jr viewed China as a strategic competitor, favored working with traditional US allies such as Japan, and saw China's military modernization as a rising threat to Taiwan. Still, Beijing had little choice but to work with Washington, given its lack of options and continuing need for a peaceful international environment that would allow it to focus on pressing domestic problems. Not long after Bush became president, the Sino-American modus vivendi was put to a severe test. In April 2001 a Chinese fighter jet and American EP-3 spy plane collided over the SCS, with the US plane making an emergency landing on Hainan Island after which China seized it and its crew. While China eventually returned the plane and crew to the US, the incident seriously damaged bilateral ties.[37]

Al-Qaeda's attack on the US five months later rescued the relationship because Washington sought Chinese support for its global war on terror (GWOT) and initiatives against Iraq and North Korea. For its part, China supported the GWOT to curry US favor, to facilitate a crackdown in restive Xinjiang, and to demonstrate that it was a responsible member of the international community. For China, warmer relations with the US were a blessing, initiating a decade of opportunity for its peaceful rise.

During the first Bush Jr administration, a bright spot in the relationship was bilateral cooperation on North Korea. Still, there were strong disagreements about how aggressive a stance should be taken to denuclearize the hermit kingdom. The US was grateful for China's role in creating the Six-Party Talks (6PT), pressuring Pyongyang to come to the bargaining table, and restricting its missile technology exports to North Korea, but wanted it to do more. Although Beijing disagreed with Washington's assumption about its actual leverage over the DPRK, a growing awareness that WMDs represented a threat to China's security and a desire to be seen as a responsible power encouraged a modicum of cooperation. Overall, the issue of North Korea promoted both cooperation and conflict, though American plans to counter North Korea through the deployment of missile defense systems only generated the latter.[38]

As one might expect, the issue generating the greatest heat during the first Bush Jr administration was Taiwan. This initially flowed from Bush's strong tilt towards Taipei as manifested by a large weapons sale in April 2001, Bush's statement during a TV interview that the US would do "whatever it takes" to help Taiwan defend itself, and close US–Taiwan military cooperation. Three years later, the root cause of tensions was Taipei, with President Chen saying in the run-up to the 2004 presidential election that he would push for a referendum modifying Taiwan's constitution. While the Taiwan legislature's vote in November 2003 to ban referenda that changed the country's name, flag, or territory calmed Beijing, Chen's statement in March 2004 that the status quo meant independence revived Beijing's anxiety. Beijing threatened force, insisted the US to adhere to the One China policy, and called for vigorous action to rein in Chen. Top US officials made clear, sometimes very bluntly, that the US opposed Taiwan independence and unilateral changes to the status quo, though it continued to sell arms to Taiwan.[39]

During Bush Jr's first term, economics provided a vital glue for the bilateral relationship.[40] By the end of 2003, trade was approaching $200 billion while American firms had invested around $45 billion in China.[41] Nevertheless, the economic relationship was a considerable source of friction from 2003 onward. One reason was the massive Sino-American trade deficit. A second, linked to the first, was a feeling that China was substantially undervaluing its currency. A third was growing dissatisfaction with China's adherence to its WTO obligations. The 2004 Congressional and presidential elections forced the Bush Jr administration to show action in all of these areas, which it did by dispatching officials to China to voice US concerns, engaging with China at the highest level, and filing, albeit rarely, WTO dispute cases against China.[42]

In the aggregate, Sino-American relations were relatively stable from 2000 to 2004. There were multiple reasons for this. In the case of the US, security issues such as the GWOT, Iraq, and North Korea encouraged Bush Jr to pursue a working relationship with Beijing. Second, to China's delight, the US adopted a relatively tough stance towards the Taiwan independence movement so it could focus on the aforementioned issues. Third, China's WTO accession in 2001 ended the circus of Congress annually approving China's MFN status. Turning to China, Beijing was focused on its leadership transition and intensifying domestic problems. Furthermore, there was a perception that the US would remain pre-eminent for many years to come. Of course, economic interests contributed to a stable relationship. China, for example, saw good relations with the US as necessary to obtain American investment, technology, and market access. Some believe, too, that stable Sino-American relations were linked, in part, to China's relatively moderate stance towards Taipei.[43]

In 2005, the relationship took a turn for the worse because of rising economic tensions, primarily over China's currency policies.[44] A key driver was the US Congress, which introduced legislation designed to punish China for its currency policies as well as subsidy programs, market access barriers, and IPR practices. Although the administration did not support such legislation, it pressed Beijing to revalue the renminbi quickly, arguing that China's currency policy was a cause of the China–US deficit. While pointing to the benefits of China's stable currency and rejecting the thesis that the trade deficit flowed from China's currency policy as opposed to other factors like American export controls, Beijing revalued, floated, and increased the daily trading band for its currency in 2005 and later in 2007, somewhat diffusing tensions.[45]

Aside from the marquee issue of China's currency policy, another big source of economic friction during Bush Jr's second term was China's success in fulfilling its IPR obligations. Ultimately, Beijing committed to increase criminal prosecutions, limit exports of pirated products, and ensure government offices only used legal software.[46] Unlike the currency issue, Bush Jr proved willing to file WTO cases against China with regard to to its IPR protection policies. A third issue was Chinese government subsidies.[47] The administration not only filed WTO cases relating to such subsidies, but also imposed countervailing duties against subsidized Chinese goods.[48] A fourth problem that emerged in 2007 was the safety of Chinese goods including fish and seafood, tires, and toys.[49] There also were problems over issues such as China's treatment of foreign investors.

Bush's second term witnessed diverse tensions linked to the Taiwan issue. For instance, Congressional efforts to increase high-level US–Taiwan government interactions, administration initiatives to strengthen US–Taiwan military ties, and China's 2005 Anti-Secession Law generated stresses.[50] In 2006, President Chen sparked new frictions when he announced plans to abolish the National Unification Council and the National Unification Guidelines. Although the US pacified China somewhat by reaffirming its One China policy and opposing a unilateral change in the status quo, it also upset China by letting Chen stop over in the US and by selling hundreds of missiles to Taiwan. China also was alarmed by the 2008 Taiwan presidential election since it included referenda calling for Taiwan to seek separate UN membership. The US strongly criticized the referenda.[51] By the end of 2008, the Taiwan issue had become a non-issue because the GMD, which focused on the economy and favored the status quo, won a legislative majority in January and the presidency in March.[52]

The second Bush Jr presidency gave newfound emphasis to China's ongoing military modernization. To illustrate, in June 2005, at a conference in Singapore, American Defense Secretary Donald Rumsfeld argued that China's military investments posed a risk to Taiwan, to American interests, and even to China's trading partners in Asia.[53] In the February 2006 Quadrennial Defense Review,

Washington singled out China as having "the greatest potential to compete militarily with the United States."[54] The worries embodied in these statements and reports tie to the de-intensification of the GWOT (which gave the administration the space to give greater attention to China), significant year-over-year increases in Chinese defense spending, and signs of China's improving military capabilities as embodied in its successful test of an anti-satellite missile.[55]

As during Bush's first term, North Korea produced both cooperation and conflict in the Sino-US relationship. As for the former, China actively tried to sustain the 6PT structure and to broker a deal.[56] In thanks, Washington lauded Beijing numerous times for serving a "constructive leadership role" as host of the 6PT and also praised its willingness to support strong and punitive UNSC measures against North Korea.[57] In terms of conflict, while pleased by Chinese support for the 6PT and UNSC measures against the DPRK, Washington still felt Beijing could have pressured North Korea more, supported stronger UNSC resolutions against Pyongyang, and done a better job enforcing approved UNSC measures.[58]

From 2004 to 2008, cooperation dominated because China and the US saw the advantages of collaborating on issues like terrorism, nuclear proliferation, and the DPRK. Still Washington found it difficult to paper over its frictions with China after the GWOT and Iraq war quieted down. Moreover, domestic pressures became more potent after Democrats took control of the US Congress. Despite displeasure over US ties with Taiwan and other issues, China found it worthwhile to cooperate with the US so it could focus on internal matters. Another factor supporting cooperation was China's desire to mollify other countries' anxieties about it. One-time events such as China's adjustment to WTO entry, the 2008 Beijing Olympics, and the onset of the 2008 financial crisis encouraged Beijing to seek an accommodative external milieu, too.[59] Even so, shifting power positions and a sense that China weathered the financial crisis well led some in China to embrace greater Chinese assertiveness and view the US less positively, creating an undercurrent of instability in the oasis of calm at the end of 2008.[60] According to some, Chinese nationalism, the Chinese military, and the Chinese public also began to weigh on the relationship as Obama took office.[61]

Conclusion

The primary goal of this chapter has been to supply a history of China–US ties. In this vein, it chronicled the relationship from 1949 to the end of 2008. It supplied details about the birth of cooperative PRC–US ties, the effort to normalize relations in the late 1970s, and the role played by the Soviet and later the Vietnam threat in these developments. Furthermore, it discussed the stress Reagan's favorable stance towards Taiwan injected into relations, the role the Soviet and Vietnamese threats and China's economic interests played in rescuing the relationship, the tumult resulting from the 1989 Tiananmen crackdown, and the 1990 Gulf War's role in staving off a major post-1989 downturn in relations. It probed human rights frictions during Clinton's first term in office, the resurgence of Taiwan as a source of tensions, and the two countries cooperation on China's WTO accession. It reported on how the GWOT and US invasion of Iraq gave an otherwise cautious Bush Jr administration reason to nurture a working relationship with China and how the moderation of both created the space for renewed US attention to China's rise.

A second purpose of this chapter has been to provide a better basis to judge the current state of the relationship. It demonstrates quite clearly that conflict and cooperation have been the norm for the relationship, though conflict may dominate over cooperation in some periods as opposed to others or in some issue areas as opposed to others. It further shows that conflict and cooperation often exist alongside each other in multiple issue areas and that conflict and cooperation can even be present concurrently within the same issue area. Given this, one should be cautious about embracing assessments that conclude the contemporary relationship is horrible or in irrevocable decline because of an increase in the breadth or intensity of bilateral frictions. On the other hand, it is inappropriate to conclude everything is fine in defined areas like economics, much less the relationship as a whole, because of extensive collaboration in these areas or massive economic cooperation. As the chapter shows, there simply are too many frictions elsewhere to support such a conclusion.

Aside from the aforementioned objectives, this chapter has aimed to detail the context surrounding the ups and downs in the China–US relationship. Of note, cooperation seems most prevalent and conflict most muted when there is a security imperative coupled with the one side needing the other to realize some objective, which may or may not be security related. It will be unsurprising to regular observers of China–US relations that cooperation seems most vigorous and strong when China and the US share a security threat or threats. This is not encouraging given the US and China's current lack of a genuine shared security threat. The past record shows that economic interests have never fueled the same kind of bonds as a security threat. Indeed, the inability of massive trade, investment, and other economic ties to mute growing frictions is striking. Another contextual transformation has been China's growing power relative to the US. The implications of this are still unfolding, but clearly it has emboldened China and made the US both anxious and cautious at the same time.

One of the limitations of this chapter is that it does not assess the impact of domestic political actors on Sino-American relations in a substantive manner. A fuller examination of bilateral interactions certainly would require a discussion of which actors have been involved and the ways in these individuals and groups have mattered. A more comprehensive treatment of ties between China and the US also would benefit from a consideration of the cultural, ideological, historical, and other noteworthy factors shaping the relationship. A proper treatment of these variables, though, requires one to consider the international and domestic contextual variables that made domestic politics and other factors relevant.

The China–US relationship now runs more than 40 years. It has had many bright spots, including a near-military alliance in the 1970s, growing economic interactions from the 1980s onward, and collaboration on issues such as North Korea. Unfortunately, the relationship also has been replete with severe problems such as large-scale direct fighting, indirect conflict through proxies, and explosive military encounters. Today, the balance seems to be shifting towards the latter and many have become concerned about the future of the relationship. However, any judgments need to be put in a historical setting. In this regard, the news is good. Conflict and cooperation often have gone together. However, historical lenses also indicate that the contextual factors that so often have undergirded cooperation are absent or disappearing. This is worrisome.

Notes

1 The author would like to thank Stanley Rosen, Simon Shen, and Robert G. Sutter for their comments on various iterations of this chapter. He remains responsible for any errors that remain. The author also would like to thank the Mr. & Mrs. S.H. Wong Foundation for research support throughout the years.
2 See, e.g., Dong Wang, *The Quarreling Brothers: New Chinese Archives and a Reappraisal of the Sino-Soviet Split, 1959–1962*, working paper no. 49 (Washington, DC: Wilson Center Cold War International History Project, n.d.).
3 Michael Schaller, *The United States and China in the Twentieth Century*, 2nd edn (New York: Oxford University Press, 1990), 66, 111, 122; Andrew J. Nathan and Robert S. Ross, *The Great Wall and the Empty Fortress: China's Search for Security* (New York: W.W. Norton, 1997), 57–9; and Jonathan D. Spence, *The Search for Modern China*, 2nd edn (New York: W.W. Norton, 1999), 459–66.
4 Nigel Thomas and Peter Abbott, *The Korean War, 1950–53* (Oxford: Osprey Publishing, 1986); Schaller, *The United States and China in the Twentieth Century*, 127–43, 148; Nathan and Ross, *The Great Wall and the Empty Fortress*, 59–62.
5 On the two Taiwan Strait Crises, useful works include Melvin Gurtov, "The Taiwan Strait Crisis Revisited: Politics and Foreign Policy in Chinese Motives," *Modern China* 2, no. 1 (January 1976): 49–103; H.W. Brands, Jr, "Testing Massive Retaliation: Credibility and Crisis Management in the Taiwan Strait," *International Security* 12, no. 4 (Spring 1988): 124–51; and Thomas J. Christensen, *Useful Adversaries: Grand Strategy, Domestic Mobilization, and Sino-American Conflict, 1947–1958* (Princeton, NJ: Princeton University Press, 1996). On the US support for Taiwan at the time, see Chi Wang, *The United States and China since World War II: A Brief History* (Armonk, NJ: M.E. Sharpe, 2013), 39–53.
6 Schaller, *The United States and China in the Twentieth Century*, 143–9; John W. Garver, *Foreign Relations of the People's Republic of China* (Englewood Cliffs, NJ: Prentice Hall, 1993), 57–64; Nathan and Ross, *The Great Wall and the Empty Fortress*, 39–42, 60–64; Robert G. Sutter, *US–Chinese Relations: Perilous Past, Pragmatic Present* (Lanham, MD: Rowman & Littlefield, 2010), 54–9; and Nancy Bernkopf Tucker, "The Evolution of US–China Relations," in *Tangled Titans: The United States and China*, ed. David Shambaugh (Lanham, MD: Rowman & Littlefield, 2013), 32–3.
7 Schaller, *The United States and China in the Twentieth Century*, 159–68; Garver, *Foreign Relations of the People's Republic of China*, 136–63, 292–301; Nathan and Ross, *The Great Wall and the Empty Fortress*, 102, 108–9; Sutter, *US–Chinese Relations*, 59–62; and Tucker, "The Evolution of US–China Relations," 33–5.
8 Schaller, *The United States and China in the Twentieth Century*, 171–86; Nathan and Ross, *The Great Wall and the Empty Fortress*, 43–6; James Mann, *About Face: A History of America's Curious Relationship with China, from Nixon to Clinton* (New York: Vintage Books, 2000), 13–52; Michael Schaller, *The United States and China*

into the Twenty-First Century (New York: Oxford University Press, 2002), 177; and Sutter, *US–Chinese Relations*, 65–75. On US thinking about better relations with China, see Gordon H. Chang, *Friends and Enemies: The United States, China, and the Soviet Union, 1948–1972* (Stanford, CA: Stanford University Press, 1990).
9 Wang, *The United States and China since World War II*, 72.
10 Harry Harding, *A Fragile Relationship: The United States and China since 1972* (Washington, DC: The Brookings Institution, 1992), 40–3: Mann, *About Face*, 22–47; and Schaller, *The United States and China in the Twenty-First Century*, 174–6, 180.
11 Patrick Tyler, *A Great Wall: Six Presidents and China* (New York: Public Affairs, 1999), 133, quoted in Wang, *The United States and China since World War II*, 85.
12 Harding, *A Fragile Relationship*, 43–4; Mann, *About Face*, 46–8; and Schaller, *The United States and China in the Twenty-First Century*, 180.
13 Charles W. Freeman, III, "The Commercial and Economic Relationship," in *Tangled Titans*, ed. Shambaugh, 181.
14 Wang, *The United States and China since World War II*, 89.
15 Mann, *About Face*, 56–65, 73–6.
16 Schaller, *The United States and China in the Twentieth Century*, 190–1, 203–7; Harding, *A Fragile Relationship*, 48–54, 67–77; Mann, *About Face*, 82–3, 85; Schaller, *The United States and China in the Twenty-First Century*, 188–90; Sutter, *US–Chinese Relations*, 77–8; and Freeman, "The Commercial and Economic Relationship," 183, 185–6.
17 Harding, *A Fragile Relationship*, 77–81; Mann, *About Face*, 83–94; and Schaller, *The United States and China in the Twenty-First Century*, 190.
18 Schaller, *The United States and China in the Twentieth Century*, 210–11; Harding, *A Fragile Relationship*, 82–7; Nathan and Ross, *The Great Wall and the Empty Fortress*, 67; Mann, *About Face*, 95; and Schaller, *The United States and China in the Twenty-First Century*, 190.
19 Schaller, *The United States and China in the Twentieth Century*, 210–13; Harding, *A Fragile Relationship*, 88–9; Mann, *About Face*, 96–100, 110–13; Schaller, *The United States and China in the Twenty-First Century*, 191–2; and Sutter, *US–Chinese Relations*, 79.
20 Harding, *A Fragile Relationship*, 87–100; Mann, *About Face*, 103–13; and Schaller, *The United States and China in the Twenty-First Century*, 192.
21 Schaller, *The United States and China in the Twentieth Century*, 215–18; Harding, *A Fragile Relationship*, 107–69; Mann, *About Face*, 115–50; Schaller, *The United States and China in the Twenty-First Century*, 193–6; and Sutter, *US–Chinese Relations*, 80–93.
22 Harding, *A Fragile Relationship*, chs 3–6; Nathan and Ross, *The Great Wall and the Empty Fortress*, 65–9; Mann, *About Face*, chs 1–7; Sutter, *US–Chinese Relations*, 67–94; and Tucker, "The Evolution of US–China Relations," 36–8.
23 Harding, *A Fragile Relationship*, 215–46; Nathan and Ross, *The Great Wall and the Empty Fortress*, 69–73; Mann, *About Face*, 175–6, 186–241; Schaller, *The United States and China in the Twenty-First Century*, 199–205; and Sutter, *US–Chinese Relations*, 95–6. The quote is from Mann, *About Face*, 192.
24 Harding, *A Fragile Relationship*, 270–80; Mann, *About Face*, 228, 248–72; Suisheng Zhao, "Beijing's Perception of the International System and Foreign Policy Adjustment after the Tiananmen Incident," in *Chinese Foreign Policy: Pragmatism and Strategic Behavior*, ed. Suisheng Zhao (Armonk, NJ: M.E. Sharpe, 2004), 146–8; Wang, *The United States and China since World War II*, 139–144; and Robert G. Sutter, *US–Chinese Relations: Perilous Past, Pragmatic Present*, 2nd edn (Lanham, MD: Rowman & Littlefield, 2013), 97–8, 105–6.
25 David M. Lampton, "America's China Policy in the Age of the Finance Minister: Clinton Ends Linkage," *China Quarterly*, no. 139 (September 1994): 597–621; Mann, *About Face*, 274–314; and Sutter, *US–Chinese Relations*, 98–106.

26 Wang, *The United States and China Since World War II*, 149.
27 Mann, *About Face*, 353–8.
28 Mann, *About Face*, 364–7. The "Three Noes" were: no support for Taiwan's independence, no support for Taiwan's admission to the UN, and no support for two Chinas.
29 Bonnie S. Glaser, "US–China Relations: Challenged by New Crises," *Comparative Connections* 1, no. 1 (July 1999), http://csiorg/files/media/csis/pubs/9901qus_china.pdf; Bonnie S. Glaser, "US–China Relations: Beginning to Thaw," *Comparative Connections* 1, no. 2 (October 1999), http://csis.org/files/media/csis/pubs/9902qus_china.pdf; and Gregory J. Moore, "Not Very Material but Hardly Immaterial: China's Bombed Embassy and Sino-American Relations," *Foreign Policy Analysis* 6, no. 1 (January 2010): 23–41.
30 Jean-Marc F. Blanchard, "The Dynamics of China's Accession to the WTO: Counting Sense, Coalitions, and Constructs," *Asian Journal of Social Science* 41, nos. 3–4 (December 2013): 263–86.
31 Bonnie S. Glaser, "US–China Relations: Progress Amidst Persisting Deep Suspicions," *Comparative Connections* 1, no. 3 (January 2000), http://csis.org/files/media/csis/pubs/9903qus_china.pdf.
32 Mann, *About Face*, 315–28; Schaller, *The United States and China in the Twenty-First Century*, 214–17; and Sutter, *US–Chinese Relations*, 98.
33 Mann, *About Face*, 328–9, 334–8; Robert S. Ross, "The 1995–96 Taiwan Strait Confrontation: Coercion, Credibility, and Use of Force," *International Security* 25, no. 2 (Fall 2000): 87–123; Schaller, *The United States and China in the Twenty-First Century*, 217–19, 224; Sutter, *US–Chinese Relations*, 98, 108–9, 222–3; and Tucker, "The Evolution of US–China Relations," 40–1.
34 Sutter, *US–Chinese Relations*, 100–3; Tucker, "The Evolution of US–China Relations," 38–40; and Robert Sutter, "Domestic American Influences on US–China Relations," in *Tangled Titans*, ed. Shambaugh, 108–10.
35 See, e.g., Mann, *About Face*, 284–9.
36 Kenneth G. Lieberthal and David M. Lampton, eds., *Bureaucracy, Politics and Policy Making in Post-Mao China* (Berkeley: University of California Press, 1992); Quansheng Zhao, "Domestic Factors of Chinese Foreign Policy: From Vertical to Horizontal Authoritarianism," *Annals of the American Academy of Political and Social Science* 519 (January 1992): 158–175; and Ning Lu, *The Dynamics of Foreign-policy Decisionmaking in China* (Boulder, CO: Westview Press, 1997).
37 This and the next paragraph draw upon Brendan Taylor, "US–China Relations after 11 September: A Long Engagement or Marriage of Convenience," *Australian Journal of International Affairs* 59, no. 2 (June 2005): 179–83; Jia Qingguo, "Learning to Live with the Hegemon: Evolution of China's Policy towards the US since the End of the Cold War," *Journal of Contemporary China* 14, no. 44 (August 2005): 395–407; Jia Qingguo, "One Administration, Two Voices: US China Policy During Bush's First Term," *International Relations of the Asia-Pacific* 6, no. 1 (2006): 23–36; Chi Wang, *George W. Bush and China: Policies, Problems, and Partnership* (Lanham, MD: Lexington Books, 2009), 11, 14–16, 79–89; Sutter, *US–Chinese Relations*, 150–4; and Tucker, "The Evolution of US–China Relations," 41–2.
38 Bonnie S. Glaser, "US–China Relations: Terrorist Strikes Give US–China Ties a Boost," *Comparative Connections* 3, no. 3 (October 2001), http://csis.org/files/media/csis/pubs/0103qus_china.pdf; Kerry Dumbaugh, *China–US Relations: Current Issues for the 108th Congress*, report no. RL31815 (Washington, DC: Congressional Research Service, 2003), 16–17, 23; Taylor, "US–China Relations after 11 September," 183–5; Wang, *George W. Bush and China*, 14–21, 67–74; and Jean-Marc F. Blanchard, "US–China Relations under Bush and Obama: Fill in the Blanks or It's the Structure, Stupid?" *Issues and Studies* 49, no. 3 (September 2013): 44.
39 Taylor, "US–China Relations after 11 September," 186–8; Sutter, *US–Chinese Relations*, 223–6; and Wang, *George W. Bush and China*, 51–63.

40 "Transcript: Powell Stresses US Wants Friendly Ties with China; July 28 interview on Chinese television," *Washington File*, July 31, 2001, http://wfile.ait.org.tw/wf-archive/2001/010731/epf203.htm.
41 Jia, "One Administration, Two Voices," 27–8.
42 Dumbaugh, "China–US Relations," 15; Neil C. Hughes, "A Trade War with China?" *Foreign Affairs* 84, no. 4 (July/August 2005): 94–106; Wang, *George W. Bush and China*, 103–4, 108–9; Blanchard, "US–China Relations under Bush and Obama," 48–55; and Wei Liang's contribution to this volume.
43 Dumbaugh, "China–US Relations," 2–5; Thomas Christensen, "PRC Security Relations with the United States: Why Things Are Going So Well," *China Leadership Monitor*, no. 8 (Fall 2003): 2–4, 6–7, http://media.hoover.org/sites/default/files/documents/clm8_tc.pdf; Robert Sutter, *China's Peaceful Rise and US Interests in Asia: Status and Outlook*, issue brief no. 27, June 24, 2004, http://csis.org/files/media/csis/pubs/pac0427.pdf; Taylor, "US–China Relations after 11 September," 187–92; and Jia, "One Administration, Two Voices," esp. 30–3.
44 Andrew Yeh, "Do More, US Urges Beijing," *Financial Times*, November 5, 2005.
45 Edward Alden and Christopher Swann, "US Set to Get Tough over Renminbi," *Financial Times*, April 8, 2005; Mark M. Spiegel, "A Look at China's New Exchange Rate Regime, 2005–23," September 9, 2005, www.frbsf.org/economic-research/publications/economic-letter/2005/september/a-look-at-china-new-exchange-rate-regime/el2005-23.pdf; "Chinese Vice Commerce Minister Calls on Joint Efforts on Balancing Sino-US Trade," *People's Daily Online*, November 25, 2005, http://english.people.com.cn/200511/25/eng20051125_223903.html, accessed November 25, 2005; Andrew Balls and Christopher Swann, "US Attacks China Peg for Trade Deficit," *Financial Times*, February 14, 2006; Eoin Callan and Richard McGregor, "US Urged to Target Chinese Exports," *Financial Times*, June 13, 2007; and Krishna Guha, "Paulson 'Frustrated' at Pace of Renminbi Reform," *Financial Times*, February 1, 2007.
46 *Xinhua*, "China, US end Annual Trade Negotiation with Consensus on IPR Protection," *People's Daily Online*, July 12, 2005, http://english.people.com.cn/200507/12/eng20050712_195494.html, accessed July 12, 2005; Richard McGregor, "US Cautious over Progress on China Trade," *Financial Times*, July 12, 2005; and Sutter, *US–Chinese Relations*, 210.
47 Steven R. Weisman, "US Toughens Its Position on China Trade," *New York Times*, April 10, 2007, accessed April 10, 2007, www.nytimes.com/2007/04/10/business/worldbusiness/10trade.html.
48 See, e.g., Eoin Callan, "US Launches Trade Dispute with China as 'Dialogue Fails,'" *Financial Times*, February 3–4, 2007; Alan Beattie, "Washington Sees Victory in China Subsidies Fight," *Financial Times*, November 30, 2007; and Steven R. Weisman, "In Big Shift, US Imposes Tariffs on Chinese Paper," *New York Times*, March 31, 2007, www.nytimes.com/2007/03/31/business/31trade.html.
49 Sutter, *US–Chinese Relations*, 202–4.
50 "China Opposes Passage of US Bill," *People's Daily Online*, July 30, 2005, accessed July 30, 2005, http://english.people.com.cn/200507/30/eng20050730_199304.html; "China Opposes US Defense Bill for Involving Taiwan Issue," *People's Daily Online*, May 28, 2005, accessed May 28, 2005, http://english.people.com.cn/200505/28/eng20050528_187201.html; "China Firmly Opposes all US–Taiwan Military Exchanges," *People's Daily Online*, October 19, 2005, accessed October 19, 2005, http://english.people.com.cn/200510/19/eng20051019_215086.html; "China Demands US Halt Arms Sale," *BBC News*, March 2, 2007, accessed March 2, 2007, http://news.bbc.co.uk/go/pr/fr/-/2/hi/asia-pacific/6412081.stm; and Suisheng Zhao, "Conflict Prevention across the Taiwan Strait and the Making of China's Anti-Secession Law," *Asian Perspective* 30, no. 1 (2006): 79–94.
51 Blanchard, "US–China Relations under Bush and Obama," 41–2.

52 Wang, *The United States and China since World War II*, 193–194.
53 Thom Shanker, "Rumsfeld Issues a Sharp Rebuke to China on Arms," *New York Times*, June 4, 2005, accessed June 4, 2005, www.nytimes.com/2005/06/04/international/asia/04rumsfeld.html.
54 "A Positive Signal Worth Attention, Comment," *People's Daily Online*, May 18, 2006, accessed May 18, 2006, http://english.people.com.cn//200605/18/eng20060518_266814.html.
55 Wang, *The United States and China since World War II*, 190.
56 Wang, *The United States and China since World War II*, 190–1.
57 "Bush Says US–China Relations Important," *People's Daily Online*, November 20, 2005, accessed November 20, 2005, http://english.people.com.cn/200511/20/eng20051120_222757.html; "Hu Stresses Peace, Stability, Opposes 'Taiwan Independence' in Talks with Bush," *People's Daily Online*, November 20, 2005, accessed November 20, 2005, http://english.people.com.cn/200511/20/eng20051120_222755.html; and Caroline Daniel, "Bush Singing from Different Song Sheet," *Financial Times*, November 20, 2005.
58 Blanchard, "US–China Relations under Bush and Obama," 44.
59 Edward Alden and Richard McGregor, "Why US–China Links are in Flux," *Financial Times*, April 16, 2006; Sutter, *US–Chinese Relations*, 128, 133–43; and Jean-Marc F. Blanchard, "Economics and Asia-Pacific Region Territorial and Maritime Disputes: Understanding the Political Limits to Economic Solutions," *Asian Politics and Policy* 1, no. 4 (October/December 2009): 682–708.
60 See, e.g., Geoff Dyer, "Paulson Receives Chinese Lecture," *Financial Times*, December 5, 2008; and Freeman, "The Commercial and Economic Relationship," 186.
61 Yufan Hao, "Domestic Chinese Influences on US–China Relations," in *Tangled Titans*, ed. Shambaugh, 125–48.

References

"A Positive Signal worth Attention, Comment." *People's Daily Online*. May 18, 2006. Accessed May 18, 2006. http://english.people.com.cn//200605/18/eng20060518_266814.html.
Alden, Edward, and Richard McGregor. "Why US–China Links Are in Flux." *Financial Times*. April 16, 2006. Accessed August 12, 2014.
Alden, Edward, and Christopher Swann. "US Set to Get Tough over Renminbi." *Financial Times*. April 8, 2005.
Balls, Andrew, and Christopher Swann. "US Attacks China Peg for Trade Deficit." *Financial Times*. February 14, 2006.
Beattie, Alan. "Washington Sees Victory in China Subsidies Fight." *Financial Times*. November 30, 2007.
Blanchard, Jean-Marc F. "The Dynamics of China's Accession to the WTO: Counting Sense, Coalitions, and Constructs." *Asian Journal of Social Science* 41, nos. 3–4 (December 2013): 263–86.
Blanchard, Jean-Marc F. "Economics and Asia-Pacific Region Territorial and Maritime Disputes: Understanding the Political Limits to Economic Solutions." *Asian Politics and Policy* 1, no. 4 (2009): 682–708.
Blanchard, Jean-Marc F. "US–China Relations under Bush and Obama: Fill in the Blanks or It's the Structure, Stupid?" *Issues & Studies* 49, no. 3 (September 2013): 35–72.
Brands, H. W., Jr. "Testing Massive Retaliation: Credibility and Crisis Management in the Taiwan Strait." *International Security* 12, no. 4 (Spring 1988): 124–51.

"Bush Says US–China Relations Important." *People's Daily Online*. November 20, 2005. Accessed November 20, 2005. http://english.people.com.cn/200511/20/eng20051120_222757.html.

Callan, Eoin. "US Launches Trade Dispute with China as 'Dialogue Fails." *Financial Times*. February 3–4, 2007.

Callan, Eoin, and Richard McGregor. "US Urged to Target Chinese Exports." *Financial Times*. June 13, 2007.

Chang, Gordon H. *Friends and Enemies: The United States, China, and the Soviet Union, 1948–1972* (Stanford, CA: Stanford University Press, 1990).

"China Demands US Halt Arms Sale." *BBC News*. March 2, 2007. Accessed March 2, 2007. http://news.bbc.co.uk/go/pr/fr/-/2/hi/asia-pacific/6412081.stm.

"China Firmly Opposes All US–Taiwan Military Exchanges." *People's Daily Online*. October 19, 2005. Accessed October 19, 2005. http://english.people.com.cn/200510/19/eng20051019_215086.html.

"China Opposes Passage of US Bill." *People's Daily Online*. July 30, 2005. Accessed July 30, 2005. http://english.people.com.cn/200507/30/eng20050730_199304.html.

"China Opposes US Defense Bill for Involving Taiwan Issue." *People's Daily Online*. May 28, 2005. Accessed May 28, 2005. http://english.people.com.cn/200505/28/eng20050528_187201.html.

"China, US End Annual Trade Negotiation with Consensus on IPR Protection." *People's Daily Online*. July 12, 2005. http://english.people.com.cn/200507/12/eng20050712_195494.html.

"Chinese Vice Commerce Minister Calls on Joint Efforts on Balancing Sino-US Trade." *People's Daily Online*. November 25, 2005. Accessed November 25, 2005. http://english.people.com.cn/200511/25/eng20051125_223903.html.

Christensen, Thomas J. "PRC Security Relations with the United States: Why Things Are Going So Well." *China Leadership Monitor*, no. 8 (Fall 2003). http://media.hoover.org/sites/default/files/documents/clm8_tc.pdf.

Christensen, Thomas J. *Useful Adversaries: Grand Strategy, Domestic Mobilization, and Sino-American Conflict, 1947–1958* (Princeton, NJ: Princeton University Press, 1996).

Daniel, Caroline. "Bush Singing from Different Song Sheet." *Financial Times*. November 20, 2005.

Dumbaugh, Kerry. *China–US Relations: Current Issues for the 108th Congress*. Report no. RL31815 (Washington, DC: Congressional Research Service, 2003).

Dyer, Geoff. "Paulson Receives Chinese Lecture." *Financial Times*. December 5, 2008.

Garver, John W. *Foreign Relations of the People's Republic of China* (Englewood Cliffs, NJ: Prentice Hall, 1993).

Glaser, Bonnie S. "US–China Relations: Beginning to Thaw." *Comparative Connections* 1, no. 2 (October 1999). http://csis.org/files/media/csis/pubs/9902qus_china.pdf.

Glaser, Bonnie S. "US–China Relations: Challenged by New Crises." *Comparative Connections* 1, no. 1 (July 1999). http://csis.org/files/media/csis/pubs/9901qus_china.pdf.

Glaser, Bonnie S. "US–China Relations: Progress Amidst Persisting Deep Suspicions." *Comparative Connections* 1, no. 3 (January 2000). http://csis.org/files/media/csis/pubs/9903qus_china.pdf.

Glaser, Bonnie S. "US–China Relations: Terrorist Strikes Give US–China Ties a Boost." *Comparative Connections* 3, no. 3 (October 2001). http://csis.org/files/media/csis/pubs/0103qus_china.pdf.

Guha, Krishna. "Paulson 'Frustrated at Pace of Renminbi Reform." *Financial Times*. February 1, 2007.

Gurtov, Melvin. "The Taiwan Strait Crisis Revisited: Politics and Foreign Policy in Chinese Motives." *Modern China* 2, no. 1 (January 1976): 49–103.

Harding, Harry. *A Fragile Relationship: The United States and China since 1972* (Washington, DC: Brookings Institution Press, 1992).

"Hu Stresses Peace, Stability, Opposes 'Taiwan Independence' in Talks with Bush." *People's Daily Online*. November 20, 2005. Accessed November 20, 2005. http://english.people.com.cn/200511/20/eng20051120_222755.html.

Hughes, Neil C. "A Trade War with China?" *Foreign Affairs* 84, no. 4 (July/August 2005): 94–106.

Jia, Qingguo. "Learning to Live with the Hegemon: Evolution of China's Policy towards the US since the End of the Cold War." *Journal of Contemporary China* 14, no. 44 (August 2005): 395–407.

Jia, Qingguo. "One Administration, Two Voices: US China Policy during Bush's First Term." *International Relations of the Asia-Pacific* 6, no. 1 (2006): 23–36.

Lampton, David M. "America's China Policy in the Age of the Finance Minister: Clinton Ends Linkage." *China Quarterly*, no. 139 (September 1994): 597–621.

Lieberthal, Kenneth G., and David M. Lampton, eds. *Bureaucracy, Politics and Policy Making in Post-Mao China* (Berkeley: University of California Press, 1992).

Lu, Ning. *The Dynamics of Foreign-policy Decisionmaking in China* (Boulder, CO: Westview Press, 1997).

Mann, James. *About Face: A History of America's Curious Relationship with China, from Nixon to Clinton* (New York: Vintage Books, 2000).

McGregor, Richard. "US Cautious over Progress on China Trade." *Financial Times*. July 12, 2005.

Moore, Gregory J. "Not Very Material but Hardly Immaterial: China's Bombed Embassy and Sino-American Relations." *Foreign Policy Analysis* 6, no. 1 (January 2010): 23–41.

Nathan, Andrew J., and Robert S. Ross. *The Great Wall and the Empty Fortress: China's Search for Security* (New York: W.W. Norton, 1997).

Ross, Robert S. "The 1995–96 Taiwan Strait Confrontation: Coercion, Credibility, and the Use of Force." *International Security* 25, no. 2 (Fall 2000): 87–123.

Schaller, Michael. *The United States and China in the Twentieth Century*. 2nd edn (New York: Oxford University Press, 1990).

Schaller, Michael. *The United States and China into the Twenty-First Century* (New York: Oxford University Press, 2002).

Shambaugh, David L. *Tangled Titans: The United States and China* (Lanham, MD: Rowman & Littlefield, 2013).

Shanker, Thom. "Rumsfeld Issues a Sharp Rebuke to China on Arms." *New York Times*. June 4, 2005. Accessed June 4, 2005. www.nytimes.com/2005/06/04/international/asia/04rumsfeld.html?pagewanted=all&_r=0.

Spence, Jonathan D. *The Search for Modern China*. 2nd edn (New York: W.W. Norton, 1999).

Spiegel, Mark M. "A Look at China's New Exchange Rate Regime, 2005–23." September 9, 2005. www.frbsf.org/economic-research/publications/economic-letter/2005/september/a-look-at-china-new-exchange-rate-regime/el2005-23.pdf.

Sutter, Robert. *China's Peaceful Rise and US Interests in Asia: Status and Outlook*. Issue brief no. 27. June 24, 2004. http://csis.org/files/media/csis/pubs/pac0427.pdf.

Sutter, Robert G. *US–Chinese Relations: Perilous Past, Pragmatic Present* (Lanham, MD: Rowman & Littlefield Publishers, 2010; 2nd edn, 2013).

Taylor, Brendan. "US–China Relations after 11 September: A Long Engagement or Marriage of Convenience." *Australian Journal of International Affairs* 59, no. 2 (June 2005): 179–99.

Thomas, Nigel, and Peter Abbott. *The Korean War 1950–53* (Oxford: Osprey Publishing, 1986).

"Transcript: Powell Stresses US Wants Friendly Ties With China; July 28 Interview on Chinese Television." *Washington File*. July 31, 2001. http://wfile.ait.org.tw/wf-archive/2001/010731/epf203.htm.

Tyler, Patrick. *A Great Wall: Six Presidents and China* (New York: PublicAffairs, 1999).

Wang, Chi. *George W. Bush and China: Policies, Problems, and Partnership* (Lanham, MD: Lexington Books, 2009).

Wang, Chi. *The United States and China since World War II: A Brief History* (Armonk, NJ: M.E. Sharpe, 2013).

Wang, Dong. *The Quarrelling Brothers: New Chinese Archives and a Reappraisal of the Sino-Soviet Split, 1959–1962*. Working paper no. 49 (Washington, DC: Wilson Center Cold War International History Project).

Weisman, Steven R. "In Big Shift, US Imposes Tariffs on Chinese Paper." *New York Times*. March 31, 2007. www.nytimes.com/2007/03/31/business/31trade.html.

Weisman, Steven R. "US Toughens Its Position on China Trade." *New York Times*. April 10, 2007. Accessed April 10, 2007. www.nytimes.com/2007/04/10/business/worldbusiness/10trade.html.

Yeh, Andrew. "Do More, US Urges Beijing." *Financial Times*. November 5, 2005.

Zhao, Quansheng. "Domestic Factors of Chinese Foreign Policy: From Vertical to Horizontal Authoritarianism." *Annals of the American Academy of Political and Social Science* 519 (January 1992): 158–75.

Zhao, Suisheng. "Beijing's Perception of the International System and Foreign Policy Adjustment after the Tiananmen Incident," in *Chinese Foreign Policy: Pragmatism and Strategic Behavior*, edited by Suisheng Zhao (Armonk, NJ: M.E. Sharpe, 2004, 146–8).

Zhao, Suisheng. "Conflict Prevention across the Taiwan Strait and the Making of China's Anti-Secession Law." *Asian Perspective* 30, no. 1 (2006): 79–94.

3 China, the US, and the transition of power

A dual leadership structure in the Asia-Pacific

Quansheng Zhao

Introduction

A new pattern of leadership has emerged following a profound power transition in Asia-Pacific Region (APR) international relations since the beginning of the twenty-first century. In the economic and financial realms, China gradually has gained the upper hand and begun to play a leading role in certain areas. In contrast, the United States remains in a hegemonic position in the military, security, and political realms – far ahead of the other major powers.[1] This emerging dual leadership structure reflects the new power configurations formed as China has risen over the past three decades. At the same time, it reflects the continued US leadership position in regional and global affairs since the end of World War II.

The dual leadership structure reflects recent trends and perceptions regarding China's rise – above all, its dramatic and persistent economic growth. China's economic growth may dramatically affect global and regional power distributions, giving China considerable new leverage relative to the US. For example, China's increasing economic strength helped to maintain economic stability in the APR in the aftermath of the 2008 financial crisis, which weakened the US. At the same time, continued US leadership in the political and military dimensions may offset China's rising influence in the APR; thus hindering China's regional leadership.

Some realists may deem the above a bipolar structure, but the dual leadership structure is distinct from this concept. It reflects fundamental *asymmetry* rather than parity. China has not moved into a position where it can challenge US leadership. Rather, it is merely starting to become more influential in the economic dimension. While this trend may eventually enhance China's power in the military and political dimensions, the transition from economic to political influence will occur over a long period of time and is difficult to measure. Therefore, it is unlikely that China will replace US leadership in both security and political dimensions, globally or regionally, any time soon.

Alternatively, for some, the dual leadership structure may appear similar to the "G2" and other related leadership concepts. However, they are conceptually and empirically different. Zbigniew Brzezinski argues strongly for the G2 model, suggesting that "the relationship between the US and China has to be truly a comprehensive global partnership, parallel [to] relations with Europe and Japan."[2] In contrast, the dual leadership structure concept refers only to a newly emerged regional structure in the APR and emphasizes the distinct strengths of the US and China in separate dimensions, namely economic vs. security. The global structure is still asymmetrical with the US remaining the sole hegemon and China far from replacing it.

The dichotomy between economic and military leadership dimensions also is reflected in public perceptions. This is exemplified by comparing trends across Gallup Research Reports on American perceptions of China's influence. In 2000, 65 percent of Americans saw the US as the world's leading economic power, while only 10 percent said China held that position. By 2014, perceptions had reversed. This time, 52 percent named China as the world's leading economic power while only 31 percent saw the US as such (see Figure 3.1).

This change in perception is due to the fact that China rode through the 2008 financial crisis fairly successfully, whereas the US, Japan, and the EU all suffered substantially. As a result of China's success, many people pay more attention to what it has to say, thereby increasing its decision-making role in international organizations such as the World Bank and International Monetary Fund (IMF). Indeed, in March 2011, the IMF passed a resolution that increased China's IMF voting power to the third largest among member countries.[3] Rising attention to China's economic might is even more visible in the APR due to the fact that virtually all surrounding economies are increasingly dependent on China's financial and trade markets.[4]

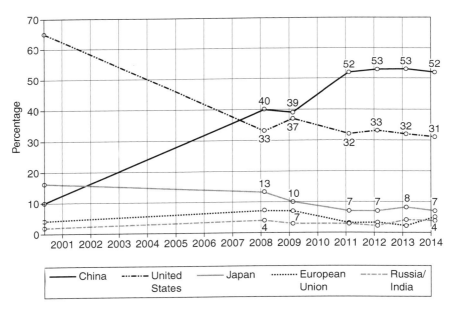

Figure 3.1 Americans' perceptions of world economic powers (source: Gallup, www.gallup.com/poll/167498/Americans-view-china-mostly-unfavorably.aspx).

This emerging dual leadership structure is a new development in contemporary international relations and has implications for the concept of power transition. Power transition theory focuses on the relationship between the rising power and the existing status quo power, particularly on how the leading status quo power deals with the rising power's ascent. One of the key drivers of a peaceful transition is the rising power's degree of satisfaction with the existing international system. The probability of conflict is greatest when the relationship can be characterized as a "zone of contention and probable war."[5] History has shown that when a rising power challenges the dominance of an existing hegemony, both war and peaceful transition are possible.[6] Some examples of peaceful transitions can be found in recent history, including the transition of power from the United Kingdom to the US in the late 1800s. According to Robert Kagan, "the most successful management of a rising power in a modern era was Britain's appeasement of the United States in the late nineteenth century, when the British effectively ceded the entire Western hemisphere (except Canada) to the expansive Americans."[7] An example of a situation that escalated into war is Japan's challenge to China's dominance during the Meiji period and throughout the beginning of World War II. Another rising power of the time was Germany, which challenged the UK's existing dominance in Europe. Moreover, despite the absence of direct war, the rise of the Soviet Union resulted in the uneasy peace between the two superpowers, punctuated by numerous proxy wars during the Cold War.[8]

Although power transition theory is not intended to be the major theoretical framework for this chapter, the dual leadership concept nevertheless reflects a step in this direction. Moreover, the dual leadership structure has emerged as a means of mediating the process of power transition as well as facilitating cooperation between the US (the leading status quo power) and China (the rising power). Both cooperation and potential conflicts have increased in recent years. The change in leadership structure in the region is conducive not only to the coordination between the two countries, but also to cooperation with other key players in the region such as Japan, Russia, the two Koreas, and the Association of Southeast Asian Nations (ASEAN). A disastrous military confrontation may yet be avoided.

Concepts of the leadership structure

In general, a country in a global leadership position should possess at least the following five elements:

- the most power in the dimension in which it is a leader;
- the ability to deliver and provide public goods at times of peace and crisis;
- a leading role in rule-making and agenda-setting;
- a leadership position in major international organizations such as the United Nations and the World Bank; and
- occupation of a high moral position.

These categories of leadership are strongly related to *perceived* influence. In many cases, a state's actual power may not be enough to significantly increase its relative position in the international system or catapult it into leadership status. In general, this leadership can be either regional or global – here we are focusing on leadership in the APR. However, a global or regional perception of increasing power that exceeds the reality of tangible power is still highly relevant because other states will be more attentive or act more deferentially, resulting in increased influence. For example, while it always was doubtful that China could "rescue" the European Union in the aftermath of the euro crisis, the perception that China possessed the economic power sufficient to weather the 2008 financial crisis and the ongoing Eurozone crisis led to much discussion about China's potential role in bolstering the EU. In this sense, "leadership" in the dual leadership structure refers to a discernible trend of influence, but not necessarily dominance, in different dimensions.

It goes without saying that China has not met all five criteria for leadership: only in the economic and financial dimensions is its increasing influence obvious and significant. China has not yet become a peer of the US and has a long way to go to become an all-around regional or global leader, though it may reach that level in the distant future. I do not comprehensively analyze the preceding five components of leadership because my argument focuses on the categories of economics and military/politics to capture this historical moment in the dynamics of regional influence.

Further, the concept of the dual leadership structure reflects current trends and perceptions in the APR rather than a prediction or judgment about the status quo. This chapter does not argue that China's economy leads the US, or that it does not have significant weaknesses. Nor does it argue that Chinese growth will continue indefinitely at the same pace. However, it highlights the observable *trend* over three decades of Chinese economic growth. Therefore, the dual leadership concept reflects the necessity of preparing for future possibilities based on the current momentum in both the economic and security dimensions. As will be seen from the analyses below, China and the US each have their own strengths and weaknesses in different dimensions.

In a dual leadership structure, coordination and cooperation between the two leading powers are the key element for successful leadership (i.e., wielding influence and achieving results). According to Robert Keohane, "Cooperation ... requires that the actions of separate individuals or organizations ... be brought into conformity with one another through a process of policy coordination." He goes on to say "this means that when cooperation takes place, each party changes his or her behavior contingent on changes in the other's behavior.... Genuine cooperation improves the rewards of both players."[9] Cooperation should not be confused with "harmony," which is "a situation in which actors' policies (pursued in their own self-interest without regard for others) automatically facilitate the attainment of others' goals ... Where harmony reigns, cooperation is unnecessary."[10] In the case of the US and China, cooperation is necessary and will be key to minimizing the risk of conflict during the process of power transition should China begin to challenge the US in the military/political realms.

In the post-Cold War era, we have seen the establishment of cooperation among capitalist powers in the form of a security community, which "means a group of states that do not expect, or prepare for, the use of military force in their relations with each other."[11] A security community involves a *normative* injunction against using violent means to resolve conflict within the community.[12] As China gains leverage through its continuing economic growth, it will be able to interact with the US on a more equal footing, creating opportunities for compromise and communication. Consistent interaction within a dual leadership structure may create the normative foundations for an effective security community with China and the US at its core, since they are the two most influential voices in the economic and military/political realms.

With regard to the emerging dual leadership structure in the APR, cooperation between the US and China is imperative. According to James Dougherty and Robert Pfaltzgraff, "cooperation may be the result of a relationship between a stronger actor and a weaker party."[13] In this case, though there is still an enormous gap in development between the US and China, the two countries are moving toward a parity in which cooperation is key.

When talking about the "leader," we must also discuss the "led." In the dual leadership structure, the leadership position is neither self-appointed nor elected; it is naturally formed through a variety of platforms and mechanisms. Over the years, there are a number of bilateral and/or multilateral mechanisms being developed that may be conducive to the formation of the dual leadership structure. Some specific examples include summit meetings, US–China Strategic and Economic Dialogue, and multilateral negotiations such as the Six-Party Talks. In most cases, the terms "leader" and "led" apply only in a relative sense. Generally speaking, great powers often have followers (or "free-riders"), but from a macro perspective, some countries have more followers in certain dimensions. In the case of the US and China, each country may be regarded as a leader in particular dimensions.

This dual leadership is different from the Cold War era zero-sum game. Rather, it indicates the necessity of two great powers that continuously coordinate and compromise, and, on many occasions, jointly assume a leadership role, although this is based on different strengths. Therefore, this new leadership structure is highly related to methods for conflict resolution. It reflects a dichotomy of economic versus military backlash and political influence to reach a win–win solution, rather than a zero-sum game.

China's emerging leadership role in economic, trade, and financial dimensions

It is in the economic dimension that the changing world configuration is most visible. Over the past few decades, the center of world economic activities has gradually shifted from the Atlantic region to the Pacific region. Following in the footsteps of Japan's economic miracle from the 1950s to the 1980s, China's economy has grown at an unprecedented rate. In 2010 China's gross domestic product (GDP) bypassed Japan's to become the second largest economy in the world.[14] China's rising economic position in relation to the rest of the world is illustrated in Table 3.1.

Although the single index of GDP is not enough to measure a country's total economic power, it is still a powerful indicator of change in world affairs. Furthermore, China's development momentum continues to be strong despite many speculations that the Chinese economy could collapse within the next several years, especially if its highly inflated real estate bubble bursts.[15] There are also a variety of predictions, including the perceptions of the American public, that China will overtake the US and become the number one economic powerhouse in the near future. This assessment is shared by the IMF, which argues that China will overtake the US economy by 2016.[16]

On the other hand, when comparing the Chinese economy with that of the US, there are still enormous gaps in terms of economic power. For example, China's nominal GDP is approximately half that of the US, while its GDP per capita is more than five times smaller than the US's.[17] Moreover, China has daunting domestic problems, such as a potential economic bubble, environmental damage, corruption, and social unrest that may slow down or even set back its economic development. Also, China has had far less influence in international organizations such as the World Bank, among others. If this is the case, how can we say that China has begun to play a leadership role in the APR economy?

First, the speed of China's economic growth is much higher than the US's. For the last 30 years – from 1980 to 2009 – the average growth of US GDP has been 2.7 percent annually, while China's average GDP growth has been 10.01 percent annually.[18] Recently, some scholars have even projected that, by 2030, relative US decline will have yielded not a multipolar world but a near-unipolar one dominated by China. By that time, it is estimated that China will account for close to 20 percent of global GDP (measured half in dollars and half in terms of real purchasing power), compared with just under 15 percent for the US.[19]

Table 3.1 Top 10 world economies by GDP (2012)

Rank	Country	GDP (nominal, US$ millions)
1	United States	15,653.37
2	China	8,250.24
3	Japan	5,984.39
4	Germany	3,366.65
5	France	2,580.42
6	United Kingdom	2,433.78
7	Brazil	2,425.05
8	Italy	1,980.45
9	Russia	1,953.56
10	India	1,946.77

Source: IMF, www.imf.org/external/data.htm.

Next, China's economy provides significant public goods to the APR and the world. China played a primary role in the process of economic recovery after the financial crisis of 2008. World GDP growth is heavily dependent upon China's GDP growth and investments.[20] In the first decade of the twenty-first century, China's economic growth accounted for 22 percent of the growth of the world economy whereas the US growth only accounted for 17 percent. In 2011, Chinese consumers' contribution to world economic growth bypassed American consumers' contribution for the first time.[21] Chinese consumption creates demand for goods and serves as a source of economic stability and wealth. Therefore, China has become one of the most important drivers of all the pillars of world economic growth, namely production, investment, and consumption.[22] China is also the world's largest creditor, owning about 21.9 percent of all foreign-owned US Treasury securities, as shown in Table 3.2.

By owning such a substantial portion of US Treasury securities, China's economy has become highly interlinked with the US economy, making both countries mutually vulnerable. For example, during the summer of 2011, after significant partisan gridlock, the US nearly failed to raise its debt ceiling, which would have made it unable to pay back its debt. If the US defaulted on its debt it would have shaken US consumer confidence and reduced demand for Chinese exports, increasing pressure on China to delink the renmimbi from the US dollar, and shaking China's confidence in the US government's ability to live up to its future commitments.[23]

With respect to the financial and monetary dimensions, China has the largest share of foreign reserves, bigger than Japan (number two) and ASEAN (number three) combined (see Table 3.3). Furthermore, China has become the number one trading partner for many countries in the region, including Japan, South Korea, India, the ASEAN nations, and Australia (see Table 3.4).[24] The US is the number one trading partner only with its two neighbor countries, Canada and Mexico. Countries in Oceania, East, Southeast, and South Asia increasingly rely on China as a trading partner, and it has also become one of the most important trading partners worldwide.

Table 3.2 Top Asia-Pacific holders of US Treasury securities (US$ billions, as of December 2013)

Rank	Country/region	Volume
1	China	1,268.9
2	Japan	1,182.5
3	Taiwan	182.2
4	Hong Kong	158.8
5	Singapore	86.2
6	Mexico	65.1
7	Canada	55.7
8	Korea	53.9
9	Thailand	51.7

Source: US Department of Treasury. www.treasury.gov/resource-center/data-chart-center/tic/Documents/mfh.txt.

Table 3.3 Official reserve assets and other foreign currency assets in Asia-Pacific (US$ billions, 2013)

Rank	Country/region	Volume
1	China*	3,821
2	Japan	1,324
3	ASEAN**	769.5
4	Taiwan***	416.9
5	S. Korea	345.5
6	Hong Kong	330
7	Mexico	180.2
8	USA	145.7
9	Canada	71.9

Source: www.safe.gov.cn/.

Notes
* The most recent data for China is from December, 2013.
** ASEAN total includes only Indonesia, Malaysia, Philippines, Singapore, and Thailand.
*** Taiwan data: www.cbc.gov.tw/ct.asp?xItem=29870&ctNode=515&mp=2.
All other data compiled from: www.imf.org/external/np/sta/ir/IRProcessWeb/colist.aspx.

China also remains the second most-desired country as a destination for foreign direct investment (FDI) after the US (see Table 3.5) in 2012. US companies like Wal-Mart continue to pump money and resources into the Chinese market. As of May 2011, Wal-Mart had 90,000 employees in China and annual sales of $7 billion.[25]

China's FDI outflow (Table 3.6) has noticeably increased in recent years, particularly in developing countries. Although it is still far behind the US, the trend indicates that China's FDI is increasing quickly, especially if Hong Kong's contribution is included in China's overall FDI outflow. Of note, China has become a leading investor in Africa, particularly in infrastructure, development, and other projects.[26] According to a *Financial Times* article,

> the China Development Bank and China Export-Import Bank signed loans of at least $110 billion to other developing country governments and companies in 2009 and 2010. The equivalent arms of the World Bank made loan commitments of $100.3 billion from mid-2008 to 2010, itself a record amount of lending in response to the financial crisis.[27]

China has also used its economic power to lead and empower the regional economic order, particularly through bilateral and regional free trade agreements (FTAs). Chinese FTAs include the ASEAN–China Free Trade Area (ACFTA), which was put into effect in 2010; the mainland and Hong Kong Closer Economic Partnership Arrangement (CEPA), which went into effect in 2003; the China–Pakistan Free Trade Agreement, in effect as of 2007; the New Zealand–China Free Trade Agreement, as of 2008 and the Taiwan Economic Cooperation Framework Agreement, a significant step in the bilateral

Table 3.4 Major partners in international trade, ranked (2011)

Country	#1	#2	#3	#4	#5	#6	#7
China	EU	USA	Hong Kong	ASEAN	Japan	S. Korea	India
USA	Canada	China	Mexico	Japan	Germany	UK	S. Korea
EU	USA	China	Russia	Switzerland	Norway	Turkey	Japan
India	UAE	China	USA	Saudi Arabia	Switzerland	Hong Kong	Germany
Hong Kong	China	USA	Japan	Taiwan	Singapore	S. Korea	India
Australia	China	Japan	USA	S. Korea	Singapore	UK	New Zealand
Japan	China	USA	S. Korea	Australia	Taiwan	Thailand	Saudi Arabia
ASEAN (2010)	China	EU	Japan	USA	S. Korea	India	Australia
S. Korea (2009)	China	Japan	USA	Saudi Arabia	Hong Kong	Australia	Singapore
Canada (2009)	USA	China	UK	Mexico	Japan	Germany	S. Korea

Sources: United States Census Bureau, National Bureau of Statistics of China, Department of Commerce, Government of India, European Commission, Trade and Industry Department, Government of Hong Kong, ASEAN Web, Department of Foreign Affairs and Trade, Australian Government, Japan External Trade Organization, etc.

Table 3.5 FDI inflows in Asia-Pacific (US$ billions, 2012)

Rank	Country/region	Value
1	USA	167.6
2	ASEAN	136.4
3	China	121
4	Hong Kong	74.6
5	Canada	45.4
6	Mexico	12.7
7	S. Korea	9.9
8	Taiwan	3.2
9	Japan	1.7

Source: United Nations Conference on Trade and Development, *World Investment Report 2013*, 213–215. http://unctad.org/en/publicationslibrary/wir2013_en.pdf.

Table 3.6 FDI outflow by country/region across Asia-Pacific (US$ billions, 2012)

Rank	Country/region	Volume
1	USA	328.9
2	Japan	122.6
4	China	84.2
3	Hong Kong	84
5	ASEAN	60.6
6	Canada	53.9
7	S. Korea	33
8	Mexico	25.6
9	Taiwan	13

Source: United Nations Conference on Trade and Development, *World Investment Report 2013*, 213–215. http://unctad.org/en/publicationslibrary/wir2013_en.pdf.

cooperation between China and Taiwan, which went into effect in early 2010.[28]

In short, China exerts significant regional influence, as other Asian countries depend on China both for investments and as an important trading partner. As Table 3.7 indicates, China is closing the gap between itself and the US. China is catching up to the US economically through its increased importance as a trading partner to other countries, large holdings of US debt and foreign exchange, and levels of FDI outflows.

Again, this chapter does not ignore the significant economic challenges that China faces. However, it is impossible to ignore the broader trend of Chinese economic growth over three decades since 1978, propelled by a manufacturing sector that earns China the moniker of "the world's factory." This pattern makes it more and more important for the region to hear China's voice on economic issues. Although China's economic power is still far behind that of the US, the APR has begun to look to China as a primary economic leader as it continues to grow.

Table 3.7 US v. China across categories

	China	USA
Foreign reserves, 2013 US$ billions	3821	145.7
Number of countries of which China/US is the largest trading partner (export), 2012	33	34
FDI inflow, 2012 US$ billions	121	167
FDI outflow, 2012 US$ billions	84.2	328.9

Source: *CIA World Factbook* www.cia.gov/library/publications/the-world-factbook/fields/2050.html.

US leadership role – military/security dimension and political influence

In the military, security, and political spheres, the US has undoubtedly maintained an absolute advantage. In 2010, US military expenses reached $687 billion, which constituted 44.1 percent of global military expenditures.[29] In 2012, US military expenditure was still as high as $682 billion. Although China is regarded as the second largest power in terms of military expenditure, it only spent $166 billion dollars, 24 percent of US spending (see Table 3.8). Furthermore, US military spending has hovered around 4 percent of its total GDP for the past few decades and the US makes the largest percentage of arms transfers worldwide. China, however, has maintained average military expenditures of around 2 percent of its GDP (see Table 3.8). This relatively low number has made it virtually impossible for China to close the gap with the US militarily in the foreseeable future.

More importantly, most APR military-security international organizations and institutions are US led or dominated. This includes bilateral security institutions such as the US–Japan and the US–South Korea security alliances. It

Table 3.8 Global military expenditures (top 10) (US$ billions, 2012)

Rank	Country	Military expenditure	% GDP (2012)
1	USA	682	4.4
2	China	166	2.0
3	Russia	90.7	4.4
4	UK	60.8	2.5
5	Japan	59.3	1.0
6	France	58.9	2.3
7	Saudi Arabia	56.7	8.9
8	India	46.1	2.5
9	Germany	45.8	1.4
10	Italy	34.0	1.7

Source: Stockholm International Peace Research Institute. http://books.sipri.org/files/FS/SIPRIFS1304.pdf.

also comprises military partnerships between US and other Asian countries such as the Philippines, Australia, New Zealand, Thailand, India, Pakistan, and Singapore as well as Taiwan. Table 3.9 below shows these relationships in more detail. The US has also developed close security ties with other regional powers such as Vietnam.

The US's most substantial APR military relationships are its alliances with Japan and South Korea. The US participates in over 100 joint military exercises annually with Japan as well as leading the "Peace-09" naval exercise (which also included China) in 2009, and naval exercises following the shelling of Yeonpyeong in 2010.[30] The US has participated in joint military exercises with South Korea since the 1970s, including the annual exercise entitled Ulchi Focus Lens.[31] Between 1976 and 1997, the US and South Korea jointly ran Operation Team Spirit.[32] In 2010, four different joint military exercises occurred, including Invincible Spirit, North Korean naval deterrence, anti-submarine exercises, an 11-day war deterrent exercise, and scheduled military drills following the shelling of Yeonpyeong.[33]

Perhaps the only initiative on the Chinese side that is similar to those above is the Shanghai Cooperation Organization, in which both China and Russia play leadership roles in Central Asia in the field of regional security. However, it is still far less institutionalized and developed compared to similar institutions such as NATO and the US–Japan alliance. The China–North Korea alliance and the China–Pakistan all-weather partnership represent other China-led or China-dominated military-security relationships. We also should acknowledge the Six-Party Talks (extensively covered in Chapter 6 by Jingdong Yuan), though China shares a leadership role with the US.

Although the US remains the leading military power globally, China has noticeably increased its defense budget and spending in the past few decades. From 1978 to 1987, China's military budget increased 3.5 percent annually. From 1988 to 1997 it increased 14.5 percent annually. And from 1998 to 2007 it

Table 3.9 US military relationships in the Asia-Pacific

Country	Relationship	Year of origin
Philippines	Security partnership – mutual defense treaty	1951
Japan	Formal alliance	1952
Australia	Security partnership – AZNUS	1952
S. Korea	Formal alliance	1953
Thailand	Security partnership – Manila Pact	1954
Taiwan	Security agreement – Taiwan Relations Act (US domestic law)	1979
India	Security partnership – Next Steps in Strategic Partnership (NSSP)	2004
Singapore	Security partnership – strategic framework agreement	2005
Pakistan	Strategic dialogue	2010

Source: US Department of State. www.state.gov/t/pm/c17687.htm.

increased 15.9 percent annually on average.[34] China is now the second most powerful nation in terms of military expenditures globally. As one can see, China has rapidly expanded its military power and increased its military expenditures.

One might question whether China can translate its economic strength into military power. Given China's increasing investment in its military capabilities, this is a legitimate concern. However, it would take considerable time and investment for China to even approach the US superiority in military capability. Meanwhile, the US will continue to advance its strategic capabilities. The US not only occupies a nearly absolute leading position in terms of military capability and equipment, but also has many more partners and followers than China. This kind of leading position is not likely to be altered any time soon even if the Chinese economy should bypass that of the US within the next decade.

The gap in political influence between the US and China is equally noticeable. This is not only because the US is still the only superpower in world affairs, but also because Washington has always paid close attention to soft power and most recently "smart power" (a phrase used by US Secretary of State Hillary Clinton). Specifically, the US has the following four advantages in terms of its soft power diplomacy:

1   It always adjusts its foreign policy in order to reflect a high moral stance.
2   It enhances and leads the news media to guide public opinion.
3   It strengthens its international credibility to maintain alliance relationships.
4   There is a constant public debate over domestic and foreign policy, creating a strong ability to self-correct, and therefore avoiding disastrous consequences caused by foreign policy errors.

While there is widespread anti-Americanism in the world, US soft power and political influence generally are much stronger than China's, particularly in terms of influencing news media and public opinion and exercising political leadership. In justifying the recent US pivot to Asia, Secretary of State Hillary Clinton noted that the US is "the only power with a network of strong alliances in the region, no territorial ambitions, and a long record of providing for the common good."[35] Furthermore, Clinton used the popular US magazine *Foreign Policy* to mark this pivot from the stronger US commitment in the Middle East to Asia, showing clever use of the media to reinforce traditional US soft power principles while demonstrating the unique US ability to self-correct from previous policy.

Despite China's repeated emphasis on peaceful rise and pursuit of a harmonious world, both the West and China's neighbors still have deep suspicions of Chinese intentions and sometimes see China's rise as a threat to them and the global political order. The soft power issue has become a weak spot in Chinese foreign policy and also complicates China's ability to defend its core interests. To illustrate, even though China has repeatedly announced that the areas of

Taiwan, Tibet, and Xinjiang are a part of its core interests, Western public opinion still reflects a lack of understanding of China's basic positions while Western sympathies typically lie with political forces such as the Dalai Lama who often oppose the Chinese government's position.[36]

The promotion of China's "peaceful rise" has been critical to China's influence and reputation within East Asia as well as the rest of the world.[37] Some of the ways China promotes its soft power is by sending doctors and teachers to work abroad, welcoming foreign students to study in China, and setting up Chinese language institutes and language program initiatives abroad. However, China's "charm offensive" has produced rather limited results.[38]

The implications of dual leadership

As indicated, the dual leadership structure reflects the development of two large regional powers with strengths in different areas. Ultimately, the future success of this newly emerged structure will depend upon whether it serves the interests of China and the US as well as major players in the region such as Japan, Russia, the two Koreas, and the ASEAN countries. Therefore, close coordination with those countries is a matter of necessity.

A dual leadership structure, by definition, means that each power has its strengths and weaknesses. As was stated, while in the economic dimension China gained momentum and moved into the upper position, in the dimensions of military and political influence, the US is still much stronger than China.[39] The two powers need to constantly adjust to, and accommodate, one another. Each should be prepared to make compromises in their weaker areas, and to be more proactive and willing to assume a clear leadership role in their stronger areas. As is often said, one cannot totally divide politics from economics so the two dimensions need to be well coordinated. Therefore, the US and China should adopt a positive 3-Cs principle entailing *coordination*, *cooperation*, and *compromise*. Put differently, both countries need to find ways accommodate each other (e.g., mutual respect of each other's core interests) and allow the two countries to exist as "stakeholders." This requires the continued institutionalization of rigorous bilateral and multilateral mechanisms for top down to lower-level leaders to regularly meet with their counterparts. By doing so, both countries can better resolve differences peacefully so that they can mutually benefit from the regional prosperity and stability.

One may contrast these positive 3-Cs with negative 3-Cs involving *competition*, *conflict*, and *confrontation*, which are more likely to occur when political pressure on domestic policy-makers constrains their ability to compromise on key issues, leading to zero-sum thinking. Whereas the positive 3-Cs are necessities for a peaceful dual structure, the negative 3-Cs will produce a divided dual structure. This paper does not argue that the emerging dual leadership structure in the APR will invariably develop positively and without conflict. However, in view of recent trends and the shared interests of the US and China, the development of the dual leadership structure under the positive 3-Cs is more likely and could create stability.

The idea of a positive 3-Cs principle tracks my earlier ideas about a "co-management approach" which discusses two conflict "hot spots" – the Korean peninsula, where Beijing and Washington followed a policy of "explicit co-management" and pursued Six-Party Talks, and the Taiwan Strait, where the two powers followed a policy of "implicit co-management."[40] This chapter goes beyond this and argues for co-management of the overall APR structure, with China and the US taking the lead, while working together with others such as Russia, Japan, North and South Korea, and ASEAN countries to discuss the region's most pressing issues and coordinate policies for regional stability and mutual benefit. As discussed above, according to the power transition theory, the most dangerous period is when the leading status quo power and the rising power reach a point of parity, which may lead to confrontation. Nick Bisley suggests that 2009–2010 "marked the beginning of a longer-run period in which the frictions and conflicts that come from overlapping interests, growing military capabilities and a regional tendency to conduct strategic policy in a militarized fashion, will become a regular feature" of the US–China relationship. At the same time, the US and China have many shared interests, which could form "the foundations of a new regional order."[41]

Different international relations perspectives can help us examine whether China's rise will result in a zero-sum game or a win–win situation. According to offensive realists, the strategic environment facing China and the US is a zero-sum game. From this view, there is little room for power-sharing, especially in the military sphere, and China's rise is a threat to the US. John Mearsheimer argues:

> The most dangerous scenario the United States might face in the early twenty-first century is one in which China becomes a potential hegemon in Northeast Asia. China and the United States are destined to be adversaries as China's power continues to grow.[42]

Indeed, there are some significant points of contention between China and the US in which the two powers may come into conflict or even military confrontation such as US arms sales to Taiwan and issues related to the South China and East China Seas, among others.

These points of contention raise serious questions about whether China and the US can truly maintain a cooperative relationship. The possibility of quarrels, debates, and conflicts between the US and China is very real. However, this does not preclude a broader trend of cooperation for reasons discussed below. It is worth pointing out that even allies do not share interests all of the time and may even disagree vociferously over certain issues. This chapter does not argue that future conflict is not possible, but argues that cooperation and co-management of difficult problems are more likely trends within a dual leadership structure.

Globalization and interdependence make a win–win scenario increasingly likely. This is evident in key differences between the Cold War zero-sum competition between the US and the Soviet Union and the current US–China relationship. First and foremost, the US and Soviet Union did not cultivate economic interdependence. In contrast, China needs US direct investment and consumption to fuel its manufacturing sector while the US needs China's market and manufacturing. China's ownership of large amounts of US debt gives it a key stake in the stability of the US economy and the state of the federal deficit. Secondly, the US–Soviet conflict of ideologies is highly unlikely to apply to the US–China relationship because China's focus is on practical modernization rather than ideology. While this does not rule out the possibility of confrontation, the national interests of China and the US in economic interdependence and pragmatic goals make win–win more likely than a zero-sum game based around the negative 3-Cs.

In comparing broader common and overlapping interests, namely regional stability and prosperity, the two powers should be able to handle their differences through peaceful means. To this end, they need to avoid conflict and further develop crisis prevention and crisis management mechanisms and institutions. We see many instances where China and the US currently cooperate such as the S&ED and 60+ bilateral dialogue mechanisms.[43] Additionally, we see frequent summits and state visits such as President Barack Obama's visit to China in 2009, President Hu Jintao's visit to Washington in 2011, Vice-President Joe Biden's visit to China in 2011, and Vice-President Xi Jinping's visit to Washington in 2012.

Co-management stresses inclusion rather than exclusion. Namely, China and the US should work together with all related powers such as Japan, Russia, and the two Koreas. In addition to the Six-Party Talks, both the US and China work closely together at the East Asian Summit (EAS), Shangri-La Dialogue, Asia-Pacific Economic Cooperation (APEC) forum meetings, and at the annual ASEAN summit. This dual leadership structure may also reduce anxiety among other players, making it less likely that they would be forced into making a choice between China and the US.

The dual leadership structure is fluid. At present, it is uncertain whether there will be changes in the political and security dimensions or whether China's leadership position will extend globally. It remains to be seen what specific institutional arrangements and mechanisms may develop to reinforce the dual leadership structure. Nevertheless, this historical moment is worthy of our recognition and attention: For the first time since World War II, China's astronomical economic growth has given it a truly influential role in the APR.

Future directions

The dual leadership structure has proven positive so far, with benefits for both the US and China. However, it remains to be seen whether the two powers can coordinate well with other powers in the region such as Japan and Russia. One possibility is that some regional mechanisms, such as the Six-Party Talks, might be expanded and institutionalized.[44] Additionally, China and the US may expand existing institutions and alliances to include each other, officially or unofficially.

Each side should be prepared for compromise in order to accommodate the other's "core national interests." For example, China may help facilitate US economic recovery. At the same time, the US may allow the "2+2" talks between two foreign ministers and two defense ministers (currently US + Japan) to become the "2+2+2" talks (US + Japan + China).

Moreover, the US and China must institutionalize regular summits between their top leaders in order to show that the bilateral relationship is the top priority. Similarly, Obama and Xi must cultivate a personal relationship in order to build the mutual trust, frankness, and understanding necessary to make cooperation a reality. Such a relationship would not only enhance the positive 3-Cs, but would be especially important in pre-empting or managing the negative 3-Cs so that potential problems do not become real or real problems do not escalate. In addition, both countries must utilize the strengths of the other to compensate for their weaknesses. For China, this may mean accepting US military dominance in order to enjoy the regional stability generated by the absence of an arms race (especially since Japanese military expansion is restrained due to the US alliance). On the other hand, the US must be willing to support a larger role for China in the economic sphere since it is becoming a major driver of the global economy and is a major export market for US companies at a time of recovery.

Looking forward, there are at least two important questions relating to the reactions of key players to the dual leadership structure. The first is whether the US would accept a dual leadership structure in the APR. Needless to say, there is a constant chorus of opposing voices in the US arguing about how to deal with the rise of China as reflected by the debate between advocates of a containment policy versus an engagement policy. This author believes the majority view among the US elite and policy-makers is that the US should do its utmost to bring China into existing international political and economic systems, making China an insider rather than a challenger.

One effort to engage China is Washington's support of a US–China consultation on the APR within the S&ED, with the first consultation held in June 2011 in Honolulu. This kind of consultation is based on the belief that "the two sides share a wide range of common interests with a shared goal of maintaining peace, stability, and prosperity in the Asia-Pacific."[45] It also emphasizes that "as part of expanded, closer, and more extensive economic cooperation, China and the United States are extending the extent of their consultation on policy actions that affect the interest of the other country." The joint statement issued after the first consultation seemed to reinforce gradual steps by the US and China towards joint leadership, making clear that "China and the US share common interests widely in the Asia-Pacific and shoulder major responsibilities of promoting peace, stability, and development in the region."[46] This wording is particularly significant because the idea that the two countries "shoulder major responsibilities" is only one step short of calling for joint leadership.

Washington's effort towards working together with China comes from the recognition that "China will have a major influence in the regions surrounding it [as it] is inherent in its geography, values, and history." Therefore, the US and

China "should seek together to define the sphere in which their peaceful competition is circumscribed."[47] These statements demonstrate that important US foreign policy elites recognize the trend of China's increasing influence and generally support working together. At the same time, both Washington and Beijing carefully watch each other, adopting a "hedging" policy in case the relationship turns in an undesirable direction caused by unexpected events or developments.

One can discern a subtle change of attitude from the US, which now seems to recognize it must work with China to address major regional and global issues. As Under Secretary of State Robert Hormats argued in March 2012, "The US and China are the world's two biggest economies and nothing can be done if they don't agree."[48] As Henry Kissinger points out, the twenty-first century's most significant issues are global in nature: proliferation, the environment, energy security, cyberspace, and the health of a world economy and the international financial systems.[49] These are not issues in the resolution in which one country wins and another country loses. They can only be resolved through US–China consultation and cooperation. It is in this context that the US and China have an opportunity to explore a new direction together beyond traditional forms of great-power rivalry. The concept of a dual leadership structure might be one of the many possible manifestations of a new direction together beyond traditional forms of great-power rivalry, reinforced by US–China consultation and cooperation.

The second important question is how to treat existing multilateral institutional arrangements such as ASEAN Plus Three, the ASEAN Regional Forum, the EAS, and, most recently, the Trans-Pacific Partnership (TPP). It is true China's Asian neighbors have some concerns about the rise of China, particularly in the security dimension. Much of this has to do with conflicts in the South China and the East China Seas, which Suisheng Zhao probes in Chapter 4. But at the same time, China has made major progress in the region, establishing close economic ties with virtually every neighboring country, as indicated. David Arase contends there is a broader China–ASEAN multilateral process which "is the most institutionally developed expression of East Asian regionalism today."[50] As Ali Rama argues, one of the most beneficial aspects of increasing Chinese strength in the region, especially in the economic dimension, is that the Chinese market may serve as an "alternative and a cushion for ASEAN countries."[51] This positive manifestation of increasing Chinese influence in the economic dimension became particularly clear after the 2008 financial crisis, when China's record high economic growth offset the US's negative growth.

As discussed at the beginning of this chapter, the leadership of the dual leadership structure is not self-appointed nor elected. It develops naturally through trends in influence. It should be emphasized that many countries can play leading roles. It is absolutely clear, though, that the US and China must work together with other regional key players such as Japan, Russia, the two Koreas, ASEAN, and India even though they currently are the leaders of this emerging APR structure.

The reason we emphasize the emergence of this new leadership is not only because it is a historical moment, but also because it will likely last for a rather long period, well into the rest of this century. China's economic power may continue to grow and US military power may continue to be dominant: one cannot replace the other in particular fields. The two countries and other players have many incentives to expect a complementary relationship between China and the US. Not only will each play a leading role in a certain field, but the dual-structure leadership may also ensure regional stability and prosperity for the years to come.

Notes

1 Robert Sutter, "Assessing China's Rise and US Leadership in Asia – Growing Maturity and Balance," *Journal of Contemporary China* 19, no. 65 (2010): 591–604.
2 Zbigniew Brzezinski, "Moving toward a Reconciliation of Civilizations," *China Daily*, January 15, 2009, www.chinadaily.com.cn/opinion/2009–01/15/content_7399628.htm.
3 "Factsheet: IMF Quotas," International Monetary Fund, accessed March 21, 2011, www.imf.org/external/np/exr/facts/quotas.htm.
4 Hiro Ito, "US Current Account Debate with Japan Then, with China Now," *Journal of Asian Economics* 20, no. 3 (May 2009): 5.
5 Ronald L. Tammen *et al.*, *Power Transitions: Strategies for the 21st Century* (New York: Chatham House Publishers, 2000): 31.
6 Christopher Layne, "China's Challenge to US Hegemony," *Current History* 107, no. 705 (2008), 16.
7 Robert Kagan, "The Illusion of 'Managing' China," Carnegie Endowment for International Peace, May 15, 2005, www.carnegieendowment.org/publications/index.cfm?fa=view&id=16939.
8 Robert J. Art, "The United States and the Rise of China: Implications for the Long Haul," *Political Science Quarterly* 125, no. 3 (2010): 366.
9 Robert O. Keohane, *International Institutions and State Power* (Boulder, CO: Westview Press, 1989),159.
10 Robert O. Keohane, *After Hegemony: Cooperation and Discord in the World Political Economy* (Princeton, NJ: Princeton University Press, 1984), 51.
11 William C. Olson and James R. Lee, *The Theory and Practice of International Relations*, 9th edn (Englewood Cliffs, NJ: Prentice-Hall, 1994), 210–11.
12 Amitav Acharya, *Constructing a Security Community in Southeast Asia: ASEAN and the Problem of Regional Order*, 2nd edn (London: Routledge, 2009), 20–1.
13 James E. Dougherty and Robert L. Pfaltzgraff, Jr, *Contending Theories of International Relations* (New York: Addison-Wesley, 2007), 419.
14 R.A., "China: Second in Line," *The Economist*, August 16, 2010, accessed February 19, 2011, www.economist.com/blogs/freeexchange/2010/08/china_0.
15 Gordon G. Chang, "China's Property Sector, just before the Crash," *Forbes*, March 3, 2013, accessed April 15, 2013, www.forbes.com/sites/gordonchang/2013/03/03/chinas-property-sector-just-before-the-crash/.
16 "Factsheet: IMF Quotas."
17 *The World Factbook*, Central Intelligence Agency, accessed April 15, 2013, www.cia.gov/library/publications/the-world-factbook/.
18 "GDP Growth (annual percent)," The World Bank, http://data.worldbank.org/indicator/NY.GDP.MKTP.KD.ZG.
19 Arvind Subramanian, "The Inevitable Superpower: Why China's Dominance Is a Sure Thing," *Foreign Affairs* 90, no. 5 (September/October 2011): 66–78.

20. Liu He and Jingzhong Wang, "China Takes Leading Role in Global Recovery: Asia Pacific Business Leaders," *People's Daily Online*, November 15, 2009, http://english.peopledaily.com.cn/90001/90776/90883/6813259.html.
21. John Berthelsen, "Will Chinese Consumers Come to the West's Rescue?" *Global Asia* 6, no. 4 (Winter 2011): 25.
22. "Roundtable: China's Surrounding Security Environment," *Zhongguo Pinglun* (*China Review*) (2011): 53–67.
23. Charles Freeman and Jeffrey D. Bean, "China's Stake in the US Debt Crisis," Center for Strategic and International Studies, July 28, 2011, https://csis.org/publication/chinas-stake-us-debt-crisis.
24. Dick K. Nanto and Emma Chanlett-Avery, *The Rise of China and Its Effect on Taiwan, Japan, and South Korea: US Policy Choices*, Report no. RL32882 (Washington, DC: Congressional Research Service, 2006), 1.
25. Berthelsen, "Will Chinese Consumers Come to the West's Rescue?" 563.
26. Yuan-kang Wang, "China's Response to the Unipolar World: The Strategic Logic of Peaceful Development," *Journal of Asian and African Studies* 45, no. 5 (October 2010): 563.
27. Geoff Dyer, Jamil Anderlini, and Henry Sender, "China's Lending Hits New Heights," *Financial Times*, January 17, 2011.
28. China FTA Network, accessed March 18, 2011, http://fta.mofcom.gov.cn/english/index.shtml.
29. Laicie Olson, "US vs. Global Defense Spending," Center for Arms Control and Non-Proliferation, May 21, 2010, http://armscontrolcenter.org/issues/securityspending/articles/US_vs_Global/.
30. "South Korea–US Military Exercises Stoke Tensions," *BBC News*, November 28, 2010, accessed February 19, 2011, www.bbc.co.uk/news/world-asia-pacific-11855162.
31. "Ulchi-Focus Lens," GlobalSecurity.org, accessed February 19, 2011, www.globalsecurity.org/military/ops/ulchi-focus-lens.htm.
32. "Team Spirit," GlobalSecurity.org, accessed February 19, 2011, www.globalsecurity.org/military/ops/team-spirit.htm.
33. Luis Martinez, "US to Join South Korean Military Exercise off North Korea Coast," *ABC News*, June 2, 2010, accessed February 19, 2011, http://abcnews.go.com/Politics/Media/us-join-south-korea-military-exercise-north-korea/story?id=10807101.
34. Andrew S. Erickson, "Chinese Defense Expenditures: Implication for Naval Modernization," *China Brief* 10, no. 8 (2010): 11–15.
35. Hillary R. Clinton, "America's Pacific Century," *Foreign Policy*, October 11, 2011. www.foreignpolicy.com/articles/2011/10/11/americas_pacific_century.
36. J. Stapleton Roy, "Foreign Service Challenge: Dealing with a Rising China" (lecture, Annual Adair Family Lecture, American University, Washington, DC, September 1, 2010).
37. Robert Sutter and Chin-hao Huang, "China–Southeast Asia Relations: China Reassures Neighbors, Wary of US Intentions," *Comparative Connections* (January 2011): 1.
38. For more on "charm offensive," see Joshua Kurlantzick, *Charm Offensive: How China's Soft Power Is Transforming the World* (New Haven, CT: Yale University Press, 2007).
39. Sutter, "Assessing China's Rise and US Leadership in Asia."
40. Quansheng Zhao, "Moving toward a Co-management Approach: China's Policy toward North Korea and Taiwan," *Asian Perspective* 30, no. 1 (2006): 39–78.
41. Berthelsen, "Will Chinese Consumers Come to the West's Rescue?" 70–3.
42. John J. Mearsheimer, *The Tragedy of Great Power Politics* (New York: W.W. Norton, 2001), 4, 401.
43. Patrick deGategno and Damien Tomkins, "US–China Strategic and Economic Dialogue," Atlantic Council, August 7, 2009, accessed March 18, 2011, www.atlanticcouncil.org/

blogs/new-atlanticist/uschina-strategic-economic-dialogue; and Bonnie S. Glaser, "The Diplomatic Relationship: Substance and Process," in *Tangled Titans: The United States and China*, ed. David Shambaugh (Lanham, MD: Rowman & Littlefield, 2013), 175–6.
44 Art, "The United States and the Rise of China: Implications for the Long Haul," 389.
45 "US–China Strategic and Economic Dialogue 2011 Outcomes of the Strategic Track," US Department of State, May 10, 2011, accessed March 21, 2012, www.state.gov/r/pa/prs/ps/2011/05/162967.htm.
46 "China and the US Hold the First Asia-Pacific Affairs Consultation in Hawaii," Embassy of the People's Republic of China in the United States of America, June 26, 2011, www.china-embassy.org/eng/zmgx/t834465.htm.
47 Henry A. Kissinger, "The Future of US–Chinese Relations: Conflict Is a Choice, Not a Necessity," *Foreign Affairs* 91, no. 2 (March/April 2012): 44–55.
48 "Coping with an Economic Juggernaut," United States Institute of Peace, March 9, 2012, accessed March 22, 2012, www.usip.org/publications/coping-economic-juggernaut.
49 Kissinger, "The Future of US–Chinese Relations," 44–55.
50 David Arase, "Non-Traditional Security in China–ASEAN Cooperation: The Institutionalization of Regional Security Cooperation and the Evolution of East Asian Regionalism," *Asian Survey* 50, no. 4 (July/August 2010): 808–33.
51 Ali Rama, "China's Emergence and Its Impact on ASEAN," *Jakarta Post*, February 4, 2010, accessed March 22, 2012, www.thejakartapost.com/news/2010/02/04/chinapercentE2percent80percent99s-emergence-and-its-impact-asean.html.

References

Acharya, Amitav. *Constructing a Security Community in Southeast Asia: ASEAN and the Problem of Regional Order*. 2nd edn (London: Routledge, 2009).
Arase, David. "Non-Traditional Security in China–ASEAN Cooperation: The Institutionalization of Regional Security Cooperation and the Evolution of East Asian Regionalism." *Asian Survey* 50, no. 4 (July/August 2010): 808–33.
Art, Robert J. "The United States and the Rise of China: Implications for the Long Haul." *Political Science Quarterly* 125, no. 3 (2010): 359–91.
Berthelsen, John. "Will Chinese Consumers Come to the West's Rescue?" *Global Asia* 6, no. 4 (Winter 2011): 25.
Brzezinski, Zbigniew. "Moving toward a Reconciliation of Civilizations." *China Daily*. January 15, 2009. www.chinadaily.com.cn/opinion/2009–01/15/content_7399628.htm.
Chang, Gordon G. "China's Property Sector, just before the Crash." *Forbes*. March 3, 2013. Accessed April 15, 2013. www.forbes.com/sites/gordonchang/2013/03/03/chinas-property-sector-just-before-the-crash/.
China FTA Network. Accessed March 18, 2011. http://fta.mofcom.gov.cn/english/index.shtml.
"China: Second in Line." *The Economist*. August 16, 2010. Accessed February 19, 2011. www.economist.com/blogs/freeexchange/2010/08/china_0.
Clinton, Hillary R. "America's Pacific Century." *Foreign Policy*. October 11, 2011. www.foreignpolicy.com/articles/2011/10/11/americas_pacific_century.
"Coping with an Economic Juggernaut." United States Institute of Peace. March 9, 2012. Accessed March 22, 2012. www.usip.org/publications/coping-economic-juggernaut.
DeGategno, Patrick, and Damien Tomkins. "US–China Strategic and Economic Dialogue." Atlantic Council. August 7, 2009. Accessed March 18, 2011. www.atlantic-council.org/blogs/new-atlanticist/uschina-strategic-economic-dialogue.

Dougherty, James E., and Robert L. Pfaltzgraff, Jr. *Contending Theories of International Relations: A Comprehensive Survey* (New York: Addison-Wesley, 2007).

Dyer, Geoff, Jamil Anderlini, and Henry Sender. "China's Lending Hits New Heights." *Financial Times*. January 17, 2011.

Erickson, Andrew S. "Chinese Defense Expenditures: Implication for Naval Modernization." *China Brief* 10, no. 8 (2010): 11–15.

Factsheet: IMF Quotas." International Monetary Fund. Accessed March 21, 2011. www.imf.org/external/np/exr/facts/quotas.htm.

Freeman, Charles, and Jeffrey D. Bean. "China's Stake in the US Debt Crisis." Center for Strategic and International Studies. July 28, 2011. https://csis.org/publication/chinas-stake-us-debt-crisis.

"GDP Growth (annual percent)." The World Bank. http://data.worldbank.org/indicator/NY.GDP.MKTP.KD.ZG.

He, Liu, and Jingzhong Wang. "China Takes Leading Role in Global Recovery: Asia Pacific Business Leaders." *People's Daily Online*. November 15, 2009. http://english.peopledaily.com.cn/90001/90776/90883/6813259.html.

Ito, Hiro. "US Current Account Debate with Japan Then, with China Now." *Journal of Asian Economics* 20, no. 3 (May 2009): 294–313.

Kagan, Robert. "The Illusion of 'Managing' China." Carnegie Endowment for International Peace. May 15, 2005. www.carnegieendowment.org/publications/index.cfm?fa=view&id=16939.

Keohane, Robert O. *After Hegemony: Cooperation and Discord in the World Political Economy* (Princeton, NJ: Princeton University Press, 1984).

Keohane, Robert O. *International Institutions and State Power* (Boulder, CO: Westview Press, 1989).

Kissinger, Henry A. "The Future of US–Chinese Relations: Conflict Is a Choice, Not a Necessity." *Foreign Affairs* 91, no. 2 (March/April 2012): 44–55.

Kurlantzick, Joshua. *Charm Offensive: How China's Soft Power Is Transforming the World* (New Haven, CT: Yale University Press, 2007).

Layne, Christopher. "China's Challenge to US Hegemony." *Current History* 107, no. 705 (2008): 13–18.

Martinez, Luis. "US to Join South Korean Military Exercise off North Korea Coast." *ABC News*. June 2, 2010. Accessed February 19, 2011. http://abcnews.go.com/Politics/Media/us-join-south-korea-military-exercise-north-korea/story?id=10807101.

Mearsheimer, John J. *The Tragedy of Great Power Politics* (New York: W.W. Norton, 2001).

Nanto, Dick K., and Emma Chanlett-Avery. *The Rise of China and Its Effect on Taiwan, Japan, and South Korea: US Policy Choices*. Report no. RL32882 (Washington, DC: Congressional Research Service, 2006).

Olson, Laicie. "US vs. Global Defense Spending." Center for Arms Control and Non-Proliferation. May 21, 2010. http://armscontrolcenter.org/issues/securityspending/articles/US_vs_Global/.

Olson, William C., and James R. Lee. *The Theory and Practice of International Relations*. 9th edn (Englewood Cliffs, NJ: Prentice-Hall, 1994).

People's Republic of China, US Embassy, "China and the US Hold the First Asia-Pacific Affairs Consultation in Hawaii." June 26, 2011. www.china-embassy.org/eng/zmgx/t834465.htm.

Rama, Ali. "China's Emergence and Its Impact on ASEAN." *Jakarta Post*. February 4, 2010. Accessed March 22, 2012. www.thejakartapost.com/news/2010/02/04/china-percentE2 percent80 percent99s-emergence-and-its-impact-asean.html.

"Roundtable: China's Surrounding Security Environment." *Zhongguo Pinglun* (*China Review* (2011): 53–67.
Roy, J. Stapleton. "Foreign Service Challenge: Dealing with a Rising China." Lecture, Annual Adair Family Lecture, American University, Washington, DC, September 1, 2010.
"South Korea–US Military Exercises Stoke Tensions." *BBC News*. November 28, 2010. Accessed February 19, 2011. www.bbc.co.uk/news/world-asia-pacific-11855162.
Subramanian, Arvind. "The Inevitable Superpower: Why China's Dominance Is a Sure Thing." *Foreign Affairs* 90, no. 5 (September/October 2011): 66–78.
Sutter, Robert. "Assessing China's Rise and US Leadership in Asia – Growing Maturity and Balance." *Journal of Contemporary China* 19, no. 65 (2010): 591–604.
Sutter, Robert, and Chin-hao Huang. "China–Southeast Asia Relations: China Reassures Neighbors, Wary of US Intentions." *Comparative Connections* (January 2011): 63–72.
Tammen, Ronald L., Jacek Kugler, Douglas Lemke, Allan C. Stam, III, Carole Alsharabati, Mark A. Abdollahian, Brian Efird, and A.F.K. Organski. *Power Transitions: Strategies for the 21st Century* (New York: Chatham House Publishers, 2000).
"Team Spirit." GlobalSecurity.org. Accessed February 19, 2011. www.globalsecurity.org/military/ops/team-spirit.htm.
"Ulchi-Focus Lens." GlobalSecurity.org. Accessed February 19, 2011. www.globalsecurity.org/military/ops/ulchi-focus-lens.htm.
"US–China Strategic and Economic Dialogue 2011 Outcomes of the Strategic Track." US Department of State. May 10, 2011. Accessed March 21, 2012. www.state.gov/r/pa/prs/ps/2011/05/162967.htm.
Wang, Yuan-kang. "China's Response to the Unipolar World: The Strategic Logic of Peaceful Development." *Journal of Asian and African Studies* 45, no. 5 (October 2010): 554–67.
World Factbook. Central Intelligence Agency. Accessed April 15, 2013. www.cia.gov/library/publications/the-world-factbook/.
Zhao, Quansheng. "Moving toward a Co-management Approach: China's Policy toward North Korea and Taiwan." *Asian Perspective* 30, no. 1 (2006): 39–78.

4 China and America
Showdown in the Asia-Pacific?

Suisheng Zhao

Home to more than 50 percent of the world's economic activity, the Asia-Pacific Region (APR) is one of the world's most dynamic power centers in the twenty-first century. It also is one of the most volatile regions. For one thing, China's re-emergence as a great power and its aspirations in the APR have given rise to uncertainties within the region. With the rapid growth of its economic, political, and military strength, China has taken a more aggressive stance in pursuing its core national interests and become more willing to back its claims by military force, as shown by a chain of incidents in 2009–14, including China's repeated attempts to prevent Vietnamese and Philippine vessels from exploring oil and gas in disputed waters in the South China Sea (SCS) and China's punitive responses to Japan's detention of a Chinese trawler captain whose boat collided with Japanese coast guard ships in the water near the disputed Diaoyu/Senkaku Islands in the East China Sea (ECS) and Japan's nationalization of some of the Diaoyu/Senkaku Islands. These incidents provoked diplomatic crises during which China displayed its naval warships to support its sovereignty claims. In November 2013, China announced, without any consultation, its air defense identification zone (ADIZ) which overlaps disputed waters with Japan and South Korea.

China's increasing assertiveness has become a source of friction not only with its APR neighbors but also with the United States. Since World War II, the US has played an indispensable role in the maintenance of regional peace and stability by providing public goods such as open sea lanes. US promotion of regional peace and stability has not only fueled the region's economic boom, but also assuaged its partners' security concerns. As China becomes stronger, the US is under increasing pressure to show its allies and partners that it is still committed to, as well as capable of, exerting influence and maintaining leadership in the region. Partially in response to China's rising power, the Obama administration reoriented US strategic priorities toward the APR to intensify America's role and reaffirm its unwavering commitment to the region after winding down wars in Iraq and Afghanistan. Some in the US and China interpret the strategic rebalance in confrontational terms, seeing it as an effort to reassert American primacy in the region, to contain China, and to having the potential to cause a showdown with China.[1] Is this an accurate assessment? Will the US strategic reorientation cause a new Cold War in the APR? This paper argues that although the strategic rebalance represents a new US attempt to secure its place in the APR, its purpose is not to contain China's rise and that a US–China showdown is not inevitable.

China's evolving policies toward APR countries

China's relations with its APR neighbors have been shaped by many factors. China's history as the region's predominant political, economic, cultural, and military power has created "a deep-rooted belief in the geopolitical centrality of China to the region."[2] Beijing cannot afford to repudiate a heritage in which all Chinese take considerable pride. At different times in history, China resorted to a variety of means – e.g., military expeditions, the bestowal of honors, the cultivation of good personal relations with ruling elite, trade promotion, and aid – to win a modicum of influence in the region and retain control of the periphery. The experience of the collapse of the Chinese empire in the nineteenth century led many Chinese elites to assign high priority to shaking off what they saw as a national humiliation of the past and restore its historical status as the APR's indispensable power. A compelling strategic lesson that the Chinese leaders learned from history was that the loss of control on the periphery repeatedly rendered China proper vulnerable to penetration and attack by hostile powers.

China's regional aspirations, however, ultimately depend upon its power capabilities relative to its neighbors. Although China would ideally like to have APR as its exclusive sphere of influence, this was obviously impractical before the twenty-first century because of China's relatively weak power position. When China started modernization drives in the 1980s, it faced chronic economic problems and acute political crisis at home and isolation abroad. From a relatively weak position, Beijing devised a *mulin zhengce* ("good neighbor policy"), building friendly relations with its neighbors to create a favorable peripheral environment for its economic development. This policy continued after the end of the Cold War in the 1990s as good relationships with neighbors provided China with not only a strategic advantage to increase its influence in regional affairs but also leverage in its relations with the US and other Western powers.

China's long-term power potential, its long history of dominating the APR culturally and politically, and its condescension toward its neighboring countries meant the success of its good neighbor policy would be fleeting. While the rhetoric of the good neighbor policy continued, China began to embark on a new pattern of aggressively asserting its sovereignty and territorial claims in the disputes with its neighbors as a result of its rapid economic growth and associated growing military might in the twenty-first century.[3] The term "China's core national interests," defined as "the bottom line of national survival,"[4] suddenly became fashionable and appeared more and more frequently in the speeches of Chinese leaders and the publications of Chinese scholars and newspaper commentators.

For many years, China's official statements on the sovereignty and territorial integrity referred almost exclusively to the issues of Taiwan, Tibet, and Xinjiang.[5] In 2009, Chinese leaders expanded China's sovereignty and territorial integrity-related core interests to include maritime territorial claims in the SCS, which are disputed by several of its neighboring countries. A private meeting between Assistant Minister of Chinese Foreign Affairs Cui Tiankai and two visiting US officials, Deputy Secretary of State James Steinberg and Senior Director of East Asian Affairs at the National Security Council Jeffery Bader in March 2010 caused a lot of uneasiness among China's Southeast Asian neighbors. According to news reports, Cui said China now viewed its claims to the SCS as its core interests, on par with its claims to Taiwan and Tibet.[6] Although this claim was not confirmed afterward by the Chinese government and even denied by some Chinese scholars close to the government,[7] a *Xinhua News* commentary said that "By adding the South China Sea to its core interest, China has showed its determination to secure its maritime resources and strategic waters."[8]

Whether or not the SCS is officially declared a core interest, China's maritime neighbors began to see a renewed and more aggressive claim of Chinese suzerainty and sovereignty over the disputed maritime territories as China increased naval patrols in the area, pressured foreign energy companies to halt operations in contested waters, and imposed fishing bans on parts of the sea. After China sent its largest fishery administration vessel, *China Yuzheng 311*, for the first time to patrol the disputed waters in the SCS in March 2009, more Chinese patrol ships followed suit and started regular patrols of the disputed areas. *China Yuzheng 311* was part of China's 1,300-vessel fisheries surveillance fleet that has been deployed to protect and manage Chinese fishing boats and monitor foreign ships in Chinese-claimed waters. While most of these vessels were relatively small, China had plans to build a number of large patrol vessels. Furthermore, it commissioned private fishing boats to operate as patrol boats in the area in a joint effort by "the government and the private sector."[9] Since then, China's patrol vessels have acted like cops on the beat, prepared to go anywhere in the SCS and ECS at any time to assert its sovereignty.

China's assertions of sovereignty over disputed territories themselves are not new. "But it is China's actions, now backed by more modern maritime enforcement capabilities and demonstrating a more assertive and decidedly nationalistic streak, that are proving to be most worrisome" to China's East Asian neighbors.[10] With its enhanced capabilities, China has shown a willingness to pursue its expanded national interests and coerce its neighbors into making concessions. As a result, tensions between China and its maritime neighbors have escalated dramatically. In the disputed SCS, Chinese vessels routinely clashed with the ships of the other claimants, causing incidents with Vietnamese oil exploration ships and Philippine naval patrol vessels. In the ECS, the territorial dispute between China and Japan over the Diaoyu/Senkaku Islands also has intensified and evolved into a crisis in the wake of a diplomatic row after Japanese coast guard vessels intercepted a Chinese fishing boat off the disputed Diaoyu/Senkaku Islands on September 7, 2010.

China's assertiveness in pursuing its core interests of state sovereignty and territorial integrity, particularly in the cases of maritime territorial disputes, has alienated many of its East Asian neighbours. But strident Chinese actions are in line with the logic of China's rise as a great power, which has not only expanded Chinese strategic and economic interests, but also enhanced its ability to pursue these interests. For a long while, China's pursuit of its maritime interests was seriously constrained because the country's military forces were mostly land based and its naval capacity could rarely reach beyond its coastal seas. But, after nearly two decades of rapid military modernization with an emphasis on naval capacity building, the People's Liberation Army Navy (PLAN) has extended its reach to the Pacific and Indian Oceans. The PLAN has developed an ability to assert exclusive control over waters within what it calls the "First Island Chain," a series of islands stretching from the ECS to the SCS. As a result, China's strategic calculation of its maritime rights and interests has expanded beyond its coastline to the resources and sea lanes far from its shores.

China's new interests also relate to the fact that more than 90 percent of the trade that drives China's growth is sea borne. It is particularly important for China to secure its position in the SCS, including the 630-mile-long Malacca Strait, through which 80 percent of China's oil imports flow. "The contribution of the marine economy to overall national development also is increasing. Ocean-related activities accounted for about 9.53 percent of total gross domestic product in 2009; in coastal areas that figure rose to 15.5 percent of regional GDP."[11] Traditionally a continental power, China looks toward the ocean for its continued economic development in the twenty-first century. China's twelfth five-year plan, a blueprint for economic and social development from 2011 to 2015, for the first time incorporated maritime economic development guidelines in a single chapter to emphasize an optimal marine industry structure that includes exploiting and utilizing maritime resources, particularly energy, in the SCS and ECS.

It is from this perspective that Zhu Feng, a Chinese scholar formerly at Beijing University, suggested:

> the strategic competition between China and major powers has gone beyond Cold War issues, such as Taiwan, Tibet, and human rights, and extended to a series of new arenas such as naval force and the maritime sphere of influence. As a result, maritime security has become a new hot-point in China's periphery security.[12]

Another Chinese scholar also urged that "China must protect its maritime resources with firm resolve to safeguard economic, security interests" because "China's marine rights and interests have been challenged by modern foreign powers." To defend its "maritime rights and interests, China is facing many urgent needs to deal with the issue of sovereignty ... These problems have seriously affected the country's maritime security and even national security." Therefore, "the necessity for China to flex its muscles on the sea appears to be nothing but pressing."[13]

The US strategic rebalance toward the Asia-Pacific

Increasingly wary of China's rising power and its vision of a traditional, hierarchical regional order, many of China's Asian neighbors began seeking the protection of the US and deepening strategic relations with each other to preserve their independence and freedom of action. Even former enemies like Vietnam and estranged friends like the Philippines and Indonesia rushed towards the US, which does not lay claim to any territory in the region and prioritizes freedom of navigation.

Scrambling to cope with the rapidly shifting balance of power and a reintensified engagement with the APR, the US forcefully reasserted itself into multilateral regional diplomacy and demonstrated a strong interest in South China Sea-related matters. Recognizing the critical importance of the Association of Southeast Asian Nations (ASEAN) to the US and demonstrating a US commitment to deepen and strengthen ties with ASEAN and its key members, Secretary of State Hillary Clinton made a point to visit Indonesia and the ASEAN secretariat in February 2009 on her first official overseas trip. President Barack Obama held the inaugural annual US–ASEAN Summit in Singapore in November 2009 and hosted the second summit in New York City the next year. Amid uncertainties surrounding the rise of China and territorial disputes in the SCS, the US accepted the ASEAN invitation to join the East Asian Summit (EAS) in 2010.

Sending a powerful message, the Obama administration waded into the territorial disputes in the SCS as dangerous incidents grew and the increasing and sometimes violent encounters between China and other disputants threatened the stability and prosperity of the region. While Washington took no sides in the disputes, Secretary Clinton, in a July 2010 speech to the ASEAN Regional Forum (ARF) that was closely watched around Asia, declared that "freedom of navigation, open access to Asia's maritime commons and respect for international law in the South China Sea" are US national interests. She also offered to help foster multilateral negotiations as a US "leading diplomatic priority." To make her points clearer, she told reporters at a news conference later in the month that increasing incidents of intimidation, such as the ramming of boats and cutting of vessels' cables, were ratcheting up tensions and raising the "cost of doing business for everyone who travels through the South China Sea. The rest of the world needs to weigh in because all of us have a stake in ensuring that these disputes don't get out of control."[14]

Secretary Clinton's statement significantly deepened Washington's involvement in the SCS disputes by sending the signal that the US does not support China's claims to maritime territories far beyond its shores. It was significant that her remarks were made in Vietnam, a country that has a long-time dispute with China over Spratly and Paracel archipelagoes and was seeking to exploit its turn as ASEAN chairman. Dan Blumenthal believed that Clinton's "comments on territorial disputes in the South China Sea mark a welcome new realism from the Obama administration."[15] At the inaugural ASEAN Defense Minister-plus-Eight (ADMM+) meeting in Hanoi in October 2010, US Secretary of Defense

Robert Gates reiterated the offer to help facilitate discussions between ASEAN and China on the code of conduct of parties in the SCS. As a result, the US boosted its relations with Vietnam and other ASEAN states in the face of shared concerns over China's willingness to wield its enhanced military capabilities in disputed waters.

The Obama administration also made efforts to strengthen and re-energize America's bilateral ties with its long time East Asian allies, particularly Japan and South Korea. The US–Japan alliance has been experiencing some friction due to the stalemate over an agreement on the relocation of the airfield and Marine bases in Okinawa. To an extent, China's diplomatic missteps helped the US and Japan overcome these difficulties. After the September 2010 diplomatic showdown with China, Japan became more reliant on the US to maintain deterrent capabilities against an increasingly powerful China. Forcing Tokyo to stand down in the worst diplomatic row between Japan and China in many years, China pushed many people in Japan from an anti-US position toward a more favorable view. Amid rising tension between Japan and China, Secretary Clinton confirmed to the Japanese Foreign Minister that the Diaoyu/Senkaku Islands administered by Japan and claimed by China were covered by Article 5 of the Japan–US security treaty. The article authorizes the US to protect Japan in the event of an armed attack "in the territories under the administration of Japan."[16]

South Korea, once drifting toward China, also was edging back towards the US following China's rejection of an international report which blamed North Korea for a March 2010 torpedo attack against the South Korean warship *Cheonan*, which killed 46 South Korean sailors, as well as China's reluctance to denounce North Korea following the latter's shelling of Yeonpyeong Islands in November 2010. China's continued opposition to planned US–South Korean military exercises further helped bolster US strategic ties with Seoul. After the sinking of the *Cheonan*, the US took a position of zero-distance from South Korea with regard to North Korea. In spite of China's protest, the US eventually sent the USS *George Washington* to the Yellow Sea to participate in US–South Korean joint military exercises in November 2010. The US also backed South Korea's rejection of China's call for resuming the Six-Party Talks until substantive inter-Korean discussions had been held. As a result, as the *Korea Times* put it, 2010 was "the best year for the US–South Korea alliance" and "the worst year for South Korea–China ties."[17] The passage of the US–Korea Free Trade Agreement in 2011 was a landmark for the relationship.

It was not just traditional allies that felt the US embrace. Obama's visit to Indonesia highlighted US support for Indonesia's democratization and was a way to reach out to Southeast Asia's 250 million Muslims. A few months before the trip, the administration announced that it was going to resume relations with Kopassus, the elite special forces of the Indonesian military, despite the unit's history of alleged atrocities and assassinations. Although restoring military ties with Indonesia prompted strong criticism from human rights advocates, a *Washington Post* article cited some analysts as saying that, "given Indonesia's transition toward democratic governance, it makes sense to re-engage with powerful elements of its military, in part to build up counterweights to China's increasing power in the region."[18]

The US also cultivated emerging regional powers such as Vietnam, which shared a historical wariness of Chinese power and an interest in balancing Chinese influence in Southeast Asia. Although Vietnam brought up feelings of loss and revulsion after a long war in which 58,000 Americans died and 1.1 million Vietnamese are estimated to have perished, the US restored normal diplomatic relations with Vietnam in 1995 and the two sides have gradually reconciled. The US and Vietnam signed a military cooperation agreement in 2005, which included plans for the US to provide military education and training to officers in the Vietnamese armed forces. After US Secretary of Defense Donald Rumsfeld visited Vietnam for the first time in June 2006, the US Congress amended its International Traffic in Arms Regulations in 2007, allowing the sale of some non-lethal defensive weapons and services to Vietnam, though such sales are to be examined and decided upon case by case.

To underscore the emerging US–Vietnam security relationship, the US dispatched a strike group of three destroyers to take part in joint exercises with the Vietnamese navy in the SCS in August 2010. At the same time, the guided missile destroyer, the USS *John S. McCain*, docked in the port city of Da Nang, and took part in a joint training exercise with the Vietnamese navy. This visit was very symbolic since the ship is named for US Senator John McCain's grandfather, an admiral, and his father, the admiral who led the Pacific Command during the Vietnam War. Senator McCain, a naval aviator, was shot down over Hanoi and spent six years as a prisoner of war. A similar symbolic visit took place earlier in November 2009 when the US navy sent missile destroyer the USS *Lassen* under the command of its first-ever Vietnamese-American captain, Hung Ba Le, on a goodwill visit to Da Nang. On March 30, 2010, the US and Vietnam signed a memorandum of understanding on the peaceful use of nuclear energy, under which the US would help Vietnam build nuclear power plants. On a related note, the US Department of Energy trained Vietnamese officials in nonproliferation and safety methods and the implementation of nuclear export controls.[19] On top of all of this, a joint statement after the annual US–Vietnam talks in Washington in June 2011 stated that "The US side reiterated that troubling incidents in recent months do not foster peace and stability within the region." It added "all territorial disputes in the South China Sea should be resolved through a collaborative, diplomatic process without coercion or the use of force."[20]

A new strategic partnership has been gradually built upon the ashes of war. It is a historical paradox that while the US partnered with China to help end the Vietnam War in the 1970s, it is now aligned with Vietnam over concern about China's escalating claims in the South China Sea. Thirty-five years after the Vietnam War, "Washington and Hanoi are cozying up in a number of areas, from negotiating a controversial deal to share civilian nuclear fuel and technology to agreeing that China needs to work with its neighbors to resolve territorial claims in the South China Sea."[21]

The US–Vietnam security cooperation was only a part of the US push to deepen military ties across Southeast Asia, including an expansion of training and military exercises in Southeast Asian countries "to enhance its ability to police international waterways, and to lift the confidence and military capabilities of smaller Southeast Asian countries."[22] At the annual Shangri-La Dialogue Asian security meeting in Singapore in June 2011, US Defense Secretary Robert Gates said that the US military would be "increasing its port calls, naval engagements and multilateral training efforts with multiple countries throughout the region" to broaden and deepen the US relationship with friends and allies and "help build partner capacity to address regional challenges."[23] On a more specific note, in January 2011, the US started a security dialog with the Philippines where it had once had key air and naval bases. Although the US lost these bases in 1992, the two countries remain linked by a 1951 mutual defense pact. US Assistant Secretary of State for East Asia and Pacific Affairs, Kurt Campbell, pledged on the first day of the security dialog that, standing ready to help the Philippines and other Southeast Asian countries bolster their ability to defend their territories, the US would set up working groups with the Philippines to study ways of increasing cooperation in territorial defense and maritime security. This would enhance the Philippine navy's capacity to patrol its waters as part of a larger goal of keeping vital sea lanes open amid the rise of China.[24]

The US thus laid down markers when China's behavior infringed on its interests in the region. As one observer suggested, "American willingness in 2009 to accommodate China and the unwillingness to do so" in 2010 "indicates that Washington is more realistic today about the kind of cooperation that it can expect from China."[25]

Chinese perceptions of the changing power balance

The US rebalance towards the APR has fueled fears among some Chinese strategists about American intentions. For many Chinese observers, the US shift is not just about the region's importance as an engine of economic growth, but, more importantly, because Washington is worried that China's rising influence will threaten US interests and challenge American supremacy.

For about two decades after the end of the Cold War, conditioned by China's limited power and geostrategic position, the Chinese leadership followed a *taoguang yanghui* policy of keeping a low profile and concentrating on building up China's national strength. With respect to relations with the US, China tried to "learn to live with the hegemon," adapting and adjusting policy to the reality of the US dominance in the international system.[26] Chinese leaders, therefore, avoided taking a confrontational posture in response to the US sanctions after Tiananmen in 1989, the inadvertent bombing of the Chinese embassy by the US in 1999, and the mid-air collision between a Chinese jet fighter and a US EP-3 surveillance plane in 2001.

Making tremendous strides in terms of national strength, China narrowed the gap with the US. This coupled with the fact that it weathered the global slowdown at the end of the 2000s better than many Western countries, a fact stressed by Quansheng Zhao in Chapter 3, led an increasing number of Chinese to see a shift in the global balance of power in China's favor. With the US in financial turmoil and seemingly desperate for cash-rich China to come to its aid, Chinese leaders became increasing confident in their ability to deal with the US. As well, they became more willing to proactively shape the external environment rather than passively react to it and more aggressive in safeguarding China's national interests.

For a long time after the end of the Cold War, China's leaders and scholars have suspected that the US was not reconciled to China's rise and have been frustrated by the perceived US intention to prevent China from achieving its rightful place. Seeing an inevitable structural conflict between China as a rising power and the US as the sole superpower, they see "containment" not just as a fact, but as the "real" US policy that the US will never abandon. A commentary in the *People's Daily* protesting US–South Korean military exercises in the ECS stated:

> it is easy for the US to say but difficult to take action to adapt to China's rise. If the US cannot find a way to recognize and accept China as a world power, Sino-US relations would continue ups-and-downs like a roller coaster.[27]

Overall, perceptions of a troubled US still bent on keeping China down have made Chinese leaders less willing to show flexibility. With increasing military capacities, Beijing has downgraded those once-central elements of its foreign policy in favor of more assertive, even aggressive, stances.

In particular, China has grown increasingly vocal in protesting and challenging US naval operations in international waters off its coast. A group of Chinese vessels intercepted an American surveillance ship, the USSN *Impeccable*, in March 2009 in the SCS where American ships frequently deployed to monitor China's military activities. Under its Freedom of Navigation Program, the US regularly asserted its rights in international waters and carried out military exercises, survey activities, and intelligence-gathering in waters seaward of China's 12-mile territorial limit. Until about a decade ago, the US essentially possessed uncontested access to the vicinity of China without any serious challenge. While Chinese always viewed US surveillance operation close to its national borders as a challenge to its national security and territorial integrity, China had never taken such high profile actions to stop US ships even in its exclusive economic zone (EEZ). According to a Chinese scholar, the incident "is a sign of new robustness in China's dealing with the West."[28]

Rejecting the results of an international investigation that found North Korea sank the South Korean ship the *Cheonan* (discussed above), Beijing took an unusually assertive position towards the joint US–South Korean military exercise in the Yellow Sea in summer 2010 designed to deter North Korea from further provocations. It argued generally that naval vessels and auxiliary ships should be restricted when operating in China's EEZ. It specifically objected to the deployment of the USS *George Washington* aircraft carrier in the Yellow Sea, an area which Chinese experts warned would place the Chinese capital within the carrier's striking distance, even though the US navy has long conducted naval exercises in the area. Between early June, when the news was revealed, and early July, when Washington confirmed the exercises, the spokesman at China's Ministry of Foreign Affairs issued six official protests with a successively tougher tone from calling on involved parties to "maintain calm and constraint," to expressing "concern" and "serious concern," then morphing into words such as "oppose" and "strongly oppose."[29] When the US ignored Chinese warnings, a *PLA Daily* commentary accused the US of carrying out hegemonism, gunshipism, and unilateralism. Noting "although we would not want to be the enemy of any country, we would not be in fear of any country which dares to ignore our solemn position and core interests," the commentary quoted Mao Zedong's saying that "If no one harms me, I harm no one, but if someone harms me, I must harm them."[30]

China was particularly upset over Secretary of State Clinton's 2010 speech that offered mediation over maritime disputes in the SCS. Seeing her speech as unwarranted outside interference in regional affairs and an attempt at containing China, the Chinese Foreign Minister issued a statement charging US internationalization of the SCS disputes and Secretary Clinton's remarks an attack on China. Asserting that the situation was not problematic in the SCS until Secretary Clinton made her unwelcome speech, China's Ministry of Defense spokesperson also made an official response to "oppose the South China Sea issue being internationalized" and reiterated that China "has indisputable sovereignty over islands in the South China Sea and the surrounding waters."[31]

Although the Philippines and Vietnam called for a multilateral solution based on the United Nations Convention on the Law of the Sea (UNCLOS), China was irked by US support for Vietnam and the Philippines and warned it to stay out of the dispute, which would allow it to deal with each of the weaker claimant states on its own. Beijing was angry, too, that the SCS was a key part of the agenda when President Obama met his ASEAN counterparts at the US–ASEAN summit and that he raised the issue at the November 2011 EAS by laying out guiding principles for dealing with challenges of maritime security in the SCS to ensure the sea lanes remained open and peaceful. While most Asian countries aligned with Washington at the summit, Chinese Premier Wen Jiabao was irritated and responded that "outside forces" had no excuse to meddle in the complex maritime dispute, a veiled warning to the US and others to keep out of the sensitive issue at multilateral venues. US efforts to strengthen its diplomatic and military relations with its APR maritime partners fueled China's fears of being encircled and pressured.

Consequently, encirclement has become a popular phrase in Chinese debates about US East Asian strategy. A *People's Daily* editorial on the China visit of Admiral Mike Mullen, the head of the US Joint Chiefs of Staff, in July 2011 complained:

the South China Sea issue has served as a mirror reflecting the complicated mentality and policies of the United States. When the South China Sea disputes escalated, the United States, which has the most powerful military presence in the region, just managed to show off its force and capitalize on the disputes instead of playing a role in cooling down them.[32]

During a meeting with South Korean Defense Minister Kim Kwan-jin in Seoul, Chen Bingde, the Chief of the PLA General Staff, raised the issue of US forces holding joint military exercises in the SCS with the Philippines and Vietnam and urged Washington to refrain from intervening in the region. In response to Admiral Mullen's statement that the US had forces in the SCS for a long time and that this commitment would continue, Chen launched into a 15-minute tirade against the US. A South Korean newspaper commented that Chen's statements were discourteous and violated diplomatic protocol.[33]

The US hedge against China's rise

Selecting a long-term strategy for dealing with China's rise has been the most difficult foreign policy challenge the US has faced since the end of the Cold War. Starting from President George H.W. Bush, each US president has struggled whether to view China as a strategic threat that requires containment or as a strategic opportunity that deserves engagement. As a result, US policy toward China has swung back and forth, leading to a cyclical pattern of ups and downs in the relationship. Every new president from the opposing party always attempts to change or reverse his predecessor's China policy. Creating new uncertainties for the US–China relationship and damaging the US interests, the new administration, after a period of dallying around, always ends up making policy adjustments.

The arrival of the Barack Obama administration in 2009 produced a swing from his predecessor President George W. Bush.[34] Charging President Bush's unilateralism had damaged US moral leadership, Obama came to office aiming to repair America's global image and reset relations with the great powers. One of his priorities was to elevate the US–China relationship through cooperation on global issues. Eschewing the balance-of-power approach and downplaying hedging strategies, Obama proposed a "positive, cooperative, and comprehensive" relationship in lieu of Bush's "cooperative, constructive, and candid" relationship with China. Using "positive" in place of "candid" reflected the Obama administration's reluctance to challenge China on issues of fundamental disagreements and its emphasis on shared interests. In February 2009, Secretary of State Clinton made explicit that the administration would not allow contentious issues such as human rights, Taiwan, and Tibet to "interfere with the global economic crisis, the global climate change crisis and the security crises."[35]

To set a good tone before his first official visit to China in November 2009, Obama made two major concessions on issues sensitive to China. One was to postpone the meeting with the Dalai Lama when the Tibetan religious leader visited Washington, DC, in October 2009, a departure from past US presidential tradition. The other was to defer the announcement on arms sales to Taiwan for 11 months. To signal US understanding of China's core interests, he signed a US–China joint statement which stated for the first time that "the two sides agreed that respecting each other's core interests is extremely important to ensure steady progress in US–China relations." Obama also did not hesitate to elevate his high-level dialog with China as "strategic" and described China as a "strategic partner," "a label much desired by Beijing."[36] Because the focus on shared interests was more or less in line with China's call for a harmonious world, the Obama administration's relationship with China enjoyed a honeymoon period.

The honeymoon, however, was short. Working assiduously in its first year to lay the groundwork for cooperation on major global challenges, the Obama administration found itself responding to one crisis after another because of mismatched interests and values. A policy adjustment thereby occurred one year after Obama assumed office. Waking up to the magnitude of China's rising power, the Obama administration shredded its "self-imposed straitjacket" and pursued "traditional American interests and principles even if George W. Bush pursued them, too."[37] The central element of the adjustment was to bring the hedge back to shape the regional context of China's rise and define the terms of engagement to which China has to respond. Acknowledging China's emergence as a world power and holding the biggest strategic and economic dialogs with the Chinese, the Obama administration began to re-energize its relationships with traditional allies and partners that shared America's values and interests.

While the hedge became the new buzzword in US strategic discourse vis-à-vis China, this did not mean engagement was rejected. Rather, the administration sought a mix in order to strike a balance between conciliation and confrontation. On the one hand, it acknowledged China's emergence as a global power, held the biggest strategic and economic dialogs with China, and continued to work with China on a broad range of issues where US interests overlap. On the other hand, the administration wielded US power, showed a willingness to act where China's behavior infringed on US interests or caused regional instability, and has worked with its allies to engage and balance China's rising power. The US is prepared for an alternative, more adversarial outcome in case the past 40 years of engagement do not work. As Joseph Nye pointed out,

> The Pentagon's East Asia Strategy Review that has guided our policy since 1995 offered China integration into the international system through trade and exchanges, but we hedged our bet by simultaneously strengthening our alliance with Japan. Our military forces did not aspire to "contain" China in a Cold War fashion, but they helped to shape the environment in which China makes its choices.[38]

The US has pursued a balanced policy because a full-out confrontation or containment policy towards China would be self-defeating. First, China is not the

Soviet Union and the US–China relationship is much more complicated and complex than was the US–Soviet relationship. China is not merely a military power and the US relationship with China focuses not only on security issues but also economic and many other important issues. Despite obvious conflicts and potential flashpoints, a significant convergence of strategic interests between the US and China has developed as "power is more equally distributed between them and each needs to cooperate with the other to address problems it deems critical to its own future."[39] Although the concept of the G-2 amounting to strategic bipolarity or a Sino-US condominium is a fantasy, it is an acknowledgement of the central importance of Sino-US relations and the need for these two states to manage their bilateral economic and security relations cooperatively. As Secretary of State Clinton indicated,

> China and the United States cannot solve all the problems of the world together. But without China and the United States, I doubt that any of our global problems can be resolved.... There is no intrinsic contradiction between supporting a rising China and advancing America's interests. A thriving China is good for America, and a thriving America is good for China.[40]

Given the increasing interdependence between the two countries, any unilateral US attempts to limit China's rise are likely to be sporadic at best.

Second, the US is not able to forge an anti-China coalition in concert with other East Asian countries because few nations, even Vietnam and Japan, could afford to antagonize a rising power and major market. None of them want to live under China's shadow and all welcome US support, but none want to make China an enemy or to be squeezed by US–China rivalry. Opting for some combination of hedging and accommodation to avoid direct confrontation with China, most of China's middle- and small-size neighbors have favored the US presence as a hedge against China's assertion of regional hegemony but also wanted to keep China fully engaged and do not want to be drawn into any tensions between the US and China. Very few East Asian countries are ready to put all their eggs in one basket. With many of them already struggling in the face of China's dominance, they do not need another great power using them as a pawn in a dangerous strategic rivalry. While recognizing a US military presence is important, they prefer the fleet remain over the horizon. They want political attention, and the assurance of US engagement as a counterweight to China, but very few of them want open confrontation with China. Maintaining delicate relationships with both of the US and China as well as other regional powers is at the heart of the balance strategy in East Asia.

Third, the Obama administration came to office at the juncture of the most important geopolitical development in the twenty-first century, i.e., the changing global distribution of power from a short-lived US unipolar dominance to multipolarity due to the rise of China and other non-Western powers. In the multipolar world, as a US National Intelligence Council report admitted, "although the US is likely to remain the single most important actor, the US's relative strength will decline and US leverage will become more constrained."[41] It is true that the US may remain the world's pre-eminent power and public goods provider for at least the next several decades as it is blessed with abundant resources, cutting-edge universities and research institutions, an innovative capitalist economy, the world's largest and most advanced military, a diverse and adaptable democratic society, a robust and reasonably efficient legal and regulatory system, attractive cultural "soft power," the most favorable demographic profile in the developed world, and excellent allies, friends, and partners with which to cooperate.[42] But it also is true that Washington faces a rapidly changing world that is becoming increasingly complex, vulnerable to disruptive trends, and diffused in power, and America's power position in the region ultimately depends on the health of its domestic economy and reforms, particularly with regard to fiscal policies. The US has to get its fiscal house in order to sustain its focus on Asia over long run.

Conclusion: showdown in the Asia-Pacific?

Walter Russell Mead pointed to both the natural strengths and the natural limits of America's position. "American power in the world has both a ceiling and a floor." If America gets too powerful and the world looks too unipolar, then countries around the world start acting in ways that cut America down to size. If China collapsed into years of internal dissension, turbulence, and instability, India, Japan, and South Korea might well take the opportunity to distance themselves from America. The US wants and needs to operate in that middle ground between feckless retreat and hubristic assertion.[43]

In this case, while the US has demonstrated its continued commitment to its allies and partners in East Asia, it is not in a position to encourage regional countries to pursue their territorial claims to the extent of defying China and increasing the risk of conflict between China and its neighbors and ultimately leading to a crisis in Sino-US relations. China is rapidly becoming too strong – not just economically and diplomatically but also militarily – for the US to maintain an unquestionable capacity to intervene successfully if necessary. Americans have to decide if they can afford the cost of backing all their Asian friends and allies in any fight they pick with China as any war in the ECS, SCS, or other areas could become very costly and dangerous for the US. As a result, for the US to avoid a direct military showdown with China, it would need to take measures aimed at discouraging not just China but also China's neighbors from adopting provocative policies.

While China looms large over the new geopolitics of East Asia, Washington could not define US engagement with the region completely in terms of a zero-sum game. It has been deepening old alliances and building new partnerships to pursue its longstanding goals: security, prosperity, and human dignity. US interests would be best served when and if the US and China work together to seriously dedicate their power and wealth to create an enduring regional security order rather than to win diplomatic or military contests with each other.

On the China side, Chinese leaders, as realists, ultimately have to accept the reality of enduring American strengths in the region. Although Americans have made many costly mistakes in their domestic and foreign policies and the US has faced serious challenges from the global financial downturn in 2008–10, its economy has showed incredible resilience. Furthermore, the US's international position remains strong in structural terms because strong and deep forces in world affairs have brought the US to its present position of influence and power and those forces cannot disappear overnight. As a 2012 National Bureau of Asian Research report indicated, despite a partial loss of autonomy, the US still is untouched when it comes to its capacity for innovation and, more generally, its technological prowess. The US remains the only country with "comprehensive national power." China has sought to develop comprehensive national power, but it still concentrated essentially on GNP growth which will ensure that its overall growth rates stay at relatively high levels. It will be a while before its growth rates translate into the increased per capita income, state capacity, institutional coherence, and military capacity necessary to sustain an international presence that others must be compelled to respect.[44]

Even in the APR, the foundations supporting US power are much stronger than those supporting China. China is still far from matching the American military and economic pre-eminence that has underwritten regional peace and prosperity for the past several decades. The US still has a remarkable advantage in soft power. With American symbols and technologies being highly valued throughout Asia, the US remains the dream society for most of the region. People want to emulate the US, whereas there are very few countries in Asia that want to become like China. Moreover, while the vast majority of East Asian states welcome the US military presence in the region, China remains distrusted by almost every APR maritime power. As Walter Russell Mead suggested, just as Soviet bullying during the Cold War strengthened the NATO alliance by reminding Europeans just how much they needed American protection, so has China's throwing of its weight around in the region pushed countries like India, Japan, South Korea, Vietnam, Singapore, Malaysia, Indonesia, and Australia towards closer cooperation with the US. China's regional allies – North Korea, Myanmar, and Pakistan – are substantially weaker and more problematic.[45] In spite of the dangerous partisan bloodletting pervasive in Washington, the US still has many of the tools needed to exercise strategic power and help from allies and partners to so-so. It also has continued to act strategically, working to institutionalize important American relationships in the APR.

Beijing cannot give up its claims of sovereignty over disputed territories because this would undermine the nationalist credentials of the communist regime. However, these territorial disputes have the potential to escalate into larger international conflicts, given the number of bilateral security commitments between regional states and the US, such as those between the US and Japan and the Philippines. Were that to happen, China's ability to use force would be constrained by the possible reactions of the US. To achieve dominance in the region may be an ultimate objective in the long run but it is not considered a serious

Chinese objective in the early twenty-first century because the presence and influence of the US and the strength of dynamic regional powers, such as Japan and India, continue to restrict the boundaries within which China's power may be asserted. As Robert Sutter discovered during a research trip to Beijing, although secret Chinese Communist Party documents over the years have continued to refer to China's general goal of Asian leadership, when asked whether China sought leadership or domination in Asia, a senior Chinese official acknowledged the constraints flowing from US power and influence and the role of many independent-minded Asian governments. These comments show an appreciation of the "realities of power that make Chinese leadership in Asia unlikely under foreseeable circumstances."[46]

Indeed, unless some unforeseen power vacuum develops in the APR, it is difficult to conceive of China assuming a hegemonic role in the region equivalent to that the US has long had in the Western hemisphere or that the Soviet Union once had in Eastern Europe. More importantly, Chinese leaders are fearful of their internal economic and political fragility. China's political stability and economic development could be threatened if China's increasing assertiveness provokes an anti-China backlash. Generally speaking, China's lack of sufficient military power and immense internal and external challenges will constrain it from taking an expansionist path in East Asia in the early twenty-first century as Japan did in the early twentieth century. Although exercising sovereignty over the disputed territories is crucial for Beijing's leaders, it would be an extremely risky decision for them to squander China's military resources and political capital to seize barren flyspecks far from China's coast. For China, the more realistic and preferred resolution to the difficult maritime territorial disputes is still diplomacy rather than the use of force.

Notes

1 朱锋 (Zhu Feng), "奥巴马政府转身亚洲战略与中美关系 (The Obama Administration's Pivot toward Asia and Sino-US Relationship)," 现代国际关系 (*Contemporary International Relations*), no. 4 (2012): 1–7.
2 Michael D. Swaine and Ashley J. Tellis, *Interpreting China's Grand Strategy: Past, Present, and Future*, report no. MR-1121-AF (Santa Monica: RAND Corporation, 2000), 3.
3 For a discussion of China's economic predominance in the APR, see Chapter 3 by Quansheng Zhao in this volume.
4 陈岳 (Chen Yue), "中国当前外交环境及应对 (The Current International Environment and the Responses)," 现代国际关系 (*Contemporary International Relations*) (2011): 4.
5 Wu Xinbo, "Forging Sino-US Partnership in the 21st Century: Opportunities and Challenges," *Journal of Contemporary China* 21, no. 75 (May 2012): 393.
6 John Pomfret, "US Takes a Tougher Tone with China," *Washington Post*, July 30, 2010, A1 section.
7 Wang Jisi, Dean of Beijing University's School of International Studies, wrote that "some Chinese commentators reportedly referred to the South China Sea and North Korea as such (China core interests), these reckless states, made no official authorization, created a great deal of confusion." Wang Jisi, "China's Search for Grand Strategy: A Rising Power Finds its Way," *Foreign Affairs* (March/April 2011): 39–48.

8 "Modernizing Navy for Self-Defense," *Xinhua*, July 13, 2010.
9 Kenji Minemura, "China to Establish Permanent Senkaku Patrols," Japan Institute of International Affairs, December 20, 2010, www.jiia.or.jp/en/commentary/.
10 Aileen S.P. Baviera, "China and the South China Sea: Time for Code of Conduct?" *RSIS Commentaries*, no. 91 (June 14, 2011). http://207.97.208.129/CHSS/History/PapersCommentariesStudies/RSIScommentaryChinaandtheSouthChinaSea.pdf.
11 Yang Mingjie, "Sailing on a Harmonious Sea: A Chinese Perspective," *Global Asia* 5, no. 4 (Winter 2010): 22–5.
12 朱锋 (Zhu Feng), "东亚安全局势：新形势，新特点与新趋势 (Security Situation in East Asia: New Situation, New Features and New Trends)," 现代国际关系 (*Contemporary International Relations*), December 2010, 12.
13 Li Jingyu, "Ocean of Dreams," *China Daily*, August 20, 2011, www.chinadaily.com.cn/usa/business/2011–08/19/content_13152341.htm.
14 "Clinton Addresses South China Sea Rifts," Boston.com, July 25, 2011, www.boston.com/news/world/asia/articles/2011/07/25/clinton_addresses_south_china_sea_rifts/.
15 Dan Blumenthal, "Reining in China's Ambitions," *Wall Street Journal*, July 27, 2010, http://online.wsj.com/article/SB10001424052748703700904575391862120429050.html.
16 "Clinton tells Maehara Senkaku Subject to Japan–US Security Pact," *Associated Press*, September 23, 2010.
17 Sunny Lee, "Can Korea 'Hedge' between US and China?" *Korea Times*, July 10, 2011, www.koreatimes.co.kr/www/news/nation/2011/07/116_90538.html.
18 John Pomfret, "US Continues Effort to Counter China's Influence in Asia," *Washington Post*, July 23, 2010, A10 section.
19 Chen Hurng-yu, "US Asserts Its Power in Indochina," *Taipei Times*, March 25, 2011, www.taipeitimes.com/News/editorials/archives/2011/03/25/2003499036/3.
20 "US, Vietnam Call for Stability, Peace," *Taipei Times*, July 19, 2011, www.taipeitimes.com/News/world/archives/2011/06/19/2003506167.
21 Margie Mason, "US–Vietnam Military Relations: Former Enemies Now Military Mates," *The World Report*, August 8, 2010, www.huffingtonpost.com/2010/08/09/us-vietnam-military-relat_n_675202.html.
22 Patrick Barta," US, Vietnam in Exercises Amid Tensions With China," *Wall Street Journal*, July 16, 2011, http://online.wsj.com/article/SB10001424052702304223804576447712748465574.html.
23 "Gates Pledges Wider US Military Presence in Asia," *USA Today*, June 4, 2011, www.usatoday.com/news/world/2011–06–03-robert-gates-china_n.htm?csp=34news.
24 "US Pledges Help for Philippine Navy," Agence France-Presse, January 27, 2011, www.abs-cbnnews.com/print/134899.
25 Frank Ching, "Hedging the Glad Hand to China," *Japan Times*, February 7, 2011, http://search.japantimes.co.jp/cgi-bin/eo20110207fc.html.
26 Jia Qingguo, "Learning to Live with the Hegemon: Evolution of China's Policy toward the US since the End of the Cold War," *Journal of Contemporary China* 14, no. 44 (August 2005): 395.
27 钟声 (Zhongsheng), "美国准备好中国作为大国登场了吗？(Is US Ready for China to Take the Stage as a World Power?)," *People's Daily*, July 29, 2010.
28 James Mikes, "China and the West, A Time for Muscle-flexing," *The Economist*, March 19, 2009.
29 Cary Huang, "PLA Ramped up China's Stand on Us–Korea Drill: Beijing Rhetoric Evolves from Neutral to Shrill Saber-Rattling," *South China Morning Post*, August 6, 2010, www.scmp.com/portal/site/SCMP/menuitem.2af62ecb329d3d7733492d9253a0a0a0/?vgnextoid=8018423df234a210VgnVCM100000360a0a0aRCRD&ss=China&s=News.
30 Luo Yuan, "武力炫耀的背后是霸道 – 评美国航母拟赴黄海参加军演 (The US Sending Aircraft Carrier to the Yellow Sea Shows Its Gunboat Policy)," 解放军报

(*PLA Daily*), August 12, 2010, http://chn.chinamil.com.cn/xwpdxw/jsyxxw/2010-08/12/content_4277766.htm.
31 Cheng Guangjin and Wu Jiao, "Sovereign Waters Are not in Question," *China Daily*, August 31, 2010, www.cdeclips.com/en/nation/fullstory.html?id=48815.
32 "To Improve Relations, Us Must Respect China's Core Interests," *People's Daily*, July 14, 2011, http://english.peopledaily.com.cn/90001/90780/91343/7440158.html.
33 "Chinese Military Chief's Rudeness Bodes Ill for the Future," *Chosun Ilbo*, July 18, 2011, http://english.chosun.com/site/data/html_dir/2011/07/18/2011071801238.html.
34 For discussion of US–China relations during George H.W. Bush, Bill Clinton, and George W. Bush's tenure in office, see Chapter 2 by Jean-Marc F. Blanchard's chapter on the history of China–US relations.
35 "Not So Obvious, The Secretary of State Underestimates the Power of Her Words," *Washington Post*, February 24, 2009, A12 section.
36 Timothy G. Ash, "Two Ways for West to Meet China," *Straits Times*, November 20, 2009, www.straitstimes.com/Review/Others/STIStory_456690.html?sunwMethod=GET.
37 Robert Kagan, "America: Once Engaged, Now Ready to Lead," *Washington Post*, October 1, 2010, www.washingtonpost.com/wp-dyn/content/article/2010/09/30/AR2010093005528.html?wpisrc=nl_pmopinions.
38 Joseph S. Nye, "A Pivot That Is Long Overdue," *New York Times*, November 21, 2011, www.nytimes.com/roomfordebate/2011/11/21/does-the-us-need-troops-in-australia/marines-in-australia-its-about-time.
39 David M. Lampton, "The United States and China in the Age of Obama: Looking Each Other Straight in the Eyes," *Journal of Contemporary China* 18, no. 62 (November 2009): 727.
40 "Hillary Clinton: Remarks at the US Institute of Peace China Conference," US Department of State, March 7, 2012, www.state.gov/secretary/20092013clinton/rm/2012/03/185402.htm.
41 "Global Trends 2025: A Transformed World – The National Intelligence Council's 2025 Project," Council on Foreign Relations, November 2008, www.cfr.org/world/global-trends-2025-transformed-world–national-intelligence-councils-2025-project/p17826. On the changing relative power position of China and the US, see Chapter 3 by Quansheng Zhao's in this volume.
42 Andrew S. Erickson, "The US Security Outlook in the Asia-Pacific Region," in *Asia Pacific Countries' Security Outlook and Its Implications for the Defense Sector*, publication no. 6 (Tokyo: National Institute for Defense Studies, 2012), www.nids.go.jp/english/publication/joint_research/series6/pdf/07.pdf.
43 Walter R. Mead, "In the Footsteps of the Kaiser: China Boosts US Power in Asia," *American Interest*, September 26, 2010, http://blogs.the-American-interest.com/wrm/2010/09/26/in-the-footsteps-of-the-kaiser-china-boosts-us-power-in-asia.
44 Ashley J. Tellis, Travis Tanner and Jessica Keough, eds., *Strategic Asia 2011–12: Asia Responds to Its Rising Powers – China and India*, issue brief (Seattle and Washington, DC: National Bureau of Asian Research, 2011).
45 Mead, "In the Footsteps of the Kaiser."
46 Robert Sutter, "Why a Rising China Can't Dominate Asia," *Asia Times Online*, September 15, 2006, www.atimes.com/atimes/China/HI15Ad02.html.

References

Ash, Timothy G. "Two Ways for West to Meet China." *Straits Times*. November 20, 2009. www.straitstimes.com/Review/Others/STIStory_456690.html?sunwMethod=GET.

Barta, Patrick. "US, Vietnam in Exercises amid Tensions With China." *Wall Street Journal*. July 16, 2011. http://online.wsj.com/article/SB10001424052702304223804576447412748465574.html.

Baviera, Aileen S.P. "China and the South China Sea: Time for Code of Conduct?" *RSIS Commentaries*, no. 91 (June 14, 2011).

Blumenthal, Dan. "Reining in China's Ambitions." *Wall Street Journal*. July 27, 2010. http://online.wsj.com/article/SB10001424052748703700904575391862120429050.html.

Chen, Hurng-yu. "US Asserts Its Power in Indochina." *Taipei Times*. March 25, 2011. www.taipeitimes.com/News/editorials/archives/2011/03/25/2003499036/3.

Chen, Yue. "中国当前外交环境及应对 (The Current International Environment and the Responses)." 现代国际关系 (*Contemporary International Relations*), November 2011.

Cheng, Guangjin, and Jiao Wu. "Sovereign Waters Are Not in Question." *China Daily*. August 31, 2010. www.cdeclips.com/en/nation/fullstory.html?id=48815.

"Chinese Military Chief's Rudeness Bodes Ill for the Future." *Chosun Ilbo*. July 18, 2011. http://english.chosun.com/site/data/html_dir/2011/07/18/2011071801238.html.

Ching, Frank. "Hedging the Glad Hand to China." *Japan Times*. February 7, 2011. http://search.japantimes.co.jp/cgi-bin/eo20110207fc.html.

"Clinton Addresses South China Sea Rifts." *Boston.com*. July 25, 2011. www.boston.com/news/world/asia/articles/2011/07/25/clinton_addresses_south_china_sea_rifts/.

"Clinton Tells Maehara Senkaku Subject to Japan–US Security Pact." Associated Press. September 23, 2010.

Erickson, Andrew S. "The US Security Outlook in the Asia-Pacific Region," in *Asia Pacific Countries' Security Outlook and Its Implications for the Defense Sector*, publication no. 6 (Tokyo: National Institute for Defense Studies, 2012), January 2012. www.nids.go.jp/english/publication/joint_research/series6/pdf/07.pdf.

"Gates Pledges Wider US Military Presence in Asia." *USA Today*. June 4, 2011. www.usatoday.com/news/world/2011–06–03-robert-gates-china_n.htm?csp=34news.

"Global Trends 2025: A Transformed World – The National Intelligence Council's 2025 Project." Council on Foreign Relations. November 2008. www.cfr.org/world/global-trends-2025-transformed-world – national-intelligence-councils-2025-project/p17826.

Huang, Cary. "PLA Ramped up China's Stand on US–Korea Drill: Beijing Rhetoric Evolves from Neutral to Shrill Saber-rattling." *South China Morning Post*. August 6, 2010. www.scmp.com/portal/site/SCMP/menuitem.2af62ecb329d3d7733492d9253a0a0a0/?vgnextoid=8018423df234a210VgnVCM100000360a0a0aRCRD&ss=China&s=News.

Jia, Qingguo. "Learning to Live with the Hegemon: Evolution of China's Policy toward the US since the End of the Cold War." *Journal of Contemporary China* 14, no. 44 (August 2005): 395–407.

Kagan, Robert. "America: Once Engaged, Now Ready to Lead." *Washington Post*. October 1, 2010. www.washingtonpost.com/wp-dyn/content/article/2010/09/30/AR2010093005528.html?wpisrc=nl_pmopinions.

Lampton, David M. "The United States and China in the Age of Obama: Looking Each Other Straight in the Eyes." *Journal of Contemporary China* 18, no. 62 (November 2009): 703–27.

Lee, Sunny. "Can Korea Hedge between US and China?" *Korea Times*. July 10, 2011. www.koreatimes.co.kr/www/news/nation/2011/07/116_90538.html.

Li, Jingyu. "Ocean of Dreams." *China Daily*. August 20, 2011. http://usa.chinadaily.com.cn/business/2011–08/19/content_13152341.htm.

Luo, Yuan. "武力炫耀的背后是霸道 – 评美国航母拟赴黄海参加军演 (The US Sending Aircraft Carrier to the Yellow Sea Shows Its Gunboat Policy)." 解放军报 (*PLA Daily*).

August 12, 2010. http://chn.chinamil.com.cn/xwpdxw/jsyxxw/2010–08/12/content_4277766.htm.

Mason, Margie. "US–Vietnam Military Relations: Former Enemies Now Military Mates." *World Report*. August 8, 2010. www.huffingtonpost.com/2010/08/09/us-vietnam-military-relat_n_675202.html.

Mead, Walter R. "In the Footsteps of the Kaiser: China Boosts US Power in Asia." *American Interest*. September 26, 2010. www.the-American-interest.com/wrm/2010/09/26/in-the-footsteps-of-the-kaiser-china-boosts-us-power-in-asia/.

Mikes, James. "China and the West, A Time for Muscle-flexing." *The Economist*. March 19, 2009. www.economist.com/node/13326082.

Minemura, Kenji. "China to Establish Permanent Senkaku Patrols." The Japan Institute of International Affairs. December 20, 2010. www.jiia.or.jp/en/commentary/.

"Modernizing Navy for Self-defense." *Xinhua*. July 13, 2010. http://news.xinhuanet.com/english2010/indepth/2010–07/13/c_13397060.htm.

"Not So Obvious, The Secretary of State Underestimates the Power of Her Words." *Washington Post*, February 24, 2009, A12 section.

Nye, Joseph S. "A Pivot That Is Long Overdue." *New York Times*. November 21, 2011. www.nytimes.com/roomfordebate/2011/11/21/does-the-us-need-troops-in-australia/marines-in-australia-its-about-time.

Pomfret, John. "US Continues Effort to Counter China's Influence in Asia." *Washington Post*, July 23, 2010, A10 section.

Pomfret, John. "US Takes a Tougher Tone with China." *Washington Post*, July 30, 2010, A1 section.

Sutter, Robert. "Why a Rising China Can't Dominate Asia." *Asia Times Online*. September 15, 2006. www.atimes.com/atimes/China/HI15Ad02.html.

Swaine, Michael D., and Ashley J. Tellis. *Interpreting China's Grand Strategy: Past, Present, and Future*. Report no. MR-1121-AF (Santa Monica: RAND Corporation, 2000).

Tellis, Ashley J., Travis Tanner, and Jessica Keough, eds. *Strategic Asia 2011–12: Asia Responds to Its Rising Powers – China and India*. Issue brief (Seattle and Washington, DC: National Bureau of Asian Research, 2011).

"To Improve Relations, US Must Respect China's Core Interests." *People's Daily*. July 14, 2011. http://english.peopledaily.com.cn/90001/90780/91343/7440158.html.

United States, Department of State. "Hillary Clinton: Remarks at the US Institute of Peace China Conference." March 7, 2012. www.state.gov/secretary/20092013clinton/rm/2012/03/185402.htm.

"US Pledges Help for Philippine Navy." Agence France-Presse. January 27, 2011. www.abs-cbnnews.com/print/134899.

"US, Vietnam Call for Stability, Peace." *Taipei Times*. June 19, 2011. www.taipeitimes.com/News/world/archives/2011/06/19/2003506167.

Wang, Jisi. "China's Search for a Grand Strategy: A Rising Great Power Finds Its Way." *Foreign Affairs*, March/April 2011.

Wu, Xinbo. "Forging Sino-US Partnership in the 21st Century: Opportunities and Challenges." *Journal of Contemporary China* 21, no. 75 (May 2012): 391–407.

Yang, Mingjie. "Sailing on a Harmonious Sea: A Chinese Perspective." *Global Asia* 5, no. 4 (Winter 2010).

Zhongsheng. "美国准备好中国作为大国登场了吗? (Is US Ready for China to Take the Stage as a World Power?)." *People's Daily* (Beijing), July 29, 2010.

Zhu, Feng. "东亚安全局势：新形势，新特点与新趋势 (Security Situation in East

Asia: New Situation, New Features and New Trends)." 现代国际关系 (*Contemporary International Relations*), December 2010.

Zhu, Feng. "奥巴马政府转身亚洲战略与中美关系 (The Obama Administration's Pivot toward Asia and Sino-US Relationship)." 现代国际关系 (*Contemporary International Relations*), no. 4 (2012): 1–7.

5 Friend or foe

Washington, Beijing and the dispute over US security ties with Taiwan[1]

Dennis V. Hickey and Kelan (Lilly) Lu

On September 21, 2011, the United States announced that it would help the Republic of China (ROC or Taiwan) upgrade its fleet of F-16 A/B warplanes and would not rule out the future sale of new fighters. Washington's continued support for Taipei, as exemplified by recent multi-billion dollar arms sales packages, has proved to be a constant source of tension between the People's Republic of China (PRC) and the US. As one prominent Chinese scholar noted, "the sale of US arms, until now, remains the most sensitive and the most destructive element in the bilateral relationship."[2]

This chapter outlines the respective US and PRC positions toward America's security relationship with Taiwan, and explains why their differing perceptions hold the potential to put the two nations on a collision course. In conclusion, the chapter suggests that some new thinking may be required if Washington, Beijing, and Taipei ever hope to realize a "peaceful resolution" of the so-called Taiwan issue.

US military ties with Taiwan: American trends and perspectives

On December 15, 1978, the US announced the establishment of full diplomatic relations with the PRC, to become effective January 1, 1979. Rejecting the Jimmy Carter administration's legislative proposal for continued "unofficial" relations with Taipei as too weak, the US Congress passed the Taiwan Relations Act (TRA) by an overwhelming majority and the Act was subsequently signed into law by the president.[3]

Although the TRA is an important piece of legislation, it is not the only document that guides US security policy toward Taiwan. As Kurt M. Campbell, then Assistant Secretary of the US Department of State's Bureau of East Asian and Pacific Affairs, explained, "the TRA, plus the so-called Six Assurances and the Three Communiqués, form the foundation of our overall approach [to Taiwan's security]."[4]

Too much ink already has been spilled analyzing the nuances of these documents. Suffice it to say that, in some respects, they do appear contradictory. When one adds official US statements, proclamations, and secret assurances to the mix, American policy appears even more confusing. In fact, critical elements in US policy toward Taiwan might best be described as "consistently inconsistent," and the provisions for Taiwan's security are almost incomprehensible.[5]

The discussion below examines America's security ties with Taiwan and shows how relations have grown closer since 1979. It also explores explanations employed by the US to justify the recent surge in arms sales to Taiwan.

Trends in US–Taiwan relations

There are some who charge that the US has "abandoned" Taiwan. This accusation has gained some traction during the past several years. For example, John Tkacik, a former US Department of State official, claims the US has "cut Taiwan loose. Taiwan is now in a phase where they basically feel they have no support in the United States."[6] Some lawmakers share this view. As Representative Dan Burton (R.-Ind.) explained, "it seems totally unacceptable that this administration and the Congress of the United States and the Government of the United States does not support Taiwan and sell them the needed equipment necessary to defend themselves."[7] Representative Ileana Ros-Lehtinen (R.-Fla.) charges that "the Obama administration to date has the worst record on Taiwan arms sales since the passage of the TRA."[8] Are such charges justified?

To be sure, key portions of US policy do appear ambiguous. However, one can still discern a consistent trend in US–Taiwan relations ever since Washington broke diplomatic relations with Taipei. Namely, the US and Taiwan have moved steadily closer during the post-normalization period. It is noteworthy that this movement is not unique to any particular US administration. The trend is evident in both Republican and Democratic administrations, and it continues to this day.

For a start, Washington has not abided by the pledges to reduce arms sales to Taipei as outlined in the August 17, 1982 US–China Joint Communiqué. In fact, in 2011, Taiwan was the largest purchaser of US defense articles and services in the world.[9] Table 5.1 outlines the items included in the 2010 and 2011 sales. The former sale included helicopters and PAC-3 "Patriot" missiles for Taiwan's air defenses, while the most notable portion of the latter package was its provision for an upgrade for Taiwan's F-16 A/B fighter fleet. The "upgrade package" is extensive. It includes:

> 176 Active Electronically Scanned Array (AESA) radar, 176 Embedded Global Positioning System Inertial Navigation Systems, 176 ALQ-123 Electronic Warfare Management systems, 128 Joint Helmet Mounted Cueing Systems, 140 AIM-9X Sidewinder missiles, 16 GBU-31V1 JDAM kits, 80 GBU-38 JDAM kits, as well as engineering, and a design study on replacing F-100 PW-220 engines with F100-PW-229 engines.[10]

US officials explain that the package will "provide improved combat capability, survivability, and reliability to Taiwan's 145 F-16 A/B aircraft" and point out that the deal also includes "an extension of the F-16 pilot training program."[11]

Table 5.1 Major US arms sales to Taiwan as notified to Congress 2010–11

Date of notification	Item or service as proposed	Value in US$ million
1/29/10	(114) PAC-3 missile defense missiles	2,810
1/29/10	(60) UH-60M Black Hawk utility helicopters	3,100
1/29/10	(12) Harpoon Block II anti-ship telemetry (training) missiles	37
1/29/10	(60) MIDS (follow-on technical support for Po Sheng C4 Systems)	340
1/29/10	(2) Osprey class mine-hunting ships (refurbished and upgraded)	105
9/21/11	Retrofit of 145 F-16 A/B fighters with 176 AESA radars, JDAMs, etc.	5,300
9/21/11	Continuation of training of F-16 pilots at Luke Air Force Base	500
9/21/11	Spare parts for F-16 A/B, F-5E/F, C-130H and IDF aircraft	52

Source: Shirley A. Kan, *Taiwan: Major US Arms Sales since 1990*, report no. RL30957 (Washington, DC: Congressional Research Service, March 7, 2012), p. 64.

US arms sales to Taiwan tell only part of the story. Beginning in the 1990s, the US and Taiwan began to hold annual meetings on national security. In some instances, Taiwan's defense minister has journeyed to the US to participate in such talks. Lower-level officials make frequent visits. For example, during an interview with one of the authors, Dr Andrew Yang, then ROC Deputy Minister of Defense, revealed that "during this year [2012] I've made at least nineteen trips to Washington and have conducted very high-level discussions with my counterparts."[12] Moreover, American military teams have been dispatched to Taiwan to assess the island's military capabilities and observe military exercises, while Taiwan's F-16 fighter pilots receive training in the US. The two sides have also boosted defense cooperation in numerous other ways. For example, a defense hotline has been established, an active duty defense attaché has been assigned to the American Institute in Taiwan (AIT), and a US Department of Defense official submitted a letter to Congress designating Taiwan as a "major non-NATO ally" in 2003.[13] Interestingly, the two sides also appear to enjoy a "cooperative intelligence-sharing agreement" whereby the US National Security Agency and the ROC National Security Bureau monitor PRC military communications from a facility that was jointly constructed on Yangmingshan Mountain north of Taipei.[14] According to media reports, Taiwan may share data acquired through its new US$1.3 billion long-range early-warning radar system in Hsinchu with the US military.[15]

In addition to growing defense links, it is noteworthy that US–Taiwan political relations have become closer – particularly after the Clinton administration's 1994 Taiwan Policy Review.[16] The name of Taiwan's "unofficial" embassy was upgraded. US cabinet-level officials visited Taiwan in 1992, 1994, 1996, 1998, and 2000. Taiwan's presidents have repeatedly visited the US. American support for Taiwan's "meaningful participation" in the World Health Organization was instrumental in helping the island become an "observer" in the global body. The US is now pushing for Taiwan to gain a "voice" in the International Civil Aviation Organization and the UN Framework Convention on Climate Change. In 2012, Taiwan was officially included in the US Visa Waiver Program.

Finally, it is significant that economic ties have not suffered during the post-normalization period. Despite its minuscule size, Taiwan is America's eleventh largest trading partner and fifteenth largest export destination for US goods (and sixth largest agricultural export market). In February 2013, the two sides agreed to resume stalled talks under the Trade and Investment Framework Agreement (TIFA) after a six-year hiatus. Taipei hopes that the negotiations will pave the way for membership in the Trans-Pacific Partnership (TPP), a "high-standard" multilateral free trade agreement.

Hillary Clinton, then US Secretary of State, was not exaggerating when she declared that "we've strengthened our unofficial relationship with Taiwan."[17] On July 12, 2012, Raymond Burghardt, AIT Chairman, outlined some of the ways in which Washington and Taipei have moved closer:

> We now have regular consultations at senior levels between both civilian and military representatives, but you don't read about this. Part of the price we pay for conducting the relationship with Taiwan discreetly is that you give people a reason to write that you are abandoning them. The fact is that we are having high-level meetings with Taiwan leaders. [Military relations are] very strong and very good. There is intelligence exchange; there are mutual assessments of defense needs; there is training that goes on. We don't talk about this stuff. Again, discretion is our biggest enemy. Maybe we should talk about it more. The military relationship is so much more than arms sales It's a good relationship and it has been strengthened a lot with more channels, more issues to work on, and more plans for collaboration.[18]

Commenting on the reluctance of US and ROC officials to openly discuss growing security linkages, Deputy Minister Yang explained, "we are not hiding from the media, but you know, its based on the need to know."[19] He warned that trumpeting recent advances in security ties would antagonize Beijing. In sum, it is clear that, despite wild claims that America has "abandoned" Taiwan, economic, political, and security ties have deepened since 1979. This trend continues.

US policy and the current dispute over arms sales

Based on the discussion above, it is possible to draw some conclusions about trends in US security ties with Taiwan. The argument up to this point has been that, while US policy may appear at times to be confusing and paradoxical, the two sides have steadily moved closer together. In order to better understand the US perspective toward the recent disputes over arms sales to Taiwan, however, it would prove useful to briefly outline US explanations proffered to justify the 2010 and 2011 deals.

In 2011, Assistant Secretary Campbell boasted that the Obama administration's arms sales to Taiwan come up to "a total of over $12 billion in sales in a two-year period – more than any comparable two-year period since the passage of the TRA."[20] Several explanations have been offered to justify the recent surge in US arms sales to Taiwan, and the likelihood of additional weapons transfers.

First, administration officials emphasize that the US must comply with the law (the TRA) and ensure that Taiwan possesses a "sufficient self-defense capability." As Campbell explained, "as part of our commitments under the TRA, we continue to provide Taiwan defensive military systems based on its needs and following our longstanding policy."[21] Moreover, during discussions with Yang Jiechi, PRC Foreign Minister, Hillary Clinton reportedly defended US policy when she explained "that the TRA is quite clear that it provides for a strong rationale for the provision of defensive capabilities and weapons to Taiwan as part of a larger context to preserve the peace and stability."[22] In other words, US officials justify arms sales to Taiwan by asserting that they have a legal obligation to sell the weapons.

Second, US authorities claim that advanced sales are required to counter China's extraordinary military build-up. As David Helvey, US Acting Assistant Secretary of Defense for East Asia, observed, despite recent improvement in cross-strait ties, "China's military shows no sign of slowing its efforts to prepare for Taiwan Strait contingencies."[23] This helps explain why US officials will not rule out additional sales. On April 26, 2012, Robert Nabors, White House Director of Legislative Affairs, wrote that a sale of additional warplanes "warrants serious consideration given the growing military threat to Taiwan."[24] He added that the administration would soon decide on a "near-term course of action on how to address Taiwan's fighter gap, including through the sale to Taiwan of an undetermined number of new US-made fighter aircraft."[25]

Third, Taiwan's democratization has stiffened American resolve to protect it. Many Americans view the island as a model to other countries – including the PRC. For example, President George W. Bush employed Taiwan as a model when calling on China to democratize in 2005. The president declared, "by embracing freedom at all levels, Taiwan has delivered prosperity to its people and created a free and democratic Chinese society."[26] Three years later, Bush stated that Taiwan serves as a "beacon of democracy."[27] President Barack Obama contends that "through the hard work of its people and its remarkable economic and political development over the past decades, Taiwan has proven to be one of the world's great success stories in Asia."[28] William Stanton, then AIT Director, has argued that these considerations explain Taiwan's "undoubted" importance to the US.[29] As Stanton observed, this is because Taiwan "shares common values such as democracy and human rights ... Taiwan is the only place among Chinese speaking people that enjoys true democracy and realizes values that the US also stands for – democracy, human rights and freedom."[30]

Fourth, many Americans – including administration officials and lawmakers in Congress – share the belief that US arms sales to Taiwan promote cross-strait reconciliation and discussion. According to this view, arms sales serve "to increase the costs of Chinese use of force and to enable the Taiwan government to negotiate with their counterparts in Beijing with confidence."[31] Moreover, as one Brookings Institution study observed, "with strengthened defense capabilities, Taiwan would more likely get favorable terms in cross-Strait negotiations and not be forced to accommodate Beijing's demands."[32]

Fifth, America's continued military support for Taiwan has long served as visible evidence that the US stands by its friends and honors its commitments. According to some accounts, "even [Chinese] mainland officials admit privately that a failure by the US to abide by its security commitments to Taiwan could weaken America's credibility with regional allies."[33] Indeed, there are some who argue that reducing security assistance for Taiwan might also raise doubts about US resolve in other regions of the world.

Sixth, American officials do not consider an escalation in US arms transfers to Taiwan as a violation of past commitments to reduce such sales. In the 1982 US–China Joint Communiqué, an agreement that committed the US to reduce arms sales to Taiwan, Beijing also declared that it embraces "a fundamental policy of striving for peaceful reunification of the motherland." However, US officials contend that "the principal metric for China's 'peaceful approach' is the nature of its military posture opposite Taiwan."[34] Deploying over 1,400 ballistic missiles opposite Taiwan is not considered a "peaceful approach" and justifies additional arms sales.

The discussion above outlines only several explanations employed to justify US policy. A more complete discussion would include other considerations that could conceivably drive policy. Despite official protestations to the contrary, a small group of analysts outside government share the late General Douglas MacArthur's assessment that Taiwan is a strategic asset to the US – an "unsinkable aircraft carrier." According to this view, Taiwan is a military asset and arms sales help "contain" the Chinese mainland.[35] Others claim that arms sales to Taiwan constitute some sort of "stimulus plan" for American workers. In fact, economic considerations were emphasized in petitions submitted to the president that called for the approval of the F-16 C/D warplane sale (47 US senators and 181 members of the US House of Representatives signed petitions urging approval of the sale).[36]

US military ties with Taiwan: the Chinese perspective

In the past, tensions between the rival governments in Beijing and Taipei have jeopardized world peace and stability on several occasions. But many people outside China do not understand the nature of this quarrel. In 2001, Fred Thompson, then US Senator (R.-Tenn.), explained:

> It is difficult for the average American to understand why something like that [unification] could be so important and why a little, small place like Taiwan would be so important to the People's Republic of China. But the

fact of the matter is, it is true, it is real, it is very important, and therefore very dangerous.[37]

A variety of arguments have been advanced seeking to explain why Beijing insists that Taiwan belongs to China, and that it must return eventually to the motherland.[38] Although numerous hypotheses may hold some explanatory value, it is important to understand that Chinese at both elite and popular levels perceive Taiwan to be an integral part of China. To be sure, domestic political considerations, shrewd strategic calculations and bureaucratic politics may influence PRC policy. But it is the shared belief that Taiwan is part of China that is the driving force behind Beijing's opposition to Washington's military support for Taipei.

China's territorial integrity

Many analysts argue that the restoration of China's territorial integrity influences all of Beijing's policies toward Taipei. Indeed, the nation's first foreign policy objective is purportedly "to restore and maintain territorial integrity" and reclaim Taiwan.[39] Chinese authorities will not renounce their claims to Taiwan and refuse to rule out the use of force to take it. As Chen Shui-bian, then ROC president, explained during an interview with one of the authors, "since the PRC was established in 1949, their leaders have come and gone, but the ambition to annex Taiwan has never changed."[40]

According to the government in Beijing, "Taiwan has belonged to China since ancient times."[41] In 1895, however, the Treaty of Shimonoseki formally ceded Taiwan to Japan after the country's defeat in the first Sino-Japanese War. For the next 50 years, Japan ruled Taiwan. The loss of Taiwan is described officially as a "wanton betrayal and humiliation [that] shocked the whole nation and touched off a storm of protest."[42] According to Henry Kissinger, former US Secretary of State, "in the Chinese mind, the humiliation of China started with the annexation of Taiwan by Japan."[43] Kissinger's claim is an exaggeration. After all, China's century of *guo chi*, or national humiliations, began when European imperialists started to dismember the country in the early nineteenth century.[44] But the country's defeat at the hands of the Japanese imperialists – including Tokyo's occupation of Taiwan – looms large in Chinese history.

On December 1, 1943, the US, the ROC, and the United Kingdom issued the Cairo Declaration proclaiming their intention to return Taiwan, Manchuria, and other "stolen" territories to China. Specifically, the document stated that the island would be "*restored* to the *Republic of China* [emphasis added]."[45] Following Japan's surrender in 1945, the ROC began to administer the island. Four years later, ROC forces loyal to the Kuomintang (KMT) government retreated to Taiwan along with the bulk of the nation's art treasures, gold, silver, and foreign exchange reserves.

Following the KMT's retreat to Taiwan, the new government of the PRC proclaimed that it must be considered the "replacement of the old regime" and that the ROC no longer existed.[46] Moreover, Beijing emphasized that "China's sovereignty and inherent territory have not changed ... so the government of the PRC naturally should fully enjoy and exercise China's sovereignty, including its sovereignty over Taiwan."[47] The besieged forces on Taiwan were not to be considered a rival government. Rather, Beijing argued that "a group of military and political officials of the KMT clique took refuge in Taiwan and, with the support the then US administration, created the division between the two sides of the Taiwan Strait."[48]

In November 1949, Chiang's exiled government first requested that American military advisers be sent to Taiwan. Following Beijing's intervention in the Korean conflict, an American military advisory group was established in Taiwan and massive amounts of US military and economic aid began to pour into the island. On November 23, 1954, Washington and Taipei concluded a mutual defense treaty and became formal allies. Beijing responded angrily to these developments and charged that "American imperialists" had "occupied" Taiwan.

In order to achieve normalization of relations with the PRC in 1979, Washington acquiesced to Beijing's three longstanding demands: (1) termination of formal diplomatic relations with the ROC, (2) abrogation of the 1954 US–ROC Mutual Defense Treaty, and (3) removal of all US troops from Taiwan. Chinese leaders were under the impression that the US had also agreed to terminate arms sales to Taiwan. When Deng Xiaoping learned that this was not the case, he was "furious" and "raged" during a meeting with US negotiators.[49] The American officials "had serious doubts as to whether Deng would agree to proceed with normalization" as China's paramount leader was only slightly mollified by assurances that arms sales during the post-normalization period would be "restrained."[50] What probably convinced Deng to proceed with the normalization process were Carter administration reassurances that reunification would likely be realized within several years.[51] Kissinger, then US National Security Adviser, had made similar assurances when, during his secret visit to Beijing in 1971, he had assured the Chinese that Taiwan's "political evolution is likely to be in the direction which Prime Minister Zhou Enlai indicated."[52] However, the two sides have not unified and the quarrel over US arms sales to Taiwan persists to this day.

PRC policy and the current dispute over US arms sales to Taiwan

Relations between Taipei and Beijing have improved enormously since Ma Ying-jeou was elected ROC president in 2008. When commenting on cross-strait relations, one PRC official gushed that the time since Ma's election "has resulted in the most peaceful and stable period in the Taiwan Strait in more than six decades."[53] Despite modifications in PRC policy and improvements in cross-strait relations, however, some facts remain constant. For example, Beijing insists that Taiwan is Chinese territory, it is determined to prevent the island from ever achieving de jure independence or being occupied by a foreign power and will not rule out the use of force to achieve unification. Moreover, Beijing continues to steadfastly oppose all foreign arms sales to Taiwan.

Washington's security ties with Taiwan 97

There are several underlying reasons for the PRC's staunch opposition to US arms sales to Taiwan. For a start, Beijing has long argued that arms transfers constitute interference in China's internal affairs and represent a threat to the nation's sovereignty. In the late 1970s, PRC officials made this position clear to their US counterparts when negotiating the establishment of diplomatic relations. In 1993, Beijing released a white paper, *The Taiwan Question and the Reunification of China*, which outlined the government's stance:

> The Chinese Government has always firmly opposed any country selling any type of arms or transferring production technology of the same to Taiwan. All countries maintaining diplomatic relations with China should abide by the principles of mutual respect for sovereignty and territorial integrity and non-interference in each other's internal affairs, and refrain from providing arms to Taiwan in any form or under any pretext. Failure to do so would be a breach of the norms of international relations and an interference in China's internal affairs.[54]

The PRC has not budged from this position. Indeed, when visiting Washington on February 14, 2012, Xi Jinping, then China's Vice-President, declared: "the Taiwan issue concerns China's sovereignty and territorial integrity and remains, as always, the most important and most sensitive issue in China–US Relations."[55]

Second, PRC authorities argue that US arms sales harm the prospects for the peaceful resolution of the Taiwan issue by providing Taipei with no incentive to agree to unification. In 1978, Deng speculated that a termination of US military support would cause Taipei to conclude that "it has no realistic choice but to reach an agreement on reunification with the mainland."[56] He warned that continuation of arms sales would mean that "a peaceful solution of the Taiwan issue would be impossible and the last alternative would be the use of force."[57]

Third, PRC officials complain that arms sales not only reduce incentives for Taiwan authorities to negotiate reunification with the Chinese mainland, but also embolden separatists on the island to push for *de jure* independence from China. Following the announcement of the 2011 decision to upgrade Taiwan's fleet of F-16 A/B fighters, Vice-Foreign Minister Zhang Zhijun told Gary Locke, then US ambassador to China, that US arms sales send "a gravely mistaken signal to pro-Taiwan independence separatist forces."[58]

Fourth, in a related vein, the Chinese contend that the US argument that arms sales provide Taipei with confidence and thereby increase the prospects for cross-strait negotiations and reconciliation lacks a serious analytical foundation. As one prominent scholar with strong ties to the PRC government explained, such claims sound "hackneyed" to many Chinese observers:

> Many in China point out that the US sold large quantities of arms to Taiwan during Chen Shui-bian's tenure (2000–2008), but did that induce Chen to talk with the mainland and help improve cross-strait relations? The answer is a clear-cut no. The arms sales package announced in 2001 by the Bush

administration sent extremely wrong signals to both China and Taiwan, and boosted Chen's secessionist arrogance, which not only created significant tension across the Strait, but also seriously affected American security interests in the area and the maintenance of peace and stability.[59]

Fifth, PRC officials have long claimed that US arms transfers to Taiwan violate past promises to curb sales. Upon learning in 1978 that America planned to continue to sell arms to Taiwan after normalization of US–PRC relations, Chai Zemin, then head of the Chinese Liaison Office, complained that "for the US to continue to sell weapons to the Chiang Clique [President Chiang Ching-kuo's government], would not be in conformity with the spirit of the 1972 Shanghai Communiqué."[60] Eventually, the dispute over arms sales prompted Deng to pressure the US to agree to yet another communiqué – the 1982 US–China Joint Communiqué. As described, in this document the US agreed to "reduce gradually its sales of arms to Taiwan, leading over a period of time to a final resolution." But this did not happen.

Rather than reduce arms sales, the US has sold roughly US\$50 billion in arms to Taiwan since 1979. As outlined in an editorial published by *Xinhua* News Service, weapons sold include everything from warships to advanced fighter planes:

> It has been almost three decades since the publication of the "August 17 Communiqué," but the pace of US arms sales to Taiwan has never stopped. The scope of arms sales involves naval, ground, and air forces, from aircraft parts and components to airborne early warning airplanes, "Patriot" missiles, antisubmarine torpedoes, main battle tanks, antisubmarine helicopters and many others. These sales are in flagrant violation of the principle of the "August 17 Communiqué" in terms of quantity, quality and performance of weapons.[61]

Not surprisingly, some Chinese feel betrayed and humiliated by the American actions. For example, after learning of the 2011 decision to upgrade Taiwan's F-16 A/B fighter fleet, Admiral Yang Yi (ret.) complained that "this US arms sale to Taiwan is lying to and making a fool of the Chinese people."[62] Such sentiments help fuel calls to retaliate against the US actions.

Sixth, some PRC analysts have objected to Taiwan's purchases of US weapons on the grounds that Taipei is wasting its money. In 2011, a pro-PRC newspaper in Hong Kong opined, "every year Taiwan spends bags of money in buying piles of toys to seek consolation … [but] the balance of power across the Taiwan Straits will inevitably lean toward the People's Liberation Army."[63] The editorial crowed, "the PLA has long had absolute strength to seize the command of the air over the Taiwan Straits and is also strong enough to blockade the Taiwan Straits with its shore-based long-range anti-ship and ground-to-air missiles."[64]

Some forms of US–Taiwan military cooperation are more likely to provoke an extremely negative reaction from Beijing than others. As noted in Chapter 10,

Beijing suspended military-to military contacts with Washington after the sale of a large package of arms to Taipei in 2008. Studies commissioned by the US arms industry contend that, while China might complain or temporarily suspend military-to-military contacts with Washington following an American arms deal with Taiwan, "past behavior indicates that China is unlikely to challenge any fundamental US interests in response to any future releases of significant military articles or services to Taiwan."[65] But this is inaccurate. Depending on the nature of the sale, a PRC response could range from a suspension in US–PRC military-to-military contacts to an actual break in diplomatic relations. Beijing might even opt to sell arms to states unfriendly to American interests. There is a precedent for such retaliation. After the US sold 150 F-16 A/B fighters to Taiwan in 1992, "China transferred M-11 missiles to Pakistan and reached a formal agreement with Iran to cooperate on nuclear energy, thus breaking its February 1, 1992, commitment to abide by the terms of the MTCR."[66] During an interview with one of the authors, a Chinese academic with close ties to the Foreign Ministry explained that a "high-profile" sale of military hardware is more likely to provoke a negative response than the transfer of technology or the sale of equipment like early-warning radar. He explained that, while a sale of advanced fighters will generate little or no impact on the cross-strait balance of power, domestic political considerations make it imperative that China's leaders respond forcefully to the more visible sales (particularly those that receive a lot of media attention).

Perceptions, policies and war or peace in the Taiwan Strait

The behavior of any given decision-maker "is shaped by the particular way in which he perceives, evaluates and interprets incoming information about events in his environment."[67] As Robert Jervis, explained, misperceptions, the selective screening out of important information, may also play a critical role in the decision-making process: "Decision-makers tend to fit incoming information into their existing theories and images. Indeed, their theories and images play a large part in what they notice. In other words, actors tend to perceive what they expect."[68] Together, perceptions and misperceptions mold the foundation upon which government policy is constructed. Therefore, it is important to gain an understanding of how the US and the PRC each perceive the issue of American arms sales to Taiwan.

To state it succinctly, despite opinions and/or evidence to the contrary, officials in both the US and the PRC *perceive* that the other side has reneged on past promises and violated past agreements pertaining to Taiwan's security. Reminiscent of rhetoric heard during the darkest days of the Cold War, some US lawmakers go so far as to warn that "China is on the march."[69] In order to counter China's military buildup and strengthen American military support for Taiwan, they are now pushing for the passage of a new law – the Taiwan Policy Act (TPA). On the other hand, China's "Netizens" are pressuring Beijing to get tough with Washington, and editorials in the state-affiliated media suggest the government retaliate by ceasing to cooperate with the US on "global issues."[70] Others claim that Beijing should dump US treasuries or otherwise employ "financial weapons" to retaliate against America.[71] Meanwhile, China's military buildup continues unabated.

Although the US and China protest that they are not engaged in an arms race, some evidence points in that direction. Taiwan plays an important part in this development. In fact, events might reach a tipping-point where Taiwan could serve either as the catalyst for a fully fledged arms race between China and the US or as a much-needed first step toward arms control and disarmament.

A cursory review of the scholarly literature focusing on arms control and disarmament reveals the disadvantages and dangers associated with an arms race. Some of these apply with special force to the arms buildup in the Taiwan Strait. For a start, the case against any large-scale arms race rests on three assumptions:

- an arms race imposes an enormous financial burden on societies and is a waste of precious resources that might be well spent elsewhere;
- an arms race ensures that if a conflict occurs, it will be more destructive than it would have been before the accumulation of additional military power; and,
- an arms race holds the potential to increase tensions and thereby enhance the likelihood of a war. In other words, arms races may cause wars.

This last point deserves further elaboration. Every student of international relations is familiar with the so-called security dilemma. Over five decades ago, John Herz, a German scholar, described the phenomenon:

> Striving to attain security from attack, [states] are driven to acquire more and more power in order to escape the power of others. This, in turn, renders the others more insecure and compels them to prepare for the worse. Since none can ever feel entirely secure in such a world of competing units, power competition ensues, and the vicious circle of security and power accumulation is on.[72]

In short, the security dilemma contributes to arms races, and recent scholarly studies confirm that arms races increase the prospects for war.[73]

Moving from the general to the specific, it is noteworthy that China's massive military buildup opposite Taiwan contributes to yet another manifestation of the security dilemma. Beijing deploys its missiles near Taiwan ostensibly to deter the island from declaring independence. Ironically, however, one of the primary dangers associated with this deployment is that these same missiles help push Taiwan away from the Chinese mainland. Public opinion polls reveal that a plurality of the Taiwan people (roughly 45 percent) believe that the mainland government is hostile toward them personally.[74] Polling data also shows that the PRC missile threat undermines support for unification.[75] Not surprisingly, support for unification (now or later) has dropped to less than 10 percent and only a fraction of the people on Taiwan now consider themselves exclusively Chinese. This development – a phenomenon that is undoubtedly driven in part by China's threatening military posture and buildup – reduces the prospects for cross-strait reconciliation, increases the sentiment for independence and thereby raises the chances for conflict.

Unfortunately, some US policies do not help matters. Rather than push for an arrangement that might reduce military deployments near the Taiwan Strait, the present US administration is straddling the fence. It is selling Taiwan new PAC-3 missiles and upgrading the military's aging fleet of F-16 A/B fighters. It is also threatening to sell Taipei additional arms.

Even more worrisome is the TPA scheme pushed by the administration's critics. This legislation calls for the sale of F-16 C/D warplanes (in addition to the F-16 A/B upgrade approved by the Obama administration), surface-to-air missiles, vertical and short take-off and landing (V/STOL) combat aircraft, submarines, mines, anti-ship cruise missiles, GPS-guided short-range rockets, unmanned air vehicles, radar and jamming equipment. Although Aegis warships are not included in the TPA, they might be included in similar legislation.

This approach to the growing military imbalance in the Taiwan Strait is unsound. First, it is questionable whether Taiwan can even afford to purchase the US equipment offered in 2010 and 2011. As Kwei-bo Huang, then a visiting scholar at the Brookings Institution, observed, "if Taiwan fully accepts the US $12 billion arms sales proposed by the US, it will not be able to pay its soldiers."[76] So, how can one reasonably assume Taipei will purchase submarines and V/STOL combat aircraft?

Second, where will the submarines and V/STOL aircraft come from? The US stopped manufacturing diesel submarines decades ago and it will probably be a decade before the problem-plagued Lockheed Martin F-35B joint strike fighters are available for export.

Third, any new F-16s will be sitting ducks for the People's Liberation Army's missiles. In a cross-strait conflict, Taiwan's runways will be pulverized and rendered inoperable in a matter of seconds. Despite arguments advanced by Lockheed Martin (the manufacturer of the F-16), the island's highways are poor substitutes for runways during a war.

Fourth, it is a matter of speculation as to whether Taipei really wants to acquire these weapons. As one Taiwanese academic said, "President Ma Ying-jeou's government is not really serious about procuring more defensive weapons from the US because he [Ma] doesn't want to irritate the PRC."[77]

Fifth, according to the 2010 National Security Strategy of the United States, "we will continue to pursue a positive, constructive and comprehensive relationship with China ... [and] we will encourage continued reduction in tension between the PRC and Taiwan."[78] Expanding on the latter point, Kurt Campbell explained that "in the period ahead, we seek to encourage more dialogue and exchanges between the two sides, as well as reduced military tensions and deployments, and we have and will continue to meet our responsibilities *under the TRA*" (emphasis added).[79] It is difficult to envision how a surge in arms transfers could encourage cross-strait dialog and exchanges or reduce military tensions and deployments – declared objectives of US national security policy. Rather, it could ramp up tensions and spark an arms race.

Finally, passage of the TPA (or other initiatives to increase arms sales) would provoke the PRC and reduce the chances for cooperation with the US in many important areas. As noted in Chapter 8, continued military-to-military cooperation helps reduce miscommunication, manage crises, and reduce tensions across the Taiwan Strait. Moreover, the US and PRC need each other's cooperation to cope with a wide range of pressing global problems including the worldwide economic tsunami, terrorism, cyber warfare, proliferation of weapons of mass destruction, environmental degradation, health issues, dwindling energy supplies and the continuing crises on the Korean peninsula, to name just a few. When combined with the fact that China is the world's second largest economy, fastest growing economy, third largest military power, and the single largest foreign holder of US government debt, it is clear that the country is important to America.

Conclusions

There are some in the US and Chinese governments who exhibit symptoms that James C. Thompson, Jr, described as "the curator mentality."[80] This sort of official "inherits from his predecessor our policy ... [and] he regards it as his function to keep that policy intact – under glass, untampered with, and dusted – so that he can pass it on in two to four years to his successor." Academics, lawmakers, and media pundits may also possess a "curator mentality" and oppose even modest adjustments to foreign or domestic policy. In short, inertia rules and innovation suffers.

As described, some charge that the present US administration is "abandoning Taiwan" or "cozying up to Beijing with a wink and a nod."[81] But this is an exaggeration. In 2009, Hillary Clinton pledged that, despite the astonishing improvement in relations between Taiwan and the Chinese mainland, there would be "no change in Washington's policy on arms sales to Taiwan under the administration of US President Barack Obama."[82] The administration has kept its word. Arms sales to Taipei continue and the administration will not rule out future sales.

In a similar vein, Chinese observers concede that relations between the mainland and Taiwan are the best in decades. However, China's massive military build-up opposite Taiwan continues as if nothing has changed. The US Department of Defense's 2012 report on China's military confirms that over the past year, the People's Liberation Army continued to build the capabilities and develop the doctrine it considers necessary to deter Taiwan from declaring independence; to deter, delay, or deny effective US intervention in a potential cross-strait conflict; and to defeat Taiwan forces in the event of hostilities.[83]

Despite the risks involved, the stakes are so high that the US and China should quietly explore ways to reduce the arms build-up in the Taiwan Strait. The two sides should explore the possibility of reaching an agreement similar to that proposed by then-President Jiang Zemin when visiting with President George W. Bush in Crawford, Texas, in 2002. Namely, Washington would agree to Beijing's proposal that it not sell new fighters, submarines, and other advanced arms to Taipei in exchange for the removal of the missiles (and their infrastructure) that China has deployed directly opposite Taiwan. In other words, the US should revisit a proposal first raised by the PRC over a decade ago. If a US administration opted to pursue this policy, it would not need to cave in to Chinese pressure and somehow "abandon" Taiwan. Rather, the US could revert to President Carter's original promise that the US intends only to continue with "the restrained sale of some very carefully selected defensive arms."[84]

Such an initiative may yield numerous dividends for both the US and China. The redeployment of China's missiles would increase warning time and help build confidence. It might even be considered as the first step toward a global ban on short-range ballistic missiles and intermediate-range ballistic missiles. Furthermore, an arms agreement could pave the way for greater cooperation between Beijing and Washington on a host of pressing international problems. Perhaps most significant for China, it would also ease tensions between the two sides of the Taiwan Strait and generate good will. Indeed, President Ma claims the removal of China's missiles is a prerequisite for the negotiation of a peace agreement.[85] Moreover, public opinion polls reveal that if China withdraws the missiles deployed opposite Taiwan, 64 percent of Taiwan's population would support a reduction in arms purchases from the US.[86] In short, Beijing should remove its missiles and Washington should curb its arms sales because such an initiative would increase the prospects for peace not only in the Taiwan Strait, but in the entire western Pacific, too.

To be sure, if an administration chose to negotiate an arms control agreement with Beijing, it must be prepared for criticism. First, the US armaments industry and its allies will oppose such an initiative. Arms sales to Taiwan are viewed as an economic stimulus plan, and US lawmakers unabashedly describe the weapons transfers in terms of jobs generated for US workers. Second, in a related vein, some will selectively cherrypick certain elements of US policy (particularly the Six Assurances) to show that it prohibits any discussions between the US and the PRC about arms sales to Taiwan, a reduction in arms sales or any concrete moves toward arms control. Third, others will complain that any agreement is useless because the missiles will not be destroyed. After all, the missiles and infrastructure could be hauled back to the coast. Finally, there is a genuine problem associated with the removal of the missiles from China's coastline. Namely, where will they be redeployed? During conversations with the authors, PRC academics and officials have repeatedly raised this issue. Wherever they go, China is going to have some unhappy neighbors.

In short, there is no perfect or happy policy. If successful, however, an arms control initiative could help reduce the chances for conflict and increase the prospects for peace. As noted in Chapter 3, US arms sales to Taiwan constitute one of the "significant points of contention between PRC and US in which the two powers may come into conflict or even military confrontation." Hopefully, an arms control initiative would lay the groundwork for other confidence-building measures – perhaps the destruction of the missiles. To be sure, this would require some new thinking in the US – particularly among ossified bureaucrats, academics, lobbyists, and media personalities. It would also require new thinking in China – especially among officers in the PLA. However, such an initiative could yield handsome dividends and is worthy of study – especially after one considers the alternatives.

Notes

1 This paper was supported with a research grant from the Taiwan Foundation for Democracy.
2 See Xu Shiquan, "30 Years On, Taiwan Arms Sales Still a Sensitive Issue," *China–US Focus*, August 15, 2012, www.chinausfocus.com/slider/30-years-on-taiwan-arms-sales-still-a-sensitive-issue/. Also see Yiwen Hua, "美对台军售如毒瘤侵蚀中美关系 还要售多久 (US Arms Sales to Taiwan is Like a Cancer Eroding the Sino-US Relationship: How Long will This Last?)," 人民日报 (*China Daily*), August 17, 2012, http://news.xinhuanet.com/tw/2012–08/17/c_123593924.htm.
3 The Carter administration's proposed law was entitled, "the Taiwan Enabling Act."
4 See testimony of Kurt M. Campbell, Assistant Secretary of the US Department of State's Bureau of East Asian and Pacific Affairs before the US House Foreign Affairs Committee in *Why Taiwan Matters*, Part II, October 4, 2011, p. 10, www.foreignaffairs.house.gov/.
5 See Dennis V. Hickey, "Rapprochement between Taiwan and the Chinese Mainland: Implications for American Foreign Policy," *Journal of Contemporary China* 20, no 69 (March 2011): 231–47.
6 See testimony of John J. Tkacik, Jr, Senior Fellow and Director of the Future Asia Project, International Assessment and Strategy Center, in *Hearing of the House Foreign Affairs Committee, Investigating the Chinese Threat, Part One: Military and Economic Aggression*, in *Federal News Service*, March 28, 2012, in Lexis/Nexis.
7 See opening statement of Representative Dan Burton (R.-Ind.) in *Why Taiwan Matters*, Part II, October 4, 2011, 5
8 See Opening Statement of Representative Ileana Ros-Lehtinen (R.-Fla.), before the US House Foreign Affairs Committee in *Why Taiwan Matters*, Part II, October 4, 2011, 10.
9 See William Lowther, "Taiwan Still a Top Buyer of US Arms," *Taipei Times*, December 22, 2011, www.taipeitimes.com/News/taiwan/archives/2011/12/22/2003521358.
10 William Lowther, "Taiwan to Receive US Arms Package," *Taipei Times*, September 23, 2011, www.taipeitimes.com/News/front/archives/2011/09/23/2003513960.
11 See testimony of Kurt M. Campbell, *Why Taiwan Matters*, Part II.
12 Dennis Hickey's interview with Dr Andrew Yang, ROC Deputy Minister of Defense, Taipei, Taiwan, Republic of China, December 24, 2012. Tape recording.
13 For more information on these and other developments, see Shirley A. Kan, *Taiwan: Major Arms Sales since 1990*, report no. RL30957 (Washington, DC: Congressional Research Service, 2012), 3–6.
14 See Wendell Minnick, "Spook Mountain: How the US Spies on China," *Asia Times*, March 6, 2003, www.atimes.com/atimes/China/EC06Ad03.html.
15 See J. Michael Cole, "New Radar Tracks North Korea Rocket: MND," *Taipei Times*, December 13, 2012, www.taipeitimes.com/News/front/archives/2012/12/13/2003550023.
16 For more information, see Dennis V. Hickey, "Reaching Out in the Darkness: The Changing Nature of US Policy Toward Taiwan," *Asian Affairs* 22, no. 3 (Fall 1995): 159–71.
17 William Lowther, "US has 'Strengthened' Relationship with Taiwan: Clinton," *Taipei Times*, March 9, 2012, www.taipeitimes.com/News/taiwan/archives/2012/03/09/2003527354.

18 See William Lowther, "US–Taiwan Relations Remain Robust: Burghardt," *Taipei Times*, July 14, 2012, www.taipeitimes.com/News/front/archives/2012/07/14/2003537694/2.
19 Dennis Hickey's interview with Dr Andrew Yang, December 24, 2012. Tape recording.
20 See testimony of Kurt M. Campbell, *Why Taiwan Matters*, Part II.
21 Ibid., 12.
22 "US Secretary of State Claims Arms Sales to Taiwan Help Preserve Cross-Strait Stability," *China Post*, September 28, 2011, www.chinapost.com.tw/taiwan/national/national-news/2011/09/28/318044/US-secretary.htm.
23 William Lowther, "Taiwan 'Focus' of Chinese Military Modernization," *Taipei Times*, May 20, 2012, www.taipeitimes.com/News/front/archives/2012/05/20/2003533262.
24 See Viola Gienger, "Taiwan Weighed for US Jet Sale at Risk of Riling China," Bloomberg, April 27, 2012, www.bloomberg.com/news/2012-04-27/u-s-to-consider-sales-of-new-f-16s-to-taiwan-white-house-says.html.
25 Ibid.
26 See Dennis V. Hickey, "The USA's Continuing Commitment to Taiwan," in *Taiwan and the International Community*, ed. Steve Y. Tsang (Oxford: Peter Lang International Academic Publishers, 2008), 96.
27 Shirley A. Kan and Wayne M. Morrison, *US–Taiwan Relationship: Overview of Policy Issues*, report no. R41952 (Washington, DC: Congressional Research Service, 2011), 4.
28 See "US Congratulates Taiwan's Ma," *ChannelNewsAsia.com*, January 15, 2012, www.channelnewsasia.com/stories/afp_world/view/1176829/1/.html.
29 "AIT Stresses Taiwan's 'Undoubted Importance to US," *China Post*, March 12, 2012, www.chinapost.com.tw/taiwan/foreign-affairs/2012/03/12/334339/AIT-stresses.htm.
30 Ibid.
31 See US–Taiwan Business Council and Project 2049 Institute, *Chinese Reactions to Taiwan Arms Sales*, (Arlington: Project 2049 Institute, 2012): 1, http://project2049.net/documents/2012_chinese_reactions_to_taiwan_arms_sales.pdf.
32 See Yuan-kang Wang, "China's Growing Strength, Taiwan's Diminishing Options," Brookings Institution, November 2010, www.brookings.edu/research/papers/2010/11/china-taiwan-wang. Also see Guiqing Chen, "美学者密集释放对台政策讯息 影响两岸关系发展 (American Scholars' Intensive Sending Signals on Taiwan Policies has Influenced Cross-Strait Relationship," 中国网 (China Net), May 9, 2013, www.china.com.cn/international/txt/2013-05/09/content_28777735_2.htm.
33 See Bonnie Glaser and Brittany Billingsley, *Taiwan's 2012 Presidential Elections and Cross-Strait Relations: Implications for the United States*, November 2011, 10, http://csis.org/files/publication/111114_Glaser_Taiwan2012_WEB.pdf.
34 See US–Taiwan Business Council and Project 2049 Institute, "Chinese Reactions to Taiwan Arms Sales," 12.
35 For an example of this kind of thinking, see Mark Stokes and Russell Hsiao, "Why the US Military Needs Taiwan," *The Diplomat*, April 13, 2012, http://thediplomat.com/2012/04/13/why-u-s-military-needs-taiwan/2/.
36 See Gerrit van der Wees, "A Lose–Lose Proposition," *Taiwan Communiqué*, no. 133 (September/October 2011): 4.
37 Fred Thompson, "Dangerous Straits," interview by Dennis Hickey, *Frontline*, Public Broadcasting System, October 18, 2001.
38 See Dennis V. Hickey, "China's Claims to Taiwan: Perceptions and Policies," in *The Routledge Handbook of Asian Security Studies*, ed. Sumit Ganguly, Andrew Scobell, and Joseph Liow (London: Routledge, 2010), 48–60.
39 See Andrew J. Nathan and Robert S. Ross, *The Great Wall and the Empty Fortress: China's Search for Security* (New York: W.W. Norton, 1997), 16.

40 Dennis Hickey's interview with Chen Shui-bian, ROC President, Taipei Taiwan, ROC, November 21, 2007. For an article containing highlights of the interview, see Dennis V. Hickey, "Reading China's 'Peace' as 'Sugar Coated Poison'," *Chicago Tribune*, January 6, 2008, section 2.
41 Taiwan Affairs Office and Information Office, The State Council of the People's Republic of China, *The Taiwan Question and the Reunification of China* (Beijing: State Council of the People's Republic of China, 1993), 1. Also see 朱树 (Zhu Shu), "台湾自古以来就是中国固有的领土 (Taiwan is the Inherent Territory of China since Ancient Times)," 大连大学学报 (*Dalian University Journal*), 1992.
42 Taiwan Affairs Office and Information Office, *The Taiwan Question*, 4.
43 Henry Kissinger, "Dangerous Straits," interview, *Frontline*, Public Broadcasting System, October 18, 2001.
44 Many consider China's defeat by the United Kingdom in the Opium War (1839–42) to be the critical event that launched the century of humiliations. See Dennis V. Hickey, "The Roots of Chinese Xenophobia," *World & I* 17, no. 7 (July 2002): 26–31.
45 The Soviet Union approved the declaration four days later at the Teheran Conference.
46 See US–China Economic and Security Review Commission, 2008 Report to Congress (Washington, DC: US Government Printing Office, 2008), 142.
47 Ibid.
48 State Council, "The Taiwan Question and the Reunification of China," 9.
49 See Ezra F. Vogel, *Deng Xiaoping and the Transformation of China* (Cambridge, MA: Harvard University Press, 2011), 331.
50 Ibid.
51 Ibid., 479.
52 See Elaine Sciolino, "Records Dispute Kissinger on His '71 Visit to China," *New York Times*, February 28, 2002, www.nytimes.com/2002/02/28/world/records-dispute-kissinger-on-his-71-visit-to-china.html. See also, Margaret MacMillan, *Nixon and Mao: The Week that Changed the World* (New York: Random House, 2007), 194.
53 "Wu-Hu Meeting Sees Major Results: China Spokesman," *China Post*, March 29, 2012, www.chinapost.com.tw/taiwan/china-taiwan-relations/2012/03/29/336120/Wu-Hu-meeting.htm. Also see Shiqing Hu and Zhenguang Li, "马英九打破"台独"围堵发展两岸关系," 环球人物杂志 (Ma Ying-jeou Breaks the 'Taiwan Independence' Containment and Develops Cross-Strait Relations," 环球人物杂志 (*Global People* magazine), May 21, 2010, http://news.sina.com.cn/c/sd/2010–05–21/092920318608_2.shtml.
54 State Council, "The Taiwan Question and the Reunification of China."
55 Alan D. Romberg, "After the Taiwan Elections: Planning for the Future," *China Leadership Monitor*, no. 37 (April 30, 2012): 15, www.stimson.org/images/uploads/CLM37AR.pdf.
56 See Vogel, "Deng Xiaoping and the Transformation of China," 326.
57 Ibid., 331.
58 See Frank Ching, "Taiwan is China's Most Important Audience," *Business Times* (Singapore), September 28, 2011.
59 Xu Shiquan, "US Arms Sales to Taiwan: Better to Assess the Costs and Recalculate," *China–US Focus*, September 15, 2011, www.chinafocus.com/print/?id+10136.
60 See Vogel, "Deng Xiaoping and the Transformation of China," 326.
61 "China Article Criticizes US Lack of 'Political Credit' in Arms Sale to Taiwan," *Xinhua*, September 22, 2011, in BBC Monitoring Asia Pacific, September 23, 2011, in Lexis/Nexis.
62 Bill Gertz, "US Selling High-Tech Arms Package to Taiwan: Republicans Critical that New F-16s not Included," *Washington Times*, September 21, 2011, 9, in Lexis/Nexis.
63 See Lu Li, "Arms Sales to Taiwan Bring Nothing But Harm," *Ta Kung Pao* (Hong

Kong), September 27, 2011, in "Arms Sales to Taiwan to Harm Sino-US Ties – Hong Kong Article," in BBC Monitoring Asia-Pacific, October 3, 2011, in Lexis/Nexis. Also see "宋楚瑜批评台湾军购 称应把两岸关系定位在和平 (James Soong Criticized Taiwan's Arms Purchase, and Claimed that Cross-Strait Relations Should be Positioned In Peace," 中国新闻网 (China News Network), September 25, 2005, http://news.sina.com.cn/c/2005–09–25/16507031380s.shtml.

64 Lu Li, "Arms Sales to Taiwan Bring Nothing but Harm." Also see Yongzheng Qiu, "台海观察：解放军空军谋求台海制空权 (Cross-Strait Observation: People's Liberation Army Air Force Seek Air Superiority over the Taiwan Strait,"青年参考 (*Youth Reference*), May 28, 2004. http://mil.news.sina.com.cn/2004–05–28/1458200631.html.
65 US–Taiwan Business Council and Project 2049 Institute, "Chinese Reactions to Taiwan Arms Sales," iv.
66 See Robert S. Ross, "The Bush Administration: The Origins of Engagement," in *Making China Policy: Lessons from the Bush and Clinton Administrations*, eds. Ramon H. Myers, Michel C. Oksenberg, and David L. Shambaugh (Lanham, MD: Rowman & Littlefield, 2001), 32.
67 Alexander L. George, *Presidential Decisionmaking in Foreign Policy: The Effective Use of Information and Advice* (Boulder, CO: Westview Press, 1989), 57.
68 Robert Jervis, "Hypotheses on Misperception," *World Politics* 20, no. 3 (April 1968): 454.
69 See opening statement of Representative Ileana Ros-Lehtinen (R.-Fla.), *Why Taiwan Matters*, Part II, 10.
70 See Frank Ching, "Taiwan is China's Most Important Audience."
71 See Ding Gang, "China Must Punish US for Taiwan Arms Sales with 'Financial Weapon'," *China Daily*, August 8, 2011, www.chinadaily.com.cn/opinion/2011–08/08/content_13069554.htm. Also see Sha Ying, "外媒：给中国提供了对付自己的核武器 (Foreign Media: Offer China with Nuclear Weapons to Deal with Itself)," 西陆网, November 26, 2011, http://junshi.xilu.com/2011/1126/news_343_215846.html.
72 See John H. Herz, "Idealist Internationalism and the Security Dilemma," *World Politics* 2, no. 2 (1950): 157.
73 See Susan Sample, "Arms Races and Dispute Resolution: Resolving the Dispute," *Journal of Peace Research* 34, no. 1 (1997): 7–22.
74 See "Beijing's Hostility Toward the ROC," Mainland Affairs Council, April, 2012, www.mac.gov.tw/public/Attachment/24249412649.gif.
75 See William Lowther, "Chinese Threats Impede Unification: US Expert," *Taipei Times*, April 28, 2013, www.taipeitimes.com/News/taiwan/archives/2013/04/28/2003560922. The news story focuses on a presentation delivered at the Center for Strategic and International Studies by Dr Emerson Niou, entitled "The China Factor in Taiwanese Politics," in April 2013. PowerPoint provided to the author by Dr Niou.
76 See "Taiwan Will Not Side with China: Expert," *Taipei Times*, May 11, 2012, www.taipeitimes.com/News/taiwan/archives/2012/05/11/2003532540.
77 Ralph Jennings, "Taiwan Offers Mixed Response to US Rejection of F-6 Fighter Sale," The Christian Science Monitor, September 22, 2011 on *Lexis/Nexis*.
78 The White House, *National Security Strategy*, report, May 2010, 43, www.whitehouse.gov/sites/default/files/rss_viewer/national_security_strategy.pdf.
79 See testimony of Kurt M. Campbell, Assistant Secretary, Bureau of East Asian Affairs, in *Asia Overview: Protecting American Interests in China and Asia*. The House Committee on Foreign Affairs Subcommittee on Asia and the Pacific, Washington DC, March 31, 2011, www.state.gov/p/eap/rls/rm/2011/03/159450.htm.
80 This term was employed by James C. Thompson in his classic study that sought to explain why American decision-makers opted to intervene in the Vietnam conflict during the 1960s and failed to consider withdrawal. See James C. Thomson, Jr, "How Could Vietnam Happen? An Autopsy," *The Atlantic*, April, 1968, www.theatlantic.com/doc/196804/vietnam.

81. Ibid.
82. See Rich Chang, "US Policy on Arms Sales Unchanged, Clinton Says," *Taipei Times*, February 18, 2009, www.taipeitimes.com/News/front/archives/2009/02/18/2003436390.
83. Office of the Secretary of Defense, *Annual Report to Congress: Military and Security Developments involving the People's Republic of China*, report (Washington, DC: US Department of Defense, 2012), iv.
84. See Vogel, "Deng Xiaoping and the Transformation of China," 326.
85. See "No Peace Unless China Removes Missiles: Ma," *China Post*, April 7, 2010, www.chinapost.com.tw/taiwan/china-taiwan-relations/2010/04/07/251444/No-peace.htm. Also see "北京不撤导弹 和平谈判难进行 (No Peace Talk Unless China Removes Missiles)," 星岛环球网 (STNN), June 19, 2008, www.stnn.cc/hk_taiwan/200806/t20080619_798262.html.
86. See Lowther, "Chinese Threats Impede Unification: US Expert."

References

"AIT Stresses Taiwan's 'Undoubted' Importance to US." *China Post*. March 12, 2012. www.chinapost.com.tw/taiwan/foreign-affairs/2012/03/12/334339/AIT-stresses.htmLn

"Beijing's Hostility Toward the ROC." Mainland Affairs Council. April 2012. www.mac.gov.tw/public/Attachment/24249412649.gif.

Chang, Rich. "US Policy on Arms Sales Unchanged, Clinton Says." *Taipei Times*. February 18, 2009. www.taipeitimes.com/News/front/archives/2009/02/18/2003436390.

Chen, Guiqing. "美学者密集释放对台政策讯息 影响两岸关系发展." 中国网. May 9, 2013. www.china.com.cn/international/txt/2013–05/09/content_28777735_2.htm.

"China Article Criticizes US Lack of 'Political Credit' in Arms Sale to Taiwan." *Xinhua*, September 22, 2011.

Chinese Reactions to Taiwan Arms Sales. Report. March 2012. http://project2049.net/documents/2012_chinese_reactions_to_taiwan_arms_sales.pdf.

Ching, Frank. "Taiwan Is China's Most Important Audience." *Business Times* (Singapore), September 28, 2011.

Cole, J. Michael. "New Radar Tracks North Korea Rocket: MND." *Taipei Times*. December 13, 2012. www.taipeitimes.com/News/front/archives/2012/12/13/2003550023.

Ding, Gang. "China Must Punish US for Taiwan Arm Sales with 'Financial Weapon.'" *China Daily*. August 8, 2011. www.chinadaily.com.cn/opinion/2011–08/08/content_13069554.htm.

George, Alexander L. *Presidential Decisionmaking in Foreign Policy: The Effective Use of Information and Advice* (Boulder, CO: Westview Press, 1989).

Gertz, Bill. "US Selling JDAM Guided Bombs to Taiwan: Republicans Critical That New F-16s Not Included." *Washington Times*. September 21, 2011. www.washingtontimes.com/news/2011/sep/21/us-selling-high-tech-arms-package-to-taiwan/?page=all.

Gienger, Viola. "Taiwan Weighed for US Jet Sale at Risk of Riling China." Bloomberg. April 27, 2012. www.bloomberg.com/news/2012–04–27/u-s-to-consider-sales-of-new-f-16s-to-taiwan-white-house-says.html.

Glaser, Bonnie, and Brittany Billingsley. *Taiwan's 2012 Presidential Elections and Cross-Strait Relations: Implications for the United States*. November 2011. http://csis.org/files/publication/111114_Glaser_Taiwan2012_WEB.pdf.

Herz, John H. "Idealist Internationalism and the Security Dilemma." *World Politics* 2, no. 2 (1950): 157–80.

Hickey, Dennis V. "China's Claim to Taiwan: Perceptions and Policies," in *The Routledge Handbook of Asian Security Studies*, edited by Sumit Ganguly, Andrew Scobell, and Joseph Liow (London: Routledge, 2010), 48–60.

Hickey, Dennis V. "Rapprochement between Taiwan and the Chinese Mainland: Implications for American Foreign Policy." *Journal of Contemporary China* 20, no. 69 (March 2011): 231–47.

Hickey, Dennis V. "Reaching Out in the Darkness: The Changing Nature of US Policy Toward Taiwan." *Asian Affairs* 22, no. 3 (Fall 1995): 159–71.

Hickey, Dennis V. "Reading China's 'Peace' as 'Sugar Coated Poison'" *Chicago Tribute*, January 6, 2008, section 2.

Hickey, Dennis V. "The Roots of Chinese Xenophobia." *World & I* 17, no. 7 (July 2002): 26–31.

Hickey, Dennis V. "The USA's Continuing Commitment to Taiwan," in *Taiwan and the International Community*, ed. Steve Y. Tsang (Oxford: Peter Lang International Academic Publishers, 2008).

Hu, Shiqing, and Zhenguang Li. "马英九打破"台独"围堵发展两岸关系." 环球人物杂志. May 21, 2010. http://news.sina.com.cn/c/sd/2010–05–21/092920318608_2.shtml.

Hua, Yiwen. "美对台军售如毒瘤侵蚀中美关系 还要售多久." 人民日报, August 17, 2012. http://news.xinhuanet.com/tw/2012–08/17/c_123593924.htm.

Jennings, Ralph. "Taiwan Offers Mixed Response to US Rejection of F-16 Fighter Jet Sale." *Christian Science Monitor*. September 22, 2011. www.csmonitor.com/World/Asia-Pacific/2011/0922/Taiwan-offers-mixed-response-to-US-rejection-of-F-16-fighter-jet-sale-video.

Jervis, Robert. "Hypotheses on Misperception." *World Politics* 20, no. 3 (April 1968): 454–79.

Kan, Shirley A. *Taiwan: Major Arms Sales Since 1990*. Report no. RL30957 (Washington, DC: Congressional Research Service, 2012).

Kan, Shirley A., and Wayne M. Morrison. *US–Taiwan Relationship: Overview of Policy Issues*. Report no. R41952 (Washington, DC: Congressional Research Service, 2011).

Kissinger, Henry. "Dangerous Straits." Interview. *Frontline*. Public Broadcasting System. October 18, 2001.

Li, Lu. "Arms Sales to Taiwan Bring Nothing but Harm." *Ta Kung Pao* (Hong Kong), September 27, 2011.

Lowther, William. "Chinese Threats Impede Unification: US Expert." *Taipei Times*. April 28, 2013. www.taipeitimes.com/News/taiwan/archives/2013/04/28/2003560922.

Lowther, William. "Taiwan 'focus' of Chinese Military Modernization." *Taipei Times*. May 20, 2012. www.taipeitimes.com/News/front/archives/2012/05/20/2003533262.

Lowther, William. "Taiwan Still a Top Buyer of US Arms." *Taipei Times*. December 22, 2011. www.taipeitimes.com/News/taiwan/archives/2011/12/22/2003521358.

Lowther, William. "Taiwan to Receive US Arms Package." *Taipei Times*. September 23, 2011. www.taipeitimes.com/News/front/archives/2011/09/23/2003513960.

Lowther, William. "US Has 'Strengthened' Relationship with Taiwan: Clinton." *Taipei Times*. March 9, 2012. www.taipeitimes.com/News/taiwan/archives/2012/03/09/2003 527354.

Lowther, William. "US–Taiwan Relations Remain Robust: Burghardt." *Taipei Times*. July 14, 2012. www.taipeitimes.com/News/front/archives/2012/07/14/2003537694/2.

MacMillan, Margaret. *Nixon and Mao: The Week That Changed the World* (New York: Random House, 2007).

Minnick, Wendell. "Spook Mountain: How US Spies on China." *Asia Times*. March 6, 2003. www.atimes.com/atimes/China/EC06Ad03.html.

Nathan, Andrew J., and Robert S. Ross. *The Great Wall and the Empty Fortress: China's Search for Security* (New York: W.W. Norton, 1997).

"No Peace Unless China Removes Missiles: Ma." *China Post*. April 7, 2010. www.chinapost.com.tw/taiwan/china-taiwan-relations/2010/04/07/251444/No-peace.htm.

Office of the Secretary of Defense. *Annual Report to Congress: Military and Security Developments Involving the People's Republic of China* (Washington, DC: US Department of Defense, 2012).

Qiu, Yongzheng. "台海观察：解放军空军谋求台海制空权." 青年参考, May 28, 2004. http://mil.news.sina.com.cn/2004-05-28/1458200631.html.

Romberg, Alan D. "After the Taiwan Elections: Planning for the Future." *China Leadership Monitor*, no. 37 (April 30, 2012). www.stimson.org/images/uploads/CLM37AR.pdf.

Ross, Robert S. "The Bush Administration: The Origins of Engagement," in *Making China Policy: Lessons from the Bush and Clinton Administrations*, edited by Ramon H. Myers, Michel C. Oksenberg, and David L. Shambaugh (Lanham, MD: Rowman & Littlefield, 2001), 21–44.

Sample, Susan. "Arms Races and Dispute Resolution: Resolving the Dispute." *Journal of Peace Research* 34, no. 1 (1997): 7–22.

Sciolino, Elaine. "Records Dispute Kissinger On His '71 Visit to China." *New York Times*. February 28, 2002. www.nytimes.com/2002/02/28/world/records-dispute-kissinger-on-his-71-visit-to-china.html.

Sha, Ying. "外媒：给中国提供了对付自己的核武器." 西陆网. November 26, 2011. http://junshi.xilu.com/2011/1126/news_343_215846.html.

Stokes, Mark, and Russell Hsiao. "Why US Military Needs Taiwan." *The Diplomat*. April 13, 2012. http://thediplomat.com/2012/04/why-u-s-military-needs-taiwan/.

The Taiwan Question and the Reunification of China (Beijing: State Council of the People's Republic of China, 1993).

"Taiwan Will Not Side with China: Expert." *Taipei Times*. May 11, 2012. www.taipeitimes.com/News/taiwan/archives/2012/05/11/2003532540.

Thompson, Fred. "Dangerous Straits." Interview by Dennis Hickey. *Frontline*. Public Broadcasting System. October 18, 2001.

Thomson, James C., Jr. "How Could Vietnam Happen? An Autopsy." *The Atlantic*. April 1968. www.theatlantic.com/doc/196804/vietnam.

United States, The White House. *National Security Strategy*. Report. May 2010. www.whitehouse.gov/sites/default/files/rss_viewer/national_security_strategy.pdf.

US Department of State, *Asia Overview: Protecting American Interests in China and Asia* (2011) (testimony of Kurt M. Campbell). www.state.gov/p/eap/rls/rm/2011/03/159450.htm.

US Department of State. *Why Taiwan Matters*, Part II (2011) (testimony of Kurt M. Campbell). www.state.gov/p/eap/rls/rm/2011/10/174980.htm.

US House of Representatives, Committee on Foreign Affairs. *Investigating the Chinese Threat, Part I: Military and Economic Aggression* (2012) (testimony of John J. Tkacik, Jr).

"US Secretary of State Claims Arms Sales to Taiwan Help Preserve Cross-strait Stability." *China Post*. September 28, 2011. www.chinapost.com.tw/taiwan/national/national-news/2011/09/28/318044/US-secretary.htm.

US–China Economic and Security Review Commission. *2008 Report to Congress*. Report (Washington, DC: US Government Printing Office, 2008).

Van Der Wees, Gerrit. "A Lose–Lose Proposition." *Taiwan Communiqué*, no. 133 (September/October 2011).

Vogel, Ezra F. *Deng Xiaoping and the Transformation of China* (Cambridge, MA: Harvard University Press, 2011).

Wang, Yuan-kang. "China's Growing Strength, Taiwan's Diminishing Options." The Brookings Institution. November 2010. www.brookings.edu/research/papers/2010/11/china-taiwan-wang.

"Wu-Hu Meeting Sees Major Results: China Spokesman." *China Post*. March 29, 2012. www.chinapost.com.tw/taiwan/china-taiwan-relations/2012/03/29/336120/Wu-Hu-meeting.htm.

Xu, Shiquan. "30 Years On, Taiwan Arms Sales Still a Sensitive Issue." *China–US Focus*, August 15, 2012. www.chinausfocus.com/slider/30-years-on-taiwan-arms-sales-still-a-sensitive-issue/.

Xu, Shiquan. "US Arms Sales to Taiwan: Better to Assess the Costs and Recalculate." *China–US Focus*, September 15, 2011. www.chinausfocus.com/print/?id=10136.

Zhu, Shu. "台湾自古以来就是中国固有的领土." 大连大学学报 (Dalian), 1992.

"北京不撤导弹 和平谈判难进行." 星岛环球网. June 19, 2008. www.stnn.cc/hk_taiwan/200806/t20080619_798262.html.

"宋楚瑜批评台湾军购 称应把两岸关系定位在和平." 中国新闻网. September 25, 2005. http://news.sina.com.cn/c/2005-09-25/16507031380s.shtml.

6 China's North Korea dilemma and Sino-US cooperation

Jingdong Yuan

Introduction

North Korea's latest provocations – the launch of an Unha-3 rocket in December 2012 and a third nuclear test in February 2013 – met with swift international condemnation. The United Nations Security Council (UNSC) passed new resolutions imposing stricter sanctions. Pyongyang's wayward behavior raises regional tension and poses a serious challenge to China and the United States. Yet, the nuclear issue also provides new opportunities for China and the US to work together to promote regional peace and stability. However, while both Beijing and Washington emphasize the importance of closer consultation and coordination, differences in their priorities and calculations have in the past prevented and may in the future impede effective common approaches. Moreover, the rapidly changing regional geo-strategic landscape, linked to China's rise and the Obama administration's rebalancing to Asia, as discussed in Chapter 4, will condition the two countries' perceptions and the end game they pursue.

Both China and the US share a common interest in resolving the North Korean nuclear issue and maintaining peninsular stability. However, their approaches differ, as do their strategic interests. Beijing emphasizes stability and opposes any actions that result in escalation and military confrontation. While China supports the important goals of denuclearization and nonproliferation, these goals are secondary to the goal of stability. In contrast, the US is most concerned with the Democratic People's Republic of Korea (DPRK's) nuclear program and the proliferation threat. Since the early 1990s when the first nuclear crisis broke out, successive US administrations, from Bill Clinton to Barack Obama, have applied various strategies, from incentives to coercion to threats, in order to prevent North Korea from acquiring nuclear weapons or transferring nuclear items to third parties. At times, Washington seems to believe regime change may be the only way to achieve these goals.

Since early 2003, China has been playing an increasingly more proactive but no less frustrating role in mediating a solution to the North Korean nuclear crisis. Specifically, Beijing was instrumental in facilitating and serving as the host of the multilateral process – the April 2003 trilateral meeting between China, the DPRK, and the US and the Six-Party Talks (6PT), launched in August 2003, which also included Japan, the Republic of Korea (ROK), and Russia. While the 6PT offered a good opportunity for China and the US to cooperate, they also imposed on China the difficult task of reconciling apparently irreconcilable positions between Pyongyang and Washington and, in the process incurred the cost of alienating both. The early Bush administration's hawkish approach stood in sharp contrast to China's emphasis on diplomacy, stability, and opposition to regime change.

The Bush administration adopted a more pragmatic stance on the North Korean nuclear issue during its second term, including direct bilateral talks with Pyongyang and better coordination with the other parties, especially China and South Korea, leading to noticeable forward movement in the peninsular nuclear disarmament process. However, the modest progress quickly evaporated as a result of Pyongyang's failure to fully implement the various joint statements and action plans as agreed during the 6PT, which eventually collapsed in late 2008. The new Obama administration indicated its willingness to negotiate with its adversaries, including North Korea. However, North Korean missile and nuclear tests in early 2009 made it impossible for any diplomatic initiative to proceed. Instead, Washington adopted a policy of "strategic patience" and strengthened its alliance with South Korea. China, meanwhile, continues to promote the three inter-related goals of stability, denuclearization, and diplomacy while focusing increasingly on expanding economic ties with North Korea.

This chapter seeks to provide an in-depth analysis of both the complexity of the North Korean nuclear issue as it impacts on US nonproliferation policy and regional stability, and China's perspectives and policy debates on this issue as a rising power in playing a more prominent role. It will outline and analyze how their common interests and differences regarding the North Korean problem both provide opportunities for cooperation and cause significant policy frictions. Key to this analysis will be an understanding of the dynamics of cooperation and competition between Beijing and Washington on the North Korean nuclear crisis and its impact on the wider bilateral relationship and regional power relations.

"Lips and teeth" relationship no more

For better or worse, China has maintained a close relationship with the DPRK for over six decades. When the Korean War broke out in 1950, PRC Chairman Mao Zedong overruled most of his senior advisors and dispatched the Chinese People's Volunteers across the Yalu River to directly confront the US.[1] What followed were two decades of hostility between China and the US as they confronted each other in Northeast Asia. Thereafter, China and North Korea maintained an ostensibly close relationship characterized as "sealed in blood and flesh," one grounded in shared ideologies, personal friendship, and common security interests.[2]

With rapprochement between China and the US in the early 1970s, the Northeast Asian strategic landscape began to change. Toward the late 1980s, after more than a decade of economic reforms and opening up, Beijing began to modify, subtly, its past rigid attitudes toward South Korea. It moved from refusing to recognize the country to acquiescing in and encouraging bilateral commercial interactions to endorsing the admission of both Koreas to the United Nations in 1991. In August 1992, over Pyongyang's objection, Beijing formally established diplomatic relations with Seoul. While China made great efforts to ease the "shock," Pyongyang still felt betrayed and the Sino-DPRK relationship entered a period of estrangement, coolness, and occasional alienation.[3] Indeed, the Soviet and Chinese establishment of diplomatic relations with Seoul without a corresponding diplomatic breakthrough between North Korea and most Western countries, Japan and the US in particular, fueled North Korean insecurities and feelings of isolation, prompting Pyongyang to speed up its nuclear weapons program.[4]

Post-Cold War Chinese policy toward the Korean peninsula has been informed by its overall strategic priorities of maintaining regional stability for economic development, which remain relatively constant over the past two decades. Beijing has focused on a number of specific issues: inter-Korea relations; the US military presence; the US–ROK military alliance; the DPRK's internal changes and regime stability as well as external behaviors; the nuclear issue; conventional armament and arms control, missile proliferation and missile defenses; the development of economically beneficial bilateral ties with South Korea; and Korean unification. All of these affect Chinese interests, some vital, and therefore require Beijing's dedicated attention and skillful diplomacy.[5]

There is strong continuity in Chinese policy toward the Korean peninsula in general and to North Korea in particular.[6] First, peace and stability on the peninsula and, of necessity, regime survival in North Korea remain the most important guiding principles underpinning Chinese policy.[7] Beijing therefore repeatedly has resisted attempts to undermine the North Korean regime. China's refusal to use its leverage – ranging from food aid to energy supplies – largely stems from its principled stand on the sanction issue but also is a reflection of its desire to encourage North Korea to come to its senses without in the process hasting its decline or provoking it to undertake irrational actions. Beijing also worries about the potential negative consequence of withdrawing support from North Korea.[8] For instance, while it endorses the nonproliferation principles relating to weapons of mass destruction (WMDs) and pledges not to allow North Korea to use China as a back door to export WMD-related items, it has declined to participate in the Proliferation Security Initiative (PSI), a US-led effort, over which it has serious concerns.[9]

North Korea has lately become one of the divisive issues facing the Chinese leadership. In fact, Beijing has on occasion shown considerable frustration with Pyongyang's wayward behavior. For instance, Chinese analysts have become increasingly critical of North Korean behavior. Some consider Pyongyang's nuclear brinkmanship as threatening China's core interests in securing a peaceful and stable environment for economic development. Others have accused Pyongyang of neglecting its Nuclear Non-Proliferation Treaty (NPT) obligations and illicitly and covertly conducting uranium enrichment programs even while it was receiving various benefits (see below) pursuant to the 1994 Agreed Framework. They deemed its behaviors – e.g., withdrawal from the NPT after the revelation of its uranium enrichment program – highly irresponsible.[10] Some scholars even suggested North Korea's nuclear brinkmanship was aimed at derailing improving Sino-US relations in the wake of the 9/11 terrorist attacks and dragging China into a DPRK–US conflict. Because North Korea's actions undermine international nuclear nonproliferation mechanisms, threaten Chinese security interests, and cause instability in Northeast Asia, some of these analysts have called on the government to consider a radical policy shift.[11]

Strategic imperatives continue to dictate Beijing's DPRK policy, with a particular emphasis on regime stability.[12] Indeed, between Kim Jong-il's reported stroke in 2008 and late 2011 when he died, there were frequent high-level exchanges between Beijing and Pyongyang. These included Kim's final four visits to China in an effort to pave the way for the succession of Kim Jong-un and to seek more Chinese economic assistance. The Chinese leadership apparently conceded to the succession arrangement for no other reasons than to ensure regime stability after Kim Jong-il and perhaps increase China's influence in the North, given Kim Jong-un's relative inexperience.[13] However, if history is any indication, "China–North Korean relations are not usual asymmetric dynamics between a great power and a smaller nation. It should be noted that a flipside of the 'teeth-to-lips' analogy is that the teeth may often bite the lips."[14] This has so far been fully borne out by the highly unpredictable Kim Jong-un regime, which has barely heeded to Beijing's wishes for the past three years.

Convergence and divergence in US–China approaches to nuclear crises

North Korea's nuclear program dates back to the mid-1950s with assistance from the Soviet Union.[15] In 1985 Pyongyang signed the NPT but it was not until 1992 that it accepted International Atomic Energy Agency (IAEA) safeguards provisions. At that time the IAEA inspections raised suspicions about a covert North Korean nuclear weapons program. A crisis ensued, with the North threatening to withdraw from the NPT and the Clinton administration preparing for military actions. The October 1994 US–DPRK Agreed Framework, which froze North Korea's plutonium-based nuclear program, brought the crisis under control. Unfortunately, the implementation of the Agreed Framework, which provided the DPRK with heavy oil shipments and two light-water reactors, encountered various political, financial, and technical obstacles.

By the time President George W. Bush came into office in 2001, the agreement was in limbo and the administration was determined to take a very different approach to dealing with North Korea than that adopted by the Clinton administration. In October 2002, the Bush administration confronted North Korea, charging that it had been engaged in a covert uranium enrichment program. After admitting to the program (an admission it later retracted), Pyongyang kicked out the IAEA inspectors, withdrew from the NPT, reactivated the Yongbyon reactor, and began reprocessing plutonium. The Agreed Framework collapsed and the second nuclear crisis began.[16]

China and the US responded to the crisis differently from the very start. Beijing's initial response to the October 2002 nuclear crisis was to call for both North Korea and the US to return to the 1994 Agreed Framework.[17] Chinese officials and analysts maintained that the key to resolving the crisis was direct dialog between North Korea and the US. Instead of blaming North Korea for the collapse of the 1994 Agreed Framework, Beijing called upon *both* Pyongyang *and* Washington to resolve their dispute through dialog.[18]

The Bush Jr administration's initial reaction to the 2002 crisis was that bad behavior should not be rewarded and instead that international pressure should be applied on the DPRK to get it to reverse course. The administration was adamant that Pyongyang should suffer the consequences of violating the norms and rules of the international nuclear nonproliferation regime. For these reasons, it steadfastly refused to engage in any bilateral negotiation with the North and demanded that Pyongyang give up its nuclear program first.[19] China, on the other hand, repeatedly emphasized the need for a peaceful resolution of the problem. Beijing's fundamental interest was in stability and it was deeply worried that Pyongyang could be pushed into taking even more reckless action. The concern over potential instability on the peninsula links to the fact that China requires a stable international environment for expanding trade and attracting foreign investment and technology transfers.[20] China therefore stated its positions on the issue as the following: (1) peace and stability on the Korean peninsula should be preserved; (2) the peninsula should remain nuclear free; and (3) the dispute should be resolved through direct diplomatic dialog between the US and the DPRK.[21]

Chinese diplomacy intensified following North Korea's withdrawal from the NPT. Then Chinese Foreign Minister Tang Jiaxuan traveled to Pyongyang to deliver China's stern warning. Subsequently, there was a secret trip by Vice-Premier Qian Qichen, who bluntly told the North Koreans to start talking to the Americans.[22] There were several factors pushing China to act. First, in the aftermath of the US invasion of Iraq in 2003, China was worried that the Bush Jr administration might consider military actions against North Korea. The second, related to the first, was Washington's pressure for Beijing to be more directly involved. However, there were differences over the format that would be used to address the North Korean nuclear issue. The Bush administration refused to engage in bilateral negotiation with North Korea, insisting that the nuclear issue was a multilateral one that required all the affected parties to be involved.[23] China preferred a trilateral arrangement but the US insisted Japan and South Korea needed to be involved. In the end, the 6PT format, with China as the host, won out.[24]

The first trilateral meeting between China, North Korea, and the US was subsequently held in Beijing in April 2003. This was followed by the 6PT in August 2003. As the host of the talks, Beijing laid out the following positions: (1) denuclearization; (2) peninsular peace and stability; (3) dialog and peaceful resolution of dispute; and (4) fair consideration for the concerns of all parties.[25]

Chinese President Hu Jintao told Kim Jong-il during the latter's April 2004 visit that China was committed to safeguarding peace and stability on the peninsula and the goal of a nuclear-weapons-free Korean peninsula, would seek a peaceful solution to the nuclear issue through dialog, and would uphold the principle that the DPRK's legitimate concerns should be addressed.[26]

China's more active diplomacy in the second nuclear crisis has been driven by its calculation of the larger strategic implications as well as the imminent security threats.[27] First and foremost, China seeks a non-nuclear Korean peninsula since a nuclear peninsula might produce more resolute US responses, including, perhaps, military options, and negatively affect regional peace and stability. In addition, regional players might nuclearize in reaction to the DPRK, which would threaten China's security interests. Second, China seeks to maintain peace and stability on the peninsula, specifically, to promote conditions that would be conducive to the resolution of the crisis and to prevent elements that could cause further escalation.

Third, the crisis provides both challenges and opportunities. The revelation of North Korea's covert nuclear weapons program, announced just prior to Chinese President Jiang Zemin's visit to Crawford, Texas, in the same month for his third summit meeting with President George W. Bush, caught China off guard. Jiang offered to cooperate with the US on working out a peaceful solution and declared China's support of a nuclear free Korean peninsula.[28]

Six rounds of 6PT meetings were held between August 2003 and December 2008. The multilateral process made some headway in moving toward denuclearization, in particular the September 2005 joint statement and the February and October 2007 action plans, which committed North Korea toward nuclear disarmament in exchange for economic assistance, security guarantees, and diplomatic normalization. In late June 2008, North Korea destroyed the cooling tower at its Yongbyon plant in a gesture to show its commitment to end the nuclear weapons program.[29] While the multilateral process for engaging North Korea had been established and both China and the US had found common grounds for continued cooperation and consultation, significant differences remained between the two countries over specific approaches and long-term objectives, which continued to strain bilateral relations during the negotiation.[30] For instance, while Washington charged Pyongyang with engaging in covert uranium enrichment program, Beijing had initially expressed doubts over the US assertion. Zhou Wenzhong, Chinese Vice-Foreign Minister and later an ambassador to the US, stated: "We know nothing about the uranium program. We don't know whether it exists. So far the US has not presented convincing evidence of this program."[31] At the same time, Beijing also saw no evidence that North Korea was to conduct nuclear tests. Assistant Foreign Minister Shen Guofang told Reuters that "there is no hard evidence proving that."[32]

Chinese analysts charge that the Bush administration was never sincere about resolving the North Korean nuclear issue. It wavered between a "Libyan" solution (i.e., regime change) and possible military operations. Never had the administration considered a return to the Clinton administration's "negotiation to buy time" strategy. The administration's basic assessment seemed to be that real nuclear dismantlement was never achievable, nor could there be any credible verification. Its high-pressure tactics became obstacles to progress since Pyongyang, always paranoid about being isolated, was constantly looking for excuses not to participate in the process unless it was absolutely certain that its security concerns would be addressed.[33]

While the Bush administration insisted on complete, verifiable, and irreversible dismantlement of North Korea's nuclear weapons program, China indicated that North Korea was entitled to peaceful use of nuclear energy once it returned to the NPT and after dismantlement of its nuclear weapons program. For instance, after the September 19, 2005 joint statement was announced, at the IAEA meeting, Chinese representative reportedly wanted the UN nuclear watchdog to mention the light water reactor as well as the other commitments.[34]

Nonetheless, Beijing reacted strongly to North Korea's first nuclear test in October 2006, apparently after it had sought to persuade Pyongyang not to conduct the test. The foreign ministry issued a strong statement, describing North Korean behavior ("flagrantly conducted a nuclear test") in terms that are usually reserved for China's putative adversaries.[35] China also supported UNSC sanctions on North Korea. However, it is not clear if Beijing has fundamentally changed its overall strategic assessment of the situation in the peninsula or maintained its traditional policy of North Korean stability over all else. Clearly, it has made some tactical adjustments and allowed more public, albeit still controlled, discussion/debates on the issue. Public opinion has understandably manifested a sense of frustration over Pyongyang's behavior since the DPRK's actions have time and again undermined China's national interests.[36]

Another US–China difference relates to tactics. Washington wants Beijing to exert more pressure on Pyongyang while Beijing believes that it has done its share in its own ways to defuse the North Korean nuclear crisis. In general, it shares the ultimate goals of a nuclear-free Korean peninsula with all the other powers. It rejects the US assertion that it is not doing enough to rein in North Korea's nuclear programs and the misperception that China cares more about peninsular stability than denuclearization. Indeed, China would say that while it appreciates Pyongyang's security dilemma, it has made very clear to its northern neighbor that it is strongly opposed to a nuclear peninsula; that the North should negotiate rather than take unilateral actions, that Pyongyang should not expect unqualified support from China, the 1961 treaty notwithstanding; and that North Korea should undertake reforms to improve its economic situations.[37]

Same goal, different approaches

One of the most important factors influencing China's approach to the North Korean nuclear issue has been the potential impact on Sino-US relations. Beijing wants to maintain a good, stable bilateral relationship with Washington that serves China's interests. Despite their differences and disputes over a range of issues, both countries share a common interest in maintaining a nuclear-free

Korean peninsula. However, their endgames for North Korea are different. For Beijing, the best outcome is a non- (or de-)nuclearized but surviving North Korean regime. For Washington, nuclear disarmament and nonproliferation are the most critical issues and to the extent that these can only be achieved through regime change then this is the way to go. At the minimum, punishment is critical to demonstrate to other potential proliferator states that proliferation does not pay. In Washington's eyes, diplomacy, at times, has become a synonym for appeasement or a reward for bad behavior.[38] It was only toward the end of the second Bush administration that diplomacy rather than threat or rhetoric began to assume greater prominence in Washington's dealing with Pyongyang, but it was too little, too late.

President Obama promised to adopt a new approach toward the DPRK nuclear issue but his hands were constrained by North Korea's May 2009 nuclear test. The policy of "strategic patience" or "benign neglect," as adopted by the administration, was intended to break the cycle of what President Obama described as "provocation, extortion, and reward" that previous administrations had to deal with since the early 1990s, or as Defense Secretary Robert Gates suggested, the US would not "pay for the same horse three times."[39] Unfortunately, the policy has so far yielded limited results, especially where US interests are concerned – seeking Pyongyang's return to the 6PT and fulfilment of the latter's commitments to nuclear disarmament/dismantlement as spelled out in the September 2005 and February 2007 joint statements and action plans.[40] If anything, the policy smacks of the earlier Bush administration approach of refusing to engage the North. Critics have characterized this approach as "a policy of doing nothing while outsourcing North Korea policy to a particularly hawkish government in Seoul ... a policy of sanctions and hostility toward Pyongyang."[41] And the longer the issue remains unresolved, the further down the road North Korea's nuclear program will become, and the world may become used to the prospect of living with a nuclear North Korea.[42]

On July 23, 2009, Secretary of State Hillary Clinton made the following statement, the clearest by then of the Obama administration's policy towards North Korea: The United States "cannot accept a North Korea that tries to maintain nuclear weapons." However, Washington would consider "full normalization, a permanent peace regime, and significant energy and economic assistance if North Korea undertakes verifiable denuclearisation." And the US "does not seek any kind of offensive [military] action against North Korea."[43]

Nor would the Obama administration close its doors to negotiations with North Korea. Former President Bill Clinton went to North Korea in August 2009 to secure the release of two detained US journalists and met with Kim Jong-il. Ambassador Stephen Bosworth, the administration's envoy on North Korea, visited the country in late 2009. Several other channels of diplomatic contacts remained open, with the so-called "Leap Day Agreement" announced on February 29, 2011, which committed North Korea to a moratorium on missile and nuclear tests and uranium enrichment activities, coupled with the readmission of IAEA inspectors. In exchange, the Obama administration pledged 240,000 metric tons of "nutritional assistance" to North Korea. Unlike its predecessor, the Obama administration has closely coordinated its North Korea policy with its key allies, South Korea and Japan. However, administration officials continue to seek a comprehensive package deal that would see complete denuclearization in exchange of diplomatic recognition and significant economic aid.[44]

But these rare occasions of conciliation were marred by the more frequent occurrences of provocations on the part of North Korea. In March 2010, the DPRK was alleged to have sunk a South Korean navy corvette *Cheonan*, resulting in the loss of 46 lives. In November of that year, North Korea shelled Yeonpyeong Island, killing civilians as well as ROK soldiers. The Obama administration's responses included unequivocal displays of alliance commitments by deploying the USS *George Washington* aircraft carrier, conducting joint military exercises in the Yellow Sea, calling for international condemnation of North Korean actions, and engaging ever-closer trilateral consultation between the US, South Korea, and Japan.[45] At the same time, the administration also prodded Beijing to do its part in exerting pressure on Pyongyang to rein in the North Koreans from further provocations. Openly showing his frustration with the tepid Chinese response to the *Cheonan* sinking and Beijing's opposition to a UNSC resolution condemning North Korea, President Obama said, "I think there's a difference between restraint and wilful blindness to consistent problems."[46] Other administration officials went further, charging that "the Chinese embrace of North Korea in the last eight months has served to convince North Korea that China has its back and has encouraged it to behave with impunity."[47]

However, not only did China resist Washington's pleas for exerting pressure on Pyongyang, Beijing responded angrily to the US–ROK military exercises. Chinese concerns were obvious: North Korea could be triggered into even more reckless behavior during a highly sensitive period of power transition in North Korea, and the exercises were too close to China's exclusive economic zone for comfort.[48] But increasingly the policy differences are more than about tactics but are linked to the broader context of emerging strategic competition between Beijing and Washington against the backdrop of a rising China and a declining US still seeking to retain its primacy in Asia, as elucidated in Chapter 4. Under this changing strategic environment, China clearly is more interested in having a stable rather than an unstable North Korea near its northeastern border, given all the uncertainties and problems a collapsing regime could bring. Understandably, Beijing has no interest in following US advice in exerting more pressure on Pyongyang, which in turn finds it convenient to exploit China's soft spot. This friction over policy reflects major differences between China and the US on how best to handle the North Korean problem. Beijing considers this largely an issue between Pyongyang and Washington to resolve through negotiation, while the US would like to see China using its leverage over North Korea to exert more pressure on the latter.[49]

Beijing's approach to North Korea, meanwhile, began to shift toward greater economic interactions and stable diplomatic ties. Since 2009, Chinese investments in and trade with North Korea have steadily increased, with China now accounting for over two thirds of all North Korea's foreign trade. In addition, the two countries have entered into agreements in developing joint special economic zones in North Korea with major Chinese investment commitments. Two thirds of North Korea's joint ventures with foreign partners are Chinese.[50] Likewise, diplomatic exchanges through high-ranking visits have continued despite North Korean missile and nuclear tests over the past few years, although top Chinese leaders and Kim Jong-un have yet to exchange visits. That said, the first foreign visitor that Kim Jong-un received since the passing away of Kim Jong-il was Wang Jiarui, the director of the Chinese Communist Party's (CCP's) International Liaison Department. CCP Politburo member and National People's Congress Vice-Chairman Li Jianguo visited North Korea in 2012. Kim Jong-un's envoy, Vice-Marshall Choe Ryong-hae, visited China and met with President Xi Jinping in May 2013 while Li Yuanchao, PRC Vice-President and also a Politburo member, was among the few foreign dignitaries present at the ceremonies in Pyongyang marking the sixtieth anniversary of the end of the Korean War in July 2013.[51]

This approach, which emphasizes encouraging Pyongyang to undertake economic reform, including establishment of special economic and development zones close to the Chinese border, and maintaining contacts with the regime even when relations may be strained, clearly reflects Beijing's strategic thinking about this rather delicate issue. In other words, China considers the North Korean nuclear issue within the broader context of regional security, its relationships with the key players, and how the escalation and containment of the problem affect and serve its national interest.[52] This places Beijing in a no-win situation. As Scott Snyder has suggested, as China works more closely with the US in exerting pressure on Pyongyang, it could actually lose influence over its unappreciative client. On the other hand, when it resists Washington's pressure for stronger measures, such as reducing or cutting off aid, then frictions ensue in Sino-US relations.[53] Beijing desires closer cooperation with Washington, but it has its own interests and priorities. And its influence over Pyongyang remains quite limited despite the fact that North Korea's dependence on China has increased significantly over the years. Indeed, despite increased assistance, there is no evidence that Beijing's leverage over Pyongyang's nuclear or missile decisions has grown. Admittedly, North Korea's extreme behaviors frustrate Beijing. At the same time, isolation of the North or any harsh actions that threaten regime survival could be highly uncertain and risky as far as broader Chinese interests are concerned. This consideration at once drives and imposes limits on its North Korea policy.[54]

Indeed, as Victor Cha observes,

> The problem today is that China is both omnipotent and impotent in North Korea. It has great material influence as the North's only patron. Yet, as the sole patron, if Beijing shut down its assistance to punish Pyongyang for its bad behavior even temporarily, it could precipitate an unraveling of the regime, which would be even more threatening to China.[55]

From Pyongyang's perspective, while it depends on China's support, especially economic assistance in food and energy supplies, it nonetheless harbors deep distrust of its patron and shuns suggestions that it adopt Chinese-style economic reforms for fear of losing political control.[56] What the outside may consider to be a viable lever – the cutoff of economic aids – could well threaten Beijing's core security interests: the preservation of the North Korean regime.

Immediate security concerns aside, China's attitude toward the Korean issue must also be seen in the context of its desire to ensure the survival of the North Korean regime and the maintenance of a strategic buffer zone. China is wary of North Korea's reckless behavior and certainly does not want the nuclear crisis to get out of control, but it also believes that Pyongyang's nuclear gamble stems from its acute sense of insecurity and vulnerability and hence any resolution must address this issue. This may explain why China has continued to provide economic assistance to North Korea. It also explains why China will be opposed to, or at least not support, any measures that might precipitate the collapse of the North.[57]

This concern over regime stability was reflected in how Beijing handled the *Cheonan* and Yeonpyeong Islands incidents. As discussed above, while Washington swiftly reacted to the provocations and firmly stood by its client, China refused to blame the North. This greatly alienated Seoul and strained their bilateral relationship.[58] Beijing's reaction must be understood in the broader context of major regional geo-strategic changes. Since 2009, after North Korea's second nuclear test and subsequent UNSC sanctions (which Beijing endorsed) and the collapse of both the inter-Korean dialog and US–DPRK negotiation, China has decided to separate the nuclear issue from its relations with North Korea. Worried about the economic and political state of its ally and desirous of preserving stability, Beijing moved to offer economic assistance and strengthen political ties such as high-level visits between the two countries.[59] At the same time, Beijing viewed Lee Myung-bak's policy toward North Korea and the US policy of strategic patience, far from being conducive to progress on denuclearization, as further heightening tensions on the peninsula. Furthermore, the strengthened US–ROK alliance and, above all, the post-*Cheonan* US–ROK military exercises in the Yellow Sea were considered by Beijing as posing a serious threat to China's security interests.[60]

Indeed, Beijing's rather awkward handling of the *Cheonan* and the Yeonpyeong Island incidents both reflects the dilemma it faces in dealing with the wayward behavior of North Korea and raises the fundamental questions of whether and for how long, can China's policy be sustained and for what purposes. There have been debates within China about Beijing's policy towards the DPRK. The first school contains both the nationalists and realists who advocate upholding the historical ties forged during the Korean War and retaining the DPRK as a strategic buffer within Chinese sphere of influence. The internationalists, on the other hand, value China's reputation in the international community and therefore support a North Korea policy in line with the commonly accepted norms – such as nuclear nonproliferation. The third school argues that, given the frustration and the fact North Korea continues to act in ways detrimental to Chinese national interests, Beijing should distance itself from the regime in Pyongyang. However, these debates have yet to result in major policy shifts since, for Beijing, the North Korean issue cannot simply be dealt with on its own merit but must be handled within the larger peninsular and regional contexts. These considerations in turn have imposed significant constraints on Beijing's ability to exert pressure and hence influence Pyongyang.[61]

The crisis of 2010 reveals significant divergence in US and China perspectives on the North Korea problem and the differences in their approaches. However, what causes the policy friction goes beyond the tactics and priorities. China's rise has led the Obama administration to seriously rethink its regional strategies, with the pivot to Asia as the clear response to a rising China and its growing influence in the region. Beijing is fully cognizant of this important US strategic shift, and hence views US and allied reactions in the aftermath of the *Cheonan* and Yeonpyeong incidents as Washington's deliberate ploy to regain and strengthen its position in Northeast Asia, and primarily as an effort to constrain China. This strategic incongruence between the two powers therefore impedes full cooperation even though both continue to share a common interest in North Korean denuclearization.[62]

Last chance or renewed hope?

North Korea's missile launch in December 2012 and its third nuclear test in February 2013 present new challenges for Beijing. For the Xi administration, the question is, how much of an asset is North Korea compared to the diplomatic and strategic toll Pyongyang's extreme behavior exacts from China? What particularly upsets Beijing is that, despite multiple serious entreaties not to pursue reckless ventures, Pyongyang nonetheless went ahead with its tests, demonstrating it could care less about what its only patron thinks.[63] While China's short-term reactions typically involve efforts to manage yet another round of North Korean provocation and prevent further escalation through a combination of signaling, including joining hands with the international community in condemning such behavior and undertaking measured actions such as UNSC resolutions and the imposition of limited and targeted sanctions, the medium- to long-term issues are how to best protect core Chinese interests while minimizing the repercussions as a result of any specific measures Beijing may take, and whether fundamental changes of China–North Korea ties are necessary. The latter further relates to the overall endgame regarding the Korean peninsula in particular and the Northeast Asian geo-strategic fallout in general.[64]

Indeed, there may be palpable changes in the making. First and foremost, there has been intensive and enhanced coordination between China and the US, including at the Obama–Xi summit in Sunnylands, California, in June 2013. North Korea topped the issues discussed by the two leaders. Both presidents agreed that North Korea has to denuclearize and neither China nor the US would accept it as a nuclear-armed state. They also agreed that enforcement is critical and on the importance of continuing to apply pressure to stop North Korea from proliferating.[65] Beijing and Washington worked closely in the drafting of the latest UNSC resolution, and US and Chinese officials have frequently exchanged views and reiterated their shared common interest in getting Pyongyang back to its 6PT obligations. Second, some specific actions have been undertaken by China to demonstrate Beijing's resolve in enforcement, including closing North Korean accounts in Chinese central banks. Third, both Chinese leaders and high-ranking officials have spoken, on various occasions, and in stronger and unequivocal terms, about the North Korean nuclear issue, giving it priority over other Chinese interests regarding the Korean peninsula – stability and diplomacy. All in all, the tensions in the aftermath of the North Korea's third nuclear test provided the opportunity for Beijing and Washington to seek closer cooperation on nonproliferation.[66]

Clearly, North Korean provocations and its growing threats to the region are detrimental to Chinese interests. There is great tension on the peninsula as shown by an escalation of rhetoric and actions by Pyongyang, Seoul, and Washington, US deployment of advanced weaponry and missile defenses, an enhanced US–ROK alliance, and the ever-growing risk of military actions as a result of either miscalculation or accident. All of this has resulted in a far less stable regional environment and a greater US presence in China's neighborhood. Should a major military confrontation break out, Beijing could face massive refugee flows from North Korea; an environmental catastrophe if chemical or even nuclear weapons were used, and a unified Korea allied to the US. Beijing would be in convulsions about how to interpret its obligations under the 1961 Sino-DPRK Treaty.[67]

External pressure and expectations from the international community for China to do something about North Korea have been building up for years but so far Beijing has maintained a steady policy of not adopting measures that could seriously destabilize the regime in Pyongyang, whether under Kim Jong-il or Kim Jong-un. Given North Korea's growing dependence on China for food and energy supplies and on trade, and with growing Chinese investments in the North, Beijing is widely perceived as having – and therefore should be capable of exercising – significant influence or leverage over Pyongyang. However, for China, the issue is less about whether it should cut off economic assistance to North Korea or threaten coercion to bring Pyongyang into line than it is about the practical impacts of such actions on Pyongyang's behavior and Chinese overall security interests in the region.[68] Indeed, as one Congressional Research Service report makes it clear,

> China's overriding priority of preventing North Korea's collapse remains firm. Beijing fears the destabilizing effects of a humanitarian crisis, significant refugee flows over its borders, and the uncertainty of how other nations, particularly the United States, would assert themselves on the peninsula in the event of a power vacuum.[69]

For Beijing, its reluctance to go beyond token measures is reflective of a careful calculation of the limited impacts on near-term North Korean behavior (e.g., stopping its missile and nuclear programs and tests) while likely contributing to an endgame that it does not see itself the beneficiary but the potential loser.

But the existing game plan is no longer effective. North Korea is not willing to pursue the kind of economic reforms that Beijing has been trying to convince it to adopt because Pyongyang fears such reforms would erode its grip on power. Without meaningful reforms, the North Korean economy will remains in a shambles and a state of constant crises which necessitate more assistance from Beijing or, worse, a regime behaving badly and provocatively to extort payments from the international community. There are serious debates among security analysts within China on a change of course on North Korea.[70] Piecemeal measures no longer work. The Xi administration should reassess its options and get itself out of this untenable situation of sustaining a regime that does not add to its overall strategic interests. But most critically, it needs to develop a strategy that sends a clear message to Pyongyang that it can no longer take its patron for granted and that its patron is willing to change course on North Korea. Of course, this assumes that other players, the US included, can assure China an outcome that enhances rather than undermines its strategic position in the aftermath of the North's collapse and the eventual Korean unification. That requires a successful management of its most important bilateral relationship, the one with the US, which is discussed next.

China's relationship with North Korea remains an enigma but is increasingly becoming a subject of debate, especially after the dramatic event in late 2013. Jang Sung-taek, presumably a close confidant of Kim Jong-un and reportedly the second most powerful figure in the hermit kingdom, was suddenly charged with multiple crimes, including conspiring against Kim, was stripped of all his positions and then summarily executed.[71] Jang was believed to have been one of the trusted few contacts between Beijing and Pyongyang and his fall from grace both reveals the dangerous liaison China reluctantly maintains with its wayward client state and highlights its diminishing influence over the latter. This phenomenon must be a conundrum of some sort and challenges the conventional wisdom most watchers of China–North Korea relations hold. On the one hand, China today has become North Korea's key supplier of food and energy and its largest trading partner. On the other hand, Beijing itself claims – and it increasingly appears to be the case – that it only has limited influence over what Pyongyang does, and indeed, the latter's occasional wayward behavior has actually embarrassed and proved deeply frustrating to its Chinese patron.

Despite all of the frustration for Beijing, including the unpredictability of Kim Jong-un, China continues to place stability first. Some analysts suggest that apart from both being communist regimes and that North Korea provides a buffer against the US, China also derives economic benefits from cooperating with Pyongyang. But fundamentally, Beijing's concern over Washington's intentions continues to inform a policy of caution and calculation, lest North Korea's collapse entraps it in conflict with the US. At the same time, Beijing also needs to reassure Pyongyang that it is not abandoning it so that defection would not take place.[72] Indeed, despite the overwhelming North Korean dependence on China for energy, food, and economic assistance, Beijing has not been able – nor is it willing – to convert its economic leverage into political influence over Pyongyang. If anything, the fear of regime collapse and the growing strategic rivalry with the US has convinced the Chinese leadership that North Korean regime survival and stability are critical. This explains why, while China has in recent years become tougher and more open in criticizing North Korean behavior and joining the international community in imposing sanctions on Pyongyang, it has not fundamentally changed its policy toward North Korea to the extent of deserting its wayward client.[73]

China and the US, two major powers with important stakes in and significant influence over the fate of peninsular peace and stability, have recently undergone leadership transitions. These changes are happening at a time when the Obama administration is "pivoting" back to East Asia and Beijing is showing newfound assertiveness in regional affairs, which could see China and the US butting heads over one of the Cold War's unresolved legacies.[74] At the same time, their ever-closer economic interdependence, mutual interests in dealing with global issues such as the financial crisis, economic recovery, and climate change offer strong incentives for the two countries to avoid open conflict over the North Korean issue.[75] To translate their common interests in ensuring North Korean nuclear disarmament and peninsular peace and stability requires mutual understanding at the strategic level and skilful diplomacy in negotiating and executing actionable deals. The challenge, if past experiences offer any guide, is if and how effectively Beijing and Washington can agree on a common approach to the North Korean issue.

In a larger context, there is another serious challenge which requires significant attention; that is, the stability of the US–China relationship during a period of power transition. Ever since the end of the Cold War, Beijing and Washington have been managing an increasingly independent yet deeply distrusting relationship. China and the US harbor different visions over regional security architecture, prefer different approaches to addressing regional security issues, and are increasingly engaged in an open competition for regional primacy. It is widely acknowledged that the two great powers have yet to develop mutual strategic trust, 40 years after the Nixon breakthrough and despite over 90 official and regular channels of dialogs and consultation. Some have argued that, given the nature of international politics, it would be impossible to develop any serious mutual trust between a rising power and a reigning power with vast differences in socio-political systems, historical experiences, geo-strategic perceptions, and divergent visions of the international and regional orders. The best that can be accomplished is to recognize these differences and develop mechanisms to manage their relationship, minimize the negative impacts of disputes, and promote and coordinate where they do share common interests.[76] For the Xi administration, an immediate task to continue the critical Strategic and Economic Dialogue in the wake of major personnel turnovers in Washington and, to a significant extent, in Beijing. The two countries also need to maintain their military-to-military contacts, which have always been vulnerable to the vicissitudes of bilateral relations but are extremely important for avoiding direct military confrontation, given the dearth of clear and reliable communication and crisis management arrangements.[77]

Addressing the North Korea issue requires close US–China policy coordination. However, whether or not this can be accomplished depends on a number of factors. Strategic mutual trust, or as Chinese leaders now often emphasize, a "new type of major power relationship," remains elusive despite the fact Beijing and Washington have over 90 ongoing official dialogs on a whole range of issues of mutual concerns, including North Korea. China is reluctant to push North Korea hard given that it risks regime collapse and a united Korea allied with the US. The US, on the other hand, is frustrated with China's unwillingness to apply pressure on Pyongyang on the nuclear issue. The US and China also differ on the tactics and priorities, with Beijing emphasizing an integrated approach while Washington focuses on denuclearization ahead of everything else. Sino-US discussions addressing these issues could go a long way toward better cooperation on North Korea.

Notes

1 On the Korean War and China's involvement, see Sergei N. Goncharov, John W. Lewis, and Xue Litai, *Uncertain Partners: Stalin, Mao, and the Korean War* (Stanford, CA: Stanford University Press, 1993); and Chen Jian, *China's Road to the Korean War: The Making of the Sino-American Confrontation* (New York: Columbia University Press, 1994). See also, David Halberstam, *The Coldest Winter: America and the Korean War* (New York: Hyperion, 2007).
2 Chae-Jin Lee and Doo-Bok Park, *China and Korea: Dynamic Relations* (Stanford, CA: Hoover Institution Press, 1996).
3 Qian Qichen, 外交十记 (*Ten Stories of a Diplomat*) (Beijing: 世界知识出版社, 2003); Jae Ho Chung, *Between Ally and Partner: Korea–China Relations and the United States* (New York: Columbia University Press, 2007).
4 Joel S. Wit, Daniel B. Poneman, and Robert L. Gallucci, *Going Critical: The First North Korean Nuclear Crisis* (Washington, DC: The Brookings Institution, 2005).
5 On Chinese policy toward the Korean peninsula since reform, see Samuel S. Kim, "The Making of China's Korea Policy in the Era of Reform," in *The Making of Chinese Foreign and Security Policy in the Era of Reform*, ed. David M. Lampton (Stanford, CA: Stanford University Press, 2001), 371–408. See also Gilbert Rozman, *Chinese Strategic Thought toward Asia* (New York: Palgrave Macmillan, 2010), 177–97.
6 Avery Goldstein, "Across the Yalu: China's Interests and the Korean Peninsula in a Changing World," in *New Directions in the Study of China's Foreign Policy*, ed. Alastair Iain Johnston and Robert S. Ross (Stanford, CA: Stanford University Press, 2006), 131–61.
7 Taeho Kim, "Strategic Relations between Beijing and Pyongyang: Growing Strains amid Lingering Ties," in *China's Military Faces the Future*, ed. James R. Lilley and David Shambaugh (Armonk, NJ: M.E. Sharpe, 1999), 321; and Scott Snyder and See-won Byun, "DPRK Provocations Test China's Regional Role," *Comparative Connections* 12, no. 4 (January 2011): 105–16.

8 Richard McGregor and Anna Fifield, "China Applies Gentlest of Flicks to Pyongyang's Reins," *Financial Times*, February 24, 2005, 7.
9 John Pomfret, "China Wary of Weapons Searches," *Washington Post*, August 23, 2003, A19 section.
10 Shi Yinhong, "论如何认识和对待朝鲜核武器 (How to View and Deal with North Korean Nuclear Crisis)," *Ta Kung Pao* (Hong Kong), January 15, 2003.
11 Deng Yuwen, "China Should Abandon North Korea," *Financial Times*, February 27, 2013.
12 Jonas Parello-Plesner, "China and North Korea: Always Neighbours – Always Close?" *ISPI Analysis*, no. 124 (July 2012): 1–6.
13 Maurice Johnstone, "Absolute Beginner: North Korea after Kim Jong-il," *Jane's Intelligence Review* 24, no. 2 (February 2012): 8–13.
14 Jae Ho Chung and Myung-hae Choi, "Uncertain Allies or Uncomfortable Neighbors? Making Sense of China–North Korea Relations, 1949–2010," *Pacific Review* 26, no. 3 (2013): 246.
15 Walter C. Clemens, Jr, "North Korea's Quest for Nuclear Weapons: New Historical Evidence," *Journal of East Asian Studies* 10 (2010): 127–54.
16 On comprehensive analyses of the two crises, see Wit *et al.*, "Going Critical"; Yōichi Funabashi, *The Peninsula Question: A Chronicle of the Second Korean Nuclear Crisis* (Washington, DC: Brookings Institution Press, 2007).
17 "AFP: PRC FM Statement on DPRK Nuclear Issue Calls for Implementation of 1994 Pact," December 25, 2002.
18 Bates Gill and Andrew Thompson, "A Test for Beijing: China and the North Korean Nuclear Quandary," *Arms Control Today* 33, no. 4 (May 2003), www.armscontrol.org/act/2003_05/gillthompson_may03.asp.
19 Victor D. Cha, *The Impossible State: North Korea, Past and Future* (New York: Ecco Press, 2012), 290–1.
20 Xiaoxiong Yi, "A Neutralized Korea? The North–South Rapprochement and China's Korean Policy," *Korean Journal of Defense Analysis* 12, no. 2 (Winter 2000): 71–118.
21 Scott Snyder, "The Second North Korean Nuclear Crisis: Assessing US and DPRK Negotiation Strategies," *Pacific Focus* 22 (2007): 49–52; Gill and Thompson, "A Test for Beijing."
22 David M. Lampton, "China and the Crisis in Korea," *The National Interest*, July 30, 2003.
23 Gilbert Rozman, "The North Korean Nuclear Crisis and US Strategy in Northeast Asia," *Asian Survey* 47, no. 4 (July/August 2007): 601–21.
24 Funabashi, "The Peninsula Questions," 271, 281–5.
25 "China Hopes the Second Round of North Korean Nuclear Talks Could Reach New Consensus," *PLA Daily*, February 5, 2004. http://pladaily.com.cn/gb/pladaily/2004/02/05/20040205001174_jryw.html.
26 Edward Cody and Anthony Faiola, "North Korean Ends 'Candid' China Visits," *Washington Post*, April 22, 2004, A22 section.
27 Junsheng Wang, *North Korean Nuclear Issue and China's Role: Pluralistic Context of Co-management* (Beijing: World Knowledge Publishing House, 2012).
28 Kelly Wallace, "N. Korea the Focus at Jiang, Bush Summit," *CNN*, October 25, 2002, http://edition.cnn.com/2002/WORLD/asiapcf/east/10/24/china.us/; Mike Allen and Karen DeYoung, "Bush Seeks China's Aid To Oppose N. Korea," *Washington Post*, October 26, 2002, A18 section.
29 "The Six-Party Talks at a Glance," Arms Control Association, May 2012, www.armscontrol.org/factsheets/6partytalks; Choe Sang-hun, "North Korea Destroys Cooling Tower at Nuclear Plant," *New York Times*, June 27, 2008.
30 Gu Guoliang, "Cooperation and Differences between China and the US in Handling the North Korean Nuclear Issue," *Korea Review* 2, no. 1 (May 2012): 63–80; Phillip

C. Saunders, "US–China Relations in a Changing Nuclear Environment," in *Sino-American Strategic Dynamics in the Early 21st Century: Prospects, Scenarios, and Implications*, ed. Jonathan D. Pollack (Newport: Naval War College Press, 2003), 159–84.
31 Joseph Kahn and Susan Chira, "Chinese Official Challenges US Stance on North Korea," *New York Times*, June 9, 2004.
32 Paul Holmes, "China Sees No Sign of N. Korea Nuclear Test," Reuters, May 24, 2005.
33 Zhu Feng, "朝核问题六方会谈前途分析（On the Future Prospects of the Six-Party Talks）," 现代国际关系（*Contemporary International Relations*）, no. 1 (2005): 26–33.
34 Anna Fifield, "China Says N Korea Entitled to Nuclear Power," *Financial Times*, September 1, 2005.
35 "Statement of the Ministry of Foreign Affairs of the People's Republic of China," October 2006.
36 Michael D. Swaine, "China's North Korea Dilemma," *China Leadership Monitor*, no. 30 (November 2009), http://media.hoover.org/sites/default/files/documents/CLM30 MS.pdf; Simon Shen, "The Hidden Face of Comradeship: Popular Chinese Consensus on the DPRK and Its Implications for Beijing's Policy," *Journal of Contemporary China* 21, no. 75 (May 2012): 427–43.
37 Interview with Chinese diplomat, Beijing, July 2005; Hui Zhang, "Don't Blame Beijing," *Bulletin of the Atomic Scientists* (September/October 2005): 23–5; Anne Wu, "What China Whispers to North Korea," *Washington Quarterly* 28, no. 2 (Spring 2005): 35–48.
38 Charles L. Pritchard, *Failed Diplomacy: The Tragic Story of How North Korea Got the Bomb* (Washington, DC: Brookings Institution Press, 2007); Fred Kaplan, "Rolling Blunder: How the Bush Administration Let North Korea Get the Nukes," *Washington Monthly* (May 2004), www.washingtonmonthly.com/features/2004/0405.kaplan.html.
39 Jeffrey A. Bader, *Obama and China's Rise: An Insider's Account of America's Asia Strategy* (Washington, DC: The Brookings Institution Press, 2012), 31.
40 Scott A. Snyder, "US Policy toward North Korea," Council on Foreign Relations, January 2013, www.cfr.org/north-korea/us-policy-toward-north-korea/p29962.
41 Dingli Shen, "Cooperative Denuclearization toward North Korea," *Washington Quarterly* 33, no. 4 (October 2009): 175–88; Charles K. Armstrong, "The Korean Peninsula on the Verge," *Current History* (September 2011): 229.
42 Bennett Ramberg, "Living with Nuclear North Korea," *Survival* 51, no. 4 (August 2009): 13–20; Christopher R. Hill, "The Elusive Vision of a Non-nuclear North Korea," *Washington Quarterly* 36, no. 2 (Spring 2013): 7–19.
43 The Korea Society and Stanford Shorenstein APARC, "New Beginnings" in the US–ROK Alliance, *Recommendations to the Obama Administration*, report (2011), 11.
44 Emma Chanlett-Avery and Ian E. Rinehart, *North Korea: US Relations, Nuclear Diplomacy, and Internal Situation*, report no. R41259 (Washington, DC: Congressional Research Service, 2013)
45 David E. Sanger, "US Implicates North Korean Leader in Attack," *New York Times*, May 22, 2010.
46 Simon Martin, "N Korea Vows to Bolster Nuclear Deterrent," AFP, June 28, 2010.
47 John Pomfret, "US Raises Pressure on China to Rein in N. Korea," *Washington Post*, December 6, 2010.
48 Jeremy Page, Jay Solomon, and Julian E. Barnes, "China Warns US as Korea Tensions Rise," *Wall Street Journal*, November 26, 2010.
49 Bonnie Glaser, "The Diplomatic Relationship: Substance and Process," in *Tangled Titans: The United States and China*, ed. David L. Shambaugh (Lanham, MD: Rowman & Littlefield, 2013), 169–170.

50 Alexander Martin, "North Korea Doubles Down on China Ties," *Wall Street Journal*, April 30, 2013.
51 Teddy Ng, "Vice-President's North Korea Trip Shows Pyongyang Still Key Partner," *South China Morning Post*, July 27, 2013.
52 Zhang Huizhi and Wang Xiaoke, "中美对朝政策竞争与合作的态势分析 (Analysis on Competition and Cooperation of China and the United States Policies toward DPRK)," 东北亚论坛 (*Northeast Asia Forum*), no. 5 (2012): 31–9.
53 Scott Snyder, "Prospects for Sino-American Policy Coordination toward North Korea," *International Journal of Korean Unification Studies* 21, no. 1 (2012): 21–44.
54 Jonathan D. Pollack, *No Exit: North Korea, Nuclear Weapons and International Security* (London: International Institute for Strategic Studies, 2011), 199–204.
55 Cha, *The Impossible State*, 344.
56 Jin Moo Kim, "North Korea's Reliance on China and China's Influence on North Korea," *Korean Journal of Defense Analysis* 23, no. 2 (June 2011): 257–71.
57 Jiang Longfan and Piao Yanhua, "中朝关系现状及展望 (The Current Status of and Prospects for Sino-North Korean Relations)," 东北亚研究 (*Northeast Asian Studies*), no. 4 (November 2002): 21–8.
58 Bader, "Obama and China's Rise," 83–93; Scott Snyder and See-Won Byun, "*Cheonan* and Yeonpyeong: The Northeast Asian Response to North Korea's Provocations," *RUSI Journal* 156, no. 2 (May 2011): 74–81.
59 Scott Snyder, "Appendix A: Diplomatic and Security Relations between China and North Korea under Kim Jong-il," in eds. Bonnie Glaser and Brittany Billingsley, *Reordering Chinese Priorities on the Korean Peninsula* (Washington, DC: Center for International and Strategic Studies, 2012), 25–46.
60 International Crisis Group, *China and Inter-Korean Clashes in the Yellow Sea*, report no. 200 (January 27, 2011); John S. Park, "Beijing's 'Sunshine Policy with Chinese Characteristics'," in *US–China Relations and Korean Unification*, ed. Choi Jinwook (Seoul: Korea Institute for National Unification, 2011), 68–79.
61 Feng Zhu, "Flawed Mediation and a Compelling Mission: Chinese Diplomacy in the Six-Party Talks to Denuclearize North Korea," *East Asia* 28 (2011): 191–218; Ren Xiao, "China Debates DPRK Policy," *PacNet*, no. 55 (Pacific Forum CSIS, 2013); Robert Marquand, "Why China Won't Help the US on North Korea," *Christian Science Monitor*, April 25, 2013.
62 Huang Fengzhi and Liu Boran, "美韩同盟强化与中国的战略应对 (The Strengthening of US–ROA Alliance and China's Strategic Response)," 国际论坛 (*International Forum*) 15, no. 2 (March 2013): 28–34.
63 "China Calls in N Korean Ambassador over Nuke Test," Associated Press, February 13, 2013.
64 Daniel Blumenthal, "China Must Weigh Its Options," *New York Times*, March 11, 2013; Hui Zhang, "China's North Korea Dilemma," *Los Angeles Times*, March 6, 2013.
65 "Press Briefing by National Security Advisor Tom Donilon," The White House, June 8, 2013.
66 ChinaFile, "Can the North Korea Challenge Bring China and the US Together?" *The Atlantic*, May 7, 2013; "North Korea's Hostile Outbursts Could Strengthen US–China Relations," Associate Press, April 5, 2013.
67 Huang Fengzhi and Liu Boran, "美韩同盟强化与中国的战略应对 (The Strengthening of US–ROA Alliance and China's Strategic Response)."
68 Ben Blanchard, "Despite Tough Talk, China's North Korea Options Are Limited," Reuters, April 8, 2013, www.reuters.com/article/2013/04/08/us-korea-north-china-idUSBRE9370BO20130408; Timothy Beardson, "China Support of North Korea Is Rational," *Financial Times*, April 23, 2013.
69 Chanlett-Avery and Rinehart, "North Korea," 13.
70 Deng, "China Should Abandon North Korea."

71 Chico Harlan, "North Korea Announces Execution of Kim Jong-un's Uncle, Jang Sung-taek," *Washington Post*, December 13, 2013.
72 Han S. Park, "North Korea as a US–China Flashpoint?" *Korea Review* 2, no. 2 (November 2012): 11–28; Nam Jong-ho, Choo Jae-woo, and Lee Jang-won, "China's Dilemma on the Korean Peninsula: Not an Alliance but a Security Dilemma," *Korean Journal of Defense Analysis* 25, no. 3 (September 2013): 385–98.
73 Zhu Feng and Nathan Beauchamp-Mustafaga, "Chinese Policy toward North Korea in the Post-Kim Jong Il Era," *Korea Review* 2, no. 2 (November 2012): 29–53.
74 For discussion, see Chapter 4 by Suisheng Zhao in this volume.
75 Anne Gearan, "US, China Agree on Korean Crisis," *Washington Post*, April 14, 2013.
76 David M. Lampton, "A New Type of Major-Power Relationship: Seeking a Durable Foundation for US–China Ties," *Asia Policy* 16 (July 2013): 51–68. A discussion of the need for mechanisms appears in Chapter 3 by Quansheng Zhao in this book.
77 On US–China military-to-military contacts see Chapter 10 by Christopher Yung in this volume.

References

"AFP: PRC FM Statement on DPRK Nuclear Issue Calls for Implementation of 1994 Pact," December 25, 2002.

Allen, Mike, and Karen DeYoung. "Bush Seeks China's Aid to Oppose N. Korea," *Washington Post*, October 26, 2002, A18 section.

Arms Control Association. "The Six-Party Talks at a Glance," May 2012. www.armscontrol.org/factsheets/6partytalks.

Armstrong, Charles K. "The Korean Peninsula on the Verge," *Current History* (September 2011): 229–35.

Bader, Jeffrey A. *Obama and China's Rise: An Insider's Account of America's Asia Strategy*. (Washington, DC: Brookings Institution Press, 2012).

Beardson, Timothy. "China Support of North Korea Is Rational," *Financial Times*, April 23, 2013.

Blanchard, Ben. "Despite Tough Talk, China's North Korea Options Limited," Reuters. April 8, 2013. www.reuters.com/article/2013/04/08/us-korea-north-china-idUSBRE9370BO20130408.

Blumenthal, Daniel. "China Must Weigh Its Options," *New York Times*, March 11, 2013.

Cha, Victor D. *The Impossible State: North Korea, Past and Future* (New York: Ecco Press, 2012).

Chanlett-Avery, Emma, and Ian E. Rinehart. *North Korea: US Relations, Nuclear Diplomacy, and Internal Situation*. Report no. R41259 (Washington, DC: Congressional Research Service, 2013).

Chen, Jian. *China's Road to the Korean War: The Making of the Sino-American Confrontation* (New York: Columbia University Press, 1994).

"China Calls in N Korean Ambassador over Nuke Test," Associated Press, February 13, 2013.

"China Hopes the Second Round of North Korean Nuclear Talks Could Reach New Consensus," *PLA Daily*. February 5, 2004. http://pladaily.com.cn/gb/pladaily/2004/02/05/20040205001174_jryw.html.

ChinaFile. "Can the North Korea Challenge Bring China and the US Together?" *The Atlantic*, May 7, 2013.

Choe, Sang-hun. "North Korea Destroys Cooling Tower at Nuclear Plant," *New York Times*, June 27, 2008.

Chung, Chae Ho. *Between Ally and Partner: Korea–China Relations and the United States* (New York: Columbia University Press, 2007).

Chung, Jae Ho, and Myung-hae Choi. "Uncertain Allies or Uncomfortable Neighbors? Making Sense of China–North Korea Relations, 1949–2010," *Pacific Review* 26, no. 3 (2013): 243–64.

Clemens, Walter C., Jr "North Korea's Quest for Nuclear Weapons: New Historical Evidence," *Journal of East Asian Studies* 10 (2010): 127–54.

Cody, Edward, and Anthony Faiola. "North Korean Ends 'Candid' China Visits," *Washington Post*, April 22, 2004, A22 section.

Deng, Yuwen. "China Should Abandon North Korea," *Financial Times*, February 27, 2013.

Fifield, Anna. "China Says N Korea Entitled to Nuclear Power," *Financial Times*, September 1, 2005.

Funabashi, Yōichi. *The Peninsula Question: A Chronicle of the Second Korean Nuclear Crisis* (Washington, DC: Brookings Institution Press, 2007).

Gearan, Anne. "US, China Agree on Korean Crisis," *Washington Post*, April 14, 2013.

Gill, Bates, and Andrew Thompson. "A Test for Beijing: China and the North Korean Nuclear Quandary," *Arms Control Today* 33, no. 4 (May 2003). www.armscontrol.org/act/2003_05/gillthompson_may03.asp.

Glaser, Bonnie S. "The Diplomatic Relationship: Substance and Process," in *Tangled Titans: The United States and China*, ed. David L. Shambaugh (Lanham, MD: Rowman & Littlefield, 2013), 151–80.

Glaser, Bonnie, and Brittany Billingsley. *Taiwan's 2012 Presidential Elections and Cross-Strait Relations: Implications for the United States* (Washington, DC: Center for Strategic and International Studies, 2011).

Goldstein, Avery. "Across the Yalu: China's Interests and the Korean Peninsula in a Changing World," in *New Directions in the Study of China's Foreign Policy*, eds. A. Iain Johnston and Robert S. Ross (Stanford, CA: Stanford University Press, 2006), 131–61.

Goncharov, Sergei N., John W. Lewis, and Litai Xue. *Uncertain Partners: Stalin, Mao, and the Korean War* (Stanford, CA: Stanford University Press, 1993).

Gurtov, Guoliang. "Cooperation and Differences between China and the US in Handling the North Korean Nuclear Issue," *Korea Review* 2, no. 1 (May 2012): 63–80.

Halberstam, David. *The Coldest Winter: America and the Korean War* (New York: Hyperion, 2007).

Harlan, Chico. "North Korea Announces Execution of Kim Jong-un's Uncle, Jang Sung-taek," *Washington Post*, December 13, 2013.

Hill, Christopher R. "The Elusive Vision of a Non-nuclear North Korea," *Washington Quarterly* 36, no. 2 (Spring 2013): 7–19.

Holmes, Paul. "China Sees No Sign of N. Korea Nuclear Test," Reuters, May 24, 2005.

Huang, Fengzhi, and Boran Liu. "美韩同盟强化与中国的战略应对 (The Strengthening of US–ROA Alliance and China's Strategic Response)," 国际论坛 (*International Forum*) 15, no. 2 (March 2013): 28–34.

International Crisis Group. *China and Inter-Korean Clashes in the Yellow Sea*. Report no. 200. (2011).

Jiang, Longfan, and Yanhua Piao. "中朝关系现状及展望 (The Current Status of and Prospects for Sino-North Korean Relations)," 东北亚研究 (*Northeast Asian Studies*), no. 4 (November 2002): 21–8.

Johnstone, Maurice. "Absolute Beginner: North Korea after Kim Jong-il," *Jane's Intelligence Review* 24, no. 2 (February 2012): 8–13.

Kahn, Joseph, and Susan Chira. "Chinese Official Challenges US Stance on North Korea," *New York Times*, June 9, 2004.
Kaplan, Fred. "Rolling Blunder: How the Bush Administration Let North Korea Get the Nukes," *Washington Monthly*. May 2004.
Kim, Jin Moo. "North Korea's Reliance on China and China's Influence on North Korea," *Korean Journal of Defense Analysis* 23, no. 2 (June 2011): 257–71.
Kim, Samuel S. "The Making of China's Korea Policy in the Era of Reform," in *The Making of Chinese Foreign and Security Policy in the Era of Reform*, ed. David M. Lampton (Stanford, CA: Stanford University Press, 2001), 371–408.
Kim, Taeho. "Strategic Relations between Beijing and Pyongyang: Growing Strains amid Lingering Ties," in *China's Military Faces the Future*, ed. James R. Lilley and David L. Shambaugh (Armonk, NJ: M.E. Sharpe, 1999), 295–321.
Korea Society and Stanford Shorenstein APARC. "New Beginnings" in the US–ROK Alliance: *Recommendations to the Obama Administration*. Report. 2011.
Lampton, David M. "A New Type of Major-Power Relationship: Seeking a Durable Foundation for US–China Ties," *Asia Policy* 16 (July 2013): 51–68.
Lampton, David M. "China and the Crisis in Korea," *The National Interest*, July 30, 2003.
Lee, Chae-Jin, and Doo-Bok Park. *China and Korea: Dynamic Relations* (Stanford, CA: Hoover Institution Press, 1996).
Marquand, Robert. "Why China Won't Help the US on North Korea," *Christian Science Monitor*, April 25, 2013.
Martin, Alexander. "North Korea Doubles Down on China Ties," *Wall Street Journal*, April 30, 2013.
Martin, Simon. "N Korea Vows to Bolster Nuclear Deterrent," AFP, June 28, 2010.
McGregor, Richard, and Anna Fifield. "China Applies Gentlest of Flicks to Pyongyang's Reins," *Financial Times*, February 24, 2005.
Nam, Jong-ho, Jae-woo Choo, and Jang-won Lee. "China's Dilemma on the Korean Peninsula: Not an Alliance but a Security Dilemma," *Korean Journal of Defense Analysis* 25, no. 3 (September 2013): 385–98.
Ng, Teddy. "Vice-President's North Korea Trip Shows Pyongyang Still Key Partner," *South China Morning Post*, July 27, 2013.
"North Korea's Hostile Outbursts Could Strengthen US–China Relations," Associated Press. April 5, 2013.
Page, Jeremy, Jay Solomon, and Julian E. Barnes. "China Warns US as Korea Tensions Rise," *Wall Street Journal*, November 26, 2010.
Parello-Plesner, Jonas. "China and North Korea: Always Neighbours – Always Close?" *ISPI Analysis*, no. 124 (July 2012).
Park, Han S. "North Korea as a US–China Flashpoint?" *Korea Review* 2, no. 2 (November 2012): 11–28.
Park, John S. "Beijing's 'Sunshine Policy with Chinese Characteristics'," in *US–China Relations and Korean Unification*, ed. Jinwook Choi (Seoul: Korea Institute for National Unification, 2011), 68–79.
People's Republic of China, Ministry of Foreign Affairs. "Statement of the Ministry of Foreign Affairs of the People's Republic of China," October 2006.
Pollack, Jonathan D. *No Exit: North Korea, Nuclear Weapons and International Security* (London: International Institute for Strategic Studies, 2011).
Pomfret, John. "China Wary of Weapons Searches," *Washington Post*, August 23, 2003, A19 section.

Pomfret, John. "US Raises Pressure on China to Rein in N. Korea," *Washington Post*, December 6, 2010.

Pritchard, Charles L. *Failed Diplomacy: The Tragic Story of How North Korea Got the Bomb* (Washington, DC: Brookings Institution Press, 2007).

Qian, Qichen. 外交十记. Beijing: 世界知识出版社, 2003.

Ramberg, Bennett. "Living with Nuclear North Korea," *Survival* 51, no. 4 (August 2009): 13–20.

Rozman, Gilbert. *Chinese Strategic Thought toward Asia* (New York: Palgrave Macmillan, 2010).

Rozman, Gilbert. "The North Korean Nuclear Crisis and US Strategy in Northeast Asia," *Asian Survey* 47, no. 4 (July/August 2007): 601–21.

Sanger, David E. "US Implicates North Korean Leader in Attack," *New York Times*, May 22, 2010.

Saunders, Phillip C. "US–China Relations in a Changing Nuclear Environment," in *Sino-American Strategic Dynamics in the Early 21st Century: Prospects, Scenarios, and Implications*, ed. Jonathan D. Pollack (Newport: Naval War College Press, 2003).

Shen, Dingli. "Cooperative Denuclearization toward North Korea," *Washington Quarterly* 33, no. 4 (October 2009): 175–88.

Shen, Simon. "The Hidden Face of Comradeship: Popular Chinese Consensus on the DPRK and Its Implications for Beijing's Policy," *Journal of Contemporary China* 21, no. 75 (May 2012): 427–43.

Shi, Yinhong. "论如何认识和对待朝鲜核武器 (How to View and Deal with North Korean Nuclear Crisis)," *Ta Kung Pao* (Hong Kong), January 15, 2003.

Snyder, Scott. "Prospects for Sino-American Policy Coordination toward North Korea," in*ternational Journal of Korean Unification Studies* 21, no. 1 (2012): 21–44.

Snyder, Scott. "The Second North Korean Nuclear Crisis: Assessing US and DPRK Negotiation Strategies," *Pacific Focus* 22 (2007): 49–52.

Snyder, Scott A. "US Policy Toward North Korea," Council on Foreign Relations. January 2013. www.cfr.org/north-korea/us-policy-toward-north-korea/p29962.

Snyder, Scott, and See-Won Byun. "*Cheonan* and Yeonpyeong: The Northeast Asian Response to North Korea's Provocations," *RUSI Journal* 156, no. 2 (May 2011): 74–81.

Snyder, Scott, and See-won Byun. "DPRK Provocations Test China's Regional Role," *Comparative Connections* 12, no. 4 (January 2011).

Swaine, Michael D. "China's North Korea Dilemma," *China Leadership Monitor*, no. 30 (November 2009).

United States, The White House, "Press Briefing by National Security Advisor Tom Donilon," June 8, 2013.

Wallace, Kelly. "N. Korea the Focus at Jiang, Bush Summit," *CNN*. October 25, 2002. http://edition.cnn.com/2002/WORLD/asiapcf/east/10/24/china.us/.

Wang, Junsheng. *North Korean Nuclear Issue and China's Role: Pluralistic Context of Co-management* (Beijing: World Knowledge Publishing House, 2012).

Wit, Joel S., Daniel B. Poneman, and Robert L. Gallucci. *Going Critical: The First North Korean Nuclear Crisis* (Washington, DC: Brookings Institution Press, 2004).

Wu, Anne. "What China Whispers to North Korea," *Washington Quarterly* 28, no. 2 (Spring 2005): 35–48.

Xiao, Ren. "China Debates DPRK Policy," *PacNet* 55 (July 22, 2013).

Yi, Xiaoxiong. "A Neutralized Korea? The North-South Rapprochement and China's Korean Policy," *Korean Journal of Defense Analysis* 12, no. 2 (Winter 2000): 71–118.

Zhang, Hui. "China's North Korea Dilemma," *Los Angeles Times*, March 6, 2013.

Zhang, Hui. "Don't Blame Beijing," *Bulletin of the Atomic Scientists*, (September/October 2005): 23–5.

Zhang, Huizhi, and Xiaoke Wang. "中美对朝政策竞争与合作的态势分析（Analysis on Competition and Cooperation of China and the United States Policies toward DPRK）," 东北亚论坛（*Northeast Asia Forum*), no. 5 (2012): 31–9.

Zhu, Feng, and Nathan Beauchamp-Mustafaga. "Chinese Policy toward North Korea in the Post-Kim Jong Il Era," *Korea Review* 2, no. 2 (November 2012): 29–53.

Zhu, Feng. "Flawed Mediation and a Compelling Mission: Chinese Diplomacy in the Six-Party Talks to Denuclearize North Korea," *East Asia* 28 (2011): 191–218.

Zhu, Feng. "朝核问题六方会谈前途分析（On the Future Prospects of the Six-Party Talks）," 现代国际关系（*Contemporary International Relations*）, no. 1 (2005): 26–33.

7 Tough love

US–China economic relations between competition and interdependence

Wei Liang

Introduction

Outgoing US Secretary of State Hillary Clinton gave a farewell address on January 31, 2013, to her colleagues at the State Department. Addressing the US–China relationship, she emphasized:

> the Pacific is big enough for both of us. We will continue to welcome China's rise if it chooses to play a constructive role in the region. The future of this relationship depends on our ability to engage across all these issues at once.[1]

President Barack Obama made a similar comment when he welcomed President Hu Jintao of China at the White House in 2011, "I absolutely believe that China's peaceful rise is good for the world, and it's good for America."[2] The US and China are at a complex and interesting crossroads in their relationship, which goes beyond a normal interstate relationship intertwined by political and economic connections. An unprecedented new dynamic exists because the relationship involves an existing superpower and a rising power in an increasingly globalized world. Both sides have seen the necessity and value of a closer and deeper relationship, but also have deep doubts about each other's intentions and ambitions.

International relations scholars have long debated the future of US–China relations in the context of the relative decline of US supremacy and Chinese ascendency. They specifically query whether China will adopt the aggressive posture predicted by realists or the cooperative and accommodating attitude forecast by neoliberal institutionalists. Realists contend that conflict between US and China is inevitable on both the political/security and economic fronts.[3] In terms of the latter, the continued relative increase in Chinese economic power poses a formidable threat to the long-term economic interest of the US. The two countries will not only contest regional dominance in the Asia-Pacific Region (APR), but also will compete in the realms of energy and commodity consumption, innovation, investment, and finance in an adversarial zero-sum game. In contrast, many neoliberal institutionalist scholars assert that China's more active participation in intergovernmental organizations such as the World Bank, the International Monterey

Fund (IMF) and the World Trade Organization (WTO) will constrain Beijing's policy options. For neoliberal institutionalists, interdependence and multilateralism push governments to abide by existing global rules and norms and to behave cooperatively.

Regardless of whether or not one is a realist or neoliberal institutionalist, the conventional wisdom is that it is relatively easier for the US and China to agree on economic issues, especially when compared to political and security relations. There is some empirical basis for this given that US–China economic relations historically have been well managed by the two countries despite the highs and lows in bilateral political relations in past decades.

Sino-US trade rose steadily after the two nations re-established diplomatic relations in 1979, signed a bilateral trade agreement (July 1979), and gave each other mutual most-favored-nation (MFN) treatment beginning in 1980.[4] In 1979, total US–China trade was only $2 billion. As of the end of 2013, it hit $562 billion.[5] China is now the second largest US trading partner (after Canada), the third largest US export market (after Canada and Mexico), and the largest source of US imports. Investment plays a large and growing role in the relationship. A significant share of China's investment in US is comprised of US securities, while foreign direct investment (FDI) constitutes the bulk of US investment in China. China's holding of US Treasury securities skyrocketed from $118 billion in 2002 to $1.27 trillion in January 2014, making China the largest foreign holder of US Treasury securities.[6] The level of FDI flows between the US and China is relatively small compared to the volume of bilateral trade with US FDI in China significantly exceeding Chinese FDI in the US. Cumulative Chinese FDI in the US through the end of 2010 was $3.2 billion while US FDI in China was $60.5 billion. Overall, US and China economic interdependence has reached unprecedented levels in the span of one mere decade.

Some, along neoliberal institutionalist lines, even argue closer economic tie can serve as the buffer to ease tensions in bilateral political relations. Following this logic, throughout the 1990s there was a broad consensus among US policy and opinion leaders that the US should engage China and draw it into the existing global order as this ultimately would make China more like the US, at least in terms of behaviors if not preferences. But this longstanding consensus is now coming apart. The reality is that even though China is now one of the most important trading countries in the world and economically globalized and liberalized in multiple ways, it has not fully adopted US-like rules or become a responsible stakeholder internationally. Instead, the visible hand of the government increasingly controls its economic activities, with adverse effects for US trade and economic interests. The WTO also has failed to reduce bilateral trade disputes and provide effective remedies to affected American domestic industries because more and more disputes now relate to China's state intervention in and regulation of the national economy rather than unfair trade practices. On top of this, the US's fiscal and economic challenges in the wake of the financial crisis have coincided with China's continued economic success. This has brought new urgency to reaching a policy consensus that not only reflects political and economic realities, but is also one that both countries can endorse. Further complicating the situation is the fact that the transformation of economic relations has taken place within the context of complex global political and economic structural change, including the global economic recession, the rise of the developing countries such as China, India, and Brazil as the new driver of global economic growth, and the deepening and flattening of global and regional production networks.[7]

This chapter reviews US–China economic relations from 1979 to 2012, highlights the principal forces causing disputes, stimulating cooperation, and encouraging change, and discusses how the two economic giants can maintain a constructive partnership that serves their interests and manages their differences. The second section overviews the evolution of US–China economic relations from late 1970s to the new century. The third lays out the key argument about why the bilateral economic relations have become more competitive today, in contrast with what many policy scholars and opinion leaders expected on the eve of China's WTO accession in 2001. The fourth section discusses what can be done to reduce conflict in the US–China economic relationship as well as to increase cooperation. The final section considers where the US–China economic relationship is headed.

Background to the US–China economic relationship

Contemporary Sino-American economic relations resulted from fundamental changes in global politics and markets, domestic and international institutions, and the domestic politics of both countries. In the 1970s and 1980s, the Soviet threat led Washington and Beijing to build up their economic links rapidly. With strong support from the US, China quickly moved back to the center of the world stage after three decades of isolation and gained membership of the United Nations, the World Bank, and the IMF.[8] In 1980, the US granted China MFN trade status, greatly lowering tariffs on Chinese imports. In addition, in the 1990s the US was the second largest investor in the Chinese market, after the overseas Chinese in Hong Kong, Taiwan, and Singapore.[9]

The end of the Cold War and particularly Beijing's squashing of the Tiananmen Square pro-democracy movement in June 1989 spurred decision-makers in both countries to re-examine bilateral relations and plan for a new post-Cold War world order. Throughout the 1990s, Chinese leaders viewed the US in the context of a US-dominated international system. Their main challenge was how to obtain space for China to focus on economic development at a time when differences with the US had become more heated. Zhu Rongji, the former Chinese premier, talked about China's incentives to apply for the WTO membership in an interview with the *Wall Street Journal* in 1999: "the reason we have made such big concessions is that we have given due consideration to the overall situation of friendly cooperation between China and the US, including China's long-term development strategy and China's international strategy."[10]

For its part, the US began to question whether it should engage or contain China since the latter no longer had its former strategic importance. One of the main factors that ultimately led the US, in the 1990s, to choose engagement over containment was China's rising economic clout coupled with its emerging economic interdependence with China. In 1990, trade with China accounted for only 2.3 percent of total US trade. That figure jumped to 6.7 percent by 2001. The same year, the US share of China's inward FDI reached 9.5 percent.[11] In the late 1990s, the US business community also began to lobby for a closer and more stable and predictable economic relationship to protect their growing economic stake in China. This was reflected by the strong business push for granting China permanent MFN status and strong support for China's WTO accession.[12] Both sides agreed to maintain and expand economic ties, which ameliorated frictions between the two states. An integral part of American engagement policy was to integrate China into extant international institutions, norms, and regimes. China's WTO accession negotiation took place in this political context. Both sides viewed China's application for WTO membership and the conclusion of Sino-American negotiations on China's WTO accession as a way to redefine bilateral relations.

Before China joined the WTO in 2001, bilateral negotiations were the main mechanism by which the two sides addressed their bilateral economic issues and solved trade disputes. Bilateralism worked well for the US because China was heavily dependent on the US market and capital. By the early 1990s, the growth of Chinese exports to the US began to catalyze complaints from US firms about Chinese protectionism and unfair trading practices. Consequently, the US pressured China to cut tariffs, eliminate quotas, drop other import-licensing restrictions on US goods, and protect intellectual property. Frustrated by incessant difficulties in opening the China market, Washington threatened to impose prohibitive tariffs on $5.4 billion of Chinese imports in early 1992.[13] At this point, US unilateralism worked well because Beijing badly coveted GATT/WTO membership and needed US approval if its quest was to succeed. Specific Chinese concessions include the 1992 Market Access Memorandum of Understanding (MOU) and intellectual property rights (IPR) agreements in 1992 and 1995. Pursuant to the latter, China agreed to change its copyright and patent laws to substantially improve protection of foreign literary works, recordings, computer software, manufacturing processes, and product designs.[14]

Undoubtedly, the most frequent source of irritation in Sino-American economic relations in the 1990s was the annual US policy debate relating to the renewal of China's MFN status and later the granting of permanent normal trade relations (PNTR) to China. By way of background, as a non-market economy, China's MFN status was subject to annual review, which essentially was perfunctory prior to 1990. After the 1989 Tiananmen massacre, Congressional and other critics of China argued that China's MFN status should be conditioned on the easing of political repression and improvements in China's human rights record.[15] President George H.W. Bush resisted these intensifying pressures, arguing the revocation of MFN would destroy Sino-American trade.[16] His successor Bill Clinton decided to renew China's MFN status with the specific condition to improve certain aspects of human rights in 1993 in order to keep his campaign promise to be tough on

China. Yet a year later, he made the announcement that he was delinking human rights from MFN once and for all.[17] Thereafter until 2000, President Clinton waffled between accommodating business groups, which lobbied hard to protect MFN, and human rights groups and the US Congress, who viewed the MFN as a useful tool to influence Chinese policies.[18] By the end of his second term, Clinton finally chose to support granting China PNTR, which cleared the way for China to win full WTO membership.

Continuity and change in the bilateral economic relationship

With the US extension of PNTR status to China in 2000 and China's accession to the WTO in 2001 bilateral economic relations began a new chapter. Comparing the subsequent period up to 2008 to the economic relationship in the 1990s, we see the US has continued its economic engagement policy toward China. Furthermore, many longstanding economic issues such as trade imbalances, market access, fairness of the playing field for foreign enterprises in China, China's managed exchange rate policy, and IPR protection have persisted. Yet, there has been change because some of these issues have become more salient. In addition, the scope and the severity of trade frictions and disputes between the two countries have grown in tandem with the growth in economic ties. This is not surprising given that competition posed by China, among other things, has resulted in job losses and a high trade deficit, and challenged the position of US firms globally. More positively, the growth in economic ties has meant rising Sino-American economic interdependence.

China poses a unique challenge to the US because of two major factors. One is China's export-oriented growth model. China maintains a high level of trade dependence, 47 percent of GDP in 2012.[19] In contrast, US trade as a percentage of GDP is only 25 percent, much lower than that of most developed countries.[20] Until China shifts away from this model toward more domestic consumption, its trade imbalances and frictions with the US will continue to grow.[21] The other factor is China's state capitalism, which is derived from China's transitional economy status, its adoption of the Asian development model, and the need to maintain rapid growth to sustain the legitimacy of the Chinese Communist Party (CCP). This model entails a full range of industrial policies involving extensive intervention in the market such as indigenous innovation requirements, local content requirements, subsidies to state-owned enterprises (SOEs), directed lending, restrictions on export of key raw materials, and currency manipulation.[22]

The George W. Bush administration addressed the new challenges and opportunities with China by engaging with China through bilateral contacts and multilateral forums. This policy choice was reinforced by the unexpected 9/11 attacks. In the aftermath of the attacks, President Bush quickly turned to China and sought to reassure it, as it was critical to include China in the US-led global war on terror (GWOT). Illustrating this, in the "National Security Strategy of the United States of America," released in September 2002, the US made clear that the US welcomes "the emergence of a strong, peaceful and prosperous China."[23]

Still, like his predecessors, Bush Jr also faced substantial pressure from the Congress and US business to "do something about China." A close examination of the agenda of the US–China Joint Commission on Commerce and Trade (JCCT) meetings during his two terms (2000–8) shows the top three US trade concerns were the worsening trade deficit, China's undervalued currency, and China's weak record of IPR protection.[24] In March 2006, Commerce Secretary Carlos Gutierrez threatened to cancel the JCCT meeting that year if the Chinese government failed to address the issue of IPR protection for DVDs and software. The danger of anti-China legislation also loomed. In 2003 and 2006 Senators Lindsey Graham (R-SC) and Charles Schumer (D-NY) introduced legislation, which eventually failed to obtain Congressional approval, to impose an across the board 27.5 percent tariff on Chinese imports unless China allowed more flexibility in its currency, the renminbi (RMB).[25] The Obama administration inherited all three of the aforementioned issues. In 2010, 12 senators introduced the Currency Exchange Rate Oversight Reform Act of 2010 (S.3134). While the attempt failed again to make it to the finish line, in March 2013 a bipartisan group of 101 lawmakers revived the effort to pass legislation that put pressure on China to change its currency policies.[26] Though it is still controversial if China should be labeled a "currency manipulator" and if the proposed action is appropriate or effective, there is little doubt that China's currency policy is a lingering issue that remains at the top of the US–China economic agenda.

Under the Obama presidency, the direction and format of US economic policy toward China has shifted. Obama has put greater focus on monitoring China's compliance with its WTO accession commitments and settling disputes through WTO litigation.[27] Washington has become more active not only because of the changing view of trade among the populace, but also because the US business community wants China to adhere to WTO rules and all its WTO accession commitments so that it has better access to and treatment in the China market. As emphasized by Obama during his re-election campaign, "we've brought trade cases against China at nearly twice the rate as the last administration."[28] The facts show he filed eight cases against China prior to the end of his first term in office. By comparison, Bush Jr's administration had filed seven cases by the end of his second term.

The Obama administration has taken a slightly different approach from the bilateralism adopted by the Bush Jr administration by circumventing China and building closer relations with China's neighbors in the Asia-Pacific region (APR). In late 2009, United States Trade Representative (USTR), Ron Kirk, announced that the US would participate in the Trans-Pacific Partnership (TPP) negotiations with Australia, Brunei, Chile, New Zealand, Peru, Singapore, Vietnam, and Malaysia. As China, Asia's economic powerhouse and the (current) largest export destination for many TPP negotiating parties, has not figured in TPP negotiations, it has fueled speculations in both Beijing and Washington that the US is trying to "pivot" in the region at the price of China.[29] This perception was reinforced when Japan decided to postpone its trilateral free trade agreement (FTA) negotiation with Korea and China and joined the TPP negotiation in March 2013. The TPP has policy importance beyond "encircling" China. It is considered a good opportunity for the US to rewrite trade rules by providing a "twenty-first century solution" to today's cross-cutting trade challenges.[30] The TPP is expected to expand the scope of WTO rules to cover investment policy, competition policy, better IPR protection, and trade issues related to government procurement and SOEs. Eventually, China will face pressure to accept these new rules if it hopes to stay deeply involved in regional production networks.

The Obama administration's policy shift posed an unexpected shock to China and its established practices vis-à-vis Asia regionalism. China took advantage of the Bush administration's focus on the Middle East and the global war on terror to develop various regional initiatives and to enhance its trade and investment ties with its APR neighbors. Not surprisingly, China prefers an "Asia-only" Asian regionalism, which was reflected in its advocacy of ASEAN+3 (China, Korea, and Japan) and its formal launching of the Regional Comprehensive Economic Partnership (RCEP) in November 2012 at the ASEAN summit in Phnom Penh, Cambodia, with the stated goal of reaching a deal to lower trade barriers across the region by the end of 2015. China only accepted Japan's proposal of ASEAN+6 (China, Korea, Japan, Australia, New Zealand, and India) after the US committed to TPP negotiation.

It seems that, in the future, there may be a competition between two concepts of APR regionalism, one the US-centered TPP and the other China's preferred RCEP. TPP will certainly solidify the US economic presence in the region and will have a direct impact on redefining the bilateral economic relationship between the US and China. Moreover, Obama's embrace of mega-FTAs, particularly the TPP negotiation and the proposed US–EU FTA negotiation, will further weaken the legitimacy and credibility of multilateralism and the possibility to put an end to the tedious Doha negotiation. The uncertainty associated with the future of the WTO may undermine the decade-long effort of the Clinton and Bush administrations to engage China in the global economy and bind it with multilateral rules.

What are the factors that have contributed to the heightened bilateral economic tensions under Obama's presidency? First, economic relations are influenced by the overall economic policy of the government. Compared to his predecessor's stance, Obama has been more cautious towards free trade. One illustration was the delayed implementation of the Colombia, Panama, and South Korea FTAs. This partially relates to concerns among some Americans that globalization and free trade have eroded jobs and wages and hurt the US.[31] Given this, it was not surprising a 2011 Pew Research Center Poll showed that more than 53 percent of Americans supported the view that the US should get tougher with China on trade and economic issues.[32] Within this context, the Obama administration adjusted its economic policy toward China, though some things have remained the same.

Second, during Obama's presidency, the link between economic and political issues loosened. In the 1990s economic issues were tightly intertwined with sensitive political issues. For example, progress (or lack of it) in regards to China's

WTO accession negotiation directly tied to political considerations and/or unexpected events such as Taiwan's GATT accession application, the 1990–1 Gulf War, the 1989 Tiananmen Square crackdown, the accidental US bombing of the Chinese embassy in Belgrade in 1999, and human rights issues.[33] Bush Jr opted to separate economic issues from political and security ones. This policy change in part reflected the increasing importance of trade and economic issues in the overall bilateral relationship. It also indicates that without a common strategic threat (like the Soviet Union during the Cold War) or shared interest, bilateral economic tensions are more likely to escalate in the US domestic realm.

The Obama administration has reinforced the absence of a linkage. While Bush's China policy was subsumed under the strategic exigencies of the GWOT, Obama has been engaged in an economic war relating to the 2008 global financial crisis. Given China's status as an indispensable global economic player, the Obama administration gave China a crucial position in its plans to address its economic recession.[34] Today, both countries pay more attention to bilateral trade and economic ties, which they no longer subordinate to "high politics." Reflecting the separation of politics and economics, the two governments created or strengthened economic-oriented high-level channels to deal with bilateral, regional and global economic issues such as the G20 summits, Asia-Pacific Economic Cooperation (APEC) meetings, JCCT meetings, etc.[35]

Third, US–China economic relations have become increasingly competitive. The size, weight, and influence of the Chinese economy today and its effect on the US are much greater than before. The bilateral deficit with China remains a source of tension given that the Chinese market is more important than ever for US export prospects and the ability of the US to reverse its declining global competitiveness. More leading US corporations have shifted large portions of their production to China or integrated into the Asian production network and supply chains, in which China plays a critical role. In the aftermath of the global financial crisis and subsequent global downturn, the magnitude of China's economic stimulus, the bilateral structural imbalance, and China's new emphasis on industrial policy have added more pressure on the US economy.

Tensions in US–China economic relations

Although majorities in both the US and China believe that growing US–China economic ties are mutually beneficial, tensions have risen over a number of outstanding issues or new challenges. Without building a common understanding on how to address these issues in the long run, they have been and will continue to be the stumbling blocks in bilateral relations. In this section I identify the main economic issues for the US, China, and both countries.

US trade deficit

Many of the thorny issues in the bilateral relationship can be traced to the evolution of the rising US trade deficit with China. This deficit rose from about $84 billion in 2000 to a record $315 billion in 2012. Although US exports to China increased by about 47.1 percent between 2002 and 2012, the widening trade deficit has become an indicator to many Americans that the trade relationship with China is both unfair and harmful to the US economy. Since 1979, the US has accumulated trade deficits of $2.98 trillion with China.[36]

Following China's WTO accession in December 2001, expectations were high that US would sharply increase its exports to China since China was obligated to reduce tariffs and increase market access. On March 29, 2000, President Clinton stated " this is a hundred-to-nothing deal for America when it comes to the economic consequences."[37] As expected, US exports to China have more than quintupled in value, but imports from China have grown even faster. There has been a dramatic rise in the levels of non-manufactured goods (such as agricultural products, raw materials, and mined natural resource products) exported by US producers to China which has led to a US trade surplus with China in non-manufactured goods.[38] However, China's comparative advantage in manufactured goods, especially where processing trade is involved, has resulted in China's exports to the US rising more significantly than the increasing imports from the US and thus led to a widening bilateral trade imbalance. The disagreements over the size and the causes of the deficit originated from many areas of consideration, including two sides' different accounting approach (i.e., including or excluding products exported and imported via Hong Kong), the role played by multinational corporations (MNCs), including US MNCs, in Chinese exports, and the actual value added to made-in-China products.

The US trade deficit with China has been a longstanding issue in bilateral economic relations. It becomes more salient when the US experiences domestic economic troubles such as the 2008 global financial crisis. The trade deficit is directly linked to job losses in the US, with critics claiming that trade deficit with China has cost the US more than 2.7 million jobs between 2001 and 2011.[39] When the Obama administration pledged to achieve the goal of doubling US exports over the five-year period ending in 2014, this implied an increase in exports from US$1.56 trillion in 2009 to over US$3 trillion by 2014. A more assertive US economic policy toward China that reduces Chinese imports to the US or expands US imports to China is crucial to meeting this goal. Given China's role as a major assembly point in global supply chains that source components from Southeast Asia, Europe, the US, and Japan, it is unlikely the US could substantially reduce US imports from China in the near future. In any event, it is not clear this would reduce the overall US trade deficit if US buyers shift purchasing from Southeast Asian countries where Chinese low-value-added manufacturers and others currently are shifting to take advantage of lower costs.[40]

China's currency policy

It seems that the more feasible option is for the US to increase its exports to China, its fastest growing export market over the last decade. But this will require a series of domestic policy adjustments in China. The most notable one is to further appreciate its undervalued currency. An undervalued RMB has the effect of making Chinese imports cheaper and American exports to China more expensive. Therefore, in concept, a revaluation would reduce the deficit by increasing US exports to China and reducing imports from China.

China's exchange rate policy topped the Obama administration's list of bilateral economic disputes and has been discussed frequently at annual Strategic and Economic Dialogues.[41] The US government and some American economists have complained that China undervalues its currency, though there is disagreement on how undervalued it is.[42] For this camp, China's undervalued currency has fueled not only China's export boom, but also American job losses and the large US trade deficit with China.[43] Given the premise that a widening trade deficit signifies growing job losses, any currency bill introduced in the US Congress also is considered a "jobs bill." In 2010, the House voted overwhelmingly to support the bill H.R. 2378, which granted the Obama administration expanded authority to impose additional tariffs on Chinese imports to the US in retaliation for the country's refusal to significantly appreciate its currency. It later was passed by Senate in 2011 but failed to win final Congressional approval. As a policy response, China has appreciated the RMB 16 percent since June 2010. Still, many in Congress believe that the undervalued RMB continues to provide unfair trade advantage to Chinese companies.[44] In March 2013, there was a renewed attempt by Congress to introduce a similar bill. This issue will not die in Congress as long as the US needs to export its way out of slow economic recovery.

In China, many believe that RMB is close to fair value and that there is little room for its further appreciation due to China's shrinking current account surplus and trade surplus.[45] Moreover, the effect of China's currency appreciation on US export and jobs is limited and China continues to run large surpluses with America despite the appreciation of the currency over the past seven years or so. In any event, Beijing is unlikely to fully comply with US pressures given compliance does not serve its own interest and it lacks viable policy alternatives. With its current transitional political and economic system, it is too risky for China to completely open up its capital market. Furthermore, the management of its exchange rate policy has given Beijing a non-WTO regulated mechanism for practicing industrial policy. Hence, this lingering bilateral tension is most likely to continue

IPR protection in China

IPR protection has been a hot-button issue in US–China economic relations. The US International Trade Commission estimated that "firms in the US IP-intensive economy that conducted business ... in 2009 reported losses of approximately $48.2 billion in sales, royalties, or license fees due to IPR infringement in China."[46] China has remained on the US Priority Watch List and subject to Section 306 monitoring for nine consecutive years. In the three main categories of IPR issue areas, trade secrets, copyrights, and patents, China has done a relatively better job of protecting trade secrets while not doing so well in regards to enforcing copyrights and patent protection. Despite China's increased enforcement efforts, counterfeiting in China remains widespread. To illustrate, products from China accounted for 72 percent of the value of the IPR infringing products seized by US Customs in fiscal year 2012.[47]

Importantly, US concerns about weak IPR protection in China have evolved over time. From 2001 to 2008, they focused on deficiencies in China's IPR regime. Hence, the USTR annual report on China's WTO implementation emphasized the gap between China commitments and its actual implementation of those laws and regulations. On a related note, in April 2007, the US initiated dispute settlement procedures relating to deficiencies in China's legal regime for protecting and enforcing copyrights and trademarks on various products. In addition, the US requested WTO dispute settlement consultation with China concerning certain other Chinese measures affecting market access and distribution for imported publications, movies, music, and audio-visual home entertainment products (e.g., DVDs and Blu-ray discs). In November 2007, a WTO panel was created to address the US complaint. For both cases, the WTO panel ruling was largely in favor of the US claims and resulted in the regulatory changes in China to bring its domestic practice in line with its WTO commitments. In 2012 China agreed to increase market access for imported films.

Since 2008, Washington's concerns about IPR have focused on China's new industrial policy and technological policy. As the USTR noted in the *2010 National Trade Estimate Report on Foreign Trade Barriers*: "A troubling trend that has emerged ... is China's willingness to encourage domestic or indigenous innovation at the cost of foreign innovation and technologies."[48] Hence, when China tried to develop its own telecommunication standards, such as TD-SCDMA, it became very controversial and raised widespread concerns among foreign MNCs on the effect on their market share in China if they opted not to embrace Chinese standards. China's indigenous innovation policies became one of the key issues discussed at the annual bilateral high-level meetings such as JCCT. In response, at the 2012 JCCT, China reaffirmed that "technology transfer and technology cooperation are the autonomous decisions of enterprises." Another new development since 2008 has been growing US concern about online piracy in China. As of mid-2013, there are more than 500 million Internet users in China, which contributes to the increasing scale of online piracy.[49]

China has made effort to enforce IPR laws in recent years because IPR eventually will have a positive impact on its own economic development. But from the US point of view, even though Chinese courts have adjudicated many more IPR cases, violations are still pervasive. Unless there is a strong push from within, US pressure alone will not dramatically change the effectiveness of China's IPR enforcement.

WTO trade dispute settlement and litigation

One of the main reasons the US accepted China's WTO accession was to bind China. After China joined the WTO, Jagdish Bhagwati concluded that China's

WTO concessions had turned China into a "paper tiger" since "China's WTO entry will make it easier for countries to shield themselves from Chinese competition that violates international norms" and "won't have to take on Beijing all by themselves."[50] However, a decade later it seems both sides are dissatisfied with the WTO regulatory framework. Although the US has won all the WTO disputes it brought against China, many Chinese trade and investment barriers persist. Existing WTO agreements do not cover or have not been effective in addressing the most important concerns of the US business community including Chinese government subsidies, IPR protection, investment restrictions, currency manipulation, and different government tax preferences and subsidies. The deadlocked Doha negotiating round and the focus of China and the US on negotiating bilateral FTAs indicate that neither has faith in the WTO and its dispute resolution mechanism as a means to solve bilateral trade disputes.

Trade disputes with China are now widening and affecting more industries, and they are more frequently targeting China's economic policies, structure, and system.[51] A closer look at all the China-related trade disputes raised through the WTO dispute settlement process shows that most are associated with the lack of market access for US companies, not trade remedies. The main disputed areas are non-tariff barriers in the Chinese market, including industrial policy, IPR protection, and government subsidies. These are the areas where WTO rules are either controversial or implicit. They are less enforceable than more "transparent" tariffs. In the near future, it is unlikely Beijing will fundamentally change its current economic policy, structure, and system. As a result, US–China bilateral trade disputes will increase over time.

China's recent behaviors seem to show it is increasingly unsatisfied about the current state of multilateralism and is irritated by the "abuse of the rules" by other WTO members against China. Since its WTO accession, China has become the most frequent target of antidumping and countervailing investigations initiated by both developed and developing countries. The non-market economy designation has allowed WTO members to evaluate Chinese dumping cases more arbitrarily and led to less favorable results for Chinese companies.[52] Through June 2013, China has been a dispute respondent in 17 cases in the WTO and lost most of the cases. As a result of all of this, China is increasingly seeking ways to revise the rules of global economic governance in order to serve its interests and has been looking for alternative regional structures it can influence. Compared to a decade ago, China seems less committed to multilateralism and economic liberalism.[53] Similarly, the Obama administration also has adopted a number of policies to protect its domestic producers and industrial policy including new subsidies as the stimulus to its economic recovery and more trade disputes with China. That has added anxiety and distrust in the relationship.

The 2008 global financial crisis and the way forward

What can be done to reduce conflict in the US–China economic relationship and to increase cooperation? Many argue that a China more like the US is the way to go.[54] Others claim that binding China by international rules such as those of the WTO will ensure its cooperation.[55] Although neither policy seems to work, we have reason for optimism. After all, the US and China have greatly benefited from the current global economic order and globalization. As well, they share a number of common goals such as a desire for global prosperity, global financial stability, and open trade. These common interests will override their bilateral disagreements and dissatisfaction and help maintain a good working relationship. Evidence of this is US–China policy coordination at G20 to ensure a quick recovery of the global economy.

Between the 1970s and 1990s, there was a considerable gap between China and the US in the weight each country attached to the bilateral economic relationship. Relations with China rarely reached the top of the US foreign policy agenda. This asymmetry in levels of interest has narrowed in the new century because of the shift of US priorities from the Middle East and elsewhere to East Asia, the 2008 global financial crisis, the increasing economic leverage of China in global governance, and, most importantly, the relative power change of the two countries from the 1990s to the 2000s.

The global financial crisis hit both the American and Chinese economies hard with high unemployment and declining exports exerting heavy political pressure on both governments. Nevertheless, the Chinese economy suffered far less than any other major economies and gradually became the engine of global economic recovery. According to the IMF, China alone contributed to 37.4 percent of world GDP growth in 2012 while the US's share was 10.2 percent.[56] Amid the slow US economic recovery, Obama put a greater focus on trade as part of his strategy for economic growth. Increasing US exports to the Chinese market is the key to fulfilling this goal.

The financial crisis also fostered the controversial concept of G2, involving joint China–US global leadership. It has many implications such as that China is now a new superpower, that China should take more international responsibility, that China and the US have many global interest, and that the US–China relationship is becoming more positive.[57] Some American scholars also interpreted it as a strategic tactic by the Obama administration to lessen the emphasis on bilateral issues and focus more on global matters.[58] Chinese analysts seem flattered that some in the US would regard them as equal to the US, having a status above all other nations, but they seem reluctant to take on the special responsibilities or to face the resentments that such a role would entail.[59] When President Obama had his state visit in China in 2009, Premier Wen Jiabao told him that China disagreed with the G2 concept.[60] Apparently China is not ready to share world leadership, or at least global responsibility. China is not a fundamentally revisionist power which tries to overthrow the existing global order, but it is increasingly interested in modifying some of the rules in its favor. Nevertheless, the US came to recognize and China came to appreciate the fact that China now is an emerging force in world affairs following the 2008 global financial crisis. Each side saw in the other an even greater interest in partnership.

In 2005, Robert Zoellick, then US Deputy Secretary of State, famously called on China to be a "responsible stakeholder" in the international community. He argued that it was time for US policy to move from inviting China to join the "membership" of the major international institutions to urging China to be a "responsible" stakeholder in the system the US created (and dominates) but which has benefited China greatly.[61] When Washington encourages Beijing to positively contribute to the strengthening of multilateral institutions, the crux of the matter is how to get Beijing to make moves its leaders do not think are good for their country.[62] If the main challenge for the US in the next decade is to ensure that China will continue to be a status quo power, then what needs to be done? The answer is that the US needs to provide more policy space for China and allow China to have more rights, not just responsibilities, in the current global system. Though China, along with other large emerging economies such as India and Brazil, has gained more influence through the reform of the IMF and the World Bank, it still has very limited rule-making power. Since China will continue to look and behave differently in the short run, it will be a challenge for the US to learn how to coexist with a country that does not share its political system, structure, values, and ideology. However, the key for a pragmatic but effective bilateral economic relationship is to ensure China remains a satisfied status quo power in the extant global and regional economic order.

Conclusion

Expanded economic ties have brought enormous benefits to the two countries. However, in contrast to the generally supportive role played in the bilateral relations in the past, the US business community now is divided as a result of the global recession and increasing competition from China. Pressure inside the US for strong actions against China has been building and will become a more consequential factor shaping the future development of bilateral economic relations. Despite the efforts by US administrations, especially from the Bush Jr to the Obama administration, China and the US are still unclear about the goal and direction of US–China economic relations in the new century. It seems that it is difficult for each to hear or understand what the other wants.

For many China specialists, trade is a net positive because the two country's economies are complementary. Furthermore, it is believed that deepening economic relations will help balance conflicting interest in other areas such as energy competition, maritime issues, and the realms of regional and global security as well as sustain a stable bilateral relationship. However, developments over the last decade show that competitive elements are prevailing over consensual ones in current bilateral economic relations. There is a dearth of policy consensus or a shared global economic vision in regards to multilateral trade liberalization and regional economic integration. There is no easy solution to existing bilateral economic tensions. The two countries should work hard to manage, if not resolve, the conflicts ahead. The rising level of economic interdependence between the two countries could bring more anxiety, discord, and mistrust if not managed well.

Notes

1 Nicole Gaouette, "Clinton Lays Out Vision of US Power in Farewell Speech," Bloomberg, January 31, 2013. www.bloomberg.com/news/2013-01-31/clinton-lays-out-vision-of-u-s-power-in-farewell-speech.html.
2 Stephanie Condon, "Obama: 'We Welcome China's Rise,'" CBS News, January 19, 2011, www.cbsnews.com/8301-503544_162-20028958-503544.html.
3 Aaron L. Friedberg, "The Future of US–China Relations: Is Conflict Inevitable?" *International Security* 30, no. 2 (Fall 2005): 7–45; and John J. Mearsheimer, *The Tragedy of Great Power Politics* (New York: W.W. Norton, 2001).
4 For a detailed analysis of the evolution of US–China political relationship, see Chapter 2 by Jean-Marc F. Blanchard in this volume.
5 Wayne M. Morrison, *China–US Trade Issues*, report no. RL33536 (Washington, DC: Congressional Research Service, 2014).
6 "Major Foreign Holders of Treasury Securities," US Department of the Treasury, www.treasury.gov/resource-center/data-chart-center/tic/Documents/mfh.txt.
7 India and China had the fastest export growth among major traders in 2011, with shipments rising 16.1 percent and 9.3 percent. *World Trade Report 2012*, www.wto.org/english/res_e/booksp_e/anrep_e/world_trade_report12_e.pdf.
8 For detailed analysis of the process of China joining these three international economic institutions, see Harold Karan Jacobson and Michel Oksenberg, *China's Participation in the IMF, the World Bank, and GATT: Toward a Global Economic Order* (Ann Arbor: University of Michigan Press, 1990).
9 Peter Morici, "Barring Entry? China and the WTO," *Current History* (September 1997): 274–7.
10 Zong Hairen, "Zhu Rongji in 1999," *Chinese Law and Government* (January/February 2002): 42.
11 Wayne M. Morrison, *China–US Trade Issues*, report no. RL33536 (Washington, DC: Congressional Research Service, 2012).
12 For a detailed analysis of the change of US domestic trade politics toward China in 1990s, see Wei Liang, "China's WTO Accession Negotiation Process and Its Implications," *Journal of Contemporary China* 11, no. 32 (August 2002): 683–719; Gary Clyde Hufbauer and Daniel H. Rosen, *American Access to Chinese Market: The Congressional Vote on PNTR*, issue brief no. 00–3 (Washington, DC: Peter G. Peterson Institute for International Economics, 2010).
13 Morici, "Barring Entry?" 274–7.
14 Office of the United States Trade Representative, *1996 National Trade Estimate-People's Republic of China*, 1996, www.ustr.gov/archive/Document_Library/Reports_Publications/1996/1996_National_Trade_Estimate/1996_National_Trade_Estimate-People's_Republic_of_China.html.
15 David Zweig, "Sino-American Relations and Human Rights: June 4th and the Changing Nature of a Bilateral Relationship," in *Building Sino-American Relations: An Analysis for the 1990s*, ed. William T. Tow (New York: Paragon House, 1991), 57–92.
16 Steven I. Levine, "Sino-American Relations: Practicing Damage Control," in *China and the World: Chinese Foreign Policy Faces the New Millennium*, ed. Samuel S. Kim (Boulder, CO: Westview Press, 1998), 106.
17 Ibid.
18 House Committee on Banking and Financial Services, *Permanent Normal Trade Relations for China (PNTR)*, 106th Cong., 2d sess., H. Bill, May 11, 2000, http://commdocs.house.gov/committees/bank/hba64509.000/hba64509_0f.htm.
19 "China Less Dependent on Foreign Trade in 2012," *People's Daily*, February 8, 2013, http://english.peopledaily.com.cn/90778/8126375.html.
20 Christopher Alessi and Robert McMahon, "US Trade Policy," Council on Foreign Relations, March 14, 2012, www.cfr.org/trade/us-trade-policy/p17859.

21 Chad P. Bown and Rachel McCulloch, *US–Japan and US–PRC Trade Conflict: Export Growth, Reciprocity, and the International Trading System*, working paper no. 158, November 2009, www.adbi.org/workingpaper/2009/11/05/3360.us.japan.us.prc. trade.conflict/.
22 *China's Industrial Policy and Its Impact on US Companies, Workers and the American Economy*, US–China Economic and Security Review Commission, March 24, 2009, http://origin.www.uscc.gov/sites/default/files/transcripts/3.24.09HearingTranscript.pdf.
23 *National Security Strategy of the United States of America*, report (Washington, DC: White House Office of the Press Secretary, 2002), 25–8.
24 The Office of the US Trade Representative and the US Department of Commerce, *The US–China Joint Commission on Commerce and Trade (JCCT) Fact Sheet*, December 11, 2007, www.ustr.gov/sites/default/files/uploads/factsheets/2007/asset_upload_file 239_13686.pdf.
25 Bonnie S. Glaser, "US–China Relations: Discord on the Eve of the Bush–Hu Summit," *Comparative Connections* 8, no. 1 (April 2006), http://csis.org/files/media/csis/pubs/0601qus_china.pdf.
26 Doug Palmer, "Lawmakers Launched New Effort to Pass China Currency Bill," Reuters, March 20, 2013. www.reuters.com/article/2013/03/20/us-usa-congress-china-idUSBRE92J11U20130320.
27 Aaditya Mattoo, *China's Accession to the WTO: The Services Dimension* (Washington, DC: The World Bank Group, 2002).
28 Charles Riley, "Obama Hits China with Trade Complaint," *CNN*, September 17, 2012, http://money.cnn.com/2012/09/17/news/economy/obama-china-trade-autos/index.html; President Obama Speaks on Enforcing Trade Rights with China, The White House, Washington, DC, March 3, 2013, www.whitehouse.gov/photos-and-video/video/2012/03/13/president-obama-speaks-enforcing-trade-rights-china.
29 For further discussion of the pivot, with an emphasis on its political and security dimensions, see Chapter 4 by Suisheng Zhao in this volume.
30 Kevin Brady, "Outlook for US Trade Policy for 2012–13" (speech). the Peter G. Peterson Institute for International Economics, Washington, DC, June 19, 2012.
31 Sara Murray and Douglas Belkin, "Americans Sour on Trade," *Wall Street Journal*, October 2, 2010.
32 "Strengthen Ties with China, but Get Tough on Trade," Pew Research Center for the People and the Press, January 12, 2011, www.people-press.org/2011/01/12/strengthen-ties-with-china-but-get-tough-on-trade/.
33 For a detailed overview of the process of US–China bilateral negotiations on China's GATT/WTO accession, see Wei Liang, "China's WTO Accession Negotiation Process and Its Implications."
34 Kerry Dumbaugh, *China–US Relations: Current Issues and Implications for US Policy*, report no. R40457 (Washington, DC: Congressional Research Service, 2009).
35 Wei Huang, "Global Governance under the G20: A Chinese Perspective," in *G20: Perceptions and Perspectives for Global Governance*, ed. Wilhelm Hofmeister (Singapore: Konrad-Adenauer-Stiftung, 2011).
36 "The Monthly Summary of US–China Trade," US–China Economic and Security Review Commission, February 8, 2013, http://origin.www.uscc.gov/sites/default/files/Research/Monthly(Dec)USCCtradereport_2–11–13.pdf.
37 Washington File, "Transcript: Clinton March 29 Comments on US–China Relations," Federation of American Scientists, March 30, 2000, http://fas.org/news/china/2000/000329-PRC–USia1.htm.
38 Joseph Casey, *Patterns in US–China Trade since China's Accession to the World Trade Organization*, report (Washington, DC: US–China Economic and Security Review Commission, 2012).
39 Robert E. Scott, *The China Toll*, report, August 23, 2012, www.epi.org/publication/bp345-china-growing-trade-deficit-cost/.

40 Ding Qingfen and Qiu Quanlin, "Higher Costs Forcing Firms to Relocate," *China Daily*, October 21, 2012. www.chinadaily.com.cn/china/2012–10/21/content_1583 4915.htm.
41 For more on dialogues, see Chapter 9 by Robert Sutter in this volume.
42 Paul Krugman, "Taking on China," *New York Times*, March 15, 2010; and Wayne M. Morrison and Marc Labonte, *China's Currency: An Analysis of the Economic Issues*, report no. RS21625 (Washington, DC: Congressional Research Service, 2011).
43 Fred Bergsten and Joseph Gagnon, *Currency Manipulation, the US Economy, and the Global Economic Order*, issue brief no. 12–25 (Washington, DC: Peter G. Peterson Institute for International Economics, 2012).
44 Doug Palmer, "Lawmakers Launched New Effort to Pass China Currency Bill," Reuters, March 20, 2013. www.reuters.com/article/2013/03/20/us-usa-congress-china-idUSBRE92J11U20130320.
45 Yiping Huang, "Krugman's Chinese Currency Fallacy," *East Asia Forum*, March 15, 2010, www.eastasiaforum.org/2010/03/15/krugmans-chinese-renminbi-fallacy/.
46 *China: Effects of Intellectual Property Infringement and Indigenous Innovation Policies on the US Economy*, publication no. 4226 (Washington, DC: US International Trade Commission, 2011), xiv.
47 USTR, *Special 301 Report*, report, May 2013, 36, www.ustr.gov/sites/default/files/05012013 percent202013 percent20Special percent20301 percent20Report.pdf.
48 USTR, *National Trade Estimate Report on Foreign Trade Barriers*, report, 2010, www.ustr.gov/sites/default/files/uploads/reports/2010/NTE/2010_NTE_China_final.pdf.
49 USTR, *Special 301 Report*, 36.
50 Jagdish N. Bhagwati, " Why China Is a Paper Tiger," Council on Foreign Relations, February 19, 2002, www.cfr.org/publication/4351/why_china_is_a_paper_tiger.html.
51 Xinquan Tu, "China Must Strive to Improve WTO rules," *People's Daily*, January 10, 2013, www.chinadaily.com.cn/cndy/2013–01/10/content_16100720.htm.
52 Ka Zeng and Wei Liang, "US Antidumping Actions against China: The Impact of China's Entry into the WTO," *Review of International Political Economy* 17, no. 3 (August 2010): 562–88.
53 The quote from Yongtu Long appears in Scott Kennedy and Fan He, *The United States, China and Global Governance: A New Agenda for a New Era* (Beijing: Rongda Quick Printing, 2013), 9.
54 John Bussey, "Trying to Make China More Like Us," *Wall Street Journal*, March 22, 2012.
55 A. Iain Johnston, *Social States: China in International Institutions, 1980–2000* (Princeton, NJ: Princeton Unviersity Press, 2007).
56 "Absent Friends: World Economic Growth Is Originating Almost Exclusively from the Emerging World," *The Economist*, January 24, 2012.
57 Yan Xuetong, "The Instability of China–US Relations," *Chinese Journal of International Politics* 3, (2010): 263–92; and C. Fred Bergsten, "A Partnership of Equals: How Washington Should Respond to China's Economic Challenge," *Foreign Affairs* 97, no. 4 (July/August 2008): 57–69.
58 Charles Freeman, "The Ambiguous Nature of the US–China Relationship," *East Asia Forum*, February 7, 2011.
59 Harry Harding, "The G-2 Chimera: Fusion or Illusion?" ("G2 at GW": The Second Conference on China's Economic Development and US–China Economic Relations, George Washington University, Washington, DC, November 20, 2009).
60 "Wen Jiabao: China Disagrees to So-called G2," *China Today*, November 19, 2009, www.chinatoday.com.cn/ctenglish/se/txt/2009–11/19/content_230354.htm.
61 Robert B. Zoellick, "Whither China: From Membership to Responsibility?" *NBR Analysis* 16, no. 4 (December 2005): 5–15. Responsible stakeholders work to protect and strengthen the international system.

62 Helene Cooper, "Asking China to Act like the US," *New York Times*, November 27, 2010. www.nytimes.com/2010/11/28/weekinreview/28cooper.html?pagewanted=all &_r=0.

References

"Absent Friends: World Economic Growth Is Originating Almost Exclusively from the Emerging World." *The Economist*, January 24, 2012.

Alessi, Christopher, and Robert McMahon. "US Trade Policy." Council on Foreign Relations. March 14, 2012. www.cfr.org/trade/us-trade-policy/p17859.

Bergsten, Fred. "A Partnership of Equals: How Washington Should Respond to China's Economic Challenge." *Foreign Affairs* 97, no. 4 (July/August 2008): 57–69.

Bergsten, Fred, and Joseph Gagnon. *Currency Manipulation, the US Economy, and the Global Economic Order*. Issue brief no. 12–25 (Washington, DC: Peter G. Peterson Institute for International Economics, 2012).

Bhagwati, Jagdish N. "Why China Is a Paper Tiger." Council on Foreign Relations. February 19, 2002. www.cfr.org/publication/4351/why_china_is_a_paper_tiger.html.

Bown, Chad P., and Rachel McCulloch. *US–Japan and US–PRC Trade Conflict: Export Growth, Reciprocity, and the International Trading System*. Working paper no. 158. November 2009. www.adbi.org/files/2009.11.06.wp158.us.japan.us.prc.trade.conflict.pdf.

Brady, Kevin. "Outlook for US Trade Policy for 2012–13" (speech). The Peter G. Peterson Institute for International Economics, Washington, DC, June 19, 2012.

Bussey, John. "Trying to Make China More Like Us." *Wall Street Journal*, March 22, 2012.

Casey, Joseph. *Patterns in US–China Trade since China's Accession to the World Trade Organization*. Report (Washington, DC: US–China Economic and Security Review Commission, 2012).

"China Less Dependent on Foreign Trade in 2012." *People's Daily*. February 8, 2013. http://english.peopledaily.com.cn/90778/8126375.html.

Condon, Stephanie. "We Welcome China's Rise." CBS News. January 19, 2011. www.cbsnews.com/8301-503544_162-20028958-503544.html.

Cooper, Helene. "The Trouble with Asking China to Act Like the US." *New York Times*. November 27, 2010. www.nytimes.com/2010/11/28/weekinreview/28cooper.html?pagewanted=all&_r=0.

Ding, Qingfen, and Quanlin Qiu. "Higher Costs Forcing Firms to Relocate." *China Daily*. October 21, 2012. www.chinadaily.com.cn/china/2012–10/21/content_15834915.htm.

Dumbaugh, Kerry. *China–US Relations: Current Issues and Implications for US Policy*. Report no. R40457 (Washington, DC: Congressional Research Service, 2009).

Freeman, Charles. "The Ambiguous Nature of the US–China Relationship." *East Asia Forum*, February 7, 2011.

Friedberg, Aaron L. "The Future of US–China Relations: Is Conflict Inevitable?" *International Security* 30, no. 2 (Fall 2005): 7–45.

Gaouette, Nicole. "Clinton Lays Out Vision of US Power in Farewell Speech." Bloomberg. January 31, 2013. www.bloomberg.com/news/2013-01-31/clinton-lays-out-vision-of-u-s-power-in-farewell-speech.html.

Glaser, Bonnie S. "US–China Relations: Discord on the Eve of the Bush-Hu Summit." *Comparative Connections* 8, no. 1 (April 2006). http://csis.org/files/media/csis/pubs/0601qus_china.pdf.

Harding, Harry. "The G-2 Chimera: Fusion or Illusion?" Speech at "G2 at GW": The Second Conference on China's Economic Development and US–China Economic Relations, George Washington University, Washington, DC, November 20, 2009.

Huang, Wei. "Global Governance Under the G20: A Chinese Perspective," in *G20: Perceptions and Perspectives for Global Governance*, ed. Wilhelm Hofmeister (Singapore: Konrad-Adenauer-Stiftung, 2011), 41–9.

Huang, Yiping. "Krugman's Chinese Renminbi Fallacy." *East Asia Forum*. March 15, 2010. www.eastasiaforum.org/2010/03/15/krugmans-chinese-renminbi-fallacy/.

Jacobson, Harold K., and Michel Oksenberg. *China's Participation in the IMF, the World Bank, and GATT: Toward a Global Economic Order* (Ann Arbor: University of Michigan Press, 1990).

Johnston, A. Iain. *Social States: China in International Institutions, 1980–2000* (Princeton, NJ: Princeton University Press, 2008).

Kennedy, Scott, and Fan He. *The United States, China and Global Governance: A New Agenda for a New Era* (Beijing: Rongda Quick Printing, 2013).

Krugman, Paul. "Taking on China." *New York Times*, March 15, 2010.

Levine, Steven I. "Sino-American Relations: Practicing Damage Control," in *China and the World: Chinese Foreign Policy Faces the New Millennium*, ed. Samuel S. Kim (Boulder, CO: Westview Press, 1998), 91–113.

Liang, Wei. "China's WTO Accession Negotiation Process and Its Implications." *Journal of Contemporary China* 11, no. 32 (August 2002): 638–719.

Mattoo, Aaditya. *China's Accession to the WTO: The Services Dimension* (Washington, DC: World Bank Group, 2002).

Mearsheimer, John J. *The Tragedy of Great Power Politics* (New York: W.W. Norton, 2001).

Morici, Peter. "Barring Entry? China and the WTO." *Current History* (September 1997): 274–7.

Morrison, Wayne M. *China–US Trade Issues*. Report no. RL33536 (Washington, DC: Congressional Research Service, 2012).

Morrison, Wayne M., and Marc Labonte. *China's Currency: An Analysis of the Economic Issues*. Report no. RS21625 (Washington, DC: Congressional Research Service, 2011).

Murray, Sara, and Douglas Belkin. "Americans Sour on Trade." *Wall Street Journal*, October 2, 2010.

Palmer, Doug. "Lawmakers Launch New Effort to Pass China Currency Bill." Reuters. March 20, 2013. www.reuters.com/article/2013/03/20/us-usa-congress-china-idUSBRE92J11U20130320.

Pew Research Center for the People and the Press. "Strengthen Ties with China, but Get Tough on Trade." January 12, 2011. www.people-press.org/2011/01/12/strengthen-ties-with-china-but-get-tough-on-trade/.

Riley, Charles. "Obama Hits China with Trade Complaint on Autos." *CNN*. September 17, 2012. http://money.cnn.com/2012/09/17/news/economy/obama-china-trade-autos/index.html.

Rosen, Daniel H. *American Access to Chinese Market: The Congressional Vote on PNTR*. Issue brief no. 00-3 (Washington, DC: Peter G. Peterson Institute for International Economics, 2000).

Scott, Robert E. *The China Toll*. Report. August 23, 2012. www.epi.org/publication/bp345-china-growing-trade-deficit-cost/.

Tu, Xinquan. "China Must Strive to Improve WTO Rules." *China Daily*. January 10, 2013. www.chinadaily.com.cn/cndy/2013-01/10/content_16100720.htm.

United States, Department of the Treasury. "Major Foreign Holders of Treasury Securities." www.treasury.gov/resource-center/data-chart-center/tic/Documents/mfh.txt.

United States, House of Representatives, Committee on Banking and Financial Services. *Permanent Normal Trade Relations for China (PNTR)*. 106th Cong., 2d sess. H. Bill. May 11, 2000. http://commdocs.house.gov/committees/bank/hba64509.000/hba64509_0f.htm.

United States, Office of the United States Trade Representative. *1996 National Trade Estimate-People's Republic of China*. Report. 1996. www.ustr.gov/archive/Document_Library/Reports_Publications/1996/1996_National_Trade_Estimate/1996_National_Trade_Estimate-People's_Republic_of_China.html.

United States, Office of the United States Trade Representative, *2013 Special 301 Report*. May 2013. www.ustr.gov/sites/default/files/05012013 percent202013percent20Special percent20301percent20Report.pdf.

United States, International Trade Commission, *China: Effects of Intellectual Property Infringement and Indigenous Innovation Policies on the US Economy*. Publication no. 4226 (Washington, DC: US International Trade Commission, 2011).

United States, Office of the United States Trade Representative. *National Trade Estimate Report on Foreign Trade Barriers*. Report. 2010. www.ustr.gov/sites/default/files/uploads/reports/2010/NTE/2010_NTE_China_final.pdf.

United States, Office of the United States Trade Representative and the US Department of Commerce. *The US–China Joint Commission on Commerce and Trade (JCCT) Fact Sheet*. Report. December 11, 2007. www.ustr.gov/sites/default/files/uploads/factsheets/2007/asset_upload_file239_13686.pdf.

United States, The White House, *National Security Strategy of the United States of America*. Report (Washington, DC: Office of the Press Secretary, 2002).

United States, The White House. "President Obama Speaks on Enforcing Trade Rights with China." March 3, 2013. www.whitehouse.gov/photos-and-video/video/2012/03/13/president-obama-speaks-enforcing-trade-rights-china.

United States, US–China Economic and Security Review Commission. "China's Industrial Policy and Its Impact on US Companies, Workers and the American Economy." March 24, 2009. http://origin.www.uscc.gov/sites/default/files/transcripts/3.24.09HearingTranscript.pdf.

United States, US–China Economic and Security Review Commission. "The Monthly Summary of US–China Trade." February 8, 2013. http://origin.www.uscc.gov/sites/default/files/Research/Monthly(Dec)USCCtradereport_2–11–13.pdf.

Washington File. "Transcript: Clinton March 29 Comments on US–China Relations." Federation of American Scientists. March 30, 2000. http://fas.org/news/china/2000/000329-PRC–USia1.htm.

"Wen Jiabao: China Disagrees to So-called G2." *China Today*. November 19, 2009. www.chinatoday.com.cn/ctenglish/se/txt/2009–11/19/content_230354.htm.

World Trade Report 2012. Report. 2012. www.wto.org/english/res_e/booksp_e/anrep_e/world_trade_report12_e.pdf.

Yan, Xuetong. "The Instability of China–US Relations." *Chinese Journal of International Politics* 3 (2010): 263–92.

Zeng, Ka, and Wei Liang. "US Antidumping Actions against China: The Impact of China's Entry into the WTO." *Review of International Political Economy* 17, no. 3 (August 2010): 562–88.

Zoellick, Robert B. "Whither China: From Membership to Responsibility?" *NBR Analysis* 16, no. 4 (December 2005): 5–15.

Zong Hairen. "Zhu Rongji in 1999," translated in *Chinese Law and Government* (January/February 2002): 36–52.

Zweig, David. "Sino-American Relations and Human Rights: June 4th and the Changing Nature of a Bilateral Relationship," in *Building Sino-American Relations: An Analysis for the 1990s*, ed. William T. Tow (New York: Paragon House, 1991): 57–92.

8 US–China relations in Asia-Pacific energy regime complexes

Cooperative, complementary, and competitive

Gaye Christoffersen

Introduction

United States–China energy relations three decades ago began with a narrow focus and limited stakeholders in a relationship that was essentially cooperative. Since then, numerous groups have become involved in the bilateral energy/environmental relationship building on the original cooperative framework, generating multiple channels of energy relations, both cooperative and competitive.

The key driver of increased US–China competition was Beijing's securitization of its dependence on oil imports, the bureaucracy's inability to control domestic energy demand, and domestic electricity shortages. Chinese analysts indicate securitization happened in 2000 when Chinese oil imports dramatically increased – 37 million metric tons (MMT) in 1999 to 72 MMT in 2000, while world oil prices tripled during that period.[1] An American analyst focuses on the energy crisis of 2003–4 which she argues had domestic determinants but nevertheless led to Beijing's concern with external threats to China's oil supply.[2] Some analysts believe the Chinese national oil company (NOC) might have promoted securitization to deflect domestic criticism of their investment strategies.[3] American analysis portrayed China's global search for oil as leading to US–China competition for scarce oil resources.[4] In the 2000s, securitization led to energy security rising to the top of the Chinese policy agenda.

Securitization of energy was reinforced with the linking of energy security to maritime security. Some Chinese analysts pinpoint Chinese securitization of energy to then President Hu Jintao's December 2003 reference to China's "*Malacca Strait wilemma*," i.e., China's dependence on the sea lines of communication (SLOC) from the Middle East for its oil supply which transit the Malacca Strait, a major choke point. The US has been the guarantor of SLOC security on which China depends. Chinese vulnerability was much discussed by Chinese and American analysts, exacerbating perceptions of an adversarial relationship.[5] The energy–maritime nexus has been a source of tension although it could have been a vehicle for collaboration in jointly guarding the SLOCs.[6] When US Admiral Michael Mullen in 2006 proposed Chinese participation in a "thousand-ship navy" global maritime partnership jointly protecting SLOCs, Beijing's response was ambiguous but not negative.

Chinese and American scholars are divided over whether cooperation is possible as competition increases. Different authors place more emphasis on one or the other, with some recognizing a mix of cooperation and competition.[7] One Chinese energy analyst has tried to explain US–China energy relations as a condition of simultaneous conflict and cooperation, with US–China competition in upstream oil development, a struggle over oil resources governed by the theoretical perspective of realism, and US–China cooperation in energy efficiency following the logic of interdependence.[8]

Cooperation occurs when there is a shared awareness of a common security interest, often called "win–win" by the Chinese. Competition occurs when either one side or both sides perceive a zero-sum situation. There are many additional situations when one side or the other is not clear on whether there are common security interests. This requires additional concepts beyond cooperation or competition.

Instead of placing US–China energy relations into rigid categories of cooperation or competition, a Chinese scholar has offered a framework that places bilateral interests in a wider array of common, complementary, conflicting, and confrontational categories, identifying different functional issues within each category.[9] Adapting this framework to energy relations provides a useful way of thinking about energy interests that are complementary, neither overtly cooperative nor confrontational, but rather moving in a parallel direction, a form of parallelism that exists simultaneously with cooperation and competition.[10] Many of the US energy initiatives in the Asia-Pacific Region (APR) have been complementary to China's energy interests, within which Chinese participate with varying degrees of enthusiasm.

Parallelism is found in US–China maritime cooperation, where since 2009 there has been parallel behavior in the Gulf of Aden fighting piracy that went through stages of increased cooperation as the Chinese learned to cooperate.[11] US–China overt cooperation did not happen until September 2012, when the US and China held their first joint anti-piracy exercise in the Gulf of Aden.[12]

A major source of contention in US–China energy relations is China's "going out" strategy, which has focused on the physical control of global oil and gas resources, threatening to close off these resources to the world oil market. American analysts have warned that Chinese acquisition of foreign oil supply, Chinese purchase of equity shares in overseas oil resources, was part of a grand strategy that would inevitably lead to US–China conflict.[13] The Chinese believe the US has too much control over the world oil market. Some Chinese would like to restructure global energy governance, creating a global energy regime according to Chinese rules rather than those created by the International Energy Agency (IEA). Despite differences, both countries have a shared interest in stability and could cooperate in constructing a producer–consumer dialog that would stabilize the market.

China has been attempting to form alternative East Asian energy regimes that exclude the US. At present, however, most Chinese initiatives for East Asian energy regimes seem uncertain. In Northeast Asia, the possibility of a China–Japan–South Korea framework that included energy, which appeared promising when agreements were signed in May 2012, faded due to maritime territorial conflicts in the East China Sea (ECS) during 2012. In Southeast Asia, the possibility of an energy regime based on ASEAN+3 faded as maritime territorial conflicts in the South China Sea (SCS) intensified. In both cases, these conflicts were driven by China, Japan, and Southeast Asia's competition for maritime energy resources.

APR energy initiatives have emerged in "energy regime complexes," defined as a mix of formal international institutions and informal networks, a patchwork of loosely linked, overlapping institutions, bilateral, minilateral, and multilateral.[14] The idea of a regime complex was suggested several decades ago as a way of thinking about regime formation based on clusters of initiatives that functioned as a regime without being fully established as a unified and fully institutionalized organization.[15]

US–China loose coordination, parallelism, is more likely to occur within a regime complex while more overt cooperation would be expected in a more institutionalized regime. This chapter will examine the patterns of US–China cooperation, competition, and parallelism in energy relations.

Pattern of cooperation[16]

The pattern of US–China cooperation began after the US Department of Energy (DOE) was created in 1977. The first Secretary of Energy, James Schlesinger, traveled to Beijing in October 1978 with a team of technical experts. Schlesinger hoped to open China to oil and gas exploration by American oil companies.[17] The Chinese Ministry of Petroleum Industry had in 1969 discovered offshore oil resources that it could not exploit with its existing technology. Deng Xiaoping and Jimmy Carter signed the "Agreement on Cooperation in Science and Technology" in January 1979. As a consequence of these developments, the US DOE and American oil companies became the initial stakeholders in US–China energy relations during the 1980s and public–private partnerships the vehicle for cooperation.

In 1987, several protocols were signed including one for a bilateral project on fossil fuels and climate change. In 1988, Lawrence Berkeley Laboratory created a bilateral project with the Chinese Energy Research Institute (ERI) of the State Planning Commission (SPC) on energy conservation.[18] The next year, the Tiananmen crackdown led to US government sanctions on China, leaving state-to-state relations contentious, and bilateral energy relations carried on by commercial interests, technical specialists, and other non-governmental entities. For example, in 1993, a non-profit, non-governmental organization (NGO), the Beijing Energy Efficiency Center, was created with funding from DOE and assistance from China's ERI, Lawrence Berkeley Laboratory, Battelle-Pacific Northwest National Laboratory and an environmental group, the World Wildlife Fund.[19]

By 1995, government-to-government energy relations were revived when DOE Secretary Hazel O'Leary led a mission to China that included government, industry, and environmental civil society organizations, following a DOE-initiated memorandum of understanding with the SPC. The mission concluded both governmental and commercial agreements that included energy efficiency and climate change. One of the agreements gave birth to the US–China Oil and Gas Industry Forum, a public–private partnership. The DOE and Enron lobbied for China to reduce oil imports by expanding natural gas production and the DOE offered technical assistance. The DOE also initiated a forum that met in April 1996, the US–China Forum on Sustainable Development, Energy, and the Environment. Additional agreements signed between the DOE and SPC strengthened the connection between energy and environment, and the May 1997 forum meeting in Beijing institutionalized the energy/environment connection. The DOE had formed teams drawn from government, industry, and NGOs to examine 10 energy areas. A forum working group, the US–China Energy Policy Working Group, met in May 1997 in Washington.[20]

In January 1997, it was proposed that the Academies of Sciences and Engineering in China and the US form a Committee on Cooperation in the Energy Futures of China and the United States, which by its very name implied that Chinese and American energy futures were linked as they faced common challenges of increasing oil import dependence, health problems from energy-related emissions, and economic barriers to deploying clean, efficient energy technologies. A primary recommendation of the committee was to find ways to better institutionalize various initiatives into a long-term cooperative program that would sustain the two countries' energy cooperation.[21] During 1997, the number of stakeholders continued to expand. To illustrate, Tsinghua University opened an Energy and Environmental Center, jointly operated by DOE and Tulane University on the American side, and Tsinghua University and the State Science and Technology Commission on the Chinese side.

In 1998, the US Departments of Energy and Commerce and the Chinese National Development and Reform Commission (NDRC) created the US–China Oil and Gas Industry Forum as a public–private partnership which met in July 1999 at the Baker Institute, Rice University, and continued to meet thereafter with representation from the DOE and the NDRC.

The George W. Bush administration's approach to US–China energy relations began with DOE Secretary Spencer Abraham discussing several energy projects with the Chinese Ambassador Yang Jiechi. The following day, April 1, 2001, the EP-3 crisis interrupted the energy dialog but it still resumed a few months later. Although these projects were kept at the DOE–NDRC level, rather than the level of government leaders, it indicated a degree of institutionalization that could withstand political ups and downs. In 2002, Bush Jr promoted energy and environmental cooperation with China during his visit to Beijing.

Despite Chinese securitization of oil import dependence, some Chinese, such as Xia Liping, argued that the US and China had common interests – maintaining the security of SLOCs to transport oil from the Middle East. Furthermore, both needed a stable world oil market, which they could create within a multilateral framework in cooperation with other net oil importers.[22]

Chinese President Hu requested a US–China Strategic Dialogue in November 2004. The first US–China Energy Policy Dialogue between the US's DOE and China's NDRC took place immediately following the sixth US–China Oil and Gas Industry Forum in June 2005.[23] This type of piggybacking on existing mechanisms is part of the pattern. The Energy Policy Dialogue built on numerous existing cooperative projects.

In September 2005, when Robert Zoellick, US Deputy Secretary of State, asked China to be a responsible stakeholder in the international system, this included working with the US in the newly created Asia-Pacific Partnership on Clean Development and Climate, working with the IEA to build strategic petroleum reserves (SPRs), and within the newly created US–China Energy Policy Dialogue.[24] Zoellick was asking China to participate in the Western-created global energy governance framework.

The seventh US–China Oil and Gas Industry Forum in September 2006 discussed strategic petroleum reserves, and was immediately followed by the second US–China Energy Policy Dialogue, which discussed China's participation in IEA programs although it was not a member of IEA because it did not have the requisite SPR. In December 2006, China hosted the Five-Country Energy Ministerial, an initiative to coordinate on SPRs between China, the US, Japan, India, and South Korea. The Five-Country Energy Ministerial met again in 2008.

The fourth US–China Strategic Economic Dialogue (SED) that met on June 17–18, 2008, produced a joint statement that committed the US–China bilateral dialog to adhere to "energy security principles embraced at the Five-Country Energy Ministerial June 7, 2008 and the *Joint Statement of Energy Ministers by the G8 Plus 3* on June 8, 2008."[25] The SED meeting produced the US–China Ten Year Energy and Environment Cooperation Framework. The framework made three breakthroughs: (1) the reduction of barriers to clean energy technology transfer; (2) the creation of several government-facilitated eco-partnerships that will deepen the institutionalization of energy cooperation; and (3) a potential for working collaboratively on emissions reductions.[26]

The pattern of US–China cooperation based on technology transfer to China had begun in the 1970s. At the fourth US–China Energy Policy Dialogue that met in September 2009, Zhang Guobao, head of China's National Energy Administration (NEA), acknowledged that technology transfer was the glue that held US–China energy cooperation together. Zhang noted that of all the energy issues the US and China discussed, clean energy came the closest to being a common interest, a basis for cooperation. Shale gas technology was another area as China by itself had not developed technologies that were commercially viable.[27] The US was leading a shale gas revolution that promised to make the US energy self-sufficient in the near future. Through technology transfer, China might also achieve greater energy self-sufficiency.

By 2011, the US DOE and China's NDRC had guided several decades of fruitful US–China energy cooperation, much of it involving technology transfer to China. Their collaboration had weathered political tensions, operating somewhat autonomously from the ongoing political crises that beset US–China relations.

However, both sides would decide to reorganize their energy bureaucracies due to increasing emphasis on climate change, clean energy, and the Chinese NOCs' going-out strategy and avoidance of dependence on oil markets, all of which required new institutions in which to collaborate.

US–China parallelism

US–China energy parallelism takes place in Asia-Pacific multilateral organizations where both countries are participating members who might frequently disagree, and they often move in parallel directions while not necessarily closely cooperating with each other.

The pattern of US–China parallelism was evident in the Asia-Pacific Economic Cooperation (APEC) organization since the time that China joined in 1991. The US and China cooperated within APEC's Energy Working Group. Yet, the US had promoted trade liberalization, which China resisted, instead promoting an alternative APEC goal, economic and technological cooperation, the ECOTECH agenda. In the past two decades, APEC has been an arena for these competing agendas. The lessons from APEC are that cooperation with China is easier when there is technology transfer. Trade liberalization, initiatives to open Chinese markets, meet resistance.

The US initiated the Asia-Pacific Partnership on Clean Development and Climate (APP) at an ASEAN Regional Forum meeting. Launched in January 2006, the APP was a project for transferring clean energy technologies whose member countries would act in accordance with the principles of the UN Framework Convention on Climate Change.[28] The APP had eight public–private task forces chaired by member countries with projects that would be invested in by the private sector. Partner countries included Japan, Canada, Australia, India, China, and South Korea. The APP is an example of US–China bilateral energy relations within an energy regime complex where there was cooperation on clean energy technology transfer but US–China differences on climate change.

Although the US DOE had had decades of cooperation with China, it also had extensive criticism regarding Chinese energy practices: it did not like China's limitations on the commercialization of energy resources, its extensive reliance on state level agreements rather than market relations, its provision of energy subsidies to state-owned enterprises, and its slowness in creating an SPR.[29]

China, as the second largest emitter of greenhouse gases, received renewed US attention, culminating with a bill put before the US House of Representatives in August 2007, called the US–China Energy Cooperation Act, part of a larger package, the US–China Competitiveness Agenda of 2007. The US–China Energy Cooperation Act was tasked with funding joint research on energy efficiency technologies and renewable energy sources, and joint energy education programs.

APP's functions reflect US policy preferences for energy security: human and institutional capacity-building in developing countries, engaging the private sector and civil society organizations, implementing work programs with benchmarks to ensure initiatives move beyond the declaratory stage, and integrating existing bilateral and regional initiatives in an effort to form an energy regime complex.[30]

The APP joined the Asian Development Bank (ADB) and the United States Agency for International Development (USAID) in the Asia Clean Energy Forum, which first met in 2006. At the forum, the ADB, ASEAN, APEC, and APP presented their energy initiatives. USAID presented its program, launched in October 2006, the ECO-Asia Clean Development and Climate Change Program, created for climate change mitigation in Asia, building Asian government capacity, leveraging private sector participation in clean energy technology, and promoting regional cooperation.[31]

The US was somewhat concerned that Japan-led East Asian energy initiatives might displace US-led Asia-Pacific energy initiatives, and was concerned Tokyo might be using the East Asian Summit in energy projects that overlapped with the APP. The US and Japan met on January 9, 2007, to review their energy cooperation and sort out which energy regimes were primary. The two allies confirmed that they cooperate through the APP, APEC's Energy Working Group, the IEA, and the International Energy Forum. They also agreed to engage China and India in these multilateral regimes.[32]

China's first white paper on energy, *China's Energy Conditions and Policies*, issued December 2007, was meant to strengthen Chinese capacity for more effective Chinese participation in multilateral energy regimes.[33] The white paper claimed China would make positive contributions to world oil security rather than pose a threat to it, stressing that China was an "active participant in international energy cooperation" and a participant in the APP.

The APP seemed as though it had potential to coordinate the APR's more than 90 initiatives into a coherent regional energy architecture. The APP emphasized that it was building on existing bilateral and multilateral initiatives with APP task forces meeting periodically and presenting progress reports on their work. The seventh meeting of the Policy and Implementation Committee met in Australia in May 2009, where China's country statement presented Beijing's achievements: a Department of Climate Change under the NDRC created in 2008, and a white paper, *China's Policies and Actions for Addressing Climate Change*, published in October 2008. The statement also mentioned that the NDRC had endorsed eight China–US bilateral cooperation projects under APP, related to building energy efficiency, cleaner fossil energy, renewable energy, and energy efficiency in some energy-intensive industrial sectors – steel, cement, and aluminum.[34]

Barack Obama's inauguration in 2009 did not create an abrupt shift in US–China energy relations, which had historically been insulated from political relations. However, in 2010, the APP Policy Implementation Committee, chaired by the US, had decided it could formally wind up the APP and shift successful APP projects to other international regimes, which it did in April 2011. China was one of the participants that indicated interest in continuing to participate in such task forces as the APP Energy Regulatory and Market Development Forum. This forum dissolved and was reconfigured as the Asia-Pacific Energy Regulatory

Forum (APER Forum) whose members included all the APP countries.[35] The forum's function is to share information on regulatory practices amongst member countries. The August 2012 meeting of APER Forum included Chinese participation from the China State Electricity Regulatory Commission.[36] Although APP itself was concluded, it was successful in spawning further networks of cooperation in the APR in new organizations.

The US and China had agreed, at the May 2012 S&ED meeting, to participate as "partners" in the August 2012 APER Forum, an indication of a more overt cooperative partnership than had been apparent in APP during its existence from 2006 to 2011. This appears to be one outcome of parallelism – the formation of partnerships after a period of moving in the same direction with an evolving sense of complementarity, which gradually culminates in an awareness of common security.

The APER Forum Work Plan 2012–14, its first work plan, had three areas of focus: transitioning to a low-carbon economy, energy infrastructure and market regulatory arrangements, and competition reform. The priority of the plan was to create a common understanding of the rules for how energy markets should operate.[37] The role of energy markets has been an ongoing contentious issue in US–China relations.

Although APP has concluded, it was an empirical example of an energy regime complex, a linking of numerous existing bilateral and multilateral regional initiatives that transferred energy technology to China. As an energy regime complex, the APP demonstrated flexibility to evolve, expand, spin off new initiatives, and then to conclude. This kind of flexibility and fluidity appears to be the advantage of a regime complex rather than a more institutionalized energy regime. During the five years of APP's existence, the US and China evolved from having complementary interests in clean energy to becoming partners in the APER Forum. The APER Forum would focus on the harder issue of market rules.

The Obama administration's rebalancing towards Asia, covered in several of the other chapters in this book, translated into greater US participation in regional energy initiatives.[38] In 2012 the APEC tenth Energy Ministerial Meeting (EMM10) instructed the Energy Working Group to review the APEC region's energy markets, in particular to increase the role of natural gas, in order to expand natural gas trade and production to assist the transition to a low-carbon economy in the region.[39]

The idea of linking the numerous Asia-Pacific energy-related organizations, a regime complex, was furthered at the East Asia Summit (EAS). Obama partnered with Brunei and Indonesia to propose the US–Asia-Pacific Comprehensive Partnership for a Sustainable Energy at the EAS held in Cambodia in November 2012, later called the US–Asia-Pacific Comprehensive Energy Partnership (USACEP). Brunei chaired the EAS in 2013 and Indonesia was chair in 2014, allowing for at least three years of continuity in implementing and institutionalizing the partnership's goals. The East Asian Summit Energy Cooperation Task Force was created in 2013 for implementing USACEP renewable energy projects.

USACEP, as a regime complex, will integrate numerous existing energy initiatives, including the APEC Energy Working Group, the East Asian Summit Energy Ministers initiative, the ASEAN–US Energy Cooperation Work Plan, and various other regional energy initiatives. US support for USACEP would be $6 billion through the US Export–Import Bank, $5 billion in export credit financing through overseas private investment corporations, $1 billion financing for sustainable energy infrastructure, through the US Trade and Development Agency programs in power generation and distribution, renewable energy connectivity to the grid, and unconventional gas development. The US State Department's Bureau of Energy Resources would administer $1 million for energy capacity building.[40] USACEP appears to have assumed the linking function that APP once had. USACEP's contribution to the regional energy regime complex will be to create a better integrated complex but it would still not be a single unified comprehensive energy regime.

People's Daily was critical of Obama's EAS diplomacy.[41] *China Energy News* had a brief comment on Obama's initiative, labeling it a US–ASEAN clean energy initiative rather than an East Asian project.[42] There was no indication that the US discussed partnering with China on this new initiative. However, China will participate in the USACEP because it links regional energy groups that China and the US already participate in such as of the APEC Energy Working Group. The ongoing pattern is initial skepticism, followed by tentative collaboration, which results in a declaration of partnership. In this way, the US and China will continue to work together within Asia-Pacific energy organizations.

US–China competitive energy relations

The US and China differ over the rules for market competition. A Chinese analyst, Xu Xiaojie, argues that China, in the process of emerging as a "petro-dragon," had become a "black energy swan," a steady source of surprise in the world oil economy due to rising oil demand and behaviors that are difficult to predict. Relations with the US were strained because the black energy swan has "incompatible cultures, conflicts of interest, and lack of shared rules" with the US during this expansion. When China had a larger role in global energy governance, it might evolve into a white energy swan, which has not happened yet. China would then become more transparent, responsible, and engaged in predictable competition, and follow international rules and practices.[43]

Distrust of markets led many Chinese analysts to warn that the US would use the "oil weapon" against China within the world oil market.[44] Some Chinese analysts claimed the US was a greater threat than China to world energy security.[45] The belief in "peak oil theory," that the world is running out of oil, is more prevalent in China than in the US.[46] Americans are much more likely to believe that technological innovation can resolve energy security issues, as the shale gas revolution has proved.

According to a Chinese analyst, Tan Yanlin, there were several factors that restricted US–China energy cooperation. Each side had different concepts of energy security, what it was and how to maintain it. The Chinese felt it was dangerous to depend on the market for energy security. Therefore government intervention in energy markets was necessary. Tan argued that American political interests viewed Chinese energy imports as a zero-sum game. The US was more willing than China to depend on SLOCs for oil transport. The Chinese felt their energy vulnerability was due to the possibility the US might interdict SLOCs, as well as market turmoil or sudden price increases. They did not trust the world oil market or the security of SLOCs.[47]

Differences over the role of the market have led to several trade disputes. The solar industry had been one of the fastest growing industries in the US and globally. Many solar companies emerged in the US and China. In 2010, the US exported $2 billion of solar products while in 2011 it registered a $1.6 billion surplus in clean energy trade with China in 2011.

Solyndra was a promising US manufacturer, whose factory had been built with a $535 million loan from the US DOE. Solyndra had also obtained a $25 million tax break from California's Alternative Energy and Advanced Transportation Financing Authority. Suntech was China's major solar panel manufacturer. China exported 95 percent of its solar panels, deeming their use domestically to be too expensive. The question became "who is winning the clean energy race?"[48] However, solar panel production expanded globally leading to overcapacity and declining prices. Solyndra filed for bankruptcy in 2011, unable to compete with its Chinese competitors' cheaper solar panels. In October 2012, Solyndra filed a $1.5 billion antitrust suit against three of China's biggest solar panel manufacturers – Suntech, Trina, and Yingli – charging them with conspiracy to drive Solyndra out of business.

The US Commerce Department in May 2012 had ruled that Wuxi Suntech Power Co., Changzhou Trina Solar Energy Co., and other Chinese companies had been dumping solar panels on the US market. The Commerce Department imposed a 31 percent tariff on these solar imports. The department had earlier ruled that the Chinese government had subsidized these panels at the rate of 2.9 percent to 4.73 percent. China responded by filing a complaint with the WTO on US import duties on 22 products that included solar panels, and also complaining that the US government had subsidized the American solar industry.

US solar panel manufacturers, a coalition of seven companies, the Coalition for American Solar Manufacturing, had lobbied the Commerce Department for this tariff, accusing the Chinese companies of dumping. American solar panel manufacturers, Solyndra, Nanosolar, and Miasolar, had charged the Chinese companies with unfair competition. An opposing coalition, the Coalition for Affordable Solar Energy (CASE), a transnational alliance of domestic solar installers and the Chinese manufacturers, had opposed the ruling.[49] CASE members included Suntech America, Trina Solar US Inc., and Yingli Americas.

In 2012, China attracted $65.1 billion investment in clean energy, while in the US clean energy investment declined 37 percent the same year. China seemed to be winning the "clean energy race."[50] However by 2013, Suntech was in a Chinese bankruptcy court, a result of plunging solar panel prices and bad management.[51]

Suntech was $2 billion in debt, defaulting on $541 million in bonds, and canceling a $1.3 billion contract with a South Korean company.[52] Yingli was also losing money.

By 2013 it was recognized that the complaints filed against Chinese solar companies' dumping in 2011 had created uncertainty in the solar industry. American companies were disappointed in the trade remedies against Chinese imports, which had not succeeded in propping up the US market. What was needed instead was for the US to put together a global solution, an agreement among US, Chinese, and European solar manufacturers for a "sustainable, mutually beneficial settlement."[53]

The *China Business Review* noted that the US and China needed to work out "how to properly compete in the clean energy sector."[54] The issue of Chinese solar panel imports had become a highly politicized and publicized trade issue with contending domestic coalitions. The solar panel dispute is not representative of the overall US–China energy relationship and is more of a trade issue than an energy issue. Most Sino-US energy issues are not so politicized. The Pew study on clean energy had framed the issue as a zero-sum competition to determine who was winning the clean energy race. However, the director of the Pew clean energy program would later note that it would be more beneficial if the US and China would collaborate on clean energy.[55]

In October 2012, China issued a white paper on China energy policy, which had different priorities than the previous energy white paper, and embodied both potential cooperation and competition with the US. It mentioned the need for a "fair and rational international energy management mechanism" as a means to maintain a stable global energy market, an indication of potential US–China competition over how to structure global energy governance. The white paper also, for the first time, referred to China's international cooperation on unconventional gas, an indirect reference to US–China cooperation on shale gas technology.[56]

Contemporary US–China energy relations

After several decades of US–China energy relations managed by China's NDRC and the US DOE, the need for a new framework and new institutions became apparent. This new phase in US–China energy relations led to the building of institutions on both sides that could better manage energy cooperation and competition.

Chinese NOCs needed the Chinese Ministry of Foreign Affairs to work with them to establish a Chinese presence overseas using energy diplomacy (能源外交) to promote Chinese NOCs in regions where they could not gain access by themselves.[57] This coordination between the Chinese NOCs and the Ministry of Foreign Affairs in cultivating relations with oil-producing states gave China a larger diplomatic presence in the Middle East, Central Asia, and Africa.[58]

Chinese energy diplomacy developed dual purposes: (1) promote the commercial interests of the Chinese NOCs, and (2) promote China's role in international organizations, introducing new norms and rules that favored emerging economies, in contention with the IEA. The IEA has been critical of China's expanding oil demand, which, with India, would account for 45 percent of the world's incremental oil demand in projections to the year 2030. China needed a greater capacity for energy diplomacy as Beijing shifted from a passive, learning phase to more active shaping behavior in international organizations, driven by dissatisfaction with their existing rules and norms.[59]

Some Chinese were annoyed that the IEA criticized Chinese energy consumption practices as China became the largest emitter of greenhouse gases, what Chinese called the "theory of China's energy responsibility" (中国能源责任论) by the IEA. Some Chinese felt these Western-created institutions did not give China a status commensurate with its position as the world's largest oil consumer. They argued China should create a new international framework.

According to Zhang Jianxin, China's energy diplomacy had many functions on the supply side: (1) to maintain political relations with oil exporting states; (2) to employ diplomacy to maintain the security of the SLOCs used to transport oil to China; (3) to fend off a third country's (America's) efforts to disrupt China's bilateral oil relations; and (4) to diplomatically block potential competitor states from imposing an oil trade embargo against China. The last is a hypothetical issue at present since there are no oil embargos in effect against China. Chinese energy diplomacy was implemented on multiple levels: Presidential diplomacy carried out by Hu Jintao, regional diplomacy in organizations such as APEC, great power diplomacy with the US and Russia, and multilateral diplomacy with the IEA.[60]

In 2006, Hu Jintao added energy security to his diplomatic agenda.[61] Hu's interest in energy diplomacy can be dated to July 2006 when he participated in the G8 energy security discussions and then in December 2006 when the Five-Country Energy Ministerial met in Beijing, according to the first Chinese volume to be published on the theory and practice of China's energy diplomacy. These meetings provided impetus for Beijing to put greater emphasis on energy diplomacy.[62]

The American capacity for energy diplomacy was also strengthened in 2006 when US Senator Richard Lugar proposed legislation to encourage greater emphasis on energy within US foreign policy.[63] The US had many venues in which to conduct energy diplomacy – through the DOE, USAID, and various offices scattered throughout the State Department – but they were not well coordinated.

It may not be coincidental that both the US and China decided in 2006 to strengthen their respective capacities for cooperative energy diplomacy. By the end of 2006, US perspectives on energy diplomacy in Northeast Asia included US–China cooperation through the Five-Country Energy Ministerial and recognition that Beijing's initiative was worthwhile and should be included in a proposed framework for a Northeast Asian multilateral energy regime.[64]

When the Obama administration took office, Secretary of State Hillary Clinton asked the State Department to review its roles and missions. This was the first time the department had done this kind of review. The result was the Quadrennial Diplomacy and Development Review, which indicated the need for better coordination of US international energy policies. The State Department's Bureau of Energy Resources (ENR) would implement coordination. The ENR became the counterpart organization of China's NEA.

US–China cooperative energy diplomacy operates within the mechanism of the US–China S&ED.[65] The July 27–28, 2009 S&ED meeting produced a Memorandum of Understanding (MOU) to Enhance Cooperation on Climate Change, Energy and the Environment, expanding cooperation under the Ten Year Framework (TYF) to include a climate change policy dialog. The MOU was chaired by the NDRC on the Chinese side and the US Department of State and DOE on the American side. Three specific initiatives were: building a joint laboratory for clean energy technologies; creating green landmark projects to test technologies for carbon capture; and training a clean energy corps in China and the US to focus on energy efficiency implementation.

The May 2010 S&ED signed the US–China Shale Gas Resource Task Force Work Plan between the US State Department and the Chinese NEA. S&ED reviewed the progress made under the US–China TYF on Energy and Environment Cooperation, and indicated publication of the action plans on clean water and air, clean and efficient electricity, clean and efficient transportation, nature reserves and wetlands protection, and energy efficiency. The S&ED issued the US–China Joint Statement on Energy Security Cooperation, recognizing their common security interests, noting that energy security and clean energy went hand-in-hand, and agreeing to work together to stabilize international energy markets. Both sides concurred on the role of the US–China Oil and Gas Industry Forum (OGIF) as the vehicle for promoting shale gas development.[66]

The fourth round of the S&ED met in May 2012. The joint statement noted progress made under the US–China TYF on Energy and Environment Cooperation. On the US–China Joint Statement on Energy Security Cooperation, both sides agreed to increase dialog in areas of common security, "stabilizing international energy markets, emergency responses, ensuring diversified energy supply, and a rational and efficient use of energy."[67] The two sides agreed to participate as "partners" in the APER Forum held in August 2012. The joint statement also noted that the first US–China shale gas assessment was completed, carried out under the Memorandum of Cooperation on Shale Gas Resources agreed to by the US State Department and the Chinese NEA. Development of shale gas in China became an important vehicle for bilateral energy cooperation.

The ENR and China's NEA cooperate under the Global Shale Gas Initiative, now called the Unconventional Gas Technical Engagement Program (UGTEP). This program shares US expertise on environmentally sound shale gas development with a select number of countries. The ENR has had dialog with the NEA on jointly analyzing the role of world energy markets, addressing a major source of US–China disagreement. The ENR and NEA share experiences on issues that cause bilateral friction – the regulatory role of the state and energy-related environmental issues.[68]

The US–China OGIF, a public–private partnership, has become a venue for focusing on shale gas exploration and development. At the twelfth US–China

OGIF, the Chinese side put forward proposals for greater cooperation on China's shale gas development plan and the strengthening of mutual coordination within multilateral frameworks, i.e., greater technology transfer.[69] China may have larger shale gas reserves than the US but it lacks the technology to exploit its reserves. In 2010 US natural gas production was larger than that of any other country in the world, raising the possibility of exporting its surplus as liquified natural gas (LNG) exports. But according to a statement from the US DOE, it was not decided at the end of 2012 whether to issue permits for LNG exports to countries that did not have a free trade agreement with the US. This would favor Japan if it joined the Trans-Pacific Partnership (TPP) while excluding China.

The July 2013 fifth round US–China S&ED produced a joint statement on the outcomes of the strategic track with 91 agreements. The statement's "Section IV Cooperation on Energy" included 17 specific areas of cooperation. These included a legal and regulatory framework for unconventional oil and gas, necessary for US companies to participate in China's shale gas development. During the S&ED, the US informed China on the application process for LNG exports to non-FTA countries such as China, decided by the US DOE according to the US Natural Gas Act. The US–China Energy Policy Dialogue was elevated to the ministerial level, chaired by the heads of US DOE and China's NEA. They finalized the First Solar Decathlon China, a decathlon for international sharing of solar technology, building solar-powered homes, that could be applied in China. It was held in August 2013. There were additional agreements on nuclear energy, renewable energy, and energy efficient technologies.[70]

One American analyst felt that the majority of the 2013 US–China S&ED agreements were "joint" agreements, reflecting a partnership with many more joint working groups, compared to previous S&ED agreements which were more "parallel," reflecting bilateral differences.[71] The working groups will meet throughout the year, a major advance in institutionalization compared to the once-a-year S&ED meeting.

Conclusion

A primary driver of continuity in US–China energy relations is the ongoing US transfer of energy technology to China. In the 1970s it was offshore oil drilling technology. In the 2000s, it is technology that allows for the safe and environmentally sustainable exploitation of shale gas. To the extent that shale gas utilization mitigates China's carbon emissions, it will be a source of common security for East Asia and the world.

This technology transfer to China has been the primary driver of US–China cooperation. The shale gas revolution is slated to further US energy self-reliance in a few years, something China would like to emulate. US transfer of shale gas technology could assist China in reducing oil imports. The possibility of US LNG exports to China could ameliorate Chinese anxieties over its energy security. Joint protection of the SLOCs would also address Chinese anxieties over the country's dependence on oil imports from the Middle East.

Continuity and cooperation are the overall trends of the past four decades, leading to increasing institutionalization of US–China energy relationship. Some of the bilateral cooperation agreements were formed out of multilateral regimes, such as the 10-year Energy and Environment Cooperation Framework, which borrowed language from the Five-Country Energy Ministerial. Asia-Pacific energy regime complexes have had the important function of fostering US–China parallelism, the practice of having complementary interests within international organizations without overt bilateral cooperation. US–China parallelism is an underappreciated aspect in much of the literature on US–China bilateral relations.

US Asia-Pacific initiatives for clean energy, US–China cooperation on clean energy, and China's shift to a low-carbon development model are embedded in regional energy regime complexes. The APP is an example of US–China bilateral energy relations within an energy regime complex that includes technology transfer. It took five years for US–China parallelism within the APP, and then the APER Forum, to transition to overt cooperation, calling themselves "partners" at the August 2012 APER Forum. The APER Forum is tasked explicitly with developing a common understanding of how energy markets should function, an issue more contentious than technology transfer.

The most significant source of change in US–China energy relations was the Chinese decision to securitize its oil import dependence, producing a socially constructed energy crisis for Chinese leaders that led to the "Malacca Strait dilemma." This securitization became the primary driver of US–China energy competition. After securitization, Chinese perceived the US as exploiting Chinese vulnerability due to expanding energy demand and dependence on oil imports.

US–China differences over the role of the market lead to different conceptions of energy security. These differences are at the core of US–China trade disputes involving energy. The Solyndra–Suntech solar panel trade dispute is remembered as a classic example of how destructive energy competition can be.

A primary factor that will continue to generate US–China energy conflict has been differences over the world oil market and the degree to which oil-importing countries should rely on it. The Chinese NOCs' going-out strategy is meant to secure physical access to oil resources and by-pass the world oil market. The Chinese will continue to prefer physical control of oil resources and rely less on market forces, which will remain a fundamental difference in US and Chinese perceptions of energy security. China uses energy diplomacy, led by the Ministry of Foreign Affairs, to facilitate Chinese NOCs' oil acquisitions in regions they would have difficulty accessing on their own.

China has experienced ongoing IEA criticism of its energy practices, which has led to a Chinese search for alternative global energy governance structures. The G-20, the Shanghai Cooperation Organization, and the BRICS (Brazil, Russia, India, China, and South Africa) have become the Chinese preferred organizations for global energy governance, although they have not had a significant impact on global energy. If Chinese energy diplomacy is used to expand

China's role within global energy governance, and China uses that expanded role to rewrite the rules and reshape the practices of global governance to reflect the interests of emerging economies, this will result in US–China competition over global energy governance.

US–China parallelism may play a role on the issue of the structure of global energy governance and the role of market forces. The US State Department's ENR seeks to "stabilize oil markets through producer-consumer dialogues," primarily between the IEA and OPEC. In contrast, China appears to treat a producer–consumer dialog as something that bypasses the world oil market, allowing for physical control of oil resources. The US and China can move in a parallel direction in encouraging a producer–consumer dialog such as the International Energy Forum, a global energy dialog between producing (OPEC), consuming (IEA), and transit states with the BRICS participating on an individual basis.[72] Their purposes may be different, but they will demonstrate parallel behavior in supporting a producer–consumer dialog, and at some point may transition to more overt cooperation, calling themselves "partners" in global energy governance.

In September 2012, at the second US–China Energy Summit, Americans and Chinese recognized the multifaceted nature of a relationship that entails both conflict and cooperation. Former US President George W. Bush encouraged further cooperation but warned that trade disputes and protectionism in violation of market forces required careful management by both sides. The Chinese Consul General in Houston stressed the numerous successful bilateral efforts at institutionalization of cooperation:

- 10-year Energy and Environment Cooperation Framework;
- US–China Renewable Energy Partnership;
- Memorandum of Cooperation on Shale Gas between the US State Department and China's NEA;
- US–China Clean Energy Forum.[73]

Sources of US–China conflict include differences over global energy governance, world oil markets, the role of the market vs. state intervention, and the boundaries of regional energy regimes. The US prefers Asia-Pacific energy regimes. China has preferred to initiate East Asian energy regimes that exclude the US and are more tightly organized. When the US and China are competing for regional leadership, and are contending over regional regimes, their energy relations appear competitive. An Asia-Pacific framework may undermine Chinese-created East Asian frameworks, but given China's need for shale gas technology, which it obtains from the US, China could be expected to be more cooperative than competitive.

The mechanisms and organizations that have done the most to institutionalize US–China energy relations include the S&ED's annual meetings which now include working groups; the decades-long relationship between the US DOE and the Chinese NDRC; the relatively new relationship between the US State Department Bureau of Energy Resources and the Chinese NEA; and Asia-Pacific

US–China energy relations 173

energy regime complexes where US–China energy parallelism often occurs. All of these organizations serve to institutionalize US–China energy relations in a positive and cooperative direction.

In the future, the US might help China rethink the securitization of its oil import dependence. Although this securitization has domestic sources, the US should continue to provide technical assistance that will strengthen the Chinese state's capacity to control domestic energy demand. With regard to Chinese anxiety over the SLOCs, the US should continue to encourage Chinese participation in the "thousand-ship navy." Joint naval exercises such as in the Gulf of Aden and RIMPAC 2014, which China has agreed to participate in, are initial steps that could lead to greater bilateral recognition of their common security interests.

Notes

1 Zha Daojiong and Hu Weixing, "Promoting Energy Partnership in Beijing and Washington," *Washington Quarterly* 30, no. 4 (Autumn 2007): 106.
2 Erica Downs, *The Brookings Foreign Policy Studies Energy Security Series: China*, report (Washington DC: The Brookings Institution, 2006).
3 Hu Shuli, "CNOOC, Unocal and the 'Go-out Strategy,'" *Caijing*, July 26, 2005, http://english.caijing.com.cn/2005–07–26/100013798.html.
4 David Zweig and Bi Jianhai, "China's Global Hunt for Energy," *Foreign Affairs* 84 (September/October 2005): 25–38.
5 Office of the Secretary of Defense, *Annual Report to Congress: The Military Power of the People's Republic of China 2005*, July 2005, www.defense.gov/news/jul2005/d20050719china.pdf. The report mentions the "Malacca Straits dilemma" and Chinese concern over the SLOCs; and Gabriel B. Collins *et al.*, eds., *China's Energy Strategy: The Impact on Beijing's Maritime Policies* (Annapolis, MD: Naval Institute Press, 2008).
6 中国现代国际关系研究院经济安全研究中心，全球能源大棋局 (*Global Energy Structure*) (北京: 时事出版社, 2005).
7 David Shambaugh, ed. *Tangled Titans: The United States and China* (Lanham, MD: Rowman & Littlefield, 2012).
8 周云亨 (Zhou Yunheng), 中国能源安全中的美国因素 (*The American Factor in Chinese Energy Security*) (Shanghai: People's Publishing House, 2012).
9 Yan Xuetong, "The Instability of China–US Relations," *Chinese Journal of International Politics* 3 (2010): 263–92.
10 Doak Barnett referred to US–China "parallelism" in 1977 to describe a security relationship with minimal explicit interaction, "Military–Security Relations between China and the United States," *Foreign Affairs* 55 (April 1977): 584–97; Henry Kissinger also spoke of US–China parallelism.
11 Gaye Christoffersen, *China and Maritime Cooperation: Piracy in the Gulf of Aden* (Berlin: Institut für Strategie-, Politik-, Sicherheits- und Wirtschaftsberatung, 2010), www.isn.ethz.ch/isn/Digital-Library/Publications/Detail/?id=111041.
12 "China, US Conduct Joint Anti-Piracy Exercise in Gulf of Aden," *People's Daily*, September 20, 2012, http://english.people.com.cn/90786/7954318.html.
13 Aaron L. Friedberg, "Going Out: China's Pursuit of Natural Resources and Implications for the PRC's Grand Strategy," *NBR Analysis* 17, no. 3 (September 2006).
14 Jochen Prantl. *Cooperating in the Energy Security Regime Complex*. MacArthur Asia Security Initiative Policy Working Paper no. 18 (2011).
15 Stephen Krasner, "Approaches to the State: Alternative Conceptions and Historical Dynamics," *Comparative Politics* 16 (1984): 223–46; see also Stephen Krasner,

"Sovereignty: An Institutional Perspective," *Comparative Political Studies* 21 (1988): 66–94; Jeff D. Colgan, Robert O. Keohane, and Thijs Van de Graaf, "Punctuated Equilibrium in the Energy Regime Complex," *Review of International Organizations* 7, no. 2 (2012): 117–43.

16 Sections of this chapter draw from Gaye Christoffersen, "US–China Energy Relations and Energy Institution Building in the Asia-Pacific," *Journal of Contemporary China* 19, no. 67 (2010): 871–89.
17 Robert S. Price, Jr, *A History of Sino-American Energy Cooperation* (Washington, DC: Woodrow Wilson International Center for Scholars, 1998), www.wilsoncenter.org/topics/pubs/ACF4C7.PDF; Robert S. Price, Jr, "A Chronology of US–China Energy Cooperation," paper presented at the US–China Energy Security Conference, Beijing, 2007. The conference was co-sponsored by Tsinghua University, the Atlantic Council of the United States, and the Institute for Sino-American International Dialogue at the University of Denver. www.acus.org/docs/A ChronologyUSChinaEnergyCooperation.pdf.
18 The commission has gone through several name changes. From the SPC, it changed to the State Planning and Development Commission (SPDC) and now is called the National Development and Reform Commission (NDRC).
19 www.beconchina.org/.
20 Price, "A Chronology of US–China Energy Cooperation."
21 National Research Council, Chinese Academy of Sciences, and Chinese Academy of Engineering, *Cooperation in the Energy Futures of China and the United States* (Washington, DC: National Academies Press, 2000), 5.
22 夏立平 (Xia Liping), 美国国际能源战略与中美能源合作 (America's International Energy Strategies and US–China Energy Cooperation), 当代亚太 (*Contemporary Asia-Pacific*) no. 1 (2005): 14–19.
23 Information on the US–China Oil and Gas Industry Forum can be found at: www.uschinaogf.org/.
24 Robert B. Zoellick, "Whither China: From Membership to Responsibility?" Remarks to National Committee on US–China Relations, New York City, September 21, 2005.
25 US Treasury Department Office of Public Affairs, "US and China Deepen Their Economic Relationship." US Department of State, June 19, 2008, http://iipdigital.usembassy.gov/st/english/article/2008/06/20080619150836xjsnommis0.2596334.html#axzz3AR0elztZ.
26 *Broadening the Bilateral: Seizing the Opportunity for Meaningful US–China Collaboration on Climate Change*, report to the Committee on Foreign Relations, United States Senate (Washington, DC: US Government Printing Office, 2009), 11–12.
27 "第四次中美能源政策对话举行 (Fourth China–US Energy Policy Dialogue Held)," *Xinhua*, September 27, 2009, http://news.xinhuanet.com/fortune/2009–09/27/content_12118183.htm.
28 The website for the organization is found at: www.asiapacificpartnership.org/.
29 Karen Harbert, Assistant Secretary, Policy and International Affairs, US Department of Energy (US Engagement in International Energy Forums, Center for Strategic and International Studies, Washington, DC, July 11, 2007), http://csis.org/event/us-engagement-international-energy-forums.
30 "Charter for the Asia-Pacific Partnership on Clean Development and Climate," US Department of State, January 12, 2006, http://2001–2009.state.gov/g/oes/rls/or/2006/59162.htm.
31 USAID, "Eco Asia." http://usaid.eco-asia.org/programs/cdcp/.
32 Japan Ministry of Economy, Trade and Industry. "United States–Japan Cooperation on Energy Security," January 10, 2007.
33 *White Paper on China's Energy Conditions and Policies* (Beijing: People's Republic of China State Council Information Office, 2007).

34 Guangsheng Gao, "Country Statement – China," Asia-Pacific Partnership on Clean Development and Climate, www.asiapacificpartnership.org/pdf/queensland/China_Country_Statement.pdf.
35 APP Energy Regulatory and Market Development Forum, Third Meeting of the Steering Committee, November 3, 2010, Sydney, Australia.
36 www.ferc.gov/aper-forum/2012-agenda.asp.
37 "Asia Pacific Energy Regulatory Forum Terms of Reference, Governance and Administrative Arrangements, Initial Work Plan 2012–14." Federal Energy Regulatory Commission, November 2011, www.ferc.gov/aper-forum/aper-governance.pdf.
38 On the Obama rebalance see Chapter 4 by Suisheng Zhao's chapter in this volume.
39 "St Petersburg Declaration – Energy Security: Challenges and Strategic Choices" (2012 APEC Energy Ministerial Meeting, St Petersburg, July 6, 2012), www.apec.org/Meeting-Papers/Ministerial-Statements/Energy/2012_energy.aspx.
40 The White House, Office of the Press Secretary, "FACT SHEET on the US–Asia Pacific Comprehensive Partnership for a Sustainable Energy," November 20, 2012, The White House, www.whitehouse.gov/the-press-office/2012/11/20/fact-sheet-us-asia-pacific-comprehensive-partnership-sustainable-energy.
41 "What's the Intention of Obama's Visit to Asia?" *People's Daily*, November 22, 2012, http://english.people.com.cn/90777/8029246.html.
42 奥巴马推动美-东南亚 清洁能源贸易协定 (Obama to Promote the United States–South East Asia Clean Energy Trade Agreement)," 中国能源报 (*China Energy Newspaper*), November 26, 2012, http://paper.people.com.cn/zgnyb/html/2012–11/26/content_1151042.htm.
43 Xu Xiaojie, "Black Energy Swan: A Global Perspective" (Hong Kong University of Science and Technology Center on Environment, Energy and Resource Policy, Hong Kong, May 17, 2012); Xu Xiaojie, *Energy Black Swan: Global Games and Chinese Options* (Beijing: China Social Sciences Press, 2011).
44 Wu Lei and Shen Qinyu, "Will China Go to War Over Oil?" *Far Eastern Economic Review* 169, no. 3 (April 2006): 38.
45 Wu Lei and Liu Xuejun, "China or the United States: Which Threatens Energy Security?" *OPEC Review* 31, no. 3 (September 2007): 215–34.
46 Feng Lianyong *et al.*, "Peak Oil Models Forecast China's Oil Supply, Demand," *Oil and Gas Journal* (January 14, 2008): 43–7; Lin Shi and Yuhan Zhang, "Rethinking peak oil," *China Dialogue*, April 23, 2012, www.chinadialogue.net/article/show/single/en/4885.
47 唐彦林 (Tang Yanlin), "奥巴马政府能源新政背景下的中美能源合作 (Sino-US Energy Cooperation in the Context of the Obama Administration's New Energy Policy)," 世界经济与政治论坛 (*Forum of World Economics and Politics*) no. 5 (2009): 82–9.
48 The Pew Charitable Trusts, "Who's Winning the Clean Energy Race? 2012 Edition," April 17, 2013, 7, www.pewenvironment.org/news-room/reports/whos-winning-the-clean-energy-race-2012-edition-85899468949.
49 Mark Clayton, "US Imposes Tariff on Chinese Solar Panels, A Victory for US Manufacturers," *Christian Science Monitor*, May 17, 2012.
50 The Pew Charitable Trusts. "Who's Winning the Clean Energy Race? 2012 Edition."
51 Wayne Ma, "The Man at the Center of Solar-Panel Maker Suntech's Fall," *Wall Street Journal*, May 3, 2013.
52 Todd Woody, "China's Suntech Has Just Broken a $1.3 Billion Contract for Solar Panel Materials," *Quartz*, April 29, 2013, http://qz.com/79379/suntech-breaks-1–3-billion-contract-with-oci-supplier-of-materials-for-solar-panels/.
53 "Wyden Eyes 'Global Solution' to Address Fallout from Solar Trade Cases," *Inside US–China Trade*, March 20, 2013.
54 Linden J. Ellis *et al.*, "Chinese Investment in Clean Energy," *China Business Review* (April–June 2012): 28.

55 Lan Lan "Energy Trade Surplus for the US," *China Daily*, March 7, 2013, 1.
56 State Council of Information Office. *China's Energy Policy 2012*, October 24, 2012, www.gov.cn/english/official/2012–10/24/content_2250497.htm.
57 Pan Guang, "30 Years of Reform and Opening up of China's Energy Diplomacy," *China International Studies*, no. 4 (Winter 2008): 85–104, www.ciis.org.cn/english/2010–11/04/content_3815122.htm.
58 Philip Andrews-Speed, *The Governance of Energy in China: Transition to a Low-Carbon Economy* (Basingstoke: Palgrave Macmillan, 2012), 151.
59 Joel Wuthnow *et al.*, "Diverse Multilateralism: Four Strategies in China's Multilateral Diplomacy," *Journal of Chinese Political Science* 17 (2012): 269–90.
60 Jianxin Zhang, *Oil Security Reshapes China's Foreign Policy*, working paper no. 9 (Hong Kong: Hong Kong University of Science and Technology Center on China's Transnational Relations, 2005).
61 James Tang, *With the Grain or Against the Grain: Energy Security and Chinese Foreign Policy in the Hu Jintao Era* (Washington, DC: The Brookings Institution, 2006), 12.
62 王海云和徐勤华 (Wang Haiyun and Xu Qinhua), 能源外交概论 (*Introduction to Energy Diplomacy*) (Beijing: 社会科学文献出版社, 2012), 4.
63 Carlos Pascual, *Briefing on the New Bureau of Energy Resources within the Department of State*, November 16, 2011, www.state.gov/e/enr/rls/rem/2011/177281.htm.
64 Carol Kessler, "US Energy Security and Energy Diplomacy." Paper presented at the conference, "Energy and Security in Northeast Asia: Towards a Northeast Asian Energy Cooperation Council," Seoul, November 16–17, 2007.
65 Robert Sutter discusses US–China non-military dialogues extensively in Chapter 9 of this volume.
66 "US–China Strategic and Economic Dialogue 2010 Outcomes of the Strategic Track," US Department of State, May 25, 2010, www.state.gov/r/pa/prs/ps/2010/05/142180.htm.
67 "Joint Statement on the US–China Strategic and Economic Dialogue Outcomes of the Strategic Track May 3–4, 2012," US Department of State, May 4, 2012, www.state.gov/r/pa/prs/ps/2012/05/189287.htm.
68 Pascual, "Briefing on the New Bureau of Energy Resources within the Department of State."
69 "第十二届中美油气工业论坛在美举行 (12th US–China Oil and Gas Industry Forum held in the United States)," 中国能源报 (*China Energy Report*), September 17, 2012, http://paper.people.com.cn/zgnyb/html/2012–09/17/content_1114396.htm.
70 "US–China Strategic and Economic Dialogue Outcomes of the Strategic Track," US Department of State, July 12, 2013, www.state.gov/r/pa/prs/ps/2013/07/211861.htm.
71 David Shambaugh, "A Big Step Forward in US–China Relations," *China–US Dialogue*, July 19, 2013, www.chinausfocus.com/foreign-policy/a-big-step-forward-in-u-s-china-relations.
72 International Energy Forum, www.ief.org.
73 "Conference in Houston Eyes Expanded China–Us Energy Cooperation," *Xinhua*, September 21, 2012.

References

Andrews-Speed, Phillip. *The Governance of Energy in China: Transition to a Low-Carbon Economy* (Basingstoke: Palgrave Macmillan, 2012).

"Asia Pacific Energy Regulatory Forum Terms of Reference, Governance and Administrative Arrangements, Initial Work Plan 2012–14." Federal Energy Regulatory Commission. November 2011. www.ferc.gov/aper-forum/aper-governance.pdf.

Asia-Pacific Partnership on Clean Development and Climate. www.asiapacificpartnership.org/.

Barnett, Doak. "Military–Security Relations Between China and the United States." *Foreign Affairs* 55 (April 1977): 584–97.
Broadening the Bilateral: Seizing the Opportunity for Meaningful US–China Collaboration on Climate Change. Report (Washington, DC: US Government Printing Office, 2009).
"China, US Conduct Joint Anti-piracy Exercise in Gulf of Aden." *People's Daily.* September 20, 2012. http://english.people.com.cn/90786/7954318.html.
Christoffersen, Gaye. *China and Maritime Cooperation: Piracy in the Gulf of Aden.* (Berlin: Institut für Strategie-, Politik-, Sicherheits- und Wirtschaftsberatung, 2010).
Christoffersen, Gaye. "US–China Energy Relations and Energy Institution Building in the Asia-Pacific." *Journal of Contemporary China* 19, no. 67 (2010): 871–89.
Clayton, Mark. "US Imposes Tariff on Chinese Solar Panels, a Victory for US Manufacturers." *Christian Science Monitor*, May 17, 2012.
Colgan, Jeff D., Robert O. Keohane, and Thijs Van De Graaf. "Punctuated Equilibrium in the Energy Regime Complex." *Review of International Organizations* 7, no. 2 (2012): 117–43.
Collins, Gabriel B., Andrew S. Erickson, Lyle J. Goldstein, and William S. Murray, eds. *China's Energy Strategy: The Impact on Beijing's Maritime Policies* (Annapolis, MD: Naval Institute Press, 2008).
"Conference in Houston Eyes Expanded China–US Energy Cooperation." *Xinhua*, September 21, 2012.
Downs, Erica. *The Brookings Foreign Policy Studies Energy Security Series: China.* (Washington, DC: Brookings Institution, 2006).
Ellis, Linden J., Devin Kleinfield-Hayes, and Jennifer L. Turner. "Chinese Investment in Clean Energy." *China Business Review* (April 2012).
Feng, Lianyong, Junchen Li, Xiongqi Pang, Xu Tang, Lin Zhao, and Qingfei Zhao. "Peak Oil Models Forecast China's Oil Supply, Demand." *Oil and Gas Journal*, January 14, 2008.
Friedberg, Aaron L. "Going Out: China's Pursuit of Natural Resources and Implications for the PRC's Grand Strategy." *NBR Analysis* 17, no. 3 (September 2006).
Gao, Guangsheng. "Country Statement – China." Asia-Pacific Partnership on Clean Development and Climate. www.asiapacificpartnership.org/pdf/queensland/China_Country_Statement.pdf.
Harbert, Karen. US Engagement in International Energy Forums, Center for Strategic and International Studies, Washington, DC, July 11, 2007. http://csis.org/event/us-engagement-international-energy-forums.
Hu, Shuli. "CNOOC, Unocal and the 'Go-out Strategy'." *Caijing*. July 26, 2005. http://%3A%2F%2Fenglish.caijing.com.cn%2F2005-07-26%2F100013798.html.
International Energy Forum. www.ief.org/.
Japan Ministry of Economy, Trade and Industry. "United States–Japan Cooperation on Energy Security." January 10, 2007.
Kessler, Carol. "US Energy Security and Energy Diplomacy." Energy and Security in Northeast Asia: Towards a Northeast Asian Energy Cooperation Council, Seoul, November 16–17, 2007.
Krasner, Stephen. "Approaches to the State: Alternative Conceptions and Historical Dynamics." *Comparative Politics* 16 (1984): 223–46.
Krasner, Stephen. "Sovereignty: An Institutional Perspective." *Comparative Political Studies* 21 (1988): 66–94.
Lan, Lan. "Energy Trade Surplus for the US." *China Daily*, March 7, 2013.

Ma, Wayne. "The Man at the Center of Solar-Panel Maker Suntech's Fall." *Wall Street Journal*, May 3, 2013.

National Research Council, Chinese Academy of Sciences, and Chinese Academy of Engineering. *Cooperation in the Energy Futures of China and the United States* (Washington, DC: National Academy Press, 2000).

Pan, Guang. "30 Years of Reform and Opening up of China's Energy Diplomacy." *China International Studies*, no. 4 (Winter 2008): 85–104. www.ciis.org.cn/english/2010–11/04/content_3815122.htm.

Pascual, Carlos. *Briefing on the New Bureau of Energy Resources within the Department of State*. November 16, 2011. www.state.gov/e/enr/rls/rem/2011/177281.htm.

People's Republic of China, State Council Information Office. *China's Energy Policy 2012*. Publication. October 24, 2012. www.gov.cn/english/official/2012–10/24/content_2250497.htm.

People's Republic of China. *White Paper on China's Energy Conditions and Policies*. (Beijing: People's Republic of China State Council Information Office, 2007).

Pew Charitable Trusts. *Who's Winning the Clean Energy Race? 2012 Edition*. April 17, 2013. www.pewtrusts.org/en/research-and-analysis/reports/2013/04/17/whos-winning-the-clean-energy-race-2012-edition.

Prantl, Jochen. *Cooperating in the Energy Security Regime Complex*. Working paper no. 18. MacArthur Asia Security Initiative, 2011.

Price, Robert S., Jr. "A Chronology of US–China Energy Cooperation." Paper presented at the US–China Energy Security Conference, Beijing, 2007.

Price, Robert S., Jr. *A History of Sino-American Energy Cooperation* (Washington, DC: Woodrow Wilson International Center for Scholars, 1998).

Shambaugh, David L. *Tangled Titans: The United States and China* (Lanham, MD: Rowman & Littlefield, 2013).

Shambaugh, David. "A Big Step Forward in US–China Relations." *China–US Dialogue*, July 19, 2013. www.chinausfocus.com/foreign-policy/a-big-step-forward-in-u-s-china-relations.

Shi, Lin, and Yuhan Zhang. "Rethinking Peak Oil." *China Dialogue*. April 23, 2012. www.chinadialogue.net/article/show/single/en/4885.

"St Petersburg Declaration – Energy Security: Challenges and Strategic Choices." 2012 APEC Energy Ministerial Meeting, St Petersburg, July 6, 2012. www.apec.org/Meeting-Papers/Ministerial-Statements/Energy/2012_energy.aspx.

Tang, James. *With the Grain or Against the Grain: Energy Security and Chinese Foreign Policy in the Hu Jintao Era* (Washington, DC: Brookings Institution, 2006).

Tang, Yanlin. "奥巴马政府能源新政背景下的中美能源合作 (Sino-US Energy Cooperation in the Context of the Obama Administration's New Energy Policy)." 世界经济与政治论坛 (*Forum of World Economics and Politics*) no. 5 (2009): 82–9.

United States, Agency for International Development. "Eco Asia." http://usaid.eco-asia.org/programs/cdcp/.

United States, Department of State. "Charter for the Asia-Pacific Partnership on Clean Development and Climate." January 12, 2006. http://2001–2009.state.gov/g/oes/rls/or/2006/59162.htm.

United States, Department of State. "Joint Statement on the US–China Strategic and Economic Dialogue Outcomes of the Strategic Track May 3–4, 2012." May 4, 2012. www.state.gov/r/pa/prs/ps/2012/05/189287.htm.

United States, Department of State. "US–China Strategic and Economic Dialogue 2010 Outcomes of the Strategic Track." May 25, 2010. www.state.gov/r/pa/prs/ps/2010/05/142180.htm.

United States, Department of State. "US–China Strategic and Economic Dialogue Outcomes of the Strategic Track." July 12, 2013. www.state.gov/r/pa/prs/ps/2013/07/211861.htm.

United States, Department of the Treasury, Office of Public Affairs. "US and China Deepen Their Economic Relationship." June 19, 2008. http://iipdigital.usembassy.gov/st/english/article/2008/06/20080619150836xjsnommis0.2596334.html#axzz3AR0elztZ.

United States, Office of the Secretary of Defense. *Annual Report to Congress: The Military Power of the People's Republic of China 2005.* July 2005. www.defense.gov/news/jul2005/d20050719china.pdf.

United States, The White House. Office of the Press Secretary. "FACT SHEET on the US–Asia Pacific Comprehensive Partnership for a Sustainable Energy." November 20, 2012. www.whitehouse.gov/the-press-office/2012/11/20/fact-sheet-us-asia-pacific-comprehensive-partnership-sustainable-energy.

US–China Oil and Gas Industry Forum. www.uschinaogf.org/.

Wang, Haiyun, and Qinhua Xu. 能源外交概论 (*Introduction to Energy Diplomacy*) (Beijing: 社会科学文献出版社, 2012).

"What's the Intention of Obama's Visit to Asia?" *People's Daily*. November 22, 2012. http://english.people.com.cn/90777/8029246.html.

Woody, Todd. "China's Suntech Has Just Broken a $1.3 Billion Contract for Solar Panel Materials." *Quartz*. April 29, 2013. http://qz.com/79379/suntech-breaks-1-3-billion-contract-with-oci-supplier-of-materials-for-solar-panels/.

Wu, Lei, and Qinyu Shen. "Will China Go to War Over Oil?" *Far Eastern Economic Review* 169, no. 3 (April 2006): 38–40.

Wu, Lei, and Xuejun Liu. "China or the United States: Which Threatens Energy Security?" *OPEC Review* 31, no. 3 (September 2007): 215–34.

Wuthnow, Joel, Xin Li, and Lingling Qi. "Diverse Multilateralism: Four Strategies in China's Multilateral Diplomacy." *Journal of Chinese Political Science* 17 (2012): 269–90.

"Wyden Eyes 'Global Solution' To Address Fallout From Solar Trade Cases." *Inside US–China Trade*, March 20, 2013.

Xia, Liping. "美国国际能源战略与中美能源合作 (America's International Energy Strategies and US–China Energy Cooperation)." 当代亚太 (*Contemporary Asia-Pacific*) no. 1 (2005): 14–19.

Xu, Xiaojie. "Black Energy Swan: A Global Perspective." Hong Kong University of Science and Technology Center on Environment, Energy and Resource Policy, Hong Kong, May 17, 2012.

Xu, Xiaojie. *Energy Black Swan: Global Games and Chinese Options* (Beijing: China Social Sciences Press, 2011).

Yan, Xuetong. "The Instability of China–US Relations." *Chinese Journal of International Politics* 3 (2010): 263–92.

Zha, Daojiong, and Weixing Hu. "Promoting Energy Partnership in Beijing and Washington." *Washington Quarterly* 30, no. 4 (Autumn 2007): 105–15.

Zhang, Jianxin. *Oil Security Reshapes China's Foreign Policy*. Working paper no. 9. Hong Kong: Hong Kong University of Science and Technology Center on China's Transnational Relations, 2005.

Zhou, Yunheng. 中国能源安全中的美国因素 (*The American Factor in Chinese Energy Security*) (Shanghai: People's Publishing House, 2012).

Zoellick, Robert B. "Whither China: From Membership to Responsibility?" Remarks to National Committee on US–China Relations, New York City, September 21, 2005.

Zweig, David, and Jianhai Bi. "China's Global Hunt for Energy." *Foreign Affairs* 84 (September/October 2005): 25–38.

中国现代国际关系研究院经济安全研究中心. 全球能源大棋局 (*Global Energy Structure*). 北京: 时事出版社, 2005.

"奥巴马推动美-东南亚 清洁能源贸易协定 (Obama to Promote the United States – South East Asia Clean Energy Trade Agreement)." 中国能源报 (*China Energy Newspaper*). November 26, 2012. http://paper.people.com.cn/zgnyb/html/2012–11/26/content_1151042.htm.

"第十二届中美油气工业论坛在美举行 (12th US–China Oil and Gas Industry Forum Held in the United States)." 中国能源报 (*China Energy Report*), September 17, 2012. http://paper.people.com.cn/zgnyb/html/2012–09/17/content_1114396.htm.

"第四次中美能源政策对话举行 (Fourth China–US Energy Policy Dialogue Held)." *Xinhua*. September 27, 2009. http://news.xinhuanet.com/fortune/2009–09/27/content_12118183.htm.

9 Dialogues and their implications in Sino-American relations[1]

Robert G. Sutter

The purpose and scope of dialogues

Dialogue has been a central feature of Sino-American relations since the United States and China opened relations under President Richard Nixon and Chairman Mao Zedong in the early 1970s. Often broad-ranging interchanges between elites in the two administrations have been complemented by legislative exchanges and interactions between other influential government and non-governmental groups. After the US cut back a variety of government exchanges with China following the Tiananmen crackdown in 1989, the two governments eventually saw the wisdom in using a few and over time more bilateral dialogues in order to reaffirm common ground and deal constructively with differences. Dialogues developed in an ad hoc way and came to be more formally structured. The two sides focused at first on such sensitive issues as human rights, but broadened the scope to entail over 60 dialogues by the first decade of the twenty-first century, capped by the annual wide-ranging leadership exchanges seen in the US–China Strategic and Economic Dialogue (S&ED) initiated in 2009.[2]

The explicit motives of the two administrations in pursuing dialogues during the past two decades were similar to earlier rationales. The exchanges were seen to help to deal with and hopefully reduce differences and gaps in interests and perceptions that divided the two countries. Some of these differences remained very sensitive and needed careful management through close leadership attention, notably during deliberations in the dialogues. American leaders and other elites at times articulated the view that American persuasiveness in the dialogues, backed by the forces of modern globalization and other circumstances, would help to persuade Chinese leaders to follow policies in line with US-supported norms. Chinese leaders generally were more circumspect regarding their motives in engaging in the dialogues, though practice showed the utility of these vehicles in managing problems in relations with the US.

There were numerous less explicit objectives in the dialogues. According to US participants in dialogues, US representatives tended to be the demanders, seeking to use the dialogues to solve problems perceived by the US.[3] The Chinese side was more inclined to use the channels to manage sensitive issues, without seeking the difficult decisions needed to solve the problems. The Americans also saw the channels as means to compel the often poorly coordinated Chinese international affairs apparatus to involve all relevant stakeholders in the Chinese administration, thereby smoothing the way to effective implementation of agreements made during the dialogues. The dialogues also required effective coordination among American government representatives in dealing with the issues addressed in the scope of specific dialogues with China. Meanwhile, American participants judged that both the Chinese and US administrations saw dialogues as useful ways to identify senior officers on each side who had the authority and inclination to solve problems that continued to emerge in the ever-broadening Sino-American relationship. These so-called "go-to" officials were sought out during crises or other stressful circumstances to help calm disputes and facilitate resolutions.

Other less explicit but broadly recognized motives of both sides in pursuing dialogues and exchanges had to do with building Sino-American interdependence in ways that would constrain one side from taking actions detrimental to the interests of the other. American specialists identified an enduring strategy involving dialogues and other exchanges used by the US, its allies, and associated states to build growing webs of relationships with rising China that would incline or compel the Chinese government to see its interests better served by cooperation rather than confrontation with them.[4] As noted above, Chinese elites and specialists were less forthright about their motives, but in practice China used dialogues and other behavior to build a range of interdependencies with the US, especially economic interdependence, that served to constrain US leaders from taking actions strongly challenging or confronting Chinese interests.[5]

Also less explicitly recognized was the common tendency of both sides to favor generally secret dialogues as ways to deal with sensitive issues out of public view. This process limited the ability of forces in both societies that opposed Sino-US collaboration and compromise on these subjects to muster support for their harder line or to otherwise complicate bilateral relations over the issue at hand. The responsible officials in these dialogues thus had more freedom of action to explore options for greater cooperation and compromise with one another, freer from constraints that would have prevailed in public discussions. The process of the various dialogues, even without meaningful progress, also was useful at times in fostering publicity that showed one side or the other was taking action on issues of importance to their respective domestic constituencies, thereby assuaging at least temporarily the pressure of these constituencies for more confrontational approaches. Thus, for example, the process of dialogues on human rights and on trade issues was useful to US administration officials seeking to assuage domestic US pressure in Congress, the media and public opinion for tougher action toward China on these issues while avoiding legislation or other substantive steps that would jeopardize broader administration interests in sustaining constructive relations with China.[6]

In recent years, the scope of the many dozens of dialogues has broadened widely, involving most relevant senior official representatives in the two countries. The scope has grown in line with the rise of China and the importance of

US–China interchange on a host of wide-ranging global and regional as well as bilateral issues. In the decade after the Tiananmen crackdown, majorities in Congress registered opposition and wariness to any engagement with China seen as beneficial to the Chinese administration. Over time, Congressional opposition declined and Congress created a variety of formal exchanges enhancing dialogue and interchange with Chinese counterparts.

The notable exception in the pattern of growing Sino-American official dialogues has been in exchanges between the two militaries, which are covered in depth in Christopher Yung's contribution to this volume (Chapter 10). Briefly, the US cut military exchanges with China after the Tiananmen crackdown. Senior-level official dialogue between the defense organizations of China and the US was slowly restored in the following decade. The dialogue was significantly constrained under the leadership of US Defense Secretary Donald Rumsfeld (2001–6) but was strongly encouraged under US Defense Secretary Robert Gates (2006–11) and Leon Panetta (2011–13) and enjoys the strong support of current Defense Secretary Chuck Hagel and his Chinese counterparts.[7] China at times has used cuts in and suspension of military exchanges to register its opposition to US decisions providing arms to Taiwan, but it has supported such exchanges more strongly over the past two years.[8]

The overall record of dialogues shows that they are important instruments in the policy "tool kit" of each side to deal with salient areas of common interests and disagreement that have broadened in scope as a result of China's rising international importance and the increasing salience of an ever-wider range of issues in US–Chinese relations in the twenty-first century. Both sides view these policy instruments positively; they serve as shock absorbers in periods of difficulty, provide the basis for actual or potential channels of informal communication in times of crisis, and promote efforts to broaden common ground in US–Chinese relations. The checkered record of military exchanges is among the array of evidence showing the reality that dialogues are subservient to the respective interests of the leaders on either side. Dialogues are instruments of improved relations but they do not compel improvement, which at bottom is decided by policy elites in Beijing and Washington. After 40 years of efforts to normalize US–China relations, those elites cooperate closely on a wide range of issues but also reflect wariness toward one another that underlines important diverging interests and differences dividing the two powers.

Specialists on both sides of the Pacific have had a tendency recently to stress the competitive aspects of Sino-American relations. The year 2012 saw a strong emphasis on mutual distrust, and developments that year tested the durability of Sino-American engagement. As shown below, dialogues were among the means used by the two powers to manage the competition and pragmatically build ties amid sometimes adverse circumstances.

This chapter briefly reviews highlights of the role exchanges and dialogues have played in US–China relations since President Nixon's visit to China in 1972. Against that background, it examines the process and significance of recent dialogues. It forecasts the likely continued importance of the dialogues, as they help to build growing common ground and deal with an ever-widening array of differences and issues prompted by China's rising international impact and the overall importance of Sino-American relations.

Past experiences and recent practice

President Nixon foreshadowed his opening to China in an article in *Foreign Affairs* prior to his election in 1968 that called for efforts to end China's isolation. As the secret efforts of the president and his National Security Adviser Henry Kissinger moved into higher gear, the president told the nation and the world in his foreign policy report of 1971 that developing a relationship with China was the challenge of the decade and that the US was prepared to establish a dialogue with Beijing. Following the president's visit in February 1972, scholar Jean Garrison found that the administration argued that:

> candid exchanges with Chinese officials lessened the risks of miscalculation and misunderstanding and thereby strengthened prospects for long-term peace.... In order to improve bilateral relations, contact would be maintained through various channels, trade would be more open, and cultural and scientific exchanges would increase.[9]

The record shows that Nixon and Kissinger took on a large share of the responsibilities for dialogue of the senior leaders of the US government in interchange with the Chinese government. They kept many of the sensitive exchanges out of public view. For example, their assurances to Chinese leaders about US policy regarding Taiwan did not become known beyond a small circle of US government officials until decades later. At the same time, the Nixon and Ford administration transferred intelligence information, promoted other security, economic and cultural exchanges, and facilitated repeated visits to China by Congressional leaders.[10]

The administration of President Jimmy Carter also adopted an approach of secret talks with Chinese leaders in reaching agreement on the normalization of US diplomatic relations with China, announced in December 1978. It followed with a broad-ranging and highly public effort to show progress in the relationship with efforts to engage different segments of the US government involved with economic and security policy in particular to interact with Chinese counterparts. It also facilitated important delegations of Congressional leaders visiting China to assess the implications of improved relations.[11]

After overcoming serious differences concerning US arms sales to Taiwan and China's shift to a more even-handed public posture between the US and the Soviet Union during the Ronald Reagan administration in the early 1980s, growing interchange between the two governments developed relatively smoothly through normal diplomatic and other channels and occasional high-level visits. This period lasted until the crisis caused by the Tiananmen crackdown. President George H.W. Bush sought to preserve key elements of constructive US engagement with China despite majorities in Congress backed by media, elite, and public opinion calling for more punitive US measures. With the strong backing of Congress, US government exchanges and interactions with Chinese counterparts were ended or curtailed. President Bush reverted to the secret channels of dialogue used by Nixon and Carter, sending his National Security Adviser on two secret missions to China in order to sustain dialogue with China's leaders.[12]

Bush seriously damaged his domestic credibility by resorting to high-level secret dialogue while publicly promising to avoid high-level official contacts with China after Tiananmen. Less controversial was the establishment of a formal dialogue with the Chinese administration on the subject of human rights. This kind of special dialogue established a pattern seen in the plethora of bilateral dialogues in US–Chinese relations evident today.[13]

Endeavoring to break out of its isolation from developed countries after the Tiananmen crackdown, the Chinese administration was sometimes willing to establish special dialogues on human rights with Western-oriented countries, including the US. In the private discussions, the two sides could lay out their competing perspectives and perhaps make some progress in narrowing differences. Under the circumstances, the salience of human rights issues as an obstacle to constructive relations was reduced and tensions over instances of controversial human rights behavior were more effectively managed. Without access to precise information on what issues were discussed and how the discussion developed, domestic constituencies favoring a harder line on human rights issues were unable to gain much traction in efforts to push for a tougher approach on human rights differences.[14]

Policy calculations in the US and a number of other countries that had sanctioned China on account of the Tiananmen crackdown evolved to a point where policy and practice came to favor constructive albeit conditional engagement with the Chinese government through dialogues, exchanges, trade, and other means. A Council on Foreign Relations compendium summarized views on such dialogues and interchange in China, the US, and among China's neighbors in the Asia-Pacific Region (APR) in the mid-1990s. It argued in favor of greater economic integration and security stabilization with rising China in so far as China abided by "ten principles" involving such issues as non-use of force, military moderation and respect for human rights. What the book's authors entitled "weaving the net of conditional engagement" involved a web of exchanges and arrangements where dialogues and other such interchange would play their role in influencing Chinese behavior in constructive directions guided by the ten principles.[15]

The Bill Clinton administration in its second term came to emphasize the belief that closer engagement through various channels, dialogues, and other interchange with China would hasten the forces of globalization and modernization seen moving China to change in directions more consistent with US-backed norms. At the time, the Chinese and US governments had shifted to a more positive posture to one another as they sought to build a cooperative strategic partnership.[16]

The George W. Bush administration initially was wary of rising China. A clash between a Chinese jet fighter and a US reconnaissance plane off China's coast on April 1, 2001, killed the Chinese pilot and forced the damaged US plane to make an emergency landing in China where the crew was detained for 11 days and the plane was held by China for months. The experience reinforced the resistance of the Bush Jr administration's defense leadership to interact with China, even though the administration's broad strategic focus shifted dramatically away from a tough line to China as the US moved to combat global terrorism following the terrorist attack on America in September 2001.[17]

By 2003, the Bush administration actively sought stability and cooperation in relations with China as the US deepened military involvement in the Middle East following the attack on Iraq in 2003 and faced a major crisis caused by North Korea's public break with past nonproliferation agreements and active push to develop nuclear weapons. For its part, China was anxious to sustain a cooperative relationship with the US and in the process build interdependencies that would constrain future US pressure against China.[18]

Soon the two governments were working together closely and dealing with differences through a rapidly growing array of official dialogues and sub-dialogues. Beginning in 2005, a so-called "senior dialogue" involved meetings more frequent that once a year between the Deputy Secretary of State and China's Executive Vice-Foreign Minister. Sometimes lasting more than one day, the dialogues covered a broad range of international issues involving China and the US and also reviewed the work of various sub-dialogues focused on specific world regions and other questions.[19]

Beginning in 2006, the US and Chinese administrations employed a "US–China Strategic Economic Dialogue" (SED) in order to deal with the wide array of often contentious economic issues between the two countries. According to the US Department of Treasury, the "essential goal" of the dialogue was to "ensure that the benefits of the growing economic relationship with China are fairly shared by the citizens of both countries." The Treasury statement appeared to reflect rising criticism on the part of the media, labor groups, Democratic Party politicians, and many in the US Congress that US economic relations with China essentially involved more cost and less benefit for the US than for China.[20]

The dialogue was led by US Treasury Secretary Henry Paulson and China's Vice-Premier Wu Yi. US Cabinet and Chinese State Council leaders involved included the heads of departments and ministries dealing with commerce, trade, finance, agriculture, health, environment, and energy, and other senior administrators. The body's broad-ranging discussions complemented ongoing dialogues on more specific issues conducted by such groups as the Joint Commission on Commerce and Trade (JCCT), the Joint Economic Committee of the US Treasury Department, and the Chinese Ministry of Finance and Joint Commission on Science and Technology, bringing together senior US and Chinese administrators in these areas.[21]

Bush administration officials and independent scholars saw great merit in what became a complicated matrix of over 60 dialogues between the US and

Chinese administrations. China scholar Thomas Christensen, who participated in many dialogues while serving for two years as Deputy Assistant Secretary of State with responsibility for China, depicted the Bush administration's many dialogues with China as a major part of an effective administration strategy to elicit cooperation from China. He saw important progress in US–China cooperation over North Korea's nuclear program, somewhat less but still significant progress on dealing with the genocide in Darfur, Sudan, and less progress in dealing with issues involving Myanmar and Iran. In economic issues, Christensen saw progress in the rise in US exports to China. He saw little progress in human rights and religious freedom issues, while China's lack of transparency in its military buildup was compounded by Beijing's suspension of military-to-military contacts on account of a US sale of a large package of arms to Taiwan in 2008.[22]

Dennis Wilder, a veteran CIA China analyst and administrator, who served for many years as the senior staff member with responsibility for China on the George W. Bush National Security Council, also argued strongly in favor of the beneficial effects of the US dialogues with China. He added to Christensen's list of accomplishments in noting that the SED saw China increase the value of its currency by 20 percent in two years, thereby offsetting building Congressional pressure for punitive trade actions against China.[23] Meanwhile, US–China relations specialist Jean Garrison judged, on the basis of her research and a one-year fellowship working with the China desk at the Department of State, that the various dialogues at the senior level had the added benefit of forcing the sometimes divided US government bureaucracies to deal with China in a more uniform and coherent manner consistent with the positive direction favored by the president.[24] Her observation complements that of US participants in the dialogues noted earlier who argued that the process had a beneficial effect in compelling the Chinese administration to involve relevant stakeholders in the often poorly integrated Chinese international affairs apparatus in order to insure effective implementation of agreements reached during the US–Chinese dialogues.

Congressional dialogues

Concurrent with the rise of official dialogues linking the US and Chinese administrations was a rise of official linkages between the US Congress and its Chinese counterparts. As seen in Dennis Wilder's observation noted above that Congress' tougher line on trade issues might have led to a trade war had not the SED intervened and prompted Chinese currency changes, the US Congress was usually depicted as more wary and negative than the US administration regarding the implications of closer relations with China.

Congress broadly welcomed Nixon's breakthrough visit to China but registered through the Taiwan Relations Act (TRA) and other means strong opposition to President Carter's decision to break all ties with Taiwan and to push ahead strongly with engagement with China. Congress was the focal point of resistance to George H.W. Bush's secret dialogue and other efforts to sustain positive engagement with China when American opinion broadly favored a punitive approach. Many in Congress were disappointed with President Clinton's shift in 1994 from a policy explicitly linking the granting of US most favored nation trade benefits to China to conditions that China improve its human rights practices in ways favored by the US. Congress was almost uniform in pressing the president to take the controversial step of allowing Taiwan's president to visit the US in 1995. Congress was the scene of a white hot and often very partisan debate on China policy for the rest of Clinton's tenure. The debate focused on such issues as Chinese spying, influence peddling, human rights and economic practices, and the threat posed by Chinese military advances. In this context, legislation was passed that restricted US defense exchanges with China that would facilitate Chinese military advances.[25]

Against this background, the exchanges that developed between Congress and Chinese counterparts in the recent decade appeared remarkable. Scholars have identified several reasons for the change. One involved pragmatic recognition that China's international importance, especially as a trade partner and place of ever-growing investment by US firms, meant that constructive US interaction with China was important to protect and foster the interests of important Congressional constituencies. A second had to do with the decline of partisanship over China policy as Republicans controlled the White House and the Congress, and did so with considerable vigor and party discipline.[26]

A third reason involved the impact of the terrorist attack on America in September 2001, the following wars in Afghanistan and Iraq and the overall war on terrorism. Preoccupied with these wide-ranging endeavors of central importance to US national security, Congress reverted to its traditional posture during such periods of national emergency and generally eschewed resistance and followed the lead of the president. The pattern of Congress asserting its rights in foreign affairs seen in the TRA and other Congressional practice since the end of Vietnam War was no more. Congress saw its interests best served by going along with the directions favored by the president. The shift to Congressional acquiescence reached a point where the results included the most serious challenges to Congressional constitutional rights in many decades carried out by Bush administration leaders in dealing with issues of war powers, use of coercive interrogation widely seen as torture, detaining suspects, and other sensitive issues. Congress did little in the face of these challenges.[27]

In short, an increasingly pragmatic, preoccupied, and acquiescent Congress saw benefit in developing channels of interchange with China in parallel with the growth of official dialogues between the two administrations. Because of the diffused authority and weak institutional structure in Congress and the fact that Congressional initiatives toward China often depended on the initiative and interests of individual members, the various forms of exchange and dialogue changed over time. But the overall increase in these constructive exchanges was clearly registered in the following ways.[28]

The US House of Representatives Inter-Parliamentary Exchange was notably active under the leadership of Representative Donald Manzullo (R.-Ill.). Manzullo led Congressional delegations to China in 2002, 2003, and 2005 for site visits and talks with Chinese officials. Chinese delegations of legislators and related officials also visited Washington, DC. The Manzullo-led delegation to China in 2005 marked the seventh US–China parliamentary dialogue which the US and Chinese sides agreed had provided "the most efficient way to deepen mutual understanding."[29]

The US Senate US–China Inter-Parliamentary Exchange program was established in 2004 with the aim of exchanging views on salient issues in US–China relations. Senate leaders Ted Stevens (R-AK) and Daniel Inoyue (D-HI) led delegations to China in 2004 and 2006, and hosted Chinese counterparts visiting Washington, DC. During the 2006 visit, Hu Jintao met with the Senate leaders and underlined that the exchanges between Chinese and US legislative bodies "served as a vigorous driving force for bilateral relations."[30]

Following a visit to China in 2005, Representative Randy Forbes (R-Va.) worked with Representative Ike Skelton (D-Mo.) to establish the Congressional China Caucus, which had a membership of 35 House members. Both Forbes and Skelton were leaders of the House Armed Services Committee and their interests seen during visits to China and interchange with Chinese counterparts focused on the strategic importance of China's rising influence in regional and world affairs as well as longstanding bilateral issues in US–China relations.

Also in 2005, Representative Mark Kirk (R-Ill.) and Representative Rick Larsen (D-Wash.) established the US–China Congressional Working Group, which had a membership of 30 House members. The group followed an active agenda of seminars, trips to China, and interchange with Chinese visitors that focused on discussion and understanding of China-related issues with the belief that "it is vital for Congress to increase its dialogue" with China.[31]

Meanwhile, the Chinese embassy sustained an active program of exchanges with Congressional staff members. The efforts began slowly in the 1980s and gradually picked up speed. By the end of the Bush Jr administration, the embassy had partnered with Chinese institutes and American non-government organizations in arranging and paying for over 100 Congressional staff delegations to visit China for consultations with relevant Chinese officials and experts and sight seeing.[32]

The Obama administration: new dialogue and mixed results

Presidential candidate Barack Obama was unusual in recent US presidential campaign politics in not making an issue of his predecessor's China policy. Like outgoing President George W. Bush, the new president steered a course with China involving pursuing constructive contacts, preserving and protecting American interests, and dealing effectively with challenges posed by rising Chinese influence and power.

A strong theme in President Obama's initial foreign policy was to seek the cooperation of other world powers, notably the world's second ranking and rapidly rising power, China, to deal with salient international concerns such as the global economic crisis and recession, climate change, nuclear weapons proliferation, and terrorism. He and his team made strong efforts to build common ground with China on these and related issues. Heading the list of these efforts was the creation of a new overarching dialogue, the S&ED. The new body replaced George W. Bush's Senior Dialogue and SED. The S&ED met annually and had two dimensions, a "strategic track" which involved consultations led by Secretary of State Hillary Clinton and Chinese State Councilor Dai Bingguo, and an "economic track," led by Treasury Secretary Timothy Geithner and Chinese Vice-Premier Wang Qishan.

The outward manifestations of high-level US–Chinese interchange seen notably in the S&ED meetings, Obama's 2009 visit to China, and Hu Jintao's 2011 visit to the US were positive with various outcomes hailed by both sides. The announcement of the results of the "strategic track" of the 2010 S&ED meeting listed "26 specific outcomes" ranging along a wide array of economic, strategic and other bilateral, regional, and global issues.[33] The announcement of the "strategic track" of the 2011 S&ED meeting listed "48 specific outcomes, and that for the 2012 S&ED listed 50 outcomes."[34]

Despite the positive announcements, however, the Obama administration came to see China's leaders offering limited cooperation. Chinese leaders seemed focused much more on their own interests than the need for global responsibility urged by President Obama. Chinese officials for their part often suspected that added global responsibilities would hold back China's economic development and modernization. And they criticized US arms sales to Taiwan, Obama's meeting with the Dalai Lama, US military surveillance along China's periphery, and a variety of US economic policies and practices.[35]

More worrisome, some Chinese actions and truculence directly challenged the policies and practices of the US. Chinese government patrol boats confronted US surveillance ships in the South China Sea (SCS). Chinese efforts to solidify relations with North Korea at a time of North Korean leadership succession, blatant North Korea nuclear proliferation, and military attacks on South Korea seemed to destroy previous common ground between China and the US and its South Korean ally on how to deal with the North Korean threats. China challenged US and South Korean military exercises designed to deter further North Korean military aggression in the Yellow Sea. Chinese reaction to US arms sales to Taiwan and Obama's meeting with the Dalai Lama was harsher than in the recent past. Chinese officials threatened to stop investing in US government securities and to move away from using the US dollar in international transactions. And the Chinese government reacted very harshly to US government interventions urging collective efforts to manage tensions in the SCS and affirming that the US–Japan alliance provides for American support for Japan over such disputed territories as islands in the East China Sea (ECS) controlled by Japan but claimed by China.[36]

The Obama government reacted calmly and firmly to what Secretary of State Clinton called these "tests" or manifestations of new assertiveness by China. It gave no ground on any of the Chinese demands. It also found that prominent

Chinese truculence with the US and neighboring Asian countries over maritime, security and other issues seriously damaged China's efforts to portray a benign image in Asia. Asian governments became more active in working more closely with the US and in encouraging an active US presence in the APR. Their interest in closer ties with the US meshed well with the Obama government's broad effort to "re-engage" with the countries of the Asia-Pacific, ranging from India to the Pacific Islands. The overall effect was a decline in China's position in the APR and a rise in the position of the US.[37]

Meanwhile, the Obama government made clear to the Chinese government and the world that the US was prepared to undertake military measures needed to deal with the buildup of Chinese forces targeting Americans and American interests in the APR. US officials also helped to move China to curb North Korea's repeated provocations by warning privately as well as publicly that the US viewed North Korea's nuclear weapons development as not just a regional issue and concern for global nonproliferation but a direct threat to the US.[38]

The period leading up to Hu Jintao's visit to Washington, January 18–20, 2011, saw actions from China designed to ease recent tensions and set a smoother course for US–China relations. The harsh rhetoric criticizing US policies and practices subsided; the Chinese put aside their objections to high-level military exchanges and Secretary of Defense Robert Gates re-established businesslike ties at the top levels of the Chinese military during a visit to Beijing in early January 2011; China used its influence to get North Korea to stop its provocations against South Korea and to seek negotiations over nuclear weapons issues; China avoided undercutting international sanctions to press Iran to give up its nuclear weapons program; China allowed the value of its currency to appreciate in recent months; and Chinese officials were more cooperative over climate change issues at an international meeting in Cancun than they were a year earlier.[39]

The successful US–China summit in January 2011, the S&ED meeting in May 2011, and subsequent high-level exchanges capped by Vice-President Xi Jinping's visit to the US in February 2012 helped to sustain positive momentum in US–China relations, even though the many differences between the two countries continued. President Obama made clear that he wanted to pursue closer engagement with China as part of his administration's overall re-engagement with the APR. His administration also made clear that it would not give in to Chinese assertiveness or pressure, and, if needed, it would respond to such Chinese actions with appropriate military, diplomatic or other means.[40]

2012: testing US–China engagement and the role of dialogues

2012 was a year of leadership transition in China and a presidential election in the US. At the 18th Congress of China's Communist Party during November, President Hu passed party and military leadership positions to Xi Jinping, who became president during the National People's Congress meeting in March 2013. President Obama ended a long and acrimonious presidential campaign, defeating

Republican nominee Mitt Romney. Meanwhile, North Korea's leadership succession following the death of Kim Jong-il in December 2011 and elections in such key regional governments as Taiwan, South Korea, and Japan influenced circumstances along the rim of China – the main arena where China and the US are encountering one another in increasingly competitive ways.

Growing divergence and competition

Growing divergence and competition in Asia headed the list of issues in 2012 that challenged and tested the abilities of American and Chinese leaders to manage their differences, avoid confrontation and pursue positive engagement. Senior US and Chinese leaders stayed in close contact with one another in an avowed effort to search for a "new type of great power relationship" which would avoid conflict and manage tensions as China's rising power and expanding interests rub against American interests, policies and practices. Nevertheless, competition for influence along China's rim and in the broader APR exacerbated an obvious security dilemma in this sensitive region featuring China's rising power and America's reaction, shown notably in the two sides' respective military build-ups. These problems and Sino-American differences on a wide range of international issues and domestic pressures on both sides led to what leading specialists Kenneth Lieberthal and Wang Jisi characterized as pervasive and deeply rooted distrust between the two governments.[41]

The Republican presidential primaries saw sharp and often hyperbolic attacks on Chinese economic and security policies. Governor Romney emerged from the pack as the party's nominee, supporting tough trade and security measures to protect US interests against China. Obama joined the fray with harsh rhetoric not seen in his presidential campaign in 2008. In the third presidential debate on October 22, 2012, veteran China specialist Donald Keyser noted that the president publicly referred to China for the first time as "an adversary" though the president added that it is a "potential partner in the international community if it follows the rules." Obama highlighted his administration's re-engagement with countries in the APR as a means to compete with China in security, economic, and other terms.[42]

The Obama government's re-engagement policy toward the APR indeed underlined a stronger American determination to compete more broadly for influence in the region. The security aspects of the so-called pivot to Asia involved US redeployment of forces from the Middle East and other areas to the APR and the determination of the American leaders to sustain and advance US security relations and power despite anticipated cuts in overall US defense spending. Actual advances in US force deployments remained modest though the scope, tempo, and intensity of US military interactions with the region continued to grow.[43]

American diplomatic activism in support of its interests was registered with an impressive advance in senior US leaders headed by President Obama traveling to the region and participating actively in bilateral relations and existing and newly emerging regional groupings involving the US. Regional problems impacting US interests in regional stability, freedom of navigation and relations with allies and partners saw the American leaders take an active role in discussing ways to manage and hopefully ease tensions over sensitive sovereignty and security concerns in disputed maritime territories along China's rim.

As President Obama indicated in his remarks in the October debate, the US also was more active in competing in support of its economic interests as part of the re-engagement with Asia. A highlight of US interest has been the proposed Trans Pacific Partnership (TPP) free trade agreement involving the US and countries on both sides of the Pacific in an arrangement seen moving forward American interests in regional and international trade liberalization. The proposed agreement is viewed as competing with groupings favored by China that require less trade liberalization and that exclude the US.

Chinese media and officials condemned the so-called China bashing seen in the American presidential and Congressional election campaigns. The Chinese leaders remained firm in deflecting American pressure on the value of China's currency and broader trade practices and strongly rebuffed US efforts to get China's cooperation in dealing with some sensitive international issues, notably the conflict in Syria. China repeatedly gave priority to sustaining ties with North Korea despite the latter's continued provocations such as long-range ballistic missile tests in April and December 2012 and a nuclear weapons test in February 2013. They equivocated in the face of US calls for greater pressure on Pyongyang.

Concurrent with the increased competition between the US and China for influence in the APR, China resorted to extraordinary demonstrations of state power, short of direct use of military force, in response to perceived challenges by US allies the Philippines and Japan regarding disputed territory in the SCS and the ECS. Chinese commentary accused the US of fostering neighboring countries to be more assertive in challenging China's claims as part of alleged American efforts to contain China under the rubric of the Obama government's re-engagement with the APR. Top Chinese leaders countered American supported efforts for dealing with the disputed claims and also highlighted regional trade arrangements that excluded the US in order to undermine American-led efforts to advance US interests through the TPP.

Against this backdrop, leading American China specialist David Shambaugh joined other commentators in concluding at the end of the year that the overall US–China relationship has becomes "more strained, fraught and distrustful." Intergovernmental meetings and dialogues meant to forge cooperation are becoming more pro-forma and increasingly acrimonious, he said; the two sides wrangle over trade and investment issues, technology espionage and cyber hacking, global governance challenges like climate change and Syria, nuclear challenges like Iran and North Korea, and their security postures and competition for influence in the APR.[44]

Cooperation and moderation

While the competitive aspects of the US–China relationship grew in 2012 and challenged the utility of Sino-American dialogues and other forms of engagement, this chapter also pays due attention to the other side of the ledger in 2012. The latter showed Sino-American developments and circumstances arguing for continued pragmatism on both sides in seeking to manage escalating competition and other differences through dialogues and other means without major incident. The overall trend of resilient and positive US–China engagement continued.

Among instruments serving to moderate the Sino-American frictions, the wide range of official Chinese–American official exchanges through an array of over 70 bilateral dialogues continued and made significant progress in several areas. They also provided mechanisms for dealing with contentious issues and advancing common ground between the two countries. The on-again off-again pattern of exchanges between the military leaders of both countries – the weakest link in the array of dialogues between the two countries – was on again with improved exchanges since 2012.[45]

The so-called Taiwan issue – historically the leading cause of friction between the US and China – has remained on a recent trajectory of easing tensions. The sharp turn by the Taiwan government from longstanding and often virulent competition to extensive engagement and cooperation with China came with the election of President Ma Ying-jeou in 2008. The change was strongly welcomed by the Chinese and American governments. Taiwan's election in January 2012 and the victory of incumbent President Ma validated the moderate continued approach to cross-strait relations, foreshadowing closer engagement along lines welcomed by both Beijing and Washington. A possible exception to US–Chinese convergence over Taiwan is American arms sales sought by Taiwan, which are always a sensitive issue in China and in recent years have at times prompted stronger Chinese reactions than in the past.[46]

Despite pervasive Sino-US distrust, there also were episodes demonstrating notable cooperation and seeming trust building between the two powers. Heading the list was the close and successful cooperation over highly sensitive issues involving sovereignty and strong national sentiment seen in the Sino-American handling of the case of Chen Guangcheng. The prominent Chinese civil rights activist in April 2012 escaped house arrest and fled from his home province to Beijing, where he eventually took refuge in the US embassy. After several days of talks between US officials working with Chen on one side and Chinese officials on the other, a deal was reached to safeguard Chen and his family and provide Chen with medical treatment. Chen subsequently changed his mind and sought to go to the US with his family. He appealed for American support, notably in a highly publicized phone conversation directed to a US Congressional committee hearing. Intensive renewed US–Chinese talks concurrent with the annual S&ED between top American and Chinese department leaders then under way in Beijing resulted in a second deal whereby Chen and his family were allowed to leave for the US on May 19. It is noteworthy that the key negotiators in this tortuous process were the leaders of a newly created and active Sino-American dialogue on Asian-Pacific matters, Chinese Vice-Foreign Minister Cui Tiankai and US Assistant Secretary of State Kurt Campbell. Cui's remarks at the end of this chapter testify to the utility of dialogues in US–Chinese relations in the period ahead.[47]

Meanwhile, the Obama government has endeavored since late 2012 to stress its interests in sustaining broader and deeper American engagement with the APR on the one hand, while on the other hand playing down emphasis in the recent past on American security and military moves that add directly to the growing security dilemma with China. Obama's trip to Southeast Asia and meetings with regional leaders at summits with Southeast Asian and Asian Pacific leaders in November 2012 received extraordinary US government publicity emphasizing sustained cooperation along a broad array of economic, diplomatic, as well as security areas and soft pedaling competition with China. Meanwhile, competition with China also was played down by other US leaders visiting Asia as the US sought to calm tensions raised by the actions of China and other claimants to disputed islands along China's rim.[48]

Finally, specialists on both the American and Chinese sides seemed to agree that effectively managing differences through a process of constructive engagement remains in the interests of both countries.[49] Thus, American specialists have noted that there are three general reasons for this judgment:

- Both administrations benefit from positive engagement in various areas. Such engagement supports their mutual interests in stability in the APR, a peaceful Korean peninsula, and a peaceful settlement of the Taiwan issue; US and Chinese leaders recognize the need to cooperate to foster global peace and prosperity, to advance world environmental conditions, and to deal with climate change and nonproliferation.
- Both administrations see that the two powers have become so interdependent that emphasizing the negatives in their relationship will hurt the other side but also will hurt them. Such interdependence is particularly strong in Sino-American economic relations.
- Both leaderships are preoccupied with a long list of urgent domestic and foreign priorities; in this situation, one of the last things they would seek is a serious confrontation in relations with one another.

Prominent Chinese specialists visiting Washington at the end of 2012 underscored the futility of conflict and the need for cooperation in a somewhat different way. They averred that the US–China relationship has become increasingly important to both sides and that three "realities" compel the two governments to seek ways to manage their differences while trying to broaden common ground. Those realities are:

- Each country is too big to be dominated by the other.
- Each country has too unique a political and social structure to allow for transformation by the other.

- Each country has become too interdependent with the other to allow conflicts to disrupt their relationship.

Outlook: continued pragmatism and dialogue amid competition

The balance of competition and accommodation reviewed above argues for cautious optimism that pragmatic considerations will remain primary in the administrations of Presidents Obama and Xi. Such optimism was boosted by the results of the informal US–China summit in California in 2013. Both governments will be constrained from harsh actions toward one another by ever-deepening interdependence; and the forecast for both involves a variety of high priority and difficult issues that will reinforce their respective interests in sustaining dialogues and avoiding serious problems with one another. Of course, the competitive aspects of the relations appear to be growing, making positive forward movement in relations more difficult.

American domestic politics promise to be an overall drag on progress in US–China relations.[50] American public opinion and media coverage that tends to reflect public opinion show a majority of Americans disapprove of the Chinese government and its policies and practices. The majority is a slim one. There also seems to be a consensus among Americans that the US government should eschew serious trouble with China.

US Congressional opinion also tends to be more negative toward China than overall public opinion. Nonetheless, many in Congress reflect the interests of business constituents who are investing in China or otherwise have an important stake in the burgeoning US–China economic relationship. And many members of Congress have been active in Congressional working groups that regularly meet and hold dialogues with Chinese counterparts, often leading to more nuanced views of China on the part of Congressional participants. Meanwhile, Congressional attention on China issues has been secondary to more important domestic issues including US budget issues, deficit reduction, and tax policy, and more pressing international crises such as North Korea, Iran, Syria, and the broader Middle East. Congress in recent years also has demonstrated a strong tendency to defer to the president and not to assert its prerogatives on China or other foreign policy issues unless there is no serious danger for the US and particularly for US military service personnel and the president's policies seem to have failed.

Reflecting pragmatism amid continued wariness about China, President Obama upon re-election did not follow Governor Romney's injunction to label China as a currency manipulator. Rather his Treasury Department followed past practice in its periodic reports on these matters with muted treatment of China. As noted above, Obama's approach to China during his visit to Southeast Asia in November 2012 was more moderate and reserved in dealing with differences with China, while officials at all levels of his administration played down the sensitive security and competitive aspects of the President's re-engagement policy.

By 2014 the deepening exchanges and array of dialogues between Chinese and US officials appeared to enhance realistic and predictable relations that reduce the chances of confrontation not in the interest of either side. The scope of the dialogues involved the following:

- 24 dialogues and sub-dialogues under the auspices of the US–China Joint Commission on Commerce and Trade. They involved 13 dialogues on trade issues; four on intellectual property rights issues; and seven on such salient sectors as agriculture, textiles and steel.
- Some of the above dialogues fed into the high-level S&ED, which had 25 other dialogues or sub-dialogues under its auspices. They involved seven dialogues dealing with energy and climate change issues, six dealing with such diplomatic issues as human rights, counter-terrorism, and broad security discussions; five dealing with various regions of the world; and seven dealing with other categories ranging from traditional Chinese medicine to export controls.
- There also were 12 other dialogues of various kinds dealing with such topics as corruption, people-to-people exchanges, and science and technology, beside four dialogues conducted by the US and Chinese militaries.[51]

The continued US commitment to close dialogue with China has seen a steady stream of cabinet-level US visits to China. The Chinese commitment to continued dialogue seemed on display in these meetings with American officials.[52] Communication by new Chinese leaders with their American counterparts also showed strong commitment to dialogue and exchanges in managing the complicated relationship. Incoming State Councilor and former Foreign Minister Yang Jiechi, a veteran of Sino-American dialogues over many years, advised Secretary of State John Kerry in early April 2013 that the two governments "should enhance dialogue and mutual trust" and "maintain high-level visits and contacts" as the two powers develop their relationship.[53]

Another veteran of dialogues with the US, former Vice-Foreign Minister and new Chinese ambassador to the US Cui Tiankai, seemed to take aim at those specialists and others in both the US and China who recently have had a tendency to emphasize differences between the two countries and to view dialogues as of marginal utility in managing tensions and improving relations. According to official Chinese media, Cui said that he "does not agree with the so-called deficit of trust between China and the United States" and that in his experience "mutual trust is growing." Against the background of his long, deep, and sometimes intense personal experience in dialogues and related exchanges with US counterparts, Cui said:

> We have worked together on so many issues, and on some of these issues we will certainly have different interests and have different policies ... but still we have managed these issues quite well and the overall relationship is still developing.

Regarding mutual trust, he advised that "Maybe the level of confidence is not as high as we would like to see, but it is certainly growing."[54]

Notes

1 An earlier version of this chapter was published in *Issues & Studies* 49, no. 3 (September 2013): 1–34, and is used in this volume with permission. This chapter benefitted greatly from comments by the editors, panel commentator Professor Wang Jianwei, and participants at the workshop "40 Years after Sino-American Normalization," Hong Kong Institute of Education, Hong Kong, December 3, 2011. The author also thanks Nicholas Bellomy for timely research and editorial assistance.
2 Overviews providing information on US leaders views include, Harry Harding, *A Fragile Relationship: The United States and China since 1972* (Washington, DC: Brookings Institution Press: 1992); James Mann, *About Face: A History of America's Curious Relationship with China, from Nixon to Clinton* (New York: Alfred Knopf, 1999); David M. Lampton, *Same Bed, Different Dreams: Managing US–China Relations 1989–2000* (Berkeley: University of California Press, 2001); Jean A. Garrison, *Making China Policy: From Nixon to G.W. Bush* (Boulder, CO: Lynne Rienner Publishers, 2005); Nancy B. Tucker, *Strait Talk: United States–Taiwan Relations and the Crisis with China* (Cambridge, MA: Harvard University Press, 2009); Robert G. Sutter, *US–Chinese Relations: Perilous Past, Pragmatic Present* (Lanham, MD: Rowman & Littlefield, 2010); and Michael D. Swaine, *America's Challenge: Engaging a Rising China in the Twenty-First Century* (Washington DC: Carnegie Endowment for International Peace, 2011). For Chinese perspectives, see Institute of American Studies, Chinese Academy of Social Science, "China–US Relations: Tending Towards Maturity," *International Spectator* 44, no. 2 (June 2009): 9–16; Yuan Peng, "Where Are Sino-US Relations Headed?," *Contemporary International Relations* (Beijing) (September 2010): 53–62; Shen Qiang, "How to Assess Obama Administration's New Geo-Strategy toward Asia," *Foreign Affairs Journal* (Beijing) 98 (Winter 2010): 28–47. For a recent assessment on how both sides view and have used dialogues, see Bonnie Glaser, "The Diplomatic Relationship: Substance and Process," in *Tangled Titans: The United States and China*, ed. David L. Shambaugh (Lanham, MD: Rowman and Littlefield, 2013), 151–80.
3 Consultations during off-the-record meetings on December 15–16, 2011, at George Washington University with 25 American and Chinese specialists; all were experts on Sino-American dialogues and several of the Americans had participated in the dialogues.
4 James Shinn, ed., *Weaving the Net: Conditional Engagement with China* (New York: Council on Foreign Relations Press, 1996).
5 Sutter, *US–Chinese Relations*, 148–54.
6 Harding, "*A Fragile Relationship*," 341–3; Sutter, *US–Chinese Relations*, 13, 74–81, 105; Tucker, *Strait Talk*, 28–152, 225.
7 "Hegel Congratulates New Chinese Defense Minister," American Forces Press Service, April 3, 2013, www.defense.gov/news/newsarticle.aspx?id=119679.
8 On US arm sales to Taiwan, see Chapter 5 by Dennis Hickey and Kelan Lu in this book.
9 Garrison, *Making China Policy*, 30–1.
10 Tucker, *Strait Talk*, 28–85; Mann, *About Face*, 65.
11 Harding, *A Fragile Relationship*, 67–106.
12 Lampton, *Same Bed, Different Dreams*, 21–30.
13 Harding, *A Fragile Relationship*, 341–3.
14 Ibid.
15 Shinn, *Weaving the Net*, 1–28.

16 Lampton, *Same Bed, Different Dreams*, 46–61.
17 Swaine, *America's Challenge*, 55. The impact of the EP-3 incident is also addressed in Chapter 11 by Simon Shen and Ryan Kaminski in this book.
18 Sutter, *US–Chinese Relations*, 153,166.
19 *Conclusion of the Fourth US–China Senior Dialogue*, media note, June 21, 2007, http://2001-2009.state.gov/r/pa/prs/ps/2007/jun/86997.htm.
20 "Fact Sheet: Creation of the US–China Strategic Economic Dialogue," September 20, 2006, US Department of the Treasury, www.treasury.gov/press-center/press-releases/pages/hp107.aspx.
21 Ibid.
22 Thomas Christensen, "Shaping the Choices of a Rising China," *Washington Quarterly* 32, no. 3 (July 2009): 89–104.
23 Dennis Wilder, "The US–China Strategic and Economic Dialogue: Continuity and Change in Obama's China Policy," *Jamestown Foundation China Brief* 9, no. 10 (May 15, 2009), www.jamestown.org/single/?tx_ttnews percent5Btt_newspercent5D =34989&no_cache=1#.U-43mFawmoc.
24 Jean Garrison, "Managing the US–China Foreign Economic Dialogue," *Asia Policy* 4 (July 2007): 165–85.
25 Sutter, *US–Chinese Relations*, 79–81, 97–146.
26 Ibid., 126–7.
27 Gordon Silverstein, "The Law: Bush, Cheney, and the Separation of Powers: A Lasting Legal Legacy?" *Presidential Studies Quarterly* 39, no. 4 (December 2009): 878–95.
28 These examples are discussed in more detail in Bates Gill and Melissa Murphy *Meeting the Challenges and Opportunities of China's Rise: Expanding and Improving Interaction between the American and Chinese Policy Communities* (Washington, DC: Center for Strategic and International Studies, 2006).
29 "China's NPC Vice-Chairman Meets US Congress Guests," Xinhua August 3, 2005 cited in Gill and Murphy, *Meeting the Challenges and Opportunities of China's Rise*, 9.
30 "Hu Jintao Meets US Senate Acting President Stevens, Pledges to Further Bilateral Ties," Xinhua August 12, 2006 cited in Gill and Murphy, *Meeting the Challenges and Opportunities of China's Rise*, 10
31 From the website of Representative Mark Kirk, cited in Gill and Murphy, *Meeting the Challenges and Opportunities of China's Rise*, 11.
32 Xiaoning Wu, "The Congressional Exchanges" (seminar paper, Georgetown University, 2011), 4, 6.
33 US Department of State, *US–China Strategic and Economic Dialogue 2010 Outcomes of the Strategic Track*, media note, May 25, 2010, www.state.gov/r/pa/prs/ps/2010/05/142180.htm.
34 US Department of State, *US–China Strategic and Economic Dialogue 2011 Outcomes of the Strategic Track*, media note, May 10, 2011, www.state.gov/r/pa/prs/ps/2011/05/162967.htm; US Department of State, *Joint Statement on the US–China Strategic and Economic Dialogue Outcomes of the Strategic Track May 3–4, 2012*, media note, May 4, 2012, www.state.gov/r/pa/prs/ps/2012/05/189287.htm.
35 Jeffrey A. Bader, *Obama and China's Rise: An Insider's Account of America's Asia Strategy* (Washington DC: Brookings Institution Press, 2012); Sutter, *US–Chinese Relations*, 161–167.
36 Bader, *Obama and China's Rise*, 69–82; Minxin Pei, "China's Bumpy Ride Ahead," *The Diplomat*, February 16, 2011, www.The-diplomat.com; Robert Sutter, *Positive Equilibrium in US–China Relations: Durable or Not? A Time of "Testing" in Sino-American Relations* (Baltimore: University of Maryland School of Law, 2010).
37 Thomas J. Christensen, "The World Needs an Assertive China," *International Herald Tribune* February 21, 2011, www.nytimes.com/2011/02/21/opinion/21iht-edchristensen21.html. Hillary R. Clinton, interview by Greg Sheridan, *Interview with Greg Sheridan of The Australian*, November 8, 2010.

38 Elisabeth Bumiller, "US Will Counter Chinese Arms Buildup," *New York Times*, January 8, 2011, www.nytimes.com/2011/01/09/world/asia/09military.html; David Sanger, "Superpower and Upstart: Sometimes It Ends Well," *New York Times*, January 22, 2011, www.nytimes.com/2011/01/23/weekinreview/23sanger.html?pagewanted=all.
39 Sanger, "Superpower and Upstart"; "Beyond the US–China Summit," Foreign Policy Research Institute, February 4, 2011.
40 Mark Landler and Martin Fackler, "US Warning to China Sends Ripples to the Koreas," *New York Times*, January 20, 2011, www.nytimes.com/2011/01/21/world/asia/21diplo.html?pagewanted=all; Bonnie Glaser, "US Pivot to Asia Leave China off Balance," *Comparative Connections* 13, no. 3 (January 2012): 29–39. Matthew Pennington, "Xi wraps up highly scripted visit to us capital," Associated Press, February 15, 2012.
41 Kenneth Lieberthal and Wang Jisi, *Addressing US–China Strategic Distrust*, monograph no. 4 (Washington, DC: Brookings Institution, 2012).
42 Don Keyser, "President Obama's Re-Election: Outlook for US–China Relations in the Second Term," Nottingham University China Policy Institute Blog, November 7, 2012, http://blogs.nottingham.ac.uk/chinapolicyinstitute/2012/11/07/present-obamas-re-election-outlook-for-u-s-china-relations-in-the-second-term/.
43 The material in this paragraph and the following three paragraphs are discussed in greater detail in Robert G. Sutter, *US–Chinese Relations: Perilous Past, Pragmatic Present*, 2nd edn (Lanham, MD: Rowman & Littlefield Publishers, 2013), chapter 7.
44 David Shambaugh, "The Rocky Road Ahead in US–China Relations," *China–US Focus*, October 23, 2012.
45 Daljit Singh, "US–China Dialogue Process: Prospects and Implications," *East Asia Forum*, November 2, 2012, www.eastasiaforum.org/2012/11/02/us-china-dialogue-process-prospects-and-implications/.
46 Richard C. Bush, *Unchartered Strait: The Future of China-Taiwan Relations* (Washington, DC: Brookings Institution Press, 2013), 213–250; and Chapter 5 by Dennis Hickey and Kelan (Lilly) Lu in this volume.
47 Bonnie S. Glaser and Brittany Billingsley, "US–China Relations," *Comparative Connections* 14, no. 1 (May 2012): 29.
48 See The White House, Office of the Press Secretary, "Remarks by National Security Advisor Tom Donilon – as Prepared for Delivery 'President Obama's Asia Policy and Upcoming Trip to Asia'," news release, November 15, 2012, www.whitehouse.gov/the-press-office/2012/11/15/remarks-national-security-advisor-tom-donilon-prepared-delivery; Su Xiaohui, "Obama Will Be 'Smarter' in Rebalancing towards Asia and Engaging China," *China–US Focus*, November 8, 2012.
49 Consultations in Washington DC involving three groups of visiting Chinese specialists, involving 12 Chinese specialists, and 30 American specialists assessing US–China relations after the US elections, November 8, 15 and 16, 2012.
50 Each of the domestic US elements noted below are reviewed in Robert Sutter, "Domestic American Influences on US–China Relations," in *Tangled Titan*, ed. Shambaugh, 114–24.
51 Glaser, "The Diplomatic Relationship: Substance and Process," 175–6.
52 Xu Song, "Li Keqiang Meets US President's Special Representative and Treasury Secretary Jacob Lew," *Xinhua*, March 20, 2013.
53 "Call for Stronger Sino-US Dialogue," *Xinhua* replayed in *China Daily*, April 5, 2013, 2.
54 Ibid.

References

Bader, Jeffrey A. *Obama and China's Rise: An Insider's Account of America's Asia Strategy* (Washington, DC: Brookings Institution Press, 2012).
"Beyond the US–China Summit." Foreign Policy Research Institute. February 4, 2011.
Bumiller, Elisabeth. "US Will Counter Chinese Arms Buildup." *New York Times*. January 8, 2011. www.nytimes.com/2011/01/09/world/asia/09military.html.
Bush, Richard C. *Uncharted Strait: The Future of China–Taiwan Relations* (Washington, DC: Brookings Institution Press, 2013).
"Call for Stronger Sino-US Dialogue." *China Daily*, April 5, 2013.
Chinese Academy of Social Science. "China–US Relations: Tending Towards Maturity." *International Spectator* 44, no. 2 (June 2009): 9–16.
Christensen, Thomas J. "Shaping the Choices of a Rising China." *Washington Quarterly* 32, no. 3 (July 2009): 89–104.
Christensen, Thomas J. "The World Needs an Assertive China." *New York Times*. February 21, 2011. www.nytimes.com/2011/02/21/opinion/21iht-edchristensen21.html.
Clinton, Hillary R. Interview by Greg Sheridan. *Interview with Greg Sheridan of The Australian*. November 8, 2010.
Garrison, Jean A. *Making China Policy: From Nixon to G.W. Bush* (Boulder, CO: Lynne Rienner Publishers, 2005).
Garrison, Jean. "Managing the US–China Foreign Economic Dialogue." *Asia Policy* 4 (July 2007): 165–85.
Gill, Bates, and Melissa Murphy. *Meeting the Challenges and Opportunities of China's Rise: Expanding and Improving Interaction between the American and Chinese Policy Communities* (Washington, DC: Center for Strategic and International Studies, 2006).
Glaser, Bonnie S. "US Pivot to Asia Leave China off Balance." *Comparative Connections* 13, no. 3 (January 2012): 29–39.
Glaser, Bonnie S. and Brittany Billingsley, "US–China Relations." *Comparative Connections* 14, no. 1 (May 2012): 29–46.
Harding, Harry. *A Fragile Relationship: The United States and China since 1972* (Washington, DC: Brookings Institution Press, 1992).
"Hegel Congratulates New Chinese Defense Minister." American Forces Press Service. April 3, 2013. www.defense.gov/news/newsarticle.aspx?id=119679.
Keyser, Don. "President Obama's Re-election: Outlook for US–China Relations in the Second Term." Nottingham University China Policy Institute blog. November 7, 2012. http://blogs.nottingham.ac.uk/chinapolicyinstitute/2012/11/07/present-obamas-re-election-outlook-for-u-s-china-relations-in-the-second-term/.
Lampton, David M. *Same Bed, Different Dreams: Managing US–China Relations 1989–2000* (Berkeley: University of California Press, 2001).
Landler, Mark, and Martin Fackler. "US Warning to China Sends Ripples to the Koreas." *New York Times*, January 20, 2011. www.nytimes.com/2011/01/21/world/asia/21diplo.html?pagewanted=all.
Lieberthal, Kenneth, and Jisi Wang. *Addressing US–China Strategic Distrust*. Monograph No. 4 (Washington, DC: Brookings Institution, 2012).
Mann, James. *About Face: A History of America's Curious Relationship with China, from Nixon to Clinton* (New York: Alfred Knopf, 1999).
Pei, Minxin. "China's Bumpy Ride Ahead." *The Diplomat*. February 16, 2011. http://thediplomat.com/2011/02/chinas-bumpy-ride-ahead/.

Pennington, Matthew. "Xi Wraps up Highly Scripted Visit to US Capital." Associated Press, February 15, 2012.
Sanger, David E. "Superpower and Upstart: Sometimes It Ends Well." *New York Times*, January 22, 2011. www.nytimes.com/2011/01/23/weekinreview/23sanger.html?pagewanted=all.
Shambaugh, David L. "The Rocky Road Ahead in US–China Relations." *China–US Focus*, October 23, 2012.
Shambaugh, David L. *Tangled Titans: The United States and China* (Lanham, MD: Rowman & Littlefield, 2013).
Shen, Qiang. "How to Assess Obama Administration's New Geo-Strategy toward Asia." *Foreign Affairs Journal* (Beijing) 98 (Winter 2010): 28–47.
Shinn, James, ed. *Weaving the Net: Conditional Engagement with China* (New York: Council on Foreign Relations Press, 1996).
Silverstein, Gordon. "The Law: Bush, Cheney, and the Separation of Powers: A Lasting Legal Legacy?" *Presidential Studies Quarterly* 39, no. 4 (December 2009): 878–95.
Singh, Daljit. "US–China Dialogue Process: Prospects and Implications." *East Asia Forum*, November 2, 2012. www.eastasiaforum.org/2012/11/02/us-china-dialogue-process-prospects-and-implications/.
Song, Xu. "Li Keqiang Meets US President's Special Representative and Treasury Secretary Jacob Lew." *Xinhua*, March 20, 2013.
Su, Xiaohui. "Obama Will Be 'Smarter' in Rebalancing towards Asia and Engaging China." *China–US Focus*, November 8, 2012.
Sutter, Robert G. *Positive Equilibrium in US–China Relations: Durable or Not? A Time of "Testing" in Sino-American Relations* (Baltimore: University of Maryland School of Law, 2009).
Sutter, Robert G. *US–Chinese Relations: Perilous Past, Pragmatic Present* (Lanham, MD: Rowman & Littlefield Publishers, 2010).
Sutter, Robert G. *US–Chinese Relations: Perilous Past, Pragmatic Present*. 2nd edn (Lanham, MD: Rowman & Littlefield Publishers, 2013).
Swaine, Michael D. *America's Challenge: Engaging a Rising China in the Twenty-First Century* (Washington, DC: Carnegie Endowment for International Peace, 2011).
Tucker, Nancy B. *Strait Talk: United States–Taiwan Relations and the Crisis with China* (Cambridge, MA: Harvard University Press, 2009).
United States, Department of State. *Conclusion of the Fourth US–China Senior Dialogue*. Media note. June 21, 2007. http://2001–2009.state.gov/r/pa/prs/ps/2007/jun/86997.htm.
United States, Department of State. *Joint Statement on the US–China Strategic and Economic Dialogue Outcomes of the Strategic Track May 3–4, 2012*. Media note. May 4, 2012. www.state.gov/r/pa/prs/ps/2012/05/189287.htm.
United States, Department of State. *US–China Strategic and Economic Dialogue 2010 Outcomes of the Strategic Track*. Media note. May 25, 2010. www.state.gov/r/pa/prs/ps/2010/05/142180.htm.
United States, Department of State. *US–China Strategic and Economic Dialogue 2011 Outcomes of the Strategic Track*. Media note. May 10, 2011. www.state.gov/r/pa/prs/ps/2011/05/162967.htm.
United States, Department of the Treasury. "Fact Sheet Creation of the US–China Strategic Economic Dialogue." News release. September 20, 2006. www.treasury.gov/press-center/press-releases/pages/hp107.aspx.
United States, The White House. Office of the Press Secretary. "Remarks by National Security Advisor Tom Donilon – as Prepared for Delivery 'President Obama's Asia

Policy and Upcoming Trip to Asia'." News release. November 15, 2012. www.whitehouse.gov/the-press-office/2012/11/15/remarks-national-security-advisor-tom-donilon-prepared-delivery.

Wilder, Dennis. "The US–China Strategic and Economic Dialogue: Continuity and Change in Obama's China Policy." *Jamestown Foundation China Brief* 9, no. 10 (May 15, 2009). www.jamestown.org/single/?tx_ttnews percent5Btt_news percent5D=34989 &no_cache=1#.U-43mFawmoc.

Wu, Xiaoning. "The Congressional Exchanges." Seminar paper, Georgetown University, 2011.

Yuan, Peng. "Where Are Sino-US Relations Headed?" *Contemporary International Relations* (Beijing) (September 2010): 53–62.

10 Continuity and change in Sino-US military-to-military relations

Christopher D. Yung

Introduction

The United States and the People's Republic of China (PRC) have one of the most important bilateral relationships of the twenty-first century. Of all the aspects of this complex relationship, the weakest is the military-to-military relationship. This chapter will discuss the history of US–China military-to-military relations from normalization in 1979 to the present. It will note past obstacles to the development and deepening of military relations, discuss emerging dynamics in the military-to-military relationship, and assess whether these new dynamics are more conducive to greater or lesser cooperation. The chapter also examines potential mechanisms and policies that might produce greater military cooperation and assesses prospects for deeper military-to-military relations.

Defining terms and the purpose of military-to-military relations

Military-to-military relations are defined here as the interactions between the armed forces of the PRC and the US. This interaction may take place between uniformed or civilian personnel affiliated with either military. Military-to-military relations should also be a long-term, sustained effort and should not simply consist of short-term, one-off interactions between the personnel of the two militaries. Following his June 2010 speech at the Shangri-la dialog in Singapore, then Secretary of Defense Robert Gates stated that the Department of Defense "wants what both Presidents Barack Obama and Hu Jintao want: sustained and reliable military-to-military contacts at all levels that can help reduce miscommunication, misunderstanding, and the risks of miscalculation."[1] The 2011 report submitted to Congress by the Department of Defense on China's military power and capabilities notes that the "fundamental purpose for the two countries to conduct military-to-military relations is to gain a better understanding of how each side thinks about the role and use of military power in achieving political and strategic objectives."[2]

The author of this chapter defines military cooperation to mean any joint effort between the two militaries to work together to accomplish common goals or to build better working relations between the two militaries. Thus, if we take the history of the relations as illustrations of how the two countries and the two militaries have cooperated with one another, it is possible to create categories or hierarchies of military cooperation. Therefore in its most basic form, military cooperation may comprise individual dialogs and interactions.

A second category could comprise agreements between the two militaries of a sustained nature which are designed to accomplish a shared goal. These include: technology transfers; sales of military equipment; joint research; joint exercises; curriculum sharing agreements; and working level exchanges to address a specific problem area – e.g., the Military Maritime Consultative Agreement (MMCA).

Finally, high-level dialogs and interactions between the two countries' military leaders and their staffs is a third category of military cooperation. Examples include the Defense Consultative and Defense Policy Consultative Talks (DCTs and DPCTs); Strategic and Economic Dialogues (S&EDs); the strategic dialogs of the two national defense universities (NDUs); and visits by the Secretaries of Defense, Chiefs of Staff, and service secretaries/chiefs.[3]

US–China military-to-military relations, 1979 to the present

The Carter administration

Although strictly speaking the history of US–China military-to-military relations began in the aftermath of President Nixon's historic trip to China in 1972, the content of these military interactions was not substantial enough to warrant a lengthy discussion here. What military-to-military interaction and cooperation did take place during the Nixon and Ford administrations often never developed further because bureaucracies on both sides consistently decided against deepening the relationship until formal normalization occurred.[4] Almost immediately following normalization in 1979, President Jimmy Carter issued Presidential Review Memorandum 24, concluding that US weapons sales to China would worsen US relations with the Soviet Union, and therefore, the US would have to review whether arms sales to China should take place.[5] Not long after, however, National Security Adviser Zbigniew Brzezinski met with the Chinese in Beijing and informed them that the US was willing to share intelligence and would not object to third-party sales to China such as those then being contemplated by Great Britain and France.[6]

Sino-US military-to-military relations gathered momentum following Vice-Premier Deng Xiaoping's January to February 1979 visit to the US when Deng discussed the possibility of US navy port visits to China. Plans were initiated for a joint monitoring facility to be established in western China to monitor Soviet compliance with arms control agreements and the two sides also discussed the possibility of US arms sales to the PRC.[7] Before this momentum could be acted upon the US Congress passed the Taiwan Relations Act (TRA) requiring the executive branch to provide sufficient weapons sales to Taiwan to assist the island in bolstering its defense against mainland China. In protest, Beijing informed Washington of its unwillingness to proceed further on military-to-military activities.[8]

Military-to-military relations improved significantly following the Soviet invasion of Afghanistan in December 1979. The Carter administration agreed to establish a ground station in China[9] for the purposes of receiving data from Landsat satellites and to sell transport aircraft, military helicopters, and communications equipment, while the Chinese agreed in principle to sell arms to the anti-Soviet mujahideen in Afghanistan.[10] High-level exchanges also began to take place at this time. The Department of Defense and the Department of Commerce agreed to issue export licenses for numerous dual-use items and military equipment to China. These included C-130 transports, Chinook helicopters, and high-speed computers for geophysical analysis and mapping. Arms sales to China were made easier when in April 1980 China was removed from the Coordinating Committee for Multilateral Export Controls (COCOM) category as a Warsaw Pact country and given its own category, which permitted China to purchase certain weapons on a case-by-case basis.[11]

The Reagan administration

Reagan administration policy-makers from the start had their doubts about the value of military-to-military relations with the PRC. The Department of Defense (DOD) under Caspar Weinberger immediately vetoed sales involving technology transfers. Upon taking office the Reagan team also announced its intention to sell military spare parts and equipment to Taiwan.[12] As a consequence, US–China military-to-military relations stalled in 1981 and the early part of 1982. Beijing immediately announced that disagreement between the two sides over the status of Taiwan arms sales would affect progress in other bilateral issue areas.[13] The Reagan policy toward China softened by the summer of 1982, however, when the two countries signed the third US–PRC joint communiqué in which the administration promised to gradually reduce arms sales to Taiwan and work toward a thorough settlement of the arms sale issue, temporarily warming the frigid military-to-military relationship.[14]

Momentum for military-to-military relations in the mid-1980s built as US navy ships made port visits at Qingdao and the US air force sent its world famous demonstration team – the Thunderbirds – to Beijing. Even the thorny obstacle of defense technology transfers seemed to have been overcome as the Reagan administration agreed to four technology transfer deals: one involving investment and construction of a munitions factory; another involving the sale of the Mk 46 torpedo; another involving the sale of artillery-locating radar; and lastly, a $500 million deal to modernize the avionics on the F-8 interceptor.[15]

By the late 1980s, this momentum was stopped short by emerging problems in the larger bilateral relationship. Within the US, concerns both within DOD and in Congress over Chinese sales of Silkworm anti-ship cruise missiles to Iran prompted a DOD re-evaluation of military ties between the two countries.[16]

The George H.W. Bush administration

The June 1989 Tiananmen Square massacre had a huge impact on all aspects of bilateral relations, including military-to-military relations. Immediately following this event which some estimates indicate involved the loss of several thousand Chinese protesters' lives, the Bush administration froze all military-related activities with the People's Liberation Army (PLA), including attaché contacts, arms sales, technology transfer agreements, and high-level visits.[17] On Capitol Hill a number of lawmakers aggressively pushed for serious reviews and alterations in China policy and a number of Bush administration officials at the DOD and Department of State began to voice opposition to any military cooperation with China.[18]

By the early 1990s, however, the Bush Sr administration had completed its review of its China policy and had concluded that it was in the US interest to loosen some of the Tiananmen restrictions or at a minimum, to gradually wind down some of these programs. At the end of 1992 the Bush Sr administration had returned the F-8 fighters in the US back to China without the avionics upgrade, approved the sales of the anti-submarine warfare torpedo, the artillery-locating radar, and the munitions plant.[19] Still, the pall of the Tiananmen Square massacre continued to hang over the larger bilateral relationship and during the latter part of the Bush Sr administration's single term in office no high-level or functional exchanges took place, nor did any port visits or "operator" level exchanges take place.[20]

The Clinton administration

Following the failure of the Clinton administration's attempt to link most favored nation (MFN) status to improvement in China's human rights record, the administration sought a new approach.[21] The new Clinton administration's approach toward China involved a significant shift in the underlying philosophy behind the bilateral relationship from that of a balancer of the Soviet Union to an important post-Cold War foreign policy actor. Believing that the two countries had strong mutual interests going into the next century, the administration pushed for a more comprehensive engagement plan with the PRC. The Clinton administration argued that through enhanced interactions the Chinese military was more likely to be open, transparent, and communicative, thereby aiding the two countries in understanding each other's intentions.[22]

In 1994, Secretary of Defense William Perry visited China and reached agreement on a Joint Defense Conversion Commission to "better enable Chinese military plants to produce civilian products."[23] In particular, the two sides agreed to a range of projects involving the modernization of China's air traffic control system. The first high-level visits since the Tiananmen restrictions had been enacted began to take place.[24]

These military-to-military developments, including the proposed visit to Washington by Minister of Defense Chi Haotian were put in abeyance in 1995 when the US State Department granted a visa to Taiwan President Lee Teng-hui to visit his alma mater, Cornell University, to give a speech.[25] The Chinese, objecting to an apparent American violation of its one-China policy, cancelled the Chi visit and later on in the summer of 1995 launched short-range ballistic missiles in the vicinity of Taiwan to signal to the electorate there that re-election of a pro-independence candidate risked military retaliation by the PLA.[26] Military ties were cut off and went into a semi-deep freeze when the Chinese conducted additional ballistic missile firings in March 1996 to further influence the upcoming Taiwan elections. In response, President Clinton dispatched two aircraft carriers to the area. The US cancelled the rescheduled Chi Haotian visit.[27] While a few lower-level DOD visits did occur, no major DOD-related visits took place until June 1996 when Undersecretary of Defense for Policy Walter Slocombe visited Beijing.[28]

A notable side effect of the Taiwan missile firings of March 1996 was the reinforcement of the negative views of many in Congress and critics of the Clinton administration's China policy that the administration not only had the basic policy wrong; that is, that "engagement had not only not served as a deterrent to aggressive Chinese action toward Taiwan, but that the administration was guilty of a whole host of sins related to China": (1) it had either by accident or by design transferred space technologies to China in return for campaign contributions; (2) it focused too much effort on interacting with the Chinese military instead of on the substance and content of those interactions; and (3) the Chinese military was displaying a blatant lack of reciprocity when the two militaries met with each other.[29]

The preceding coupled with the Wen Ho Lee incident in which a Chinese American working at Los Alamos National Laboratory was accused by the FBI of disclosing nuclear weapons test data to the Chinese, and the release of the Cox Report, whose sponsoring committee was initially convened to investigate the "campaign contributions-space technology sale" controversy, led to the FY 2000 National Defense Authorization Act (NDAA 2000) which directed that the Secretary of Defense not authorize military contacts that might give the PLA inappropriate military capabilities.[30] The NDAA 2000 banned "inappropriate contacts" in the areas of force projection, nuclear weapons, logistics, chemical-biological defense and operations, and other weapons of mass destruction (WMD) areas. The bill also required that the DOD submit to Congress an annual report, which evaluated current and projected Chinese military capabilities.[31] The restrictions laid down by NDAA 2000 and its descendants still govern the DOD's interactions with the Chinese military today.

Ironically, the Taiwan Straits missile crisis convinced many Clinton administration officials that military-to-military relations were important in preventing misunderstandings and miscalculations between the two countries.[32] By the end of 1997 the two countries had agreed to restore functional exchanges at the lower levels and higher-level defense visits. The two countries also agreed to multilateral dialogues and discussions of confidence-building measures. During an October 1997 visit by Chinese President Jiang Zemin, the two countries agreed to establish a mechanism to discuss safe maritime operations – the MMCA – and agreed to share information in cases of humanitarian assistance and disaster relief.[33] The end of 1997 also brought the first US–China Defense Consultative Talks or DCTs. These talks, initially held by Deputy Chief of General Staff Xiong Guangkai and Undersecretary of Defense Slocombe, were designed to provide a venue to discuss security and defense related matters at the official policy level.[34]

By 1999 the military-to-military relationship was at its most robust since the 1980s. US officials had visited numerous PLA facilities and bases, including logistics units, PLA navy bases, and military defense academies. PLA visits by students, general officers and other military related officials, and functional experts were at an all-time high.[35] In 1999, however, yet another event shook the foundations of both bilateral and military-to-military relations. During the American bombing of Belgrade during the Kosovo campaign to convince then Serbian President Slobodan Milosevic to cease his genocidal policies, the US air force accidentally bombed the Chinese embassy in Belgrade, leading to the deaths of three Chinese reporters and injuring 20 embassy staff. The incident caused such an outrage in China with numerous "spontaneous" protests at the US embassy and US consulates in China in addition to Chinese acts of vandalism against US property, that the Chinese government immediately halted military-to-military relations.[36] This freeze of military relations lasted for most of the rest of 1999, until the Chinese agreed to permit a US ship to visit Hong Kong in September 1999. No military-to-military activities of note took place within this time frame. In November 1999 Kurt Campbell, the Deputy Assistant Secretary of Defense for Asia-Pacific Affairs, traveled to China to attempt to restart the defense relationship.[37] Secretary of Defense Cohen visited Beijing in July 2000 and announced that the two sides were planning a joint humanitarian assistance exercise, that a new round of US navy ship visits was being discussed, and that a delegation of Chinese army medical professionals were to visit the US.[38]

George W. Bush administration

Given the amount and intensity of the criticism received by the Clinton administration, the G.W. Bush administration entered office with a skeptical view of the value of military-to-military contacts with China. New Secretary of Defense Donald Rumsfeld conducted a thorough review of the military relationship "so as to institute discipline into the management of military contacts and to enable the US military to better respond to China's lack of reciprocity and transparency."[39] Rumsfeld was in the midst of this review in early 2001 when military-to-military relations received yet another shock following the "EP-3 incident" in which a Chinese F8-ii sent to intercept a USN EP-3 electronic surveillance plane struck the EP-3 flying in the South China Sea near Hainan Island.[40] Rumsfeld froze the military-to-military relationship in response and in May 2001 the DOD announced that it would review all military-to-military contacts on a case-by-case basis. By September 2001 only such military-to-military discussions as the

MMCA convened in order to discuss "rules of the road" and other important operational-level issues expected to emerge between navies and militaries operating in close proximity to one another.[41]

By the end of 2001, however, the relationship had sufficiently thawed that the Chinese approved the first US navy ship port visit since the EP-3 incident. Despite the resumption of military-to-military relations, one observer of the first term of the second Bush administration characterized the military-to-military relationship as "modest" and one that had purposely set low expectations of the value from these interactions.[42] However, former members of the Bush team contend that within the Pentagon there was an active interest in engaging in military-to-military relations and indeed made headway in the relationship.[43] For example it was during the Bush administration that the Chinese agreed to set up a hotline between the two countries. Whether expectations for the relationship were modest or not, they had to reflect another characteristic of the Bush administration's China policy; that, unlike the Clinton administration which saw positive value in engagement with the Chinese, the G.W. Bush administration insisted on reciprocity and taking the adversarial nature of the relationship into account.[44] As a consequence, some observers point out that the Bush Jr administration placed high importance on using military interactions to bolster deterrence of Chinese actions harmful to US national interests and to the interests of the region.[45]

At the same time, aided by Chinese and US commonality in prosecuting a war on terrorists and insurgents following the September 11 Al-Qaeda attacks, US–China military relations thawed with successive visits to China by several high-ranking administration officials, culminating in Secretary of Defense Rumsfeld's visit in October 2005. This period, however, was not without major disruptions in the military-to-military relationship. Starting as early as the initial election of Chen Shui-bian to the presidency of Taiwan in 2000, the Chinese had become increasingly concerned about the Taiwan independence issue. For close to a decade the Chinese sought US assistance in "reining in Chen." This had the unfortunate effect of giving the Chinese the erroneous impression that the US could control political events on Taiwan. Just prior to the March 2008 elections in Taiwan in which the then ruling Democratic People's Party called for a referendum on whether the people of Taiwan supported joining the UN under the name of Taiwan instead of as the Republic of China, the US government, including those in the US military, were getting strong signals from the Chinese that the US must help China to "keep this problem in its box."[46] Secretary Gates' visit to China took place in November 2007 and he assured his Chinese hosts that the US did not support instability in cross-straits relations. Just after Secretary Gates left China the US announced that it would sell 12 surplus Orion P3-C maritime patrol aircraft and SM-2 Block 3A Standard anti-aircraft missiles to Taiwan.[47] According to one China expert then at the US embassy in Beijing, the resulting shock waves ran through the PLA and the entire Chinese system.[48] The PLA was convinced that the US did not care about stability in cross-straits relations. Consequently, the Chinese froze all bilateral military activities.[49] This included the infamous cancellation of the aircraft carrier *Kitty Hawk*'s planned

November 2007 port visit to Hong Kong and the denial of emergency docking rights to two US minesweepers which had run into extremely difficult weather conditions.[50]

It took renewed effort through visits by the Pacific Command commander and high officials in the Bush administration to thaw the relationship and eventually, close to the end of the Bush administration's tenure, Sino-American military relations were marked by the visits of a number of high-ranking visits to each country.[51] These gradually improved military-to-military relations were all undertaken within the context of a larger US–China bilateral relationship which seemed to be improving. Starting in 2003, the US sought to get China's support in reining in North Korea's nuclear ambitions through the Six-Party Talks and had been engaged in constant dialogs with Chinese counterparts. The first two rounds of the SED, President Hu Jintao's visit to Washington in 2006, and, lastly, the improved relationship between the PRC and Taiwan following the election of Ma Ying-jeou and the Kuomintang's (KMT's) return to power in 2008, contributed to improved US–China bilateral relations.

The Obama administration

Once in office, President Obama's defense and foreign policy teams sought to improve US–China bilateral relations as part of a larger effort to improve US foreign relations in general. The Obama administration also sought to avoid what it perceived as the mistakes of past administrations by getting its China policy off to a positive start from the beginning instead of having to spend effort during most of the first year repairing a relationship that had gotten off to a poor start. Obama's November 2009 summit in Beijing was one of the first foreign trips made by this administration, and the Defense Policy Consultative Talks (DPCT), held by Undersecretary of Defense Michelle Fluornoy, were promptly resumed. According to current members of the Obama team, the administration's objectives in military-to-military relations were to increase cooperation between the two militaries in such areas as peacekeeping, humanitarian assistance and disaster relief, and counter-piracy; to institutionalize the military-to-military relationship; and to increase mutual understanding in an increasingly complex security environment.[52]

Despite these efforts, Sino-American bilateral relations ran into a number of disruptions by the second year of the administration. These included the Dalai Lama's visit to the White House, US complaints about China's currency policy, and a diplomatic spat over US declaration of a "national interest" in freedom of navigation in the South China Sea. The event, however, which ultimately led to the most serious disruption in US–China military relations since the EP-3 incident was the announcement in February 2010 that the US would be following through on a Bush administration US$6.4 billion arms sale deal with Taiwan.[53]

The Taiwan arms sales incensed the Chinese who subsequently argued that given improvements in cross-strait relations, the US motive in selling arms to Taiwan had to be to sow discord between mainland China and Taiwan. This arms sale announcement even prompted some notable retired members of the PLA to call for China to initiate "economic retaliation" against the US.[54] Although higher-level defense policy talks continued during this time frame, a number of planned visits by delegations were suspended by the Chinese. These types of activities did not fully resume until Deputy Assistant Secretary of Defense Michael Schiffer's September 2010 visit to Beijing.[55] During that visit Schiffer and his team sought to stabilize the military relationship by advancing principles of the military-to-military relationship which the two militaries should abide by in interacting with one another. These principles included: mutual respect; mutual trust; reciprocity; mutual interest; continuous dialog; and mutual risk reduction.[56]

Once military-to-military relations appeared to be back on track, the successful visit to Beijing by Deputy Assistant Secretary Schiffer was followed up by the resumption of the MMCA meetings in Hawaii, another round of DPCTs in Washington, Secretary of Defense Gates' visit in January 2011 and President Hu's summit visit at the end of January 2011.[57]

In September 2011, the Obama administration announced that another round of arms sales to Taiwan were to take place involving a US$5.8 billion package deal. Although many in the Chinese press warned that the arms deal would completely derail US–China military-to-military relations, the effective reaction from China was less severe than China's reactions to the 2010 Taiwan arms sale announcement. As of this writing, other high-ranking military-to-military exchanges have taken place, including the May 2012 visit to the US of China's Minister of Defense Liang Guanglie and his successor, Chang Wanquan, in August 2013, the August 2012 visit to the US of the Deputy Chief of General Staff, General Cai Yingting, and the April 2013 visit to the PRC by General Martin Dempsey, the US Chairman of the Joint Chiefs of Staff, to name but a few. Positive military-to-military relations were affirmed as an objective by both US and Chinese leaders at the Obama–Xi summit at Sunnylands, California, in June 2013.

Continuity in Sino-American military-to-military relations

A deeper examination of the military relationship between the US and China since 1979 reveals a number of factors negatively affecting this relationship. Some of these factors have remained remarkably persistent over time. This section discusses at length those factors which emerged from the beginning of the military-to-military relationship and are expected to continue to deeply influence it.

The military-to-military relationship as a "political football"

The description of Sino-American military-to-military relations as a "political football" might be considered too simplistic. However, there is no question that since normalization, the military relationship has been subordinate to the larger political and strategic objectives of the two countries. Immediately after normalizing the relationship the Carter administration limited arms sales and technology transfers to the PRC out of concern over the impact on the US relationship with the Soviet Union. The Chinese for their part put a halt to deepening military-to-military relations following the passage of the TRA, and then later during the Reagan administration put a stop to military-to-military contacts when the new administration announced arms sales to Taiwan.

Although both sides have initiated cutoffs in the military relationship, the Chinese have done so much more frequently. Some China watchers argue that this simply reflects the fact that China values the military relationship less than the US. If it did not, the PLA would act to protect the relationship as China does with other elements of the bilateral relationship. Other China watchers disagree and point out that China uses the military-to-military relationship just as it does other elements in its strategic tool kit. That is, the Chinese engage in a cost–benefit analysis and if they conclude that a larger strategic goal is attained by cutting off the military relationship they will do so; however, if strategic goals require the military-to-military relationship be intact, the Chinese will follow that path.[58] Advocates of this school of thought frequently point out that the Chinese now see continued value in maintaining high-level contact with the DOD. They note that the Chinese appear to have accepted the argument put forth by the US that in times of crisis and difficulty between the two countries military relations should not be cut off completely; this is when sustained relationships are most valuable.[59] As a consequence, the Chinese now do not talk of freezing or suspending the relationship, they now refer to such actions as "dialing back the intensity of the contacts" and they note that high-level dialogs such as DCT went on as planned following the most recent arms sales announcements.[60]

In similar fashion, when the larger political relationship is going well the bilateral military relationship follows. Following the Obama–Hu summit of 2011, and the declared intention of both leaders to improve the relationship of the militaries, the military-to-military relationship has involved a number of high-level military exchanges. Additionally, when the political leadership in Beijing stated that it intended to develop a "new kind of major power relationship" with the US, China's military leadership began talk of a "new kind of major military relationship" with the US.[61]

Taiwan

A second recurring theme in the military-to-military relationship is that the Taiwan issue has been at the heart of most of the disruptions in military ties. The first halting of the progress in the military relationship during the Carter presidency took place following the passage of the TRA. The next disruption followed the Reagan announcement of arms sales to the island. Despite robust ties during the Clinton administration, the military-to-military relations were cut off by both sides following the Taiwan missile crisis of the mid-1990s and successive Taiwan arms sales announcements have also led to freezes in the military-to-military relationship. Of course other external shocks have led to the cutoff of ties (e.g., the Belgrade bombing, the EP-3 incident), but Taiwan has been the most prominent cause of the disruption.

Curiously, this has also been the case even when cross-straits relations have been relatively good. Following the election of President Ma Ying-jeou and the return of the KMT to power in 2008, the bilateral relationship between mainland China and Taiwan had been steadily improving. Yet despite these good relations the Obama administration's announcement in 2010 that it would be selling weapons systems to Taiwan led to an eight-month freeze in the military-to-military relationship.[62]

Cultural and political systems differences

Another issue that has persisted over time as a stumbling block is the existence of significant cultural and political system differences. An example of this is the apparent cultural disconnect between American and Chinese interlocutors over how to best overcome disputes, disagreements, and differences in interests. A number of observers of the military-to-military relationship identified this phenomenon in the mid-1990s as a "top-down" versus "bottom-up" difference by the two sides over how to develop the military relationship.[63] They noted that once trust was built between the two countries' top leaders, this cooperation was expected by the Chinese to flow down toward subordinates. By contrast, Americans prefer and indeed expect cooperation across all levels of both systems, but especially at the lowest levels, to take hold before the top leaders can develop trust. As one veteran China hand noted, this distinction in how two countries build trust is a significant cultural obstacle. For Americans trust must be earned, he said, and this comes about through repeated interactions at all levels of the system. For the Chinese, trust is earned at the highest levels and can only be mandated from the top; once it has been authorized by the top of the system those lower down in the bureaucracy can act.[64]

Differences in culture and in the system in which Chinese and American representatives operate also manifest themselves in the approaches the two sides appear to take in solving problems. The previously mentioned China expert[65] noted that Americans are essentially problem solvers. They will look at a bilateral problem and seek a direct bilateral solution where everyone has a stake in overcoming that problem, and everyone is expected to "give and take" equally Americans are thus willing to identify where their own positions are flawed and where they can compromise.[66] Essentially, Americans seek immediate "point solutions." The Chinese consensus-based system not only seeks to overcome the specific difficulty at hand, but also seeks to incorporate into the negotiation a process which is acceptable to an entire network of interests back in Beijing.[67] As such it is difficult to build trust between the two sides when each takes vastly different approaches to solving immediate political problems and overcoming immediate obstacles to the relationship.[68]

Cultural differences also matter in the disagreement between the two sides over what constitutes appropriate transparency. For the US, displays of transparency are a sign that two countries are developing mutual trust between them. For the Chinese, transparency is the tool of the strong, which can be used to deter potential adversaries. Deception and obfuscation are the tools of the weaker side.[69] Additionally, when the two sides sit down to discuss transparency it has often been the case that the Chinese stress transparency of intentions over transparency of capabilities, while Americans tend to focus on transparency of capabilities.[70] Finally, Saunders and Kiselycznyk have noted that, for the Chinese, transparency is relative – its scope and characteristics are tailored to accomplish national security interests, while for the US transparency is an absolute state, which can be pointed to and measured in tangible ways.[71]

Change in Sino-American military-to-military relations: greater cooperation or conflict?

While a number of obstacles identified above have persisted over time, new dynamics have also emerged which have made the relationship more competitive or at least less cooperative in its nature. These are now discussed.

The PLA's changing military capabilities

For decades US military capabilities have eclipsed those of the PLA. This asymmetry has caused a stumbling block in the US military-to-military relationship with China. The oft-repeated argument put forth by the Chinese in this regard is that as long as China is the weaker party, it would be reluctant to be as transparent and forthcoming in forming a substantial relationship with the US.

As China's economy grows, and as the PLA becomes much more capable as a joint force, should this not have a positive effect on the military relationship? Certainly, the Chinese argument that the weaker party is forced to rely on secrecy when interacting with a stronger party starts to weaken. It is also the case that, as China's military develops, it will start forming strong incentives to learn from, interact with, and engage with militaries that can help in the PLA development. A good illustration of this dynamic might be the acquisition of the *Liaoning* – the PLA navy's aircraft carrier. Does China's possession of this representation of China's modern maritime power make the Chinese more inclined to cooperate with the US navy or less? It is unclear.

Reciprocity

Some observers of the military relationship have pointed out that the US military has shown the PLA what it has asked for, while the US military has at times been shown a much less impressive display of Chinese capability.[72] This returns us to the issue of reciprocity which the Clinton administration had been so severely criticized over. Others have commented that the Chinese military has over time shown new and useful military capabilities to American military officials.[73] The Chinese also dispute the non-transparent and non-reciprocal characterization and have insisted that they have shown the US military what it has asked for. However, the Chinese also directly argue that the intrinsic value of transparency and reciprocity is different for both sides. For the US, transparency and reciprocity is valued not only because it provides intelligence for US assessments, but also because when the US is transparent it has the additional benefit of showing China American military power – hence enhancing US deterrence. The Chinese also argue that it is a matter of proportionality. If the US has 100 rooms and shows 10 rooms to the Chinese, it has shown 10 percent of what it has. If China only has two rooms and it shows the US one room, then it has shown half of what it has.[74]

The reciprocity issue can be disruptive if it becomes the obsessive focus of the military-to-military relationship. When the US NDU was overseeing the reciprocal visit by the PLA NDU to Washington in the summer of 2011, the Chinese, possibly owing to a Confucian or cultural sense of the importance of ritual or appropriate conduct, refused to visit the State Department unless they were received by someone with at least a three-star rank, essentially an Assistant Secretary of State – this despite the fact that the lesser-ranking individuals the NDU was lining up for the Chinese to meet could probably talk more substantively on the subjects of direct interest to the PLA.[75] Similarly, with regard to this same visit, the US Joint Staff, probably with good reason, refused to approve proposed visits to various commands in the Midwest until the staff had scrutinized what the past US CAPSTONE[76] visit to the PRC received from the Chinese. It can probably be safely argued that the Joint Staff would not have been so fixated on the rigid interpretation of reciprocity if reciprocity were not such a hot button political issue which could be used by critics to beat up on an administration's China policy.

Mutual suspicion and the absence of mutual strategic trust

Another noteworthy change has been the increase in mutual suspicion between the two countries. When the US and China normalized relations over 30 years ago, the relationship between the two countries could be defined unofficially as "aligned" if not as an alliance. As China's economic, political, and military power have expanded in the twenty-first century, and as China starts to assert itself regionally and globally, there has naturally been suspicion within the US over China's ultimate intentions. Similarly on the Chinese side, there is a deep-rooted suspicion that the US's ultimate intentions are to contain China's rise and to thwart any effort China may make to reattain its status as a great power.

The roots of mutual suspicion appear to be structural. Despite personal ties being developed by the presidents of the two countries, connections forming between the Chairman of the Joint Chiefs and the Chief of General Staff, and the development of other high-level bonds, the two countries are still operating in a deficit of trust. The reasons for this persistence of suspicion are that there are either significant differences in the interests of the two countries, or there are differences in the geopolitical positions of the countries within the region, that are difficult to overcome: a major hegemon versus its rising challenger; one country has an interest in access to global commons, another in demarcating its territory and preventing others from having access; one country (the US) is an Asia-Pacific power dependent on an alliance system with other Asian powers who happen to also be in competition with the largest single Asian regional power (China); and finally, American interest in a peaceful outcome for the Taiwan situation as well as indirect moral support to an Asian democracy, the Chinese interest in maintaining territorial integrity and ensuring that China remain intact (to include the use of force to make that a certainty).

The three obstacles

Another recent development in military-to-military relations is what the Chinese call the "three obstacles to military relations." One of the obstacles is not new – it is the persistent problem of Taiwan arms sales discussed above. However, the other two obstacles raised by the Chinese in discussions with both their DOD counterparts and the open press have not been persistent problems. One of these obstacles, the NDAA 2000 was mentioned previously; however, the Chinese have now specifically cited it as a major obstacle to deeper military-to-military relations.[77] NDAA 2000, which calls for an annual report to Congress from DOD specifying and itemizing China's growing military capabilities, is said by PLA representatives to be a major irritant in the military relationship. In addition, NDAA 2000 mandates that the DOD undertake no activity that would enhance the military capabilities of the PLA. Thus, arms sales and other technology transfers are no longer possible. This aspect of NDAA 2000, if applied conservatively, has also had the dampening effect of preventing PLA students from attending the US NDU and has possibly curtailed certain types of joint exercises.

The third obstacle cited by the Chinese is the persistent problem of US surveillance and reconnaissance operations (SRO) within China's exclusive economic zones (EEZs). The US has, as is its right, conducted air and maritime surveillance operations within international waters (but within China's recognized EEZs) as a hedge against future possible conflict with the PLA. These SROs take many forms, but essentially, they are efforts by the US military to map out the operational environment that it might have to operate in if the PLA and the US military come to blows over Taiwan. PLA interlocutors have complained that these operations have taken place too close to China's coastlines, are far too frequent, and represent the fact that the US really considers China to be a future adversary and not a friend.[78] The Chinese have responded with PLA aircraft intercepts (as illustrated by the 2001 EP-3 incident in which an F8ii collided with a US navy EP-3 conducting surveillance operations off of Hainan Island); and civilian law enforcement vessels harassing US navy ships (as illustrated by such harassment of the USNS *Bowditch* and the USNS *Impeccable*). The bottom line is that the PLA has repeatedly stated that until these three obstacles are resolved, it will not be possible to deepen the military-to-military relationship or make it more robust.

Mechanisms and policies conducive to deeper military-to-military relations

Given the difficulties of deepening military-to-military relations laid out in this chapter, there are still actions both the US and China can undertake to strengthen them. However, these actions cannot directly address the specific obstacles that the Chinese consider the major impediments to the military relationship. To start off with, circumventing or altering two of the obstacles noted by the PLA (TRA and NDAA 2000) would require changing, evading, or ignoring laws passed by the US. The third obstacle, the SROs, while not mandated by US law, simply makes sense from an American strategic and operational point of view. It might be possible to curtail the number of such SRO activities or even to alter the specific locations where they occur, but that should be a matter for greater dialog between the two militaries, not an excuse to cut down on the interaction.

In a recent article in *Asia Policy* RAND China analyst Scott Harold argued that if enhanced military-to-military ties are the objective, then one strategy should be to enhance the ties so as to raise the cost to the Chinese of cancellation.[79] Some concrete areas of improved coordination and cooperation between the two militaries are already being discussed and in some cases, being implemented. The trip of the US Chairman of the Joint Chiefs of Staff to China in April 2013 involved a discussion on a proposal for a secure video teleconference capability between the two militaries; and the aforementioned direct line between the US and Chinese militaries was reportedly utilized in the spring of 2013 between General Dempsey and his counterpart in China, General Fang Fenghui, for a one-hour conversation on topics related to Asia-Pacific security.[80]

One obvious recommendation for deeper military-to-military relations is to have the two militaries and their associated universities/think tanks conduct joint studies to address common challenges. Expanding military student exchanges is another area that can enhance the military-to-military relationship right now. At present, the PLA permits US military personnel to attend its international course in Beijing. This cooperative effort could be enhanced if the PLA permitted the US to attend the course it offers its own officers.

Another possible area conducive to deepening the relationship is to increase the frequency and scope of joint exercises. Given China's sensitivities to maritime sovereignty issues and other issues in China's "backyard," these cooperative efforts might be possible outside of what China calls its "Near Seas." Some of this has also already begun; a joint exercise in the Gulf of Aden took place in September 2012, and the PLA navy participated in the Rim of the Pacific (RIMPAC) exercises in the summer of 2014. Finally, the two militaries could conduct cooperative operations in mission areas of concern to both countries and to the international community as a whole: humanitarian assistance and disaster relief operations; direct cooperation in counter-piracy operations; non-combatant evacuation operations table-top exercises, followed by joint exercises practicing the real thing; building partner capacities of developing states combating terrorism; and sea lines of communication protection.

Conclusion

What then are the prospects for improved, deepening and more robust military-to-military relations? To start off with, the earlier observation that the military-to-military relationship is essentially dependent on the status of the larger bilateral relationship still stands. If the overall relationship between China and the US is going well we can expect an improvement and a deepening of the military relationship. The military relationship will have its limits, restricted both by political considerations at home, and also by the persistence of mutual suspicion. Additionally, as has happened throughout the history of the military-to-military relationship, it can be expected that a sudden shock to the larger bilateral relationship will lead to a freeze. This has consistently been the case through the decades.

As this chapter has shown, a number of factors have consistently served as stumbling blocks to the military relationship. Taiwan has persisted as the most disruptive issue for military-to-military relations either through US arms sales announcements, the prospects of a pro-independence candidate being elected into the presidency in Taiwan, or some other Taiwan-related issue which threatens Beijing's sense of security on the issue. However, it is also the case that other unexpected turns of events have led to disruptions in the military relationship. Finally, the cultural differences between the two sides and their divergent methods over how to best manage disagreements, disputes, and different interests also get in the way of the development of a robust military-to-military relationship.

This chapter also concludes that the larger relations today between the PRC and the US have many more elements of conflict than has been the case in the past, which complicates efforts to deepen and make robust the military-to-military relationship. Increasing Chinese military capability, the rise in mutual suspicion, the absence of mutual strategic trust, and China's stated "three obstacles to military relations" have all made the task of military cooperation much more challenging to manage than was the case only two decades ago. Despite this fact, the current US administration and its counterparts in China appear to be taking steps to advance the military-to-military relationship through a number of joint and cooperative mechanisms: the S&ED; DCTs and DPCTs; MMCA meetings; reciprocal visits by the Chairman of the Joint Chiefs of Staff and the PLA Chief of General Staff; US NDU–PLA NDU strategic dialogs; and NDU student visits, to name but a few.

The management of the Sino-US military relationship is starting to move away from the attempt to accomplish big things with the military-to-military relationship and to move toward establishing limited but achievable goals. Instead of an American attempt to transform the Chinese military and political system through defense cooperation, the focus is starting to be on tempering competition on the margins and developing useful mechanisms for competition and crises. The lowering of expectations will probably have a positive effect on the military-to-military relationship since this new approach is less likely to lead to American disappointment. The emphasis on managing competition could also have the side benefit of building trust between the two sides. From the Chinese point of view, military-to-military relations have always had a much less ambitious and expansive objective in comparison to American objectives. China has always seen the military-to-military relationship as a direct tool for accomplishing political and strategic objectives vis-à-vis the US. If good military relations help China attain larger political objectives then the PLA will make the effort to promote good relations. If China wishes to show its displeasure over some larger political problem between China and the US, then the PLA will act accordingly with regard to the military relationship.

China watchers are split on whether the Sino-US military-to-military relationship is on an upward trajectory or simply going around in circles. There is evidence to support both points of view. That the military-to-military relationship is subordinate to the larger bilateral relationship appears to be a given. If the overall bilateral relationship continues on a positive track, it should be the case that the military-to-military relationship will also continue positively. If the larger relationship sours, however, history has shown that the military-to-military relationship is one of the earliest, if not the first, bilateral relationship to suffer. There is some evidence that the Chinese are preserving the higher-level defense contacts even during times of larger military-to-military freezes. For the China–US military relationship to deepen and develop, however, the Chinese will have to recognize, as their American counterparts have urged, that in difficult times, there is intrinsic value in a continued robust relationship at most if not all levels between the two militaries. The next few years will reveal if this will turn out to be the case.

Notes

1 *Annual Report to Congress: Military and Security Developments Involving the People's Republic of China 2011*, report (Washington, DC: Office of the Secretary of Defense, 2011), 53.
2 Ibid.
3 For an analysis of S&EDs and similar non-military focused dialogues and interactions, see Chapter 9 by Robert Sutter in this book.
4 Michel Oksenberg, "The Dynamics of the Sino-American Relationship" in *The China Factor: Sino-American Relations and the Global Scene*, ed. Richard Solomon (Englewood Cliffs, NJ: Prentice-Hall, 1981), 57–9.
5 Kevin L. Pollpeter, *US–China Security Management: Assessing the Military-to-Military Relationship*, monograph (Santa Monica: RAND Corporation, 2004), 7.
6 Strobe Talbott, "The Strategic Dimension of the Sino-American Relationship: Enemy of Our Enemy, or True Friend?" in *The China Factor*, ed. Solomon, 91; Pollpeter, *US–China Security Management*, 7–8.
7 Pollpeter, *US–China Security Management*, 8.
8 Pollpeter, *US–China Security Management*, 8–9. Readers wishing to know more about the Taiwan issue in the Sino-American relationship including US arms sales to Taiwan might want to consult Dennis Hickey and Kelan Lilly Lu's contribution to this book (Chapter 5).
9 Talbott, "The Strategic Dimension of the Sino-American Relationship," 92.

10 Ibid., 91.
11 Pollpeter, *US–China Security Management*, 10–11. COCOM was established by the Department of Commerce in coordination with other agencies of the US government following the Second World War. Its purpose was to limit the flow of weapons and technology to the Warsaw Pact countries.
12 Talbott, "The Strategic Dimension of the Sino-American Relationship," 93; Pollpeter, *US–China Security Management*, 11.
13 Steven Levine, "China and the United States: The Limits of the Interaction," in *China and the World: Chinese Foreign Policy in the Post-Mao Era*, ed. Samuel Kim (Boulder, CO: Westview Press, 1984), 119.
14 Pollpeter, *US–China Security Management*, 10–1.
15 Ibid.
16 Eden Woon, "Chinese Arms Sales and US–China Military Relations," *Asian Survey* 29, no. 6 (June 1989): 613, as noted in Pollpeter, *US–China Security Management*, 14.
17 Shirley A. Kan, *US–China Military Contacts: Issues for Congress* (Washington, DC: Congressional Research Service, 2011): 1; Pollpeter, *US–China Security Management*, 14
18 Kan, *US–China Military Contacts*, 1.
19 Ibid., 2.
20 Ibid., 2.
21 James Mann, *About Face: A History of America's Curious Relationship with China, from Nixon to Clinton* (New York: Alfred Knopf, 1999), 274–313, 343–5.
22 Kurt Campbell and Richard Weitz, "The Limts of US–China Military Cooperation: Lessons from 1995–1999," *Washington Quarterly* 29, no. 1 (Winter 2005): 172; Pollpeter, *US–China Security Management*, 16–17.
23 Kan, *US–China Military Contacts*, 44; Pollpeter, *US–China Security Management*, 16.
24 Excluding National Security Adviser Brent Scowcroft's secret visits to China in 1989. Kan, *US–China Military Contacts*, 44.
25 Ibid., 45.
26 Ibid.
27 Ibid., 46; Pollpeter, *US–China Security Management*, 18.
28 Kan, *US–China Military Contacts*, 46.
29 Mann, *About Face*, 349–51, 363–7.
30 Ibid., 180.
31 Pollpeter, *US–China Security Management*, 24.
32 Ibid., 19.
33 Kan, *US–China Military Contacts*, 48–9.
34 Ibid., 49.
35 Pollpeter, *US–China Security Management*, 21.
36 Kan, *US–China Military Contacts*, 52.
37 Ibid., 53.
38 Ibid., 54.
39 Ibid., 25.
40 Ibid., 55. It should also be noted that Chinese aircraft had exhibited a pattern of close air intercepts and harassment of EP-3 surveillance flights preceding this collision.
41 Pollpeter, *US–China Security Managemen*t, 25.
42 Campbell and Weitz, "The Limits of US–China Military Cooperation," 181–3.
43 Interview with Mr Abe Denmark, former China Desk Officer, Office of Assistant Secretary of Defense for Asia-Pacific Affairs, February 14, 2012.
44 Ibid.; Campbell and Weitz, "The Limits of US–China Military Cooperation," 183.
45 Campbell and Weitz, "The Limits of US–China Military Cooperation," 183.
46 Interview with Commander (USN) Leah Bray and Mr. John Schaus, Office of Secretary of Defense, February 27, 2012.

47 Bonnie Glaser, "US–China Relations: China Signals Irritation with US Policy," *Comparative Connections* 9, no. 4 (January 2008): 25–35.
48 Interview with CDR (USN) Leah Bray, Office of Secretary of Defense, February 27, 2012.
49 Ibid.
50 Ibid.
51 Kan, *US–China Military Contacts*, 65.
52 Interview with CDR (USN) Leah Bray and Mr. John Schaus, Office of Secretary of Defense, 27 February 2012. This obviously accords with the Department of Defense Report to Congress on Chinese Military Power or MILPOWER Report. See *Annual Report to Congress: Military and Security Developments Involving the People's Republic of China 2012* (Washington, DC: Office of the Secretary of Defense, 2012), 13.
53 Peter Ford, "US Arms Sales to Taiwan Stifle US–China Military Engagement," *Christian Science Monitor*, February 2, 2010, www.csmonitor.com/world/2010/0202/US-arms-sales-to-Taiwan-stifle-US–China-military-engagement.
54 The two most notable of these were Major General Luo Yuan and Rear Admiral Yang Yi. See "Analysts Defend China Government's Sanctioning of US Companies Selling Arms to Taiwan," *People's Daily*, February 5, 2010; Chris Buckley, "Senior Chinese Military Officers Urge Economic Punch against US," Reuters, February 2, 2010, www.retuers.com/article/2010/02/09/us-china-usa-pla-idUSTRE6183KG20100209.
55 Larry Shaughnessy, "Official: US–China Military Relations 'Back on Track'" in *CNN*.com, September 29, 2010, as found in http://articles.cnn.com/2010–09–29/us/china.military_1_chinese-militaries-military-relations.
56 Michael Schiffer, Deputy Assistant Secretary of Defense for East Asia, "Building Cooperation in the US–China Military-to-Military Relationship" (address, Institute for International Strategic Studies, Washington, DC, January 6, 2011).
57 Kan, *US–China Military Contacts*, 66–8.
58 Interview with CDR Leah Bray and Mr. John Schaus of the Office of the Secretary of Defense-Policy on February 27, 2012.
59 Ibid.
60 Ibid.
61 Defense analysts and representatives started hearing about a new kind of major power relationship on visits to China in the spring of 2012. General Cai Yingting, the Deputy Chief of General Staff, on his visit to NDU in August 2012 used the phrase a "new kind of military power relationship" and subsequent exchanges between the two militaries has involved the use of that phraseology.
62 "US: Freeze in China Military Relations Over," *Voice of America*, September 29, 2010, www.voanews.com/content/us-china-military-relations-freeze-over-104018559/166437.html.
63 David Finkelstein and John Unangst, *Engaging DOD: Chinese Perspectives on Military Relations with the United States* (Alexandria, VA: CNA Corporation, 1999): 17; Interview with Abe Denmark, Senior Policy Director for East Asia, National Bureau of Asian Research, February 14, 2012.
64 Interview with Col. (USA, ret.) Frank Miller, Senior Defense Intelligence Officer for China, March 2012.
65 Ibid.
66 Ibid.
67 Ibid.
68 Miller goes on to point out that in successive negotiations or discussions, the Chinese will repeatedly bring up past admissions of American errors or deficiencies as starting bids in the next round of military-to-military discussions; whereas because the Chinese had not made a similar admission, the American interlocutor was often at a disadvantage.

69 See Luo Yuan, "China to Increase Military Transparency," *China Daily*, October 25, 2007, accessed March 7, 2012, www.chinadaily.com.cn/opinion/2007–10/25/content_6205574.htm.
70 Michael Kiselycznyk and Phillip Saunders, Assessing Chinese Military Transparency, China Strategic Perspectives #1, NDU Press, Washington, DC, June 2010, pp. 4–5.
71 Ibid.
72 Campbell and Weitz, "The Limits of US–China Military Cooperation," 175;
73 Kan, *US–China Military Contacts*, 31; For a detailed examination of exactly what the Chinese have been shown, what the US military has been shown, and which units/capabilities are new, see Pollpeter, *US–China Security Management*, 59–60.
74 Chinese participants in a conference on trilateral (US–China–Japan) maritime security cooperation held at the Shanghai Academy of Social Sciences in September 2010 made this argument when pressed by the author on the unbalanced nature of US–China military transparency.
75 The author's direct experience arranging for the visit of the PLA NDU Strategic Course to the US NDU in June 2011.
76 CAPSTONE is a course designed to prepare US military officers for the kinds of responsibilities they are likely to encounter as general or flag officers. Part of the course involves a visit to the People's Republic of China.
77 Major General Zhu Chenghu during the annual PLA NDU–US NDU strategic dialog in March 2012 raised the issue of the "three obstacles" and specifically noted that NDAA 2000 was a major irritant to the military relationship. See also "中美军交流仍有3大障碍美防长将稍后访华," *Sina*, May 5, 2012, http://news.sina.com.cn/o/2012–05–05/160824372440.shtml.
78 PLA NDU strategic dialog with US NDU, March 2012. Similar remarks were made to the author on a research trip to Beijing for discussions with the Naval Research Institute and PLA NDU in April 2012.
79 Scott Harold, "A Strategy for Improving US–China Military-to-Military Relations," *Asia Policy*, no. 16 (July 2013): 112.
80 Kevin Bacon, "Pentagon's China Guru David Helvey: Friction is 'Inevitable' but Mil-Mil Relations Are 'As Good As Its Been'," *Foreign Policy*, May 8, 2013. http://e-ring.foreignpolicy.com/posts/2013/05/08/pentagon_s_china_guru_david_helvey_friction_is_inevitable_but_mil_mil_relations_are.

References

"Analysts Defend China Government's Sanctioning of US Companies Selling Arms to Taiwan." *People's Daily*. February 5, 2010.
Bacon, Kevin. "Pentagon's China Guru David Helvey: Friction Is 'Inevitable' but Mil-Mil Relations Are 'As Good As Its Been.' " *Foreign Policy*. May 8, 2013. http://e-ring.foreignpolicy.com/posts/2013/05/08/pentagon_s_china_guru_david_helvey_friction_is_inevitable_but_mil_mil_relations_are.
Buckley, Chris. "Senior Chinese Military Officers Urge Economic Punch against US." Reuters. February 2, 2010. www.retuers.com/article/2010/02/09/us-china-usa-pla-idUSTRE6183KG20100209.
Campbell, Kurt, and Richard Weitz. "The Limts of US–China Military Cooperation: Lessons from 1995–1999." *Washington Quarterly* 29, no. 1 (Winter 2005): 169–86.
Finkelstein, David M., and John Unangst. *Engaging DOD: Chinese Perspectives on Military Relations with the United States* (Alexandria: CNA Corporation, 1999).
Ford, Peter. "US Arms Sales to Taiwan Stifle US–China Military Engagement." *Christian*

Science Monitor. February 2, 2010. www.csmonitor.com/world/2010/0202/US-arms-sales-to-Taiwan-stifle-US–China-military-engagement.

Glaser, Bonnie. "US–China Relations: China Signals Irritation with US Policy." *Comparative Connections* 9, no. 4 (January 2008): 25–35.

Harold, Scott. "A Strategy for Improving US–China Military-to-Military Relations." *Asia Policy*, no. 16 (July 2013): 112.

Kan, Shirley A. *US–China Military Contacts: Issues for Congress*. Report no. RL32496 (Washington, DC: Congressional Research Service, 2001).

Levine, Steven. "China and the United States: The Limits of the Interaction," in *China and the World: Chinese Foreign Policy in the Post-Mao Era*, ed. Samuel Kim (Boulder, CO: Westview Press, 1984), 119.

Luo, Yuan. "China to Increase Military Transparency." *China Daily*. October 25, 2007. Accessed March 7, 2012. www.chinadaily.com.cn/opinion/2007–10/25/content_6205574.htm.

Mann, James. *About Face: A History of America's Curious Relationship with China, from Nixon to Clinton* (New York: Alfred Knopf, 1999).

Pollpeter, Kevin L. *US–China Security Management: Assessing the Military-to-Military Relationship* (Santa Monica: RAND Corporation, 2004).

Schiffer, Michael. "Building Cooperation in the US–China Military-to-Military Relationship." Address, Institute for International Strategic Studies, Washington, DC, January 6, 2011.

Solomon, Richard H., ed. *The China Factor: Sino-American Relations and the Global Scene* (Englewood Cliffs, NJ: Prentice-Hall, 1981).

United States, Office of the Secretary of Defense. *Annual Report to Congress: Military and Security Developments Involving the People's Republic of China 2011* (Washington, DC: Office of the Secretary of Defense, 2011).

United States, Office of the Secretary of Defense. *Annual Report to Congress: Military and Security Developments Involving the People's Republic of China 2012* (Washington, DC: Office of the Secretary of Defense, 2012).

"US: Freeze in China Military Relations Over." *Voice of America*. September 28, 2010. www.voanews.com/content/us-china-military-relations-freeze-over-104018559/166437.html.

Woon, Eden. "Chinese Arms Sales and US–China Military Relations." *Asian Survey* 29, no. 6 (June 1989).

"中美军事交流仍存3大障碍 美防长将稍后访华." *Sina*. May 5, 2012. http://news.sina.com.cn/o/2012–05–05/160824372440.shtml.

11 From the EP-3 incident to the USS *Kitty Hawk–Song* class submarine encounter

The evolution of Sino-US crisis management communication mechanisms[1]

Simon Shen and Ryan Kaminski

Introduction

United States-Sino relations have been no stranger to serious diplomatic and military crises over the years.[2] Over the previous decade, these have included, among others, the accidental bombing of China's embassy in Belgrade (1999), the EP-3 spy plane incident (2001), and the USS *Kitty Hawk–Song* class submarine encounter (2006). Unfortunately, the conventional interpretation of such events on both sides of the Pacific has been one of deep pessimism. Each crisis, occurring out of the blue, is often taken as evidence of one state's inherently malign strategic intentions against the other, despite the usual unpreparedness recorded, no matter the specifics of the event. However, as a consequence of previous crises, a subtle change has occurred with respect to Sino-US crises: they have become better crisis managers.[3]

On March 9, 2009, for instance, five Chinese patrol ships surrounded the USS *Impeccable*, an unarmed US surveillance vessel, off the coast of China's Hainan Island. A few of the Chinese ships came within 25 feet of the *Impeccable* while attempting to snag its sonar buoy. To prevent a collision, the US crew sprayed several of the Chinese ships with its water cannon. While various media outlets and commentators claimed the incident was proof that the US–China relationship was destined for conflict and similar misunderstandings, what happened in the days following the incident, however, suggests otherwise. US President Barack Obama urged expanding the two nations' military-to-military dialog while China's Foreign Minister Yang Jiechi suggested that both countries "shelve" their differences and work to enhance their bilateral relationship.[4] Privately, some US officials hinted the US would likely reconsider some its military related patrols in the South China Sea (SCS) to prevent a repeat of the incident.[5] Another Chinese analyst stated, "Overall, this won't have a major impact, because the US and China need each other."[6] Trust levels between the two powers remained respectable in 2010 when the US launched controversial military exercises in the Yellow Sea, though they have declined substantially in the second Obama administration due to alleged Chinese cyber warfare activities against the US and the subsequent Edward Snowden incident. In any event, the question is: what has led to the state of rational and measured interaction between the two powers?

Using the EP-3 crisis and the USS *Kitty Hawk* encounter as case studies, by remapping their courses and aftermath from primary sources, this chapter argues that, rather than presenting insurmountable roadblocks to cooperation, crises have given both states significant learning opportunities and thus later helped them avoid mistakes that otherwise might have functioned to inadvertently escalate a crisis into something worse.[7] In this chapter we expound on this change, laying out how China and the US have become better equipped to weather future crises that carry the potential to seriously damage this critical bilateral relationship.

This chapter is organized as follows. After noting past crises in Sino-US relations and offering a succinct literature review, we provide a brief overview of our two case studies. Subsequently, we undertake a comparative analysis of the handling of the two cases. This analysis will explain how the cases could be grafted upon the contemporary US-Sino relationship, revealing the capacity for China and the US to learn from crisis encounters and mitigate the potential for serious escalation and miscalculation in future scenarios. Three significant policy areas illustrating this change will be identified, namely their initial crisis communications, crisis resolutions, and immediate post-crisis reactions. Finally, three key factors will be identified as responsible for catalyzing this transition.

Historical background and literature review

Crises are not an unusual occurrence in Sino-US relations. Since the founding of the People's Republic of China (PRC) in 1949, the Chinese have repeatedly surprised the US, such as with their entry into the Korean War (1950) and bombardments of the Taiwan Strait (1954, 1958). For its part, America's involvement in the Vietnam War deeply alarmed the Chinese. The Shanghai Communiqué signaled an end to repeated Sino-American crises, though a mechanism facilitating both sides' direct communication remained absent.

As Michael Swaine has pointed out, policy-makers struggle during a political-military crisis to protect the interests of the country without escalating the conflict as well as to "signal conciliation without conveying weakness."[8] Since the end of the Cold War, China and the US have acquired further crisis management experience, particularly through the resolution of the 1995 Taiwan Strait crisis and the NATO bombing of the Chinese embassy in Belgrade in 1999.[9] The crisis management maxim in Sino-US relations has been described as "reasonable, beneficial, and with restraint (*youli, youli, youjie*) in response to shape, deter or reverse political gestures in political-military crises."[10] In the post-Deng Xiaoping era, Beijing primarily thinks in terms of negotiating with Washington when it comes to issues like trade, prevention of the proliferation of weapons of mass destruction (WMDs), and counter-terrorism, though this is not the case in regards to territorial and sovereignty issues.[11]

Some international affairs analysts believe China and the US are already engaged in a twenty-first-century quasi Cold War. For these realists, crises are not to be understood as unfortunate misunderstandings between the two powers, but instead as portents of what will inevitably turn into a major conflict that might even affect the balance of power.[12] Others see room for cooperation between the two states in the areas of trade, counter-terrorism, denuclearizing North Korea, among others while recognizing there is serious potential for military conflict on issues like Taiwan, the Spratly Islands, or Japan.[13] While acknowledging that significant security challenges exist between the two nations, the latter view posits that there remain significant opportunities to improve relations. Influenced by the success of crisis management communication between the US and the Union of Soviet Socialist Republics (USSR) during the Cold War in the aftermath of the Cuban Missile Crisis, it sees crises or, more specifically crisis management communication, as a useful platform to enhance Sino-American cooperation.[14] However, in comparison to the US–USSR Cold War era case where there often was intense hostility associated with political-military crises, many Chinese and Western scholars suggest that Sino-US crisis management reflects a duality where confrontational stances are associated with close collaboration that allows for the attainment of foreign policy objectives during a crisis.[15]

Many current Chinese observers argue that the new generation of Chinese leaders will mean a more favorable environment for crisis communication as they are more attentive to international law and Western institutions in dealing with crises. Michael Swaine adds that "in China, the importance of organizational structures and processes in crisis decision-making has apparently increased as the Chinese political system has become more bureaucratic and functionally specialized."[16]

The most comprehensive studies of the US and China crisis management structures by analyzing various crises in contemporary US-Sino history have been done by Michael Swaine, on the US side and Xinbo Wu on the Chinese side.[17] However, by focusing on individual cases, they have paid relatively less attention to analyzing the effectiveness of reforms or changes within crisis management systems over time. In *Managing Sino-American Crises*, for example, Swaine clarifies crisis management terminology as well as analyzing the impact of crisis management mechanisms during specific crises. Despite obvious strengths, this approach inadequately considers reforms that have taken place during the interludes between crises.[18] Although there is no issue on the horizon that has the immediate potential to spark conflict between China and the US, the complex North Korean situation and China's territorial and maritime tensions with Japan and various SCS claimants have the potential to bring about a direct Sino-US confrontation. Thus, there clearly is a need for further research on Sino-American crisis management mechanisms.

Reconstructing the Sino-US crisis management communication mechanism

Case overviews

On April 1, 2001, a US EP-3 reconnaissance plane operating in the SCS collided with a PLA J-811 Interceptor fighter jet causing the former, with a crew of 24, to make an emergency landing on China's Hainan Island. The US plane landed safely, albeit without permission from Chinese authorities, and its crew immediately proceeded to destroy sensitive technology aboard the aircraft. In short order, Chinese officials boarded the plane and detained the crew. The PLA fighter, along with its pilot, Wang Wei, went down. Eleven days later, the EP-3 crew was permitted to return to the US while the plane was shipped back to the US in pieces. Beijing argued that the US should take full responsibility, whereas claims from Washington that Wang Wei was responsible for the crash are supported by the fact that it was unquestionably more maneuverable than the clunky EP-3.[19]

The second case, whose handling starkly contrasted with the first case, happened on October 27, 2006, when a PLAN *Song* class submarine surfaced within five miles of the USS *Kitty Hawk* aircraft carrier operating near Okinawa. A US military aircraft conducting a routine reconnaissance flight around the *Kitty Hawk*'s perimeter detected the sub. While there was no weapons fire or physical contact between the vessels, the incident was considered a significant blow to perceptions regarding both the US and Chinese navies. To the US, it shattered dreams of an invincible state-of-the-art naval detection grid, with one US navy official admitting, "It was not detected."[20] For China, the encounter was emblematic of an extraordinary technological advancement as the *Song* class ship was the first submarine to be completely designed and constructed by the PLAN.[21] Commodore Stephen Saunders, a former British Royal Navy anti-submarine specialist, claims it "was certainly a wake-up call for the Americans."[22] Contributing to the seriousness of the situation was the potential that the USS *Kitty Hawk*'s crew could have misperceived the Chinese sub's surfacing as evidence that it was preparing to attack.[23] Admiral William Fallon, Commander of US forces in the Pacific at the time, noted that the surfacing could have triggered an "unforeseen incident."[24]

While there is quite a bit of literature on the EP-3 incident, there is very little discussing the 2006 USS *Kitty Hawk–Song* class submarine encounter, not to mention the relationship between the two cases.[25] The literature concerning the former tends to be too focused on the technical details and the timeline of the incident while disregarding what the US and China may have learned from one another's response in the aftermath of the crisis.[26] Yet, what perhaps was the most interesting part of the latter incident was Washington and Beijing's failure to take escalatory measures or even acknowledge a serious incident in its wake. The event only became public weeks later when a November 13 *Washington Times* article quoted anonymous US officials discussing the incident, and it almost went unnoticed.[27] Similarly, even Chinese nationalists did not notice the event.

While the 2001 spy plane collision quickly exploded into a serious public conflict, both powers appeared determined to forgive and forget the USS *Kitty Hawk* incident. US officials tended to obfuscate when asked about the surfacing event and most Chinese officials refused to admit the encounter had even happened. Reflecting back on the events of 2001, it is curious why high-ranking US officials did not publicly condemn the Chinese government for brazenly risking an attack from a confused USS *Kitty Hawk* and it is also interesting to explore why Beijing did so little to promote its tremendous naval accomplishment domestically.

We now turn to our comparative analysis of the two cases.

Initial crisis communication – the blame game

The EP-3 incident

Following the EP-3's emergency landing on Hainan Island, both China and the US claimed the other side was responsible not only for the collision itself, but also for various violations of international law. The intensity with which each side blamed the other not only likely squandered attempts at establishing a genuine dialog to resolve the crisis, but probably further alienated and provoked the opposite party, too. Whoever was to blame for the EP-3 collision, according to one analyst, it represents, "the deepest crisis between the two Pacific superpowers for a decade or more."[28]

China suggested that, even if the EP-3 aircraft was flying over international waters when the accident occurred, the US was violating international norms by monitoring communications within China's territory.[29] In fact, despite the various euphemisms put forth by the US military on what the aircraft was doing prior to the collision, it is clear the EP-3 was spying. Indeed, the US has annually engaged in at least 200 similar missions for the purposes of monitoring China's military and government-related communications and resumed this activity following the return of the EP-3 crew. Moreover, the US position regarding the unacceptability of Chinese officials boarding its aircraft was undermined by a similar incident involving a Soviet MIG in 1976.[30]

Three days after the incident, a spokesperson from the Chinese Ministry of Foreign Affairs, providing no evidence, charged, "by veering and ramming the Chinese jet at a wide angle, against flight rules, the US surveillance plane caused the crash of the Chinese jet."[31] Chinese Foreign Minister Yang Jiechi, then China's ambassador to the US, declared, "our side has said it perfectly, that the US side should share all the responsibility and apologize to the Chinese side."[32] Beijing's response puzzled observers. Given the US pilots' past encounters with Wang Wei, it is unclear why they suddenly chose to ram his plane. China's claim that the US violated international law by flying within its exclusive economic zone (EEZ) is undermined by the fact that Japan had recently lodged a protest against China for engaging in similar surveillance activities within Japan's EEZ, and that much of the international community does not recognize China's SCS territorial claims.[33]

The US charged that, despite its best attempts to contact China in the immediate aftermath of the incident, neither the PLA nor the Ministry of Foreign Affairs (MFA) returned high-level phone-calls.[34] The upper echelons of power within Beijing appeared to experience institutional backlog while many US officials grew aggravated over what appeared to be a genuine communications blackout with China's PLA, MFA, and other levels of the Chinese leadership. For instance, it took 12 hours before the US ambassador to China could meet with representatives from the MFA to discuss the issue. Some attributed this lag to China's top leadership being away from Beijing for a tree-planting ceremony and the lack of a formal crisis management structure within the bureaucracy. David Lampton even speculated that the Chinese government actually banned the PLA from engaging in talks with the US State Department during the crisis.[35]

Getting the top leadership together in one place as well as establishing an ad hoc crisis management apparatus significantly slowed down the ability of China to act during the crisis.[36] James Mulvenon, a specialist in Chinese military affairs, has eloquently argued that due to the "stove-pipe" structure of the PLA, it is highly probable that the Politburo Standing Committee, China's highest decision-making organ, was receiving faulty information about the collision. Specifically, as the data and analysis from the crash had to navigate through five different departments in the Chinese bureaucracy before arriving at the desk of China's top leadership, Beijing may have been receiving "massaged" information, ignoring the potential role Wang Wei played in causing the EP-3 collision.[37] Minxin Pei, Senior Associate at the Carnegie Endowment for International Peace, concludes that "confusion, internal division, and indecision" within various layers of China's government, rather than an intrinsically hostile view of the US, acted to complicate China's ability to engage in diplomacy during the crisis.[38] Doug Paal, President of the Asia Pacific Policy Center in Washington, quite rightly summarized as follows:

> In the first few days, the Chinese leadership was getting information, much of which American officials believe was bad information, from their military commanders in the South where the incident occurred, and staking very large statements on that bad information. And the United States was issuing broadsides back to try to open the channels. What we had not succeeded in doing in the very initial phase was getting together with the people who, in the foreign ministry or the trade ministry and elsewhere, have a stake in making the relationship work so we can accomplish things together.[39]

The initial US response was equally unhelpful in resolving the situation. Despite being in the awkward position of defending themselves while engaging in China-specific surveillance activities, various US agencies and high-ranking officials unabashedly argued that fault for the incident did not lie at their doorstep. US

Secretary of State Colin Powell declared, "I have heard some suggestion of an apology but we have nothing to apologize for. We did not do anything wrong. Our airplane was in international airspace."[40] White House Press Secretary Ari Fleischer firmly stated that "the accident took place over international airspace, over international waters, and we do not understand any reason to apologize ... the United States did not do anything wrong."[41]

Chairman of the US Armed Services Committee, Senator Joseph Lieberman, even blamed China for the crisis, arguing that the collision occurred as result of "an aggressive game of aerial chicken being played by the Chinese air force."[42] Admiral Denis Blair, Commander in Chief of the Pacific Command, publicly added, "it's not normal practice to play bumper cars in the air."[43] In an address to the nation on April 2, following a meeting with the National Security Council, President George W. Bush not only ignored allegations from Beijing that the US had violated international law, he also claimed the collision occurred as a result of the PLA fighter "shadowing" the spy plane. Absent from the early official US response was any acknowledgement of the US violating China's territorial integrity by landing at the Hainan airbase or that is was in fact spying on China. Instead, to Washington, China had violated international law by boarding the aircraft, which should have been considered an extension of US territory.

While Secretary Powell did eventually write a personal letter to China's vice-premier expressing "deep regret" over the collision and the assumed loss of Wang Wei's life, the diplomatic significance of his statements were mitigated by the statements made from Press Secretary Fleischer, Senator Lieberman, and other US officials. Adding to the confusion was the early decision by US officials to delegate the handling of the crisis to the Department of Defense, which was not predisposed to conduct international negotiations, rather than the State Department, for the first four days of the crisis. Instead of appointing a special envoy or negotiator to exclusively handle the crisis and reach out to Chinese officials, the US government instead relied on traditional diplomatic means through the State and Defense Departments.[44] Even if such practices are efficient for non-crisis-related foreign relations with China, they likely were too bureaucratic and slow in the exceptionally critical days following the EP-3 incident. The Chinese also noted such internal confusion. For instance, Wu Xinbo, then Deputy Director for American Studies at Fudan University, argues Bush's harsh rhetoric in this chaos acted both to escalate the crisis and limit the negotiating room of China's top leadership.[45]

Good communication channels are obviously one of the key elements to effective crisis management.[46] In the case of EP-3 incident, it was obvious that both China and the US lacked rapid and reliable means to communicate accurately and evaluate the impacts on both countries. In their rush to completely absolve their militaries of guilt during the EP-3 crisis, the situation between the two powers in the days following the crisis deteriorated. Their mutual failure to recognize the possibility that neither party likely premeditated the collision made resolving the crisis increasingly difficult.

The Kitty Hawk *incident*

In contrast, communication between the US and China following the USS *Kitty Hawk–Song* submarine encounter clearly differed from in the EP-3 case. Officials from both sides not only prevented any escalation, they also were able to sustain productive bilateral military dialogs during and after news of the encounter went public.

Immediately following the encounter, US and Chinese officials attempted, as much as possible, to avoid blaming one another. Admiral Gary Roughead, Commander of the US Pacific Fleet who happened to be in China on a military-to-military exchange when news of the encounter broke in the *Washington Times*, publicly accepted that the incident took place in international waters and clarified, "[the submarine] was operating in a manner that did not hazard any vessel or cause any problems for any vessel."[47] Publicly, Beijing remained evasive about the incident, and in some cases even denied any event had occurred at all. China's MFA spokesman, Jing Yu, once evasively claimed, "I have not heard of such a report … China has always had a defensive national defense policy. We are an adamant force in maintaining peace and stability in the Asia-Pacific region as well as the world at large."[48] Beijing also did not confirm whether Washington had posited a formal diplomatic complaint regarding the incident.[49] When the *Washington Times* broke the incident publicly, Chinese officials were still able to directly communicate with their US counterparts first.

Calm, controlled communication helped crisis management greatly, as explained by Wu Xinbo:

> Quiet diplomacy is always preferred to overt vociferation. Public actions usually only reduce the maneuvering room of each side and harden the stance of the other government. In contrast, interacting behind the scenes will not only allow each side to save face, but also reduce pressure from the general public.[50]

Beijing in particular deserves credit as it appeared unwilling to acknowledge its strategic achievement of piercing the US Pacific defense screen. No public statements from any other official – in either the MFA or the PLAN – ever hinted at blaming the US. In response, while some US military officials privately told some news outlets that they did not believe in China's claim of innocence, they never went as far as to publicly criticize China. Apparently, communication networks of governmental officials or "hotlines" seem to have developed as conflict resolution mechanisms for crisis management.

Crisis resolution – communication coherence and empathy

The EP-3 incident

Besides early attempts by both Beijing and Washington to paint the other as culpable for the collision, structural problems and prejudices related to both sides' crisis communication apparatuses acted to significantly aggravate an already tense situation. On one hand, responses from the Chinese government and state-run media acted to confuse US officials about the intentions and position of Beijing. As talks were taking place in order to resolve the crisis and return the EP-3 crew to the US, various Chinese state-run media outlets increasingly limited or redefined the position of the Chinese government. This included misrepresenting Secretary Powell's expression of "regret" with an apology and not reporting on US offers to help search for Wang Wei, remaining silent about the numerous mayday calls made by the EP-3 crew that went unanswered on Hainan Island, and disregarding the idea that the collision did not actually happen within Chinese airspace. Commentary and public statements from the PLA – even if not directed towards US officials – acted to confuse the US about China's expectations during the crisis. For example, while the MFA appeared to become increasingly conciliatory as the crisis wore on, comments from the PLA were generally hostile to the US and embraced canonizing Wang Wei as a martyr.[51] Whatever the case, Chinese authorities could have done more not only to present a more coherent response to the US government, but also to make sure one hand was watching the other.

Conversely, the US did not appear to seriously consider how its response could be interpreted by China's general public, which tends to be wary of anything resembling foreign bullying, limiting Beijing's ability to compromise and negotiate.

Given China's experience with imperialism and growing nationalist sentiments since Tiananmen, the EP-3 incident produced a heated response from the country's population. Headlines in Chinese news sources following the incident that particularly shocked the Western audiences included "Wang Wei Where Are You?" "Americans Invade Chinese Airspace," and "Chinese People Condemn American Hegemonism."[52] Chinese online message boards were quickly filled with extreme anti-US rhetoric and calls to charge the American crew with spying. Because of the diverse assortment of political actors and interests in Beijing vying for influence, it would be difficult for those in positions of leadership to go against popular opinion and extend an olive branch to the US, even if a desirable course of action.

The Kitty Hawk *incident*

In contrast, the crisis resolution after the USS *Kitty Hawk–Song* class submarine encounter was generally coherent and organized. In private, Chinese military officials reportedly told their US counterparts that the incident happened entirely by chance, and that the submarine had only surfaced to avoid a potential misunderstanding with *Kitty Hawk*.[53] Forgoing an opportunity to spin the event as a victory for Chinese technological and military know-how, the Chinese media played little to no role in the days after the crisis. This general lack of acknowledgment was anomalous, given the extraordinary coverage of the EP-3 crisis.

While the US was a little more upfront publicly about what transpired near Okinawa, it never crossed the line of throwing direct jabs at Beijing. Michael Perkinson, the US Naval Liaison Officer in Hong Kong who managed the case at that time, found the crisis management of both sides "exceptional" in the sense that both the US and Chinese officials seemed to have the understanding to assess the situation by gathering thorough information from all channels, rather than reacting instantly.[54] This understanding nonetheless received some criticisms from the US side; for instance, Lou Dobbs, a conservative news commentator with *CNN*, called the US military's reserved response "particularly ... bizarre" and "unmilitary" like.[55]

Post-crisis behaviors

The EP-3 incident

Immediately following the return of the EP-3 crew to the US and the ebbing of the spy plane crisis, the US and China both attempted to come out on top one last time. The effect was to not only further exacerbate a tense situation, but also to decrease the prospects of mutual reconciliation.

China demanded that the US pay a US$1 million bill for the time the crew spent in Hainan, despite the US having paid more than US $5 million to an independent contractor to have the plane disassembled and sent back to the US.[56] The request was met with widespread skepticism and even indignation in the US. One State Department official privately joked, "it proves the Chinese still have a sense of humor." Other officials called the bill "highly exaggerated."[57] Legislation was introduced in the US Congress to prevent Washington from paying Beijing the sum. Later, the US Department of Defense offered China US$34,657 (a little more than 3 percent of what China originally asked for) for services rendered during the crisis. China rejected the offer outright, but the act already made Beijing appear desperate. Ultimately, for its efforts, China only won itself an increasingly large group of hostile US legislators as well as several confused and disappointed US foreign policy officials.

The US also attempted to retaliate by deciding to limit its military-to-military exchange program with China to a case-by-case basis.[58] This was obviously counter-productive and was severely criticized by observers like Bates Gill, who argued that the incident should have led to increased and expanded exchanges between the two nations:

> I think it strengthens all the more the case that we should do as much as we can to learn even more about this organization and not just in a strictly military, technical sense, but what its role is, precisely – politically and within the decision-making councils of power inside China. We need to be able to better and more effectively deal with this constituency in our relationship with China, because I think we can expect over time to have – not precisely similar occasions as we've just had in the past 10 or 12 days, but

certainly, encounters will intensify over time, and the PLA will remain an important player for us to try to know.[59]

The Kitty Hawk *incident*

The US and China acted quite differently following the USS *Kitty Hawk* incident. Neither side publicly called for any sort of material compensation. Military-to-military exchanges, occurring between the two countries when the incident broke out, proceeded as planned. Admiral Fallon even used the incident to promote continuing the military exchanges, claiming that "it illustrates the primary reason why we are trying to push, to have better military-to-military relationships."[60] After his visit to China and being questioned about the submarine encounter by the US media, Fallon claimed the exchange had bettered his ability to "pick up the telephone and call someone I know" in China should a crisis or other serious situation break out between the two powers.[61] Roughead, like Fallon, defended the navy-to-navy exchange program he was participating in with Chinese officials as follows:

> Enhancing our navy-to-navy relationships is especially important so we can cooperate in our many areas of mutual interest ... Through routine dialogue and exercise, our navies can improve the ability to coordinate naval operations in missions such as maritime security, search and rescue, and humanitarian relief.[62]

According to the *Washington Times*, while the incident was discussed during the six-day exchange, the bilateral consultations were considered overwhelmingly cordial.[63]

Reasons for the evolution of Sino-US crisis management communication

While a combination of communications blockages, deficient bilateral resolutions, and a lack of follow-up contributed to the general aggravation of the EP-3 incident, the experience with the USS *Kitty Hawk* was remarkably different. Three main factors explain this stark contrast between the two incidents. The changes flowing from these factors have contributed to a refined crisis management communication mechanism that will serve a stabilizing function in future crises.

Sino-US military-to-military exchanges[64]

The first factor driving change has been the regularization of Sino-US military-to-military exchanges, which started after the EP-3 incident. Such exchanges, which have occurred sporadically since 2003, are designed to improve "communication, conflict prevention, and crisis management; transparency and reciprocity; tension reduction over Taiwan; weapons proliferation; strategic nuclear and space talks; counter-terrorism; and accounting for POW/MIAs" between the US and China. In 2004, US Deputy Secretary of State Richard Armitage admitted that while the exchange program encountered some early setbacks, "it's come pretty much full circle ... [and] we're getting back on track with the military-to-military relationship."[65] In 2005, Fallon called for expanding the program to higher and lower military ranks and for increased cooperation with China in the areas of natural disaster response, the avian flu, and other unique areas.[66]

Of particular significance has been increased Sino-US maritime cooperation. Chinese officials have attended lectures and training at various US Coast Guard academies, permitted port calls by US ships, hosted various US military officials during trips to China, and observed US military exercises at the invitation of their US counterparts.[67] Qian Lihua, Deputy Director of the Foreign Affairs Office of China's Defense Ministry, claimed that Sino-US collaboration in a naval exercise near Hawaii "symbolizes more substantial cooperation between the armed forces of China and the United States, which is very important to the future development of military relations."[68]

The program has not been immune from criticisms from both sides. Yet, while some US legislators and military personnel have complained the exchange programs are only used by the Chinese officials to ascertain US defense vulnerabilities and that the US is disproportionately open with exchanges within its territory, many others defended the program as it has continued to expand. One report by two US military attachés concluded,

> The US military does learn something about the PLA from every visit ... [and] the United States should fully engage China in a measured, long-term military-to-military exchange program ... Even though the PLA minimizes foreign access to PLA facilities and key officials, the United States has learned, and can continue to learn, much about the PLA through its long-term relationship.[69]

Perkinson contends the US can reap significant rewards from the exchanges while also "keeping its eyes open" to make sure China is not getting a free ride.[70]

On the Chinese side, according to a report written by the US Center for Naval Analyses, the PLA once firmly believed that it would be "ludicrous" to risk showing the US anything that might reveak its military strengths and weaknesses.[71] However, as time goes by, the Chinese participants, despite avoiding public commentary, have privately given high credits to the program.

Mutual trust developed from the program obviously played a great role in the changes in the *Kitty Hawk* handling in 2006. As previously discussed, such exchanges not only survived the crisis, but may have also served directly as a communication platform behind the crisis. One should note that the news of the submarine encounter came about precisely when a delegation of high-ranking US military officials was visiting Beijing.[72] Although the exact content of discussion of the delegation is not known publicly, the very fact that the delegation could be present in Beijing during the crisis was already a sign of improved Sino-US bilateral communication. Indeed, cooperation and relations between Beijing and Washington actually increased in the weeks and months following that incident. In August 2007, for instance, US Rep. Ike Skelton (R-Mo.), Chairman of the US House Armed Services Committee, toured a Chinese navy destroyer and a Second Artillery Brigade in Beijing along with an eight-member US Congressional delegation.[73] Three months later, US Secretary of Defense Robert Gates traveled to China for the purposes of establishing a hotline between the two countries' militaries.[74] A number of high-level military exchanges were arranged in 2011, including Chief of General Staff, commanders and military class of both countries. In September 2012, the then Secretary of Defense traveled to China to meet with the incoming Chinese President, Xi Jinping, among other high-level officials. Of course, Sino-American military-to-military relations also link to the two countries' larger bilateral relationship.[75]

Reforms within China's national security apparatus

Another structural factor contributing to variation between the two cases is the reforms carried out within China's national security apparatus after 2001. As a direct result of Beijing's disorganized response during the EP-3 crisis, many foreign relations analysts at that time forecast that China would be forced to take a hard look at certain practices that might have exacerbated an already tense situation with the US.[76] Some Chinese officials have privately admitted that the Chinese crisis management system did not work to their advantage. The incident became a stimulus for China to develop an integrated National Security Council, resembling the US National Security Council, to better coordinate its responses in future crises. Other proposals considered by China included establishing "counter-emergency" response mechanisms or "leadership small groups," which are meant to sideline the bureaucracy and emulate the functions of a Chinese national security council.[77] While the actual functions of such bodies remain opaque to the public, they were clearly in place after 2001, as judged by the US side, and likely played a role in the USS *Kitty Hawk–Song* submarine encounter.[78]

Another reform after 2001 has been the introduction of "crisis management" lessons at the Central Party School of the Chinese Communist Party (CCP), the foremost CCP cadre training institution.[79] On a related note, Mulvenon points out that the CCP has increasingly promoted PLA members with whom they have deep bonds of trust, in the hopes of avoiding a repeat of the internal misinformation that may have affected China's response following the EP-3 collision.[80]

Besides military exchanges, China and the US also engaged in other military cooperative activities afterwards. For instance, the Sino-US Military Maritime Consultation Mechanism (*Zhongmei haishang junshi anquan cuoshang jizhi*) held its first session in Guam in September 2001 and it was here that military dialog after the EP-3 crisis was promptly resumed.[81] Moreover, China's Central Military Commission agreed to initiate joint naval maritime search and rescue exercises with the US from 2006 and regular exchange programs have also been since held by the two states.[82]

Evolution of the US's handling of security measures with China

Since 2001, perceptions within US agencies concerning how to engage China in crisis situations have steadily evolved. According to Perkinson, there was a "creeping recognition that relations between these two countries are too important for people to freelance or engage in proud talk," and interrelated interest "in being more measured in public statements."[83]

Supplementing this new framework, there has been substantially increased cooperation between the two states in the realm of security generally and counter-terrorism specifically. Notably, the earliest evidence of this took place after 9/11, i.e., only five months after the EP-3 incident. After China nominally joined the US-led anti-terror coalition, cooperation between Beijing and Washington in counter-terrorism suddenly escalated significantly. Considering the scale of change in such a short time, the single week after 9/11 should be considered as representing one of the most dramatic U-turns in Chinese diplomatic history, though Chinese assistance to the US sometimes took a low profile because of concerns that the about face was too sensitive. For instance, one of the most substantial Chinese contributions, the green light given to the shaping of close post-9/11 relations between the US and Pakistan, was never revealed by the official press.[84] The relevance of such Chinese cooperation was that it was viewed most favorably by the US. According to the US Congressional Research Service, "the counter-terrorism campaign helped to stabilize US–PRC relations up to the highest level."[85]

The participation of the Chinese ports of Hong Kong and Shenzhen with the US-sponsored Container Security Initiative in 2003 and 2005 respectively added a new layer to the extent of Sino-US security cooperation. Commemorating Hong Kong's entrance into the agreement, which attempts to block the illegal smuggling of weapons of mass destruction, the US Commissioner of Customs and Border Protection, Robert Bonner, enthusiastically declared, "China and the United States stand shoulder-to-shoulder in the world war on terrorism and in our mission to protect the global trading system."[86] As compared with 2001, these institutionalized cooperation initiatives ensure greater space for effective and open mediums of communications between two countries should another crisis occur in the future.

Final words

Returning to the example of the Cuban Missile Crisis mentioned at the beginning, Robert McNamara and his associate James Blight once noted:

> It is becoming increasingly apparent that the greatest threats to Great Power security, and to the peace of the world, derive not from threats uttered or

implied at the moment, but inadvertence – from unintended consequences of hugely complicated interactions of policies, pronouncements, and actions taken over time by a multilateral cast of players.[87]

During the height of the Cold War, the US and the Soviet Union could have unwittingly initiated a global nuclear holocaust not because they wanted to, but because of a faulty communications system. McNamara and Blight also remind us that crisis situations can happen even among friends. Whether friends, enemies, or something in between, the geopolitical influence and interests of Washington and Beijing will invariably increasingly intersect as China's political, economic, and military prowess continues to expand. Traditionally, the US and China do not share in-depth military information with one another on a regular basis. Nor do they have robust institutions to facilitate communication and mutual exchange of information between their militaries. Fortunately, regardless of the complexities of the Sino-US relationship, both sides have shown a capacity to engage in critical self-evaluation and have worked, at least to some extent, to adjust practices that acted to inadvertently escalate crisis situations from 2001 to 2006. Through growing military-to-military exchanges and significant reforms to both China and the US's crisis management systems, neither country has remained inert in attempting to understand and interact with the other.

The immensely dissimilar responses of both states in 2001 and 2006 provide hope that if another crisis situation occurs between the US and China, the two countries can navigate their way through the storm even if the ride is a bit choppy. It is true that after the 2006 *Kitty Hawk* incident, a few small-scale jolts in Sino-US relations have occurred. These include the Chinese government's last-minute decision to cancel a scheduled port call by the USS *Kitty Hawk* in Hong Kong in 2007, China's brief suspension of its participation in its military-to-military exchange program with the US as a result of US–Taiwan arms sales in 2008, and the USS *Impeccable* incident in 2009, among others. Yet none of these frictions escalated into a crisis on the scale of 2001, as revamped Sino-American crisis management mechanisms functioned well. Using the minimal scope of crisis defined in the introduction, there has not been another occurrence of military conflict or intensification of scope of hostility between the parties. The Sino-US crisis management mechanism seems to have adjusted and been well executed.

Given the Obama administration's re-engineering of its diplomatic focus to the Asia-Pacific from 2010 onwards, as discussed in Chapter 4 by Suisheng Zhao, establishing crisis management communication mechanisms between Beijing and Washington becomes increasingly essential, particularly in cyberspace where the two powers now regularly grapple. As shown, the existence of direct bilateral communication mechanism, the management of both country's citizenry's expectations, the coordination of the decision-making process and its relative transparency, among others, are critical to satisfactory crisis management. Given the ability of the US and USSR to compromise immediately following the crisis that almost brought both countries – if not the world – to a smoldering ruin, we can presume that China and the US can work with one another to an even better degree. This, though, requires dynamic engagement, regular contact, and a commitment to proactive reflection and, if necessary, reform.

There is reason for optimism as shown by Xi Jinping's Sunnylands summit with Barack Obama in June 2013, where both leaders were able to build trust or even friendship. Besides, Sunnylands laid the foundation for more summits between two leaders in the future.[88] At Sunnylands, Xi also established the idea of "new type of great-power relations" (*xinxing daguo guanxi*) between China and the US. Building trust and a regular communication channel between the leaders of China and the US appears easier since Obama has taken a softer stance towards China following the departure of Secretary of State Hillary Clinton.

The Sino-US Strategic and Economic Dialogues (S&ED), one of the most regular communication channels between both powers over the past five years, took place in Washington a month later. The S&ED's purpose was to seek common ground and areas of cooperation vis-à-vis bilateral issues and regional challenges. However, following the shuffling of China's top-level decision-making team, some observers are worried about the inexperienced Chinese top officials in handling the relationship with the US.[89] Another threat to Sino-US relation was Edward Snowden's revelations about US cyber spying. Still, the S&ED scored a surprising success in providing a venue for the two countries to discuss cyber security.

Despite general goodwill displayed by leaders of both countries, there are a number of crosscutting winds. First, there is a lack of trust between the two countries, especially among front-line officials. Second, communication channels are maintained when relations are good yet military exchanges often become a casualty when the Sino-American relationship turns bad. Third, the 2008 global financial crisis, which has stoked fears about China being a major rival, has diluted some of the factors that created China and the US's satisfactory crisis management mechanism. For China, the "new type of great-power relationship" requires the US to accept China's role in parts of the world that the US used to play. At the same time, it requires American respect of China's "core interests" – US support for Japan in the Diaoyu/Senkaku Islands dispute and Southeast Asian countries in the SCS dispute was seen not just as a difference of opinion but as a breach of trust.[90]

Regarding the potential ways to reinforce the crisis management mechanism, the system should be institutionalized and operated regardless of political turbulence in order to avoid a heightening of tensions among front-line officials. The norms of mutual deterrence and transparency should also be enhanced, for example, through establishing notification mechanisms on military exercises in nearby regions.

Following Snowden's revelations, the next Sino-American crisis seems more likely to emerge in the cyber world, which requires the US and China to build a brand new bilateral protocol. Recent accusations that the PLA owns a Chinese hacker group under Unit 61398 which targeted explicitly American defense contractors have elevated the cyber conflicts between two countries to a higher level.[91] In terms of possible ways of improving the existing communication channels, a regular summit at the ministerial level should be established to govern the execution of such protocol. Both sides should also consider the possibilities of extraditing wanted individuals who violated such protocol, as listed by the other. It is essential for Beijing and Washington to have a serious discussion on this topic. Otherwise, in an atmosphere of nationalists from both sides being increasingly suspicious of one another, a new round of crises with unpredictable consequences is likely to take place out of the blue when China's comprehensive national strength eventually catches up with that of the US.

Notes

1 The authors acknowledge Saturnia Kwok's research assistance and Michael Perkinson's advice and comments. They also acknowledge the Hong Kong Institute of Asia-Pacific Studies of the Chinese University of Hong Kong for publishing an earlier version of the paper and thank their Hong Kong Institute of Education colleagues for their contructive feedback.
2 According to the *Oxford Dictionary*, a crisis is a time when a difficult or important decision must be made.
3 Chinese studies see crisis management as the dynamic process of a crisis manager's effort to minimize the threats of damage to an organization and its stakeholders through crisis information analysis and implementation of planned crisis response strategies. This, in particular, is executed to ensure the integrity and sustainability of the entire system. Dong Zhuanyi, 危机管理学 (*Studies on Crisis Management*) (Beijing: 中国传媒大学出版社, 2007), 17.
4 Foster Klug, "Obama Calls for More Military Talks with China," Associated Press, March 12, 2009.
5 Paul Richter and Julian Barnes, "Sea Encounter Prompts Vow by US, China," *Los Angeles Times*, March 12, 2009.
6 Yu Meng, "Protest Lodged against US Incursion," *China Daily*, March 11, 2009, 1.
7 The authors have engaged a number of Chinese and American informants in formal interviews and informal conversations, but at the request of the interviewees most names and identities have not been disclosed. Nonetheless, the content of this article draws extensively on their viewpoints and therefore the authors would sincerely like to acknowledge their assistance and cooperation.
8 Michael D. Swaine, "Understanding the Historical Record," in *Managing Sino-American Crises: Case Studies and Analysis*, ed. Michael D. Swaine, Tuosheng Zhang, and Danielle F. S. Cohen (Washington, DC: Carnegie Endowment for International Peace, 2006), 5.
9 Xia Ping, "Crisis Management in China and in the United States: A Comparative Study," in *Managing Sino-American Crises*, ed. Swaine *et al.*, 149–78.
10 Swaine, "Understanding the Historical Record," 23.
11 Ibid., 18–19.
12 See John Mearsheimer, "The Future of the American Pacifier," *Foreign Affairs* 80, no. 5 (September/October, 2001): 46–61.
13 Thomas Christensen has written extensively on the potential areas for US–China cooperation. Aaron Friedberg concludes the relationship between the US and China could be marked by a complex mix of realism and liberalism in "The Future of US–China Relations," *International Security* 30, no. 2 (Fall 2005): 7–45.

14 Following the 1962 Cuban Missile Crisis, the US and the Soviet Union took numerous steps to prevent similar incidents happening again. One was to replace the inefficient mode of postal communication between Washington and Moscow with the infamous hotline. Another step was to restart negotiations concerning banning nuclear tests, which ultimately led to both sides ratifying the 1963 Limited Test Ban Treaty. James A. Nathan, *Anatomy of the Cuban Missile Crisis* (Westport, CT: Greenwood, 2001), 8.
15 Zhang Tuosheng, Shi Wen, eds., 对抗·博弈·合作: 中美安全危机管理案例分析 (*Confront, "Go Chess," Cooperate: The Sino-US Crisis Management Cases Studies*) (Beijing: 世界知识出版社, 2007), 5–6; and Thomas Christensen and Michael Glosny, "China: Sources of Stability in US–China Security Relations," in *Strategic Asia 2003–04: Fragility and Crisis*, ed. Richard J. Ellings, Aaron L. Friedberg, and Michael Wills (Seattle: National Bureau of Asian Research, 2003), 53–6.
16 Swaine, "Understanding the Historical Record," 48.
17 Xinbo Wu, "Managing Crisis and Sustaining Peace between China and the United States." Washington, DC: United States Institute of Peace Press, April 2008. www.usip.org/sites/default/files/resources/PW61_FinalApr16.pdf.
18 Swaine *et al.* eds., *Managing Sino-American Crises*.
19 Ed Vulliamy and John Gittings, "The Top Gun Spies," *The Observer* (April 8, 2001).
20 "Song Class-Peoples Liberation Army Navy," GlobalSecurity.org, January 12, 2007. www.globalsecurity.org/military///world/china/song.htm.
21 Wayne McDonald, "Chinese Submarine Beats Navy's Best SONAR Operators," Associated Content, November 23, 2006. http://wikicars.org/en/Chinese_Submarine_Beats_Navy_s_Very_Best_Sonar_Operators.
22 Matthew Hickley, "The Uninvited Guest," *Mail Online*, November 10, 2007.
23 Joe Buff, an expert on national security issues at the US Society for Risk Analysis, claims,

> No PLAN submarine captain in his right mind would surface in such conditions unless he wanted to be absolutely sure that his presence, previously undetected within the carrier's inner defense zone, was made unmistakably clear to theater US admirals and their higher-ups inside the Beltway.
> (Joe Buff, "Is China Stalking US?" Military.com, November 28, 2006. www.freerepublic.com/focus/f-news/1746207/posts)

24 "US Commander Says Chinese Sub Came Close to US Ship in the Pacific," Associated Press, November 14, 2006.
25 See James Mulvenon, "Civil–Military Relations and the EP-3 Crisis: A Content Analysis," *China Leadership Monitor*, no. 1 (Winter 2001): 1–11; John Keefe, *Anatomy of the EP-3 Incident, April 2001* (Alexandria, VA: CAN Corporation, 2002); and Zhang Tuosheng, "The Sino-American Aircraft Collision: Lessons for Crisis Management," in *Managing Sino-American Crises*, ed. Swaine *et al.*, 391–421.
26 Shirley A. Kan *et al.*, *China–US Aircraft Collision Incident of April 2001: Assessments and Policy Implications*. Report no. RL30946 (Washington, DC: Congressional Research Service, 2001).
27 "China Sub Stalked US Fleet," *Washington Times*, November 13, 2006.
28 Derek Brown, "The US China Spy Plane Row," *The Guardian*, April 4, 2001.
29 Dexin Tian and Chin-Chung Chao, "The American Hegemonic Responses to the US–China Mid-Air Plane Collision," *International Journal of Communication*, 2 (2008): 9.
30 In 1976, following the aircraft's landing in Japan, American and Japanese officials – ignoring Soviet protests – boarded and disassembled the plane to examine its contents. The MIG also was sent back to the USSR in pieces.
31 "Chinese FM Spokesperson Gives Full Account of Air Collision," *Xinhua*, April 4, 2001.
32 "China Unmoved by US 'Regrets'," *CNN*, April 5, 2001.

33 Nicholas Lardy et al., *The Surveillance Plane Crisis: Implications and Next Steps for US–China Relations* (Washington, DC: The Brookings Institution, 2001).
34 Shirley A. Kan, *US–China Military Contacts: Issues for Congress*, report no. RL32496 (Washington, DC: Congressional Research Service, 2008), 18.
35 David M. Lampton, *Same Bed, Different Dreams: Managing US–China Relations, 1989–2000* (Berkeley: University of California Press, 2002), 453–4.
36 Wu, "Managing Crisis," 21, 25.
37 Mulvenon, "Civil–Military Relations and the EP-3 Crisis," 4.
38 Lardy et al., *The Surveillance Plane Crisis*.
39 Ibid.
40 Tian and Chao, "The American Hegemonic Responses," 9.
41 "Powell Sends Personal Letter to Chinese Vice Premier," *CNN*, April 5, 2001.
42 "Lieberman: China Played 'Aggressive Game of Aerial Chicken'," *CNN*, April 4, 2001.
43 Vulliamy and Gittings, "The Top Gun Spies."
44 Simon Shen, *Redefining Nationalism in Modern China: Sino-American Relations and the Emergence of Chinese Public Opinion in the 21st Century* (Basingstoke: Palgrave Macmillan, 2007), 12.
45 Wu, "Managing Crisis," 16–17.
46 Charles F. Hermann, "Types of Crisis Actors and Their Implications for Crisis Management," in *International Crises and Crisis Management: An East–West Symposium*, ed. Daniel Frei (Farnborough: Saxon House, 1978), 29–41.
47 "US Admiral Says China Submarine Incident Not Dangerous," Associated Press, November 17, 2006.
48 "Chinese Sub Comes Close to US Ships in the Pacific," *CBS News*, November 14, 2006.
49 "China Sub Stalked US Fleet," *Washington Times*, November 13, 2006.
50 Xinbo Wu, "Understanding Chinese and US Crisis Behavior," *Washington Quarterly* 31, no. 1 (Winter 2007–8): 74.
51 Mulvenon, "Civil–Military Relations and the EP-3 Crisis," 7.
52 Rupert Wingfield-Hayes, "Spy Plane Row Stokes Chinese Passions," *BBC News*, April 5, 2001.
53 "US Officials Press China on Armed Submarine Encounter," *Washington Times*, January 10, 2007.
54 Personal interview, Hong Kong, April 3, 2009.
55 Lou Dobbs, "US Navy Trying to Downplay Confrontation between Chinese Submarine and USS *Kitty Hawk*," *Lou Dobbs Tonight*, November 15, 2006.
56 Kan et al., *China–US Aircraft Collision Incident of April 2001*, 7–8.
57 Alan Sipress and Thomas Ricks, "China Bills US over Collision," *Washington Post*, July 7, 2001.
58 Kan, "US–China Military Contacts," 3.
59 Lardy et al., *The Surveillance Plane Crisis*.
60 "Chinese Sub Comes Close to US Ships in the Pacific," *CBS News*, November 14, 2006.
61 Kan, "US–China Military Contacts," 18.
62 "Chinese Sub Comes Close to US Ships in the Pacific."
63 "US Officials Press China on Armed Submarine Encounter," *Washington Times*, January 10, 2007.
64 For an in-depth treatment of Sino-US military-to-military exchanges, see Chapter 10 in this volume.
65 Kan, *US–China Military Contacts*, 3.
66 Kan, *US–China Military Contacts*, 3.
67 Kenneth W. Allen and Eric A. McVadon, *China's Foreign Military Relations* (Washington, DC: Henry L. Stimson Center, 1999).

68 "China, US Enjoy Active Military Exchanges in 2006," *People's Daily Online*, December 28, 2006. http://english.people.com.cn/200612/28/eng20061228_336342.html
69 Allen and McVadon, *China's Foreign Military Relations*.
70 Personal interview, Hong Kong, April 3, 2009.
71 Kan, *US–China Military Contacts*, 17.
72 "China Sub Stalked US Fleet": "US Pacific Fleet Commander Visits China," US Pacific Fleet Public Affairs, November 13, 2006.
73 Andrew S. Erickson, "New US Maritime Strategy: Initial Chinese Responses," *China Security* 3, no. 4 (2007): 40–61.
74 Edward Cody, "China and US to Establish Military Hotline," *Washington Post*, November 6, 2007.
75 On this, see Chapte 10 by Christopher Yung in this volume.
76 Lardy *et al.*, *The Surveillance Plane Crisis*.
77 Frank Miller and Andrew Scobell, "'Decisionmaking under Stress' or 'Crisis Management'? In Lieu of a Conclusion," in *Chinese National Security: Decisionmaking under Stress*, ed. Andrew Scobell and Larry M. Wortzel (Carlisle Barracks: US Army War College Strategic Studies Institute, 2005), 233.
78 Personal interview, Hong Kong, April 3, 2009.
79 Cheng-yi Lin, "US–China Military Hotline a Model for Cross-Strait CMB," *Jamestown Foundation China Brief* 7, no. 23 (December 2007). www.jamestown.org/programs/chinabrief/single/?tx_ttnews%5Btt_news%5D=4583&tx_ttnews%5Bback Pid%5D=197&no_cache=1#.VHVO2dKUdsU.
80 Mulvenon, "Civil–Military Relations and the EP-3 Crisis," 4.
81 "2002年中国的国防 (China's Military Defense in 2002)," *People's Daily*, December 10, 2001, 7.
82 "China, US Enjoy Active Military Exchange in 2006," People.com, December 28, 2006. http://english.people.com.cn/200612/28/eng20061228_336342.html.
83 Mike Perkinson interview, Hong Kong, April 3, 2009.
84 David M. Lampton, *Chinese and American Mutual Perceptions and National Strategies after 9–11 and the Leadership Transition in China* (Hong Kong University of Science and Technology, Hong Kong, March 6, 2003).
85 Shirley Kan, *US–China Counter-Terrorism Cooperation: Issues for US Policy*. CRS Report for Congress RS21995 (Washington, DC: Congressional Research Service, 2010), 4.
86 "US Official Praises HK, Mainland for Cooperation against Terrorism," Embassy of the People's Republic of China in the United States of America, August 1, 2003, www.china-embassy.org/eng/zt/mgryzdzg/t36538.htm.
87 Robert McNamara and James Blight, *Wilson's Ghost: Reducing the Risk of Conflict, Killing and Catastrophe in the 21st Century* (New York: Public Affairs, 2001).
88 "America and China: The Summit," *The Economist*, June 8, 2013.
89 "Wrestling in Sino-US Strategic and Economic Dialogues," *South China Morning Post*, July 11, 2013.
90 "One Model, Two Interpretations," *The Economist*, September 28, 2013.
91 "China–US Cyber Spying Row Turns Spotlight Back on Shadowy Unit 61398," Reuters, May 20, 2014.

References

"2002 年中国的国防 (China's Military Defense in 2002)." *People's Daily*, December 10, 2001.

Allen, Kenneth W., and Eric A. McVadon. *China's Foreign Military Relations* (Washington, DC: Henry L. Stimson Center, 1999).

"America and China: The Summit." *The Economist*, June 8, 2013.
Brown, Derek. "The US China Spy Plane Row." *The Guardian*, April 4, 2001.
Buff, Joe. "Is China Stalking US?" Military.com. November 28, 2006.
"China Sub Stalked US Fleet." *Washington Times*, November 13, 2006.
"China Unmoved by US 'Regrets'." *CNN*. April 5, 2001.
"China–US Cyber Spying Row Turns Spotlight Back on Shadowy Unit 61398." Reuters, May 20, 2014.
"China, US Enjoy Active Military Exchanges in 2006." *People's Daily*. December 28, 2006. http://english.people.com.cn/200612/28/eng20061228_336342.html.
"China and US to Establish Military Hotline." *Washington Post*, November 6, 2007.
"Chinese FM Spokesperson Gives Full Account of Air Collision." *Xinhua*, April 4, 2001.
"Chinese Sub Comes Close to US Ships in the Pacific." *CBS News*. November 14, 2006.
Christensen, Thomas, and Michael Glosny. "China: Sources of Stability in US–China Security Relations," in *Strategic Asia 2003–04: Fragility and Crisis*, eds. Richard J. Ellings, Aaron L. Friedberg, and Michael Wills (Seattle: National Bureau of Asian Research, 2003): 53–80.
Dobbs, Lou. "US Navy Trying to Downplay Confrontation between Chinese Submarine and USS *Kitty Hawk*." *Lou Dobbs Tonight*. November 15, 2006.
Dong, Zhuanyi. 危机管理学（*Studies on Crisis Management*）(Beijing: 中国传媒大学出版社, 2007).
Erickson, Andrew S. "New US Maritime Strategy: Initial Chinese Responses." *China Security* 3, no. 4 (2007): 40–61.
Friedberg, Aaron. "The Future of US–China Relations." *International Security* 30, no. 2 (Fall 2005): 7–45.
Hermann, Charles F. "Types of Crisis Actors and Their Implications for Crisis Management," in *International Crises and Crisis Management: An East–West Symposium*, ed. Daniel Frei (Farnborough: Saxon House, 1978), 29–41
Hickley, Matthew. "The Uninvited Guest." *Mail Online*. November 10, 2007. www.dailymail.co.uk/news/article-492804/The-uninvited-guest-Chinese-sub-pops-middle-U-S-Navy-exercise-leaving-military-chiefs-red-faced.html.
Kan, Shirley A. *US–China Military Contacts: Issues for Congress*. Report no. RL32496 (Washington, DC: Congressional Research Service, 2008).
Kan, Shirley A. *US–China Counter-Terrorism Cooperation: Issues for US Policy*. CRS Report for Congress RS21995 (Washington, DC: Congressional Research Service, 2010).
Kan, Shirley A., Richard Best, Christopher Bolkcom, Robert Chapman, Richard Cronin, Kerry Dumbaugh, Stuart Goldman, Mark Manyin, Wayne Morrison, Ronald O'Rourke, and David Ackerman. *China–US Aircraft Collision Incident of April 2001: Assessments and Policy Implications*. Report no. RL30946 (Washington, DC: Congressional Research Service, 2001).
Keefe, John. *Anatomy of the EP-3 Incident, April 2001* (Alexandria, VA: CNA Corporation, 2002).
Klug, Foster. "Obama Calls for More Military Talks with China." Associated Press, March 12, 2009.
Lampton, David M. "Chinese and American Mutual Perceptions and National Strategies after 9–11 and the Leadership Transition in China." Hong Kong University of Science and Technology, Hong Kong, March 6, 2003.
Lampton, David M. *Same Bed, Different Dreams: Managing US–China Relations, 1989–2000* (Berkeley: University of California Press, 2002).

Lardy, Nicholas, Michael Armacost, Bates Gill, Douglas Paal, and Minxin Pei. *The Surveillance Plane Crisis: Implications and Next Steps for US–China Relations* (Washington, DC: The Brookings Institution, 2001).

"Lieberman: China Played 'Aggressive Game of Aerial Chicken'." *CNN*. April 4, 2001.

Lin, Cheng-yi. "US–China Military Hotline a Model for Cross-Strait CMB." *Jamestown Foundation China Brief* 7, no. 23 (December 2007). www.jamestown.org/programs/chinabrief/single/?tx_ttnews%5Btt_news%5D=4583&tx_ttnews%5BbackPid%5D=197&no_cache=1#.VHVO2dKUdsU.

McDonald, Wayne. "Chinese Submarine Beats Navy's Best SONAR Operators." Associated Content. November 23, 2006. http://wikicars.org/en/Chinese_Submarine_Beats_Navy_s_Very_Best_Sonar_Operators.

McNamara, Robert S., and James G. Blight. *Wilson's Ghost: Reducing the Risk of Conflict, Killing and Catastrophe in the 21st Century* (New York: Public Affairs, 2001).

Mearsheimer, John. "The Future of the American Pacifier." *Foreign Affairs* 80, no. 5 (September/October 2001).

Meng, Yu. "Protest Lodged against US Incursion." *China Daily*, March 11, 2009.

Miller, Frank, and Andrew Scobell. "'Decisionmaking under Stress' or 'Crisis Management'? In Lieu of a Conclusion," in *Chinese National Security: Decisionmaking under Stress*, eds. Andrew Scobell and Larry M. Wortzel, (Carlisle Barracks: US Army War College Strategic Studies Institute, 2005), 229–48.

Mulvenon, James. "Civil–Military Relations and the EP-3 Crisis: A Content Analysis." *China Leadership Monitor*, no. 1 (Winter 2001): 1–11.

Nathan, James A. *Anatomy of the Cuban Missile Crisis* (Westport: Greenwood Press, 2001).

"One Model, Two Interpretations." *The Economist*, September 28, 2013.

Peoples' Republic of China, Embassy in the United States. "US Official Praises HK, Mainland for Cooperation against Terrorism." August 1, 2003. www.china-embassy.org/eng/zt/mgryzdzg/t36538.htm.

"Powell Sends Personal Letter to Chinese Vice Premier." *CNN*. April 5, 2001.

Richter, Paul, and Julian Barnes. "Sea Encounter Prompts Vow by US, China." *Los Angeles Times*, March 12, 2009.

Shen, Simon. *Redefining Nationalism in Modern China: Sino-American Relations and the Emergence of Chinese Public Opinion in the 21st Century* (Basingstoke: Palgrave Macmillan, 2007).

Sipress, Alan, and Thomas Ricks. "China Bills US over Collision." *Washington Post*, July 7, 2001.

"*Song* class-Peoples Liberation Army Navy." GlobalSecurity.org. January 12, 2007. www.globalsecurity.org/military///world/china/song.htm.

Swaine, Michael D., Tuosheng Zhang, and Danielle F. S. Cohen, eds. *Managing Sino-American Crises: Case Studies and Analysis* (Washington, DC: Carnegie Endowment for International Peace, 2006).

Tian, Dexin, and Chin-Chung Chao. "The American Hegemonic Responses to the US–China Mid-Air Plane Collision." *International Journal of Communication*, no. 2 (2008): 1–19.

"US Admiral Says China Submarine Incident Not Dangerous." Associated Press. November 17, 2006.

"US Commander Says Chinese Sub Came Close to US Ship in the Pacific." Associated Press, November 14, 2006.

"US Officials Press China on Armed Submarine Encounter." *Washington Times*, January 10, 2007.

"US Pacific Fleet Commander Visits China." US Pacific Fleet Public Affairs, November 13, 2006.

Vulliamy, Ed, and John Gittings. "The Top Gun Spies." *The Observer*, April 8, 2001.

Wingfield-Hayes, Rupert. "Spy Plane Row Stokes Chinese Passions." *BBC News*. April 5, 2001.

"Wrestling in Sino-US Strategic and Economic Dialogues." *South China Morning Post*, July 11, 2013.

Wu, Xinbo. "Managing Crisis and Sustaining Peace between China and the United States." Washington, DC: United States Institute of Peace Press, April 2008. www.usip.org/sites/default/files/resources/PW61_FinalApr16.pdf.

Wu, Xinbo. "Understanding Chinese and US Crisis Behavior." *Washington Quarterly* 31, no. 1 (Winter 2007–8): 61–76.

Zhang, Tuosheng, and Wen Shi, eds. 对抗·博弈·合作: 中美安全危机管理案例分析 (*Confront, "Go Chess," Cooperate: The Sino-US Crisis Management Cases Studies*) (Beijing: 世界知识出版社, 2007).

12 Conclusion

Stanley Rosen

Introduction

In 1996, a year before paramount leader Deng Xiaoping's death, the late MIT professor Lucian Pye began an op-ed article in the *New York Times* by noting that it was a tough time in relations between the United States and China, given China's conviction that the US was a superpower in decline and determined to contain China, while China was a superpower on the rise. Washington's reaction, he suggested, reflected ambivalence on how to deal with a China whose policies on a variety of issues did not conform to the hopes and expectations of Americans. Going further, he explained that:

> the fact that relations with China are troubled should not be surprising for the relationship has rarely been close, except for the brief period of near alliance against Soviet expansionism. There are just too many fundamental obstacles in political culture, history and ideologies for the political relationship to be a warm one.[1]

While some of the specific issues have changed – for example, following the return of the Kuomintang (KMT) to power in Taiwan in 2008, under President Ma Ying-jeou, Beijing is no longer engaging in saber-rattling in the Taiwan Strait – the larger issue on both sides has remained the management of the relationship between a rising power and an entrenched superpower.

The intervening years have seen the ties between China and the US deepening in a wide variety of areas, along with China's continued upward trajectory and growing confidence. However, as perceptive observers on both sides pointed out with increasing concern, the fact that Beijing and Washington sought to build a constructive partnership for the long run, understood well each other's position on all major issues, and had extensive dealings with each other, had not produced a level of trust with regard to either side's long-term intentions.[2] The complexity of the problem has been compounded by the self-images of two nations that tend toward moral righteousness. The US has a long history of what has been called American exceptionalism, which holds that the US is:

a special, chosen nation created to play a unique role in history as the redeemer of an inferior, corrupt and oppressed world ... and has the responsibility to help other peoples follow the model laid out by the chosen few.[3]

What this means in practice is that American leaders generally do not view their policies to be driven by selfish motives, the pursuit of hegemony, or the desire to subjugate other nations, but rather reflect more altruistic impulses, including the dissemination of universal values that all will want to share if given the opportunity. Moreover, one of the key findings that emerged from a conference devoted to American images of China was that this self-image has influenced American perceptions of China perhaps more than any one action or set of actions on the part of the Chinese, and that US images of China have gone through cycles of optimism and pessimism, with similar love–hate cycles characterizing Chinese images of the US.[4] It is useful to bear this in mind in evaluating the recent history and likely future developments in the relationship since, as suggested below, any actions undertaken by either side will be interpreted through pre-existing conceptions of the other.

The Chinese self-image also emphasizes benevolent behavior toward others. For example, in response to concerns of a rising China or what Chinese call the "China threat theory" (*zhongguo weixie lun*), Du Ruiqing, former president of Xi'an International Studies University, noted at a forum,

> It's high time to make ourselves better understood by the world's people. Once they come to know the Chinese people better, they will find out that harmony is an essential part of Chinese tradition and a country that highly values harmony will absolutely pose no threat to the rest of the world.[5]

Ironically, this sounds eerily similar to a comment made by then President George W. Bush when he was informed of the high levels of anti-Americanism in many countries, protesting that if only they really understood us, they would love us. These self-images are derived from very different political histories. If we can say that belief systems in the US are marked by a strong belief that democracy is the natural and most desirable state of affairs for all mankind, in China one could argue that Chinese belief systems are marked by a fear of chaos and disorder, of the dangers that come when the central government is weak and can be manipulated, whether by warlords, foreigners, or despotic or corrupt leaders, leading to the pursuit of social stability as the primary value. If we extrapolate this to foreign policy, it can be argued that while the US may see China's behavior in defending what it considers its core territorial interests as overly harsh in dealing with domestic minorities in Tibet and Xinjiang, and overly assertive in areas of contested sovereignty such as the South China Sea (SCS) and East China Sea (ECS), China's self-image sees the country, as Andrew Nathan and Robert Ross note, as vulnerable, internally and externally, crowded on all sides by powerful rivals and potential foes, facing immense security problems in defense of its territorial integrity.[6]

By 2013, with the re-election of Barack Obama to a second term and the ascendance of Xi Jinping as China's new leader, the time appeared ripe for, in Xi's own words, "a new type of great power relationship," with the two powers now at a "critical juncture."[7] The two leaders met in a highly publicized and closely watched summit for two days of intensive discussions on June 7 and 8, 2013, at Sunnylands, an estate east of Los Angeles, to try and build a personal rapport and define the relationship between the two countries. Virtually all the issues raised in this volume were on the table for discussion, including North Korea, the global economy, SCS and ECS territorial disputes, cybersecurity, and the mounting distrust between the American and Chinese militaries. Indeed, this latter issue was a major focus of President Obama's then National Security Adviser Tom Donilon when he traveled to Beijing to prepare the agenda for the California summit meeting. Before meeting with the Vice-Chairman of the Central Military Commission, General Fan Changlong, Donilon repeated the Obama administration's desire for stronger communications between the two militaries and for joint, rather than competitive, efforts to deal with regional problems in Asia.[8] Not surprisingly, given the potential importance of this meeting and the likelihood that Xi will be leading China for the next 10 years, the Chinese, American, and international media devoted extensive commentaries and suggestions on the positions each side should adapt for these discussions, with academics from both sides also weighing in.[9]

What can we learn from the research presented in the chapters in this volume and elsewhere that help us understand such key issues as change and continuity in Sino-American relations, the roots and causes of conflict and cooperation, and the future course of the relationship? China's desire for a new great power relationship reflects its quest for more respect from the US in terms of its legitimate rights and interests in the global order, starting with but not limited to what China has defined as its "core interests." This includes sovereignty issues in terms of Tibet, Xinjiang, Taiwan, and the SCS and ECS. While the US wants China to be a "responsible stakeholder" in the largely American-designed rules of the game and norms that mark the current international order, the Chinese want to have more of a say in redesigning those rules, as part of their proposed new relationship. Thus, a prior discussion and understanding of the worldviews of the two leaders is essential before specific issue areas that divide the two countries are raised. To paraphrase the concluding line from a recent assessment of China's rapid rise and its global impact, can we expect China to adapt to the world or will it be the other way around?[10]

Many of the chapters in this volume, for example Wei Liang on US–China economic relations, Jingdong Yuan on the North Korean challenge, Gaye Christoffersen on energy policy, and Christopher Yung on military-to-military relations, offer suggestions on how to reconcile divergent Chinese and American interests to bring about greater cooperation and a sustainable integration of China within an evolving international system. The answer is likely to be different in each of these issue areas, particularly since China's rise has been rapid in some areas, particularly economics, but less so in other areas, including soft or cultural power and military power.[11] Related to this, some authors encourage Washington, in the interest of improving cooperation with China, to allow China to exercise more rights and privileges in the evolving global order, while others worry that allowing this to occur will more likely increase competition than promote cooperation; nevertheless, many chapters reflect a cautious optimism. Reflecting the geographical area where much of interaction between the two countries has taken place and will take place in the future, most of the chapters focus heavily on the Asia-Pacific Region (APR).

Because she is dealing with an arena of China's greatest success, Wei Liang notes that if Washington wants to encourage Beijing to contribute positively to the strengthening of multilateral institutions, which may require Chinese leaders to adopt policies they feel are not necessarily in Beijing's best interests, the US has to persuade Beijing by offering something substantive in return.[12] As Liang concludes, one way to do this would be to provide more policy space for China and allow China to have more rights, not just responsibilities, in the current global system. To be successful, the US has to accept that China will continue to look different and behave differently, at least in the short run. Can Washington learn to coexist with a country that does not have a similar system, structure, values, and ideology? In her discussion of the likelihood of Sino-American cooperation on energy issues, Gaye Christoffersen notes the limitations that come from different strategies in relation to world markets and energy security, suggesting that if Chinese energy diplomacy is used to expand China's role within global energy governance, and China uses that expanded role to rewrite the rules and reshape the practices of global governance to reflect the interests of emerging economies, then US–China competition could be expected to have global implications. China will continue to prefer physical control of oil resources while relying less on market forces, which will remain a fundamental difference in US and Chinese perceptions of energy security. Such differences over the role of markets lead to different concepts of energy security. While both sides have strengthened their capacity for energy diplomacy, they have done so for different purposes. China uses energy diplomacy to facilitate oil acquisitions in regions they would have difficulty accessing on their own. China's going-out strategy is meant to secure physical access to oil resources and bypass the world oil market. The US uses energy diplomacy to support and stabilize the world oil market. Christoffersen concludes that it remains unclear whether these strengthened capacities will promote US–China cooperation or US–China competition.

Reflecting their different perspectives over the prospects for cooperation or competition, the writers here also differ in their analysis of current trends in the relationship. In looking at Sino-US crisis management mechanisms over time, Shen and Kaminski are quite optimistic about the future, a particularly striking conclusion since they are studying the military-to-military relationship, which, as Robert Sutter notes in his chapter, has been the most notable exception to the increase in Sino-American dialogs. Contrasting the responses that followed the EP-3 plane collision incident on April 1, 2001, when a reconnaissance aircraft operating in the SCS collided with a PLA J-811 Interceptor fighter jet causing the former, with a crew of 24, to make an emergency landing on China's Hainan Island, and the USS *Kitty Hawk* incident on October 27, 2006, when a PLAN *Song* class submarine surfaced within five miles of an American aircraft carrier operating near Okinawa, Shen and Kaminski demonstrate that new factors in the military relationship, including regularized military-to-military exchange programs, reforms carried out in China's national security apparatus, and the evolution of perceptions in the US on how to engage China in crisis situations, have combined to produce more rational behavior in this crucial relationship. In the aftermath of 9/11, there was yet another reason for Sino-American cooperation on security issues.

Shen and Kaminski therefore conclude that, despite the continuing lack of shared information on military matters on a regular basis, and the lack of robust institutions to facilitate communication, both sides worked hard between 2001 and 2006 to adjust practices so that crisis situations would not escalate. Examining more recent unanticipated events at sea that could have escalated into serious crises, they credit the revised crisis management communication mechanism for avoiding a repeat of the 2001 standoff, which makes the authors optimistic that, even with the American pivot or rebalancing toward the Asia-Pacific, future tensions can also be managed.

While their argument is based on careful research, it is also possible to look at some of the same events and suggest less optimistic conclusions about the future. Indeed, in his examination of the APR rivalry, Suisheng Zhao appears less sanguine, primarily because his focus is not crisis management, but rather the implications of Chinese perceptions of the changing power balance. For Zhao, Chinese leaders are in essence realists and, responding to Deng Xiaoping's teaching of *taoguang yanghui*,[13] or keeping a low profile in international affairs, have attempted to "learn to live with the hegemon," making adaptation and policy adjustments to the reality of US dominance in the international system.[14] For Zhao, therefore, Chinese leaders avoided taking a confrontational posture in response to American sanctions after Tiananmen in 1989, the embassy bombing in 1999, and the mid-air collision in 2001. In this sense, Zhao appears to view the 2001 crisis as less serious than Shen and Kaminski. However, the US rebalance toward Asia has convinced a number of Chinese strategists that this new American focus reflects Washington's concern that the rising influence of China in the region will threaten US interests and challenge American supremacy. As Zhao and Chinese insiders such as Wang Jisi note, there is an influential policy school in China that argues that the world balance of power has begun to shift toward China and it may be time to abandon the passive *taoguang yanghui* policy and assert China's core interests more forcefully. Thus, if Zhao sees the 2001 crisis as less dangerous than Shen and Kaminski, he sees the more recent naval confrontations as deliberately more confrontational and therefore potentially much more dangerous, reflecting what a Chinese scholar called "the new robustness in China's dealing with the West."[15]

Indeed, this comes through in some semi-official Chinese assessments published in high-profile Western publications on the eve of the Xi–Obama summit.

For example, He Yafei, a former Vice-Minister of Foreign Affairs, characterized the debate in both countries over the future of the relationship in terms of its "downright pessimism, with only a sliver of optimism," and with a "huge deficit of strategic trust." Noting the "great deal of suspicion" in China over the "ill-thought-out policy of rebalancing," he warned that a continuation of that policy and a worsening of the security environment would lead to an inevitable arms race. He also noted that "it is clear to all that the world's balance of power is shifting in favor of China and other emerging countries," and that "the United States is the only power capable of creating a negative external environment for China," likely suggesting to readers that his call for a new type of great power relationship in the Asia-Pacific would be mostly on Chinese terms.[16] Informed American specialists have also noted how Beijing increasingly sees the US as "hostile, aggressive, and determined to block Beijing's rise," as a cover blurb in the journal *Foreign Affairs* characterized the conclusions of an article in that issue.[17]

There is another reason why a comparison of the differing responses to the 2001 and 2006 events may not be a strong predictor of future cooperation. As with the crisis that occurred after the May 1999 bombing of the Chinese embassy in Belgrade, the April 2001 crisis led to a loss of Chinese life, in this case the Chinese pilot Wang Wei, who was lionized as a hero in the Chinese media, necessitating a relatively strong response. Moreover, unlike the 2006 USS *Kitty Hawk* incident, which was kept under wraps by both sides, the 2001 crisis could not be removed from public knowledge. Jumping to the present, where we are now in the social media age, highlighted by the increasing importance of microblogs or *weibo*, which not only make it far more difficult to conceal events, but also can push the regime into more nationalistic responses than it might want to undertake, and it is easy to see the potential for crisis escalation.[18]

Are past (or present) models useful in understanding the Sino-American rivalry?

Although the analysis above suggests some of the different perspectives that mark the individual chapters in this volume, which should not be surprising given the complexity and unpredictability of the US–China relationship, at the same time there are a number of key themes that emerge and are worth highlighting. First, we should be very cautious in comparing the Sino-American "rivalry" in terms of past models. As Quansheng Zhao makes clear in his discussion of power transition theory, history has shown that when a rising power challenges the dominance of an existing hegemonic power, it can mean either war or a peaceful transition. Will China's rise result in a zero-sum game or a win–win situation? Noting that "offensive realists" such as John Mearsheimer portray the strategic environment facing China and the US as a zero-sum game, with little room for shared power, especially military power, Zhao recognizes the dangers of confrontation posed by such key points of contention as US arms sales to Taiwan and divergent perspectives on how to manage China's territorial disputes in the SCS and ECS, among other issues. However, he makes a persuasive case that cooperation and co-management of difficult problems are more likely trends than conflict within the dual leadership structure currently being created by China and the US. In pointing to globalization and interdependence as key factors that make a win–win scenario increasingly likely, he stresses the differences from the Cold War zero-sum competition of the US and the Soviet Union. While the US and Soviet Union did not cultivate a relationship of economic interdependence, China needs US direct investment and consumption to fuel its manufacturing sector, and the US needs China's market and manufacturing. Moreover, China's possession of US debt gives it a key stake in the stability of the US economy and the state of the federal deficit.

Zhao also suggests that the US–Soviet conflict of ideologies is highly unlikely to apply to the US–China relationship because China's focus is on practical modernization rather than ideology. The national interests of China and the US in economic interdependence and pragmatic goals make a win–win based on coordination, cooperation, and compromise (his positive 3-Cs) more likely than a zero-sum game based around the negative 3-Cs of competition, conflict, and confrontation. While Zhao's argument is compelling, an alternative argument can be presented that the issue of ideology has not entirely disappeared, albeit it now takes a different form than it did during the US–Soviet rivalry. Indeed, there is considerable debate in the academic and popular literature, as well as the Western media, on whether one can define a Chinese "model" in contrast to an American one and, if so, whether there is a deliberate attempt by China to propagate that model internationally and, further, whether such an attempt is likely to succeed.

This debate often pits what Joshua Cooper Ramo dubbed the new "Beijing Consensus" in contrast to the older "Washington Consensus."[19] Emphasizing developmental characteristics that pit China's growth strategy in opposition to the status quo represented by US hegemony, Ramo's initial characterization of China's path to modernization was then more fully elaborated into a "model" by those who followed, although there was wide divergence in characterizing its components, or whether there really was a consistent, operational Chinese model.[20] While the debate in the academic literature questioned the coherence of an exportable model and even how successful China has been in projecting its power internationally,[21] some observers saw the rise of China as seemingly inevitable[22] and, in some cases, as a clear threat to American hegemony, by essentially "beating the West at its own game," by adopting a Chinese brand of capitalism and a Chinese conception of the international community that are opposed to and substantially different from their Western version.[23] James Mann, the former Beijing Bureau Chief of the *Los Angeles Times*, goes further and views the "China Model" as an existential threat to the future of liberal democracy, noting that its emergence stemmed from the interaction of two independent developments which, taken together, "has been especially toxic for democratic values." The first development has been the failure of US foreign policy, symbolized by the war in Iraq, and the second has been the staying power and economic success of the Chinese Communist Party (CCP), despite all the predictions of the Western pundits in the aftermath of the military crackdown on the protesters in Tiananmen Square in 1989. Mann notes that China serves as a blueprint, not just economically but also politically, for authoritarian leaders around the world seeking to maintain their grip on power.[24]

Mann's argument suggests another fundamental issue in the Sino-American relationship that will have an impact on the sustainability of cooperation, an issue that others have also raised. Mann's opening sentence in an op-ed piece hints at this when he boldly states: "The Iraq war isn't over, but one thing's already clear: China won." He intends this as a critique of those policy-makers in the US who emphasize military power and the spread of democracy through the use of force, with the Iraq example suggesting that this American "model" provides neither security nor prosperity, leading to the erosion of America's appeal worldwide. Even when there is some success, as has happened in Iraq with the vast increase in oil output since the overthrow of Saddam Hussein in 2003, often it is China that benefits, not the US. Thus, China now buys more than half of Iraqi oil and that figure is expected to increase, reflecting the strategy toward energy security noted by Christoffersen.[25] Kenneth Lieberthal, in a memorandum intended for President Obama as he began his second term, noted how this separation between security and economic issues was being played out in Asia, a region where the US "rebalancing" or "pivot" brings it in much closer contact with China. Acknowledging that American friends and allies have encouraged the rebalancing, and how this has been a success story thus far for US policy, Lieberthal also noted that these same countries are tying their economic futures to China's growth, so that the US is "in danger of having Asia become an ever greater profit center for China (via economic and trade ties) and a major cost center for the United States (via security commitments)." He suggests that the key to a successful policy would be to "solidify and strengthen the core bilateral relationship with China while continuing to provide reassurances to allies and partners of US staying power in the region," so that Asian nations are not compelled to take sides in any US–China confrontation.[26] In short, even though we are no longer in a Cold War zero-sum game with an implacable ideological adversary like the Soviet Union, the threat from China may be even greater since they have shown they have none of the economic weaknesses that were major contributors to the collapse of Soviet communism, but may in fact be better capitalists than we are, with an ideology that is far more pragmatic and flexible.[27]

Has the Sino-American relationship really evolved?

A second key theme, one that appears in one form or another in all the chapters, is the evolution of the Sino-American relationship over time, with its highs and lows. Some authors review the entire 40-year record, as Wei Liang does for the economic relationship, while others highlight more specifically those events that led to significant alterations in the relationship, often for the worse. For example

Christopher Yung addresses the crucial military-to-military relationship – the least well developed of all the relationships and one important focus of the recent Obama–Xi summit – where predictable irritants such as periodic US arms sales to Taiwan will trigger a negative response and a likely suspension of military contacts, and unanticipated incidents such as the NATO bombing of the Chinese embassy in May 1999 during the Kosovo War, or the EP-3 plane collision incident over Hainan Island in April 2001, will impact the relationship more seriously. As Yung suggests at the end of his chapter, "China watchers" are divided on whether the Sino-US military-to-military relationship is on an upward trajectory or simply going around in circles since it is easy to find evidence to support both assessments. Indeed, more than any other aspect, the military-to-military relationship is subordinate to the overall bilateral relationship.

It is important, therefore, hearkening back to Lucian Pye's admonition cited at the beginning of this chapter, to note the various obstacles that have made a stronger Sino-American relationship elusive. Suisheng Zhao provides an important instance of this problem in his discussion of the "swings" in American policy toward China through various presidential administrations, and even within individual administrations, and the difficulties of escaping from this oscillating cycle. Thus, Zhao notes how the arrival of the Obama administration in 2009, with its criticism of President Bush's "unilateralism" and the resulting damage to America's "moral leadership," began with Obama's desire to elevate the US–China relationship through cooperation on global issues of consequence to both countries and shared interests, but in the end simply resulted in a new swing. Proposing a "positive, cooperative, and comprehensive" relationship to replace Bush's "cooperative, constructive, and candid" relationship with China, and stating a reluctance to challenge China on issues of fundamental disagreements, the administration dispatched Secretary of State Hillary Clinton to Beijing where she made it clear that contentious issues such as human rights, Taiwan, and Tibet should not be allowed to interfere with the global economic crisis, the global climate change crisis, and the security crisis. Moreover, Obama's actions backed up the rhetoric, and included postponing a meeting with the Dalai Lama, deferring an announcement on arms sales to Taiwan, and signing a joint statement with China in which the US acknowledged for the first time that "the two sides agreed that respecting each other's core interests is extremely important to ensure steady progress in US–China relations," while also noting that China was a "strategic partner."[28] Despite this apparent willingness to engage China as a strategic partner in dealing with major global challenges, Zhao notes how the wide divergence in interests and values compelled the Obama administration to respond to a series of crises, leading to policy adjustments within a year after taking office. In the face of what was determined to be a lack of reciprocity and China's rising power, the Obama administration abandoned its self-imposed restrictions and pursued "traditional American interests and principles even if George W. Bush pursued them, too."[29] Becoming more proactive, re-energizing traditional alliances with allies and partners, the US began a "pivot" or "rebalancing," forcing China to respond to these new American initiatives in the APR.[30]

Zhao's assessment resonates well with Robert Sutter's conclusions in his chapter on Sino-American dialogs. Recognizing their usefulness, Sutter is also well aware of their limitations in the face of the overall context of the relationship, marked by strategic mistrust of intentions, an issue that is most apparent in military-to-military exchanges, where interactions through dialogs have been weakest. Like Zhao, Sutter notes how the Obama administration's efforts at new dialog produced, at best, only mixed results. As a presidential candidate, Obama was unusual in recent American presidential campaign politics in not making an issue of his predecessor's China policy and, once in office, took initiatives such as the creation of a new, overarching dialog, the US–China Strategic and Economic Dialogue, begun in 2009. However, as Sutter suggests, citing Jeffrey Bader, the former senior director for East Asian Affairs at the National Security Council, despite some positive developments, the Obama administration came to see China's leaders as offering only limited cooperation since they seemed focused much more on their own interests than the need for global responsibility urged by President Obama. Chinese officials for their part often suspected that the added global responsibilities they were being urged to adopt would only hold back China's economic development and modernization.[31]

A similar point could be made about the seemingly intractable problem of North Korea, although here there are at least some common interests that unite the US and China, primarily the denuclearization of the Korean peninsula, re-emphasized at the Xi–Obama summit. However, as Jingdong Yuan notes in his chapter, because China and the US harbor different visions over regional security architecture, prefer different approaches to addressing regional security issues, and are increasingly engaged in open competition for regional primacy, their strategies toward North Korea also substantially diverge. A consistent Chinese interest has been the avoidance of a regime collapse, particularly one that led to its replacement by a united, democratic Korea that would be allied militarily with the US. At the same time, with China's more assertive policies pushing its APR neighbors closer to a rebalancing US, China also needs to prevent the kind of North Korean bellicosity that would help create an axis that pitted South Korea and Japan against a Beijing seen as too supportive of the North. This delicate balance in terms of what Beijing is willing to do to constrain Pyongyang has produced an unending cycle and a virtual stalemate.

The replacement of Hu Jintao by Xi Jinping, widely seen in China and the West as a more confident leader willing to depart from a prepared script and pursue a more enduring relationship with the US, has fueled expectations for the future. Prior to President Xi's visit to southern California for the June 2013 summit with President Obama, one influential "scholar-official" suggested that Obama once again take the initiative, this time in offering Xi a "game-changing opportunity" that will reassure Beijing of American intentions while also advancing important US interests.[32] What was interesting, aside from the specific recommendations on how to build strategic trust, was the admonition that "Beijing is bureaucratically incapable of taking the initiative to suggest the ideas recommended" and that "Xi will want the United States to put cards on the table to which he can then respond," allowing the US to shape the opening agenda, after which China may or may not want to begin a reciprocal negotiation.[33]

The importance of systemic and cultural differences

This suggestion of the differences in negotiation styles highlights the often overlooked factor of systemic and cultural differences, although such differences have played a key role in defining the relationship, and are addressed in a number of the chapters in this volume. For example, Christopher Yung has detailed the impediments of cultural and political system differences to a closer military relationship, noting the Chinese insistence on agreement on matters of principle prior to resolving individual issues; the Chinese desire to build trust and promote cooperation at the top before subordinates down below are given their marching orders, in contrast to the American preference for cooperation to begin at lower levels first and trust to be earned by extensive interactions at all levels of the system; the American preference to solve individual problems bilaterally through a mutual give-and-take and to demonstrate a willingness to admit previous mistakes, while their Chinese counterparts seek to incorporate into the negotiation a process which is acceptable to an entire network of interests back in Beijing, as well as a far greater reluctance to admit any previous errors; and the very different views on the meaning of "transparency" by the two sides, to cite only some of the insights from that chapter.

In like manner, Dennis Hickey and Kelan (Lilly) Lu's assessment of the triangular relationship between Beijing, Washington, and Taipei, citing the work of Robert Jervis, brings in cultural factors in the form of perceptions and misperceptions as an important variable in the behavior of each participant. In this case, the selective screening of important information plays a critical role in the decision-making process, as relevant actors fit incoming information into their existing theories and images, with actors perceiving what they expect. As Hickey and Lu suggest, officials in both the US and the PRC *perceive* that the other side has reneged on past promises and violated past agreements pertaining to Taiwan's security. Because of this perception, some American lawmakers urge a strengthening of military support for Taiwan to counter China's military buildup, while one can find a variety of suggestions on the Chinese Internet, in op-ed and editorial pages, and in comments from military officials on the types of retaliatory measures China should take in response to American military support for Taiwan.

Hickey and Lu's reference to the work of Jervis as an explanation for what they view as a potentially escalating arms race over Taiwan can be applied more broadly to the Sino-American relationship, and also has explanatory power for understanding the continuing strategic mistrust between the two countries. In his study of Chinese Internet politics, Zhou Yongming conducted a case study of a website of military fans in China and found that the majority of its members were well educated, very knowledgeable of how to circumvent censorship methods in order to access forbidden websites, and therefore were very well informed, yet at the same time they were nationalistic and anti-Western. He wondered why such Chinese Internet surfers who are so well informed about the outside world found nationalistic thinking much more appealing than ideas of democracy and freedom; worse still, why did they treat the latter ideas with disbelief and sarcasm? His answer was that even though the Chinese people have become more informed, they have also adopted a new interpretive framework that acknowledges the pursuit of national interest as the best measure for understanding state behavior and international relations more generally. Within such a "reception context," information emanating from Western media sources is viewed skeptically by well-informed young Chinese, who assume that such reporting is merely attempting to further a pro-Western agenda.[34]

Following the logic of this conceptualization, if the US promotes human rights or democratization in China it would not be doing so because of a belief in universal values, but only because promoting such rights advances the American national interest, with these appeals perhaps intended to divide China internally and promote instability, thereby aiding the US in its efforts to remain the world's only superpower. In like manner, American protestations that its rebalancing strategy is not directed against China's rise would be interpreted as self-serving rhetoric. In other words, simply having free information available in China will not make much difference if the reception context of national interest remains. Only a new reception context that makes democratic values more attractive would make a difference, and these values should not be linked with US policy. Zhou's insightful argument resonates well with James Mann's explanation of why the Iraqi intervention has been so devastating for the promotion of American values through its foreign policy.

Indeed, one of the ironies in examining the attitudes and behavior of young Chinese and its influence on Sino-American relations over the last 30 years is the seeming paradox that an increasing knowledge of and influence from the outside world has been accompanied by a rising tide of nationalism. In the 1980s Chinese students knew far less about international affairs and often accepted, quite naively, reports from Western media sources. In an era marked by student unrest and distrust of Chinese media reports – with major demonstrations in 1985, 1986, and of course 1989 – students turned to the British Broadcasting Corporation (BBC) and the Voice of America (VOA) for "unbiased" accounts. The more the regime sought to block information from outside, the more the students sought it out. This unabashed, uncritical internationalism of that time has been gradually eroded, and can be traced only in part to the patriotic education campaign launched in 1991, with discourse focused on the national humiliations of the past, to foster love for the motherland. Arguably even more important have been the specific actions taken by the US that have reinforced the CCP's message that the West has continued its long-term strategy to deny China its rightful place in the world. A number of surveys have documented the rise in negative attitudes toward the US since 1993 when the American Congress passed a resolution urging the International Olympic Committee not to award China the Games in the year 2000 because of human rights violations. This was

260   S. Rosen

followed shortly after by an incident in which the American navy shadowed and eventually searched a Chinese ship suspected of carrying chemicals that could be used to manufacture weapons to Iran. When no such chemicals were found, the government-controlled press – as they had after Beijing lost out to Sydney in the Olympic decision – took the lead in excoriating the US for groundlessly violating Chinese sovereignty and attempting to police the world. The effect of these events is reflected in two surveys conducted in Beijing, one in 1988 and the other in 1996. Those who showed a liking for the US dropped from 48 percent to 23 percent over this period, while those who disliked the US increased from 14 percent to 27 percent.[35]

However, no event shaped attitudes toward the US as forcefully as the NATO bombing of the Chinese embassy in Belgrade, Yugoslavia, in May 1999, in which three Chinese citizens were killed. Far more than the image of the lone young man in front of the Chinese tank in June 1989 – an image that still strongly influences American attitudes toward China – the attack on the Belgrade embassy arguably remained the key image of hostile American foreign policy intentions for patriotic Chinese youth for many years, and reinforced the CCP's message that the US, and the West more generally, could not be trusted. In another example of the influence of perceptions and reception contexts, the American explanation that the bombing was an "accident" found virtually no believers among the Chinese audience, with admittedly non-scientific surveys published in the Chinese media showing that a large percentage of the survey informants (68 percent in a survey published in *Beijing Youth Daily*) viewed the US to be "hypocritical."[36] As Christopher Yung demonstrates in his chapter, the bombing occurred, ironically, at a high point in the US–China military relationship, revealing the ever-present danger of accidents and unanticipated events, and why the military-to-military relationship remains the most fragile and underdeveloped.

Conflict or cooperation? Potential pitfalls on the road ahead

As detailed in the various chapters, given its complexity there are elements in the Sino-American relationship that can suggest either optimism or pessimism. Offensive realists using history and international relations theory warn of the virtual inevitability of conflict between a rising power and an entrenched power while other analysts point to the possibility of cooperative security strategies, particularly in the nuclear age where conflict carries unthinkable risks.[37] Since many of the chapters here, understandably, take a normative position and focus on how a cooperative relationship between China and the US might be fashioned, it is useful to examine some of the factors that make sustainable cooperation so challenging.

First, some factors, which on the surface would appear to be quite positive, may in fact actually complicate the Sino-American relationship. For example, while Chinese policy-makers and analysts have struggled over the years to understand where power resides in the messy American federal system marked

Conclusion 261

by a separation of powers and media independence,[38] it used to be easier to determine who spoke for China in the realm of foreign policy since public discourse was so tightly controlled. However, over time an increasing number of actors have been allowed access to the Chinese media, suggesting a pluralization of voices and interests gaining representation, which some have seen, at least potentially, as a precursor to a developing civil society if not democratization. On the downside, the multiplication of viewpoints has made it more difficult to determine authoritatively China's core interests, despite the frequent use of that expression. As Wang Jisi has noted, while the need to identify an organizing principle to guide Chinese foreign policy is widely recognized in Chinese policy circles and the scholarly community, defining China's core interests according to the "three prongs of sovereignty, security and development, which sometimes are in tension, means that it is almost impossible to devise a straightforward organizing principle."[39] Wang details the widely differing proposals on how to deal with the US, noting that the variety of views among political elites has greatly complicated efforts to devise a grand strategy based on political consensus. In contrast to much of what appears in both Chinese and Western media, Wang suggests that, apart from the issue of Taiwan, the Chinese government has never officially identified any single foreign policy issue as one of the country's core interests. Chinese commentators, without official authorization, who have made "reckless statements" referring to the SCS and North Korea as core interests have "created a great deal of confusion."[40] This confusion is exacerbated when those making such incendiary statements in print, on their blogs, or in other forums are high-ranking military officials. Should they be interpreted as trial balloons that have at least tacit government backing, as representative of general thinking in the military, or simply as personal views? Who speaks for China and which groups have the most influence, and on which specific issues, in formulating Chinese foreign policy?

A recent example of how the pluralization of voices has complicated outside understanding of Chinese policy initiatives was provided when two academics from the Chinese Academy of Social Sciences published an article in *Renmin ribao* (*People's Daily*) in which they stated that the Ryukyu kingdom, which is today's Okinawa prefecture, was a Chinese "vassal state" during the Ming and Qing dynasties. Owing to the weakness of the Qing dynasty, China "was robbed of Taiwan and its affiliated islands, including the Senkakus, the Pescadores and the Ryukyus" by Japan.[41] Since the article appeared in the authoritative *People's Daily*, Japan launched a formal protest and Western and Japanese analysts speculated on whether the Chinese government was using the academics to put pressure on Japan over the Diaoyu/Senkaku dispute or using this venue as a precursor to making an official claim for Okinawa. Internet voices and some Chinese media outlets began to call for China to "recapture Okinawa." It became necessary for the authors to deny to a Japanese newspaper that they had any Chinese government backing and the deputy chief of the general staff, Lieutenant General Qi Jianguo, was compelled to announce at a security conference in Singapore that China does not dispute Japanese sovereignty over Okinawa and that recent comments in Chinese newspapers that might suggest otherwise merely represented the views of some academics.[42]

Second, implicit or explicit in virtually all the chapters is the recognition of a mutual lack of trust in the Sino-American relationship. In their analysis of the growing strategic distrust between China and the US, Lieberthal and Wang trace the problem to three fundamental sources:

> different political traditions, value systems, and cultures; insufficient comprehension and appreciation of each others' policy-making processes and the relation between the government and other entities; and a perception of a narrowing gap in power between the US and China.[43]

Acknowledging that the first source of distrust stems from structural and deep-rooted elements in each country, they focus on the latter two sources in their recommendations for improvement. Their suggestions for military affairs, the least developed aspect of the relationship, demonstrate the difficulties of narrowing this gap. Their major recommendations include better mutual understanding on such issues as the long-term possibilities in the Korean peninsula, agreements on mutual restraint in deployment, and

> [a] sustained, deep dialogue to discuss what array of military deployments and normal operations will permit China to defend its core security interests and at the same time allow America to continue to meet fully its obligations to friends and allies in the Asia-Pacific region.[44]

While dialog and understanding are of course crucial, will they be enough to produce a policy that will allow China to defend its core security interests, as it defines them, and also allow the US to meet its obligations? Indeed, as suggested above, because of the perception in China of a narrowing gap in power, and a lack of clarity on China's core interests, such interests may easily expand over time; moreover, based on at least some Chinese commentary such as He Yafei's essay in *Foreign Policy* cited above, China would prefer to see a scaling back of American "obligations" in the APR. As China increases its naval strength will it make greater efforts, as offensive realists would suggest, to "persuade" the US to reconsider its obligations to countries such as Japan and disputed areas like Taiwan?

In his chapter on military relations and his discussion of the "three obstacles," Christopher Yung provides an additional reason why it will be extremely difficult to build sustainable trust. One of the obstacles is the longstanding problem of arms sales to Taiwan, which under the Taiwan Relations Act represents an American obligation to provide Taiwan with the weaponry it needs to defend itself. The second obstacle is the 2000 National Defense Authorization Act (NDAA), which calls for an annual report to Congress from the Department of Defense (DOD) specifying and itemizing China's growing military capabilities and which mandates that the DOD undertake no activity which would enhance the military capabilities of the PLA. Thus, arms sales and other technology transfers to China are no longer possible. Yung suggests that, strictly applied, this could also have the dampening effect of preventing PLA students from attending the US National Defense University and curtailing certain types of joint exercises. The third obstacle is the persistent problem of US surveillance and reconnaissance operations within China's exclusive economic zones (EEZs). While the US sees these air and maritime surveillance operations within international waters (but within China's recognized EEZs) as perfectly legitimate in pursuit of its APR obligations, as well as a hedge against future possible conflict with the PLA, the Chinese respond that such actions demonstrate that the US considers China to be a future adversary rather than a partner. The air and sea "incidents" that have occurred, such as the 2001 airplane collision and various naval encounters, were the result of Chinese countermeasures to such US surveillance. As Yung notes, the PLA has repeatedly stated that until these three obstacles are resolved, it will not be possible to deepen or make the military-to-military relationship more robust. Finally, the vast difference in training and experience of Chinese and American military officers contributes to very different mindsets. For example, PLA officers go to military colleges and have little or no experience outside China while American military officers have a far broader education and have often traveled much more widely. One American communications specialist who lectures to both groups in an effort to reduce tensions and misunderstanding noted in an interview how striking he found their different perspectives on world affairs.[45]

All of this suggests, and a close reading of the individual chapters confirms, that we should be realistic in our expectations and focus primarily on the management of the relationship so as to prevent irritants that will inevitably arise from escalating into serious crises, while still seeking to build and sustain greater trust, through dialog, mutual understanding, and respect for each other's core interests and obligations.

Notes

1 Lucian Pye, "China's Quest for Respect," *New York Times*, February 19, 1996, A15.
2 Kenneth Lieberthal and Wang Jisi, *Addressing US–China Strategic Distrust*, (Washington, DC: Brookings Institution, 2012), vi.
3 Nancy Bernkopf Tucker, "America First," in *China in the American Political Imagination*, ed. Carola McGiffert (Washington, DC: The CSIS Press, 2003): 17–18. The essays in this outstanding collection were originally presented at a conference held at the Center for Strategic and International Studies in Washington, DC, in December 2002, and examine the origins of American images of China throughout modern history and their implications for US foreign policy toward China. For a companion volume that examined the US from Chinese perspectives, see Carola McGiffert, ed., *Chinese Images of the United States* (Washington, DC: CSIS Press, 2005).
4 McGiffert, *Chinese Images of the United States*, xvi.
5 "Culture Promoted Overseas to Dissolve 'China Threat'," *Xinhua*, May 28, 2006.
6 Andrew J. Nathan and Robert S. Ross, *The Great Wall and the Empty Fortress: China's Search for Security* (New York: W.W. Norton, 1997).

7 Jane Perlez, "Chinese President to Seek New 'Power Relationship' in Talks with Obama," *New York Times*, May 29, 2013, A6.
8 Ibid.
9 For example, on the American side see David M. Lampton, "A New Type of Major-Power Relationship: Seeking a Durable Foundation for US–China Ties," *Asia Policy* 16 (July 2013): 51–68; Jeremy Page and Colleen McCain Nelson, "US–China Summit Reveals Beijing's Drive," *Wall Street Journal*, June 2, 2013; David Ignatius, "A Power Test for the US and China," *Washington Post*, May 31, 2013; and Kenneth Lieberthal, "Bringing Beijing Back In," in *Big Bets and Black Swans: Policy Recommendations for President Obama's Second Term by the Foreign Policy Scholars at Brookings*, ed. Martin Indyk, Tanvi Madan, and Thomas Wright (Washington, DC: Brookings Institution, 2013): 5–8. On the Chinese side, see He Yafei, "How China See US Pivot to Asia," *Foreign Policy*, May 23, 2013; Research Center of the Socialism with Chinese Characteristics Theory Group, Chinese Academy of Social Sciences, "Construct a New Great Power Relationship," *Renmin ribao*, June 4, 2013; and "Sino-American Relations Needs to Change the Old Thinking: Neither Alliance Nor Opposition," *Jiefang ribao*, May 5, 2013 (reprinted in *Renminwang*, May 5, 2013). More generally, see the cover story in *The Economist*, June 8–14, 2013, in which the California location is likened to Hollywood film titles ("The Summit," starring Barack Obama and Xi Jinping; "He Stole His Heart (and then his intellectual property)"; "'Team America' Meets 'Kungfu Panda'"), 11, 38, and 48–49 and *Time* magazine, June 17, 2013 ("The World According to China"), 26–33.
10 Heriberto Araujo and Juan Pablo Cardenal, "China's Economic Empire," *New York Times Sunday Review*, June 1, 2013.
11 David L. Shambaugh, *China Goes Global: The Partial Power* (Oxford: Oxford University Press, 2013); Fareed Zakaria, "China Is Not the World's Other Superpower," *Washington Post*, June 5, 2013; and Chapter 3 by Quansheng Zhao in this volume.
12 Helene Cooper, "The Trouble with Asking China to Act like the US," *New York Times*, November 27, 2010. www.nytimes.com/2010/11/28/weekinreview/28cooper.html?pagewanted=all&_r=0.
13 On *taoguang yanghui* as one of a number of alternative schools of thought among Chinese political elites on devising a grand strategy, see Wang Jisi, "China's Search for a Grand Strategy: A Rising Great Power Finds Its Way," *Foreign Affairs* 90, no. 2 (March/April 2011): 68–79.
14 Jia Qingguo, "Learning to Live with the Hegemon: Evolution of China's Policy toward the US since the End of the Cold War," *Journal of Contemporary China* 14, no. 44 (August 2005): 395, as cited in Zhao's chapter.
15 James Mikes, "China and the West, A time for Muscle-flexing," *The Economist*, March 19, 2009, as cited in Zhao's chapter.
16 He, "How China Sees US Pivot to Asia." He is currently the Deputy Director of the Overseas Chinese Affairs Office of the State Council.
17 Andrew Nathan and Andrew Scobell, "How China Sees America: The Sum of Beijing's Fears," *Foreign Affairs* 91, no. 5 (September/October 2012): 32–47.
18 The role of public opinion and popular nationalism as a factor in state–society relations and foreign policy decision-making is a highly contested subject. For those who see a relatively weak Chinese state in the face of an assertive public, see Susan L. Shirk, *China: Fragile Superpower* (Oxford: Oxford University Press, 2007) and Peter Hays Gries, *China's New Nationalism: Pride, Politics and Diplomacy* (Berkeley: University of California Press, 2004). For a view of the state very much in command despite a strong society, see James Reilly, *Strong Society, Smart State: The Rise of Public Opinion in China's Japan Policy* (New York: Columbia University Press, 2012).
19 Joshua Cooper Ramo, *Beijing Consensus: Notes on the New Physics of Chinese Power* (London: Foreign Policy Center, 2004). For the origin of the term "Washington

Consensus" see John Williamson, "What Washington Means by Policy Reform," in *Latin American Adjustment: How Much Has Happened?* ed. John Williamson (Washington, DC: Institute for International Economics, 1989). www.petersoninstitute.org/publications/papers/paper.cfm?researchid=486. For a good comparison of the "two consensuses" see Barry Naughton, "China's Distinctive System: Can It Be a Model for Others?" *Journal of Contemporary China* 19, no. 65 (June 2010): 437–60.

20 Minglu Chen and David S. G. Goodman, "The China Model: One Country, Six Authors," *Journal of Contemporary China* 21, no. 73 (January 2012): 169–85, argue, for example, that there is very little evidence that there is a replicable China model, that the development of the PRC since 1978 is the result of unique circumstances. Skepticism also marks the symposium in "Debating the China Model of Modernization," *Journal of Contemporary China* 19, no. 65 (June 2010), including Suisheng Zhao, "The China Model: Can It Replace the Western Model of Modernization?": 419–436, Naughton, "China's Distinctive System: Can It Be a Model for Others?" and Scott Kennedy, "The Myth of the Beijing Consensus": 461–77.

21 Shambaugh, *China Goes Global*. Eric X. Li, "The Life of the Party: The Post-Democratic Future Begins in China," *Foreign Affairs* 92, no. 1 (January/February 2013): 34–46, sees China as a successful political model, but one that "will never supplant electoral democracy because, unlike the latter, it does not pretend to be universal. It cannot be exported" (46). Li's views are critiqued in Yasheng Huang, "Democratize or Die: Why China's Communists Face Reform or Revolution," *Foreign Affairs* 92, no. 1 (January/February 2013): 47–54.

22 Martin Jacques, *When China Rules the World: The End of the Western World and the Birth of a New Global Order* (New York: Penguin Press, 2009) is the most widely cited example.

23 Stefan Halper, *The Beijing Consensus: How China's Authoritarian Model Will Dominate the Twenty-First Century* (New York: Basic Books, 2010), 11.

24 James Mann, "A Shining Model of Wealth without Liberty," *Washington Post*, May 20, 2007. Mann's book-length works spell out his argument and his assessment of Sino-American relations more fully. See *The China Fantasy: How Our Leaders Explain Away Chinese Repression* (New York: Viking, 2007) and *About Face: A History of America's Curious Relationship with China, from Nixon to Clinton* (New York: Alfred Knopf, 1998).

25 Tim Arango and Clifford Krauss, "China Is Reaping Biggest Benefits of Iraq Oil Boom," *New York Times*, June 3, 2013, A1.

26 Lieberthal, "Bringing Beijing Back In."

27 Giovanni Arrighi argues that the China model is the very antithesis of neoliberalist capitalism, with a strong role for the state in the economy. See *Adam Smith in Beijing: Lineages of the Twenty-First Century* (London: Verso, 2007) and the useful comparisons among Jacques, Halper, Arrighi and others in Chen and Goodman, "The China Model."

28 See Chapter 4 by Suisheng Zhao in this volume for the key distinctions between the Bush and Obama administrations' strategies for dealing with China.

29 Robert Kagan, "America: Once Engaged, Now Ready to Lead," *Washington Post*, October 1, 2010, A19.

30 For an assessment of Sino-American relations from an insider, which criticizes the Western media for its undue attention to the tensions, fluctuations, and frictions in the relationship instead of focusing on the management of relations to promote mutual global interests, see Jeffrey A. Bader, *Obama and China's Rise: An Insider's Account of America's Asia Strategy* (Washington, DC: Brookings Institution Press, 2012).

31 Ibid.

32 Lieberthal, "Bringing Beijing Back In."

33 Ibid. Mindful of the lack of reciprocity from Hu Jintao with Obama's 2009 initiatives, Lieberthal notes that his proposed agenda would not commit the US to take any unilateral actions in the absence of a positive Chinese response.

34 Zhou Yongming, "Understanding Chinese Internet Politics," in *China and Democracy: A Contradiction in Terms?* (Washington, DC: Woodrow Wilson International Center for Scholars, 2006), 21–5.
35 This paragraph draws heavily from Stanley Rosen, "Chinese Media and Youth: Attitudes toward Nationalism and Internationalism," in *Chinese Media, Global Contexts*, ed. Chin-Chuan Lee (London: Routledge, 2003), 97–118. The survey data is cited in Zheng Yongnian, "Nationalism, Globalism, and China's International Relations," in *China's International Relations in the 21st Century: Dynamics of Paradigm Shifts*, ed. Weixing Hu, Gerald Chan, and Dajiong Zha (Lanham, MD: University Press of America, 2000), 104.
36 Rosen, "Chinese Media and Youth," 109–13. The *Beijing Youth Daily* survey is discussed in the newspaper on May 19, 1999, 8.
37 John J. Mearsheimer, *The Tragedy of Great Power Politics* (New York: W.W. Norton, 2001). More directly, see the special report in *Foreign Policy* (January/February 2005): 43–58 entitled "China Rising," which included a "debate" on "whether the United States and China are destined to fight it out." Brzezinski uses the title "Make Money, Not War" (46–7) and Mearsheimer counters with "Better to be Godzilla than Bambi" (47–8), followed by multiple rejoinders by each of them attempting to refute the other's arguments (48–50). Also see David M. Lampton, *The Three Faces of Chinese Power: Might, Money and Minds* (Berkeley: University of California Press, 2008), 13–15 for a presentation of Mearsheimer's argument and the response, both supportive and critical, from scholars in China, and Lampton, "A New Type of Major-Power Relationship," 6, where he notes that offensive realists rarely consider "the political and military resources available to achieve or maintain dominance or hegemony, the likelihood of domestic exhaustion in the course of such efforts, and the reaction of others in the international system to such steps."
38 Many examples of Chinese confusion over how things work in the US could be cited. For example, after Bill Clinton proposed "constructive engagement" as the "only option of American policy on China," and agreed to work more closely with Jiang Zemin, a senior Chinese foreign ministry official summoned American reporters to a lavish banquet where he set out China's position on a variety of issues such as Tibet, Taiwan, and Tiananmen and lectured them that the only thing wrong with US–China relations is demonization of China by the American media. He told them that Chinese reporters had been told what to write to support the relationship and that he expected American reporters would follow President Clinton's example and only write articles that would improve the relationship between Washington and Beijing. See Patrick Tyler, "With an Eye on Politics, China Fetes US Press," *New York Times*, January 20, 1997. Similar sentiments have been expressed on other occasions, including the argument that American reporters should see the improvement of the Sino-American relationship as an important goal of their work. Those who wrote articles that could potentially be damaging to the relationship were irresponsible at best.
39 Wang Jisi, "China's Search for a Grand Strategy," 71–2.
40 Ibid., 71.
41 Zhang Haipeng and Li Guoqiang, "Discussions on Treaty of Maguan (Shimonoseki) and Diaoyu Islands," *Renmin ribao*, May 8, 2013, cited in Atsushi Okudera, "Authors Deny Beijing's Role in Commentary Doubting Japan's Sovereignty of Okinawa," *Asahi Shimbun* (Asahi.com), May 29, 2013.
42 "China not Disputing Japan Sovereignty over Okinawa," Reuters, June 2, 2013.
43 Lieberthal and Wang, *Addressing US–China Strategic Distrust*, x–xi.
44 Ibid., xii.
45 Interview in Los Angeles, June 10, 2013.

References

Arango, Tim, and Clifford Krauss. "China Is Reaping Biggest Benefits of Iraq Oil Boom." *New York Times*, June 3, 2013, A1 section.
Araujo, Heriberto, and Juan Pablo Cardenal. "China's Economic Empire." *New York Times Sunday Review*, June 1, 2013.
Arrighi, Giovanni. *Adam Smith in Beijing: Lineages of the Twenty-First Century* (London: Verso, 2007).
Bader, Jeffrey A. *Obama and China's Rise: An Insider's Account of America's Asia Strategy* (Washington, DC: Brookings Institution Press, 2012).
Brzezinski, Zbigniew, and John Mearsheimer. "China Rising." *Foreign Policy*, January/February 2005, 43–58.
Chen, Minglu, and David S. G. Goodman. "The China Model: One Country, Six Authors." *Journal of Contemporary China* 21, no. 73 (January 2012): 169–85.
"China Not Disputing Japan Sovereignty over Okinawa." Reuters. June 2, 2013.
Cooper, Helene. "The Trouble with Asking China to Act Like the US" *New York Times*. November 27, 2010. www.nytimes.com/2010/11/28/weekinreview/28cooper.html?pagewanted=all&_r=0.
"Culture Promoted Overseas to Dissolve 'China Threat'." *Xinhua*. May 28, 2006.
Gries, Peter H. *China's New Nationalism: Pride, Politics and Diplomacy* (Berkeley: University of California Press, 2004).
Halper, Stefan A. *The Beijing Consensus: How China's Authoritarian Model Will Dominate the Twenty-First Century* (New York: Basic Books, 2010).
He, Yafei. "How China See US Pivot to Asia." *Foreign Policy*. May 23, 2013.
Huang, Yasheng. "Democratize or Die: Why China's Communists Face Reform or Revolution." *Foreign Affairs* 92, no. 1 (January/February 2013): 47–54.
Ignatius, David. "A Power Test for the US and China." *Washington Post*. May 31, 2013.
Jacques, Martin. *When China Rules the World: The End of the Western World and the Birth of a New Global Order* (New York: Penguin Press, 2009).
Jia, Qingguo. "Learning to Live with the Hegemon: Evolution of China's Policy toward the US since the End of the Cold War." *Journal of Contemporary China* 14, no. 44 (August 2005): 395–407.
Kagan, Robert. "America: Once Engaged, Now Ready to Lead." *Washington Post*, October 1, 2010, A19 section.
Kennedy, Scott. "The Myth of the Beijing Consensus." *Journal of Contemporary China* 19, no. 65 (June 2010): 461–77.
Lampton, David M. "A New Type of Major-Power Relationship: Seeking a Durable Foundation for US–China Ties." *Asia Policy*, no. 16 (July 2013): 51–68.
Lampton, David M. *The Three Faces of Chinese Power: Might, Money and Minds* (Berkeley: University of California Press, 2008).
Li, Eric X. "The Life of the Party: The Post-Democratic Future Begins in China." *Foreign Affairs* 92, no. 1 (January/February 2013): 34–46.
Lieberthal, Kenneth. "Bringing Beijing Back In," in *Big Bets and Black Swans: Policy Recommendations for President Obama's Second Term by the Foreign Policy Scholars at Brookings*, eds. Martin Indyk, Tanvi Madan, and Thomas Wright (Washington, DC: Brookings Institution, 2013), 5–8.
Lieberthal, Kenneth, and Jisi Wang. *Addressing US–China Strategic Distrust* (Washington, DC: Brookings Institution, 2012).

Mann, James. *About Face: A History of America's Curious Relationship with China, from Nixon to Clinton* (New York: Alfred Knopf, 1999).
Mann, James. *The China Fantasy: How Our Leaders Explain Away Chinese Repression* (New York: Viking, 2007).
Mann, James. "A Shining Model of Wealth without Liberty." *Washington Post*, May 20, 2007.
McGiffert, Carola, ed. *Chinese Images of the United States* (Washington, DC: CSIS Press, 2005).
Mearsheimer, John J. *The Tragedy of Great Power Politics* (New York: W.W. Norton, 2001).
Mikes, James. "China and the West, A Time for Muscle-flexing." *The Economist*, March 19, 2009.
Nathan, Andrew J., and Robert S. Ross. *The Great Wall and the Empty Fortress: China's Search for Security* (New York: W.W. Norton, 1997).
Nathan, Andrew, and Andrew Scobell. "How China Sees America: The Sum of Beijing's Fears." *Foreign Affairs* 91, no. 5 (September/October 2012): 32–47.
Naughton, Barry. "China's Distinctive System: Can It Be a Model for Others?" *Journal of Contemporary China* 19, no. 65 (June 2010): 437–60.
Perlez, Jane. "Chinese President to Seek New 'Power Relationship' in Talks with Obama." *New York Times*, May 29, 2013, A6 section.
Pye, Lucian. "China's Quest for Respect." *New York Times*, February 19, 1996, A15 section.
Ramo, Joshua C. *Beijing Consensus: Notes on the New Physics of Chinese Power* (London: Foreign Policy Center, 2004).
Reilly, James. *Strong Society, Smart State: The Rise of Public Opinion in China's Japan Policy* (New York: Columbia University Press, 2012).
Research Center of the Socialism with Chinese Characteristics Theory Group, Chinese Academy of Social Sciences. "Construct a New Great Power Relationship." *Renmin Ribao*. June 4, 2013.
Rosen, Stanley. "Chinese Media and Youth: Attitudes toward Nationalism and Internationalism," in *Chinese Media, Global Contexts*, ed. Chin-Chuan Lee (London: Routledge, 2003), 97–118.
Shambaugh, David L. *China Goes Global: The Partial Power* (Oxford: Oxford University Press, 2013).
Shirk, Susan L. *China: Fragile Superpower* (Oxford: Oxford University Press, 2007).
"Sino-American Relations Needs to Change the Old Thinking: Neither Alliance Nor Opposition." *Jiefang Ribao*. May 5, 2013.
Tucker, Nancy B. "America First," in *China in the American Political Imagination*, ed. Carola McGiffert (Washington, DC: CSIS Press, 2003): 16–21.
Tyler, Patrick. "With an Eye on Politics, China Fetes US Press." *New York Times*. January 20, 1997.
"US–China Summit Reveals Beijing's Drive." *Wall Street Journal*. June 2, 2013.
Wang Jisi. "China's Search for a Grand Strategy: A Rising Great Power Finds Its Way." *Foreign Affairs* 90, no. 2 (March/April 2011): 68–79.
Williamson, John. "What Washington Means by Policy Reform," in *Latin American Readjustment: How Much Has Happened?* ed. John Williamson (Washington, DC: Institute for International Economics, 1989). www.petersoninstitute.org/publications/papers/paper.cfm?researchid=486.
"The World According to China." *Time*, June 17, 2013, 26–33.

Zakaria, Fareed. "China Is Not the World's Other Superpower." *Washington Post*, June 5, 2013.

Zhang, Haipeng, and Guoqiang Li. "Discussions on Treaty of Maguan (Shimonoseki) and Diaoyu Islands." *Renmin Ribao*, May 8, 2013.

Zhao, Suisheng. "The China Model: Can It Replace the Western Model of Modernization?" *Journal of Contemporary China* 19, no. 65 (June 2010): 419–36.

Zheng, Yongnian. "Nationalism, Globalism, and China's International Relations," in *China's International Relations in the 21st Century: Dynamics of Paradigm Shifts*, eds. Weixing Hu, Gerald Chan, and Daojiong Zha (Lanham, MD: University Press of America, 2000): 93–116.

Zhou, Yongming. "Understanding Chinese Internet Politics," in *China and Democracy: A Contradiction in Terms?* (Washington, DC: Woodrow Wilson International Center for Scholars, 2006), 21–5.

Index

Page numbers in *italics* denote tables, those in **bold** denote figures.

2 + 2 talks 61
3-Cs principle 9, 58–61, 254
6PT *see* Six-Party Talks (6PT)
9/11 terrorist attacks 115, 140, 238, 252

activists 194–5
Africa and Chinese foreign direct investment (FDI) 52
Agreed Framework (1994) 115–16
Air Defense Identification Zone (ADIZ) 5, 68
American Institute in Taiwan (AIT) 91, 92
American perception of China: influence 46, **46**, 50; self-image 249
anti-Americanism 233, 249, 259–60
anti-China legislation 141, 145
anti-piracy 25, 158
Anti-Secession Law (2005) 34
anti-terrorism *see* global war on terror (GWOT)
Armitage, Richard 236
Arms Sale Communiqué (1982) 29–30
arms sales by China 99, 206
arms sales to China 205–6
arms sales to Taiwan: military relations 210–14, 217, 256, 262; nuclear crisis 115–27; US arms sales to Taiwan 4, 29–30, 89–90, *91*, 91–104; US economic stimulus 94, 103
ASEAN–China Free Trade Area (ACFTA) 52
Asian Development Bank (ADB) 163
Asia-Pacific Economic Cooperation (APEC) 162
Asia-Pacific Energy Regulatory Forum (APER Forum) 163–4

Asia-Pacific Partnership on Clean Development and Climate (APP) 161, 162–3
Asia-Pacific Region (APR): balance of power 68–9, 75–8; Chinese evolving policies 69–71; dual leadership structure 47–9, 61–3; energy initiatives 159, 163; foreign direct investment (FDI) 54, *54*; re-engagement by US 191, 192–3, 195, 196; Trans-Pacific Partnership (TPP) 141–2; US military relationships 72–5; US rebalance 1, 141–2; US strategy to Chinese build up 78–83
Association of Southeast Asian Nations (ASEAN) 62, 72, 77, 142, 162, 165

Bader, Jeffrey 70
balance of power: Chinese perception 75–8, 252; global financial crisis (2008) 148; military imbalance 101; rebalance 188–9, 192, 252–3, 255, 256; trade imbalance 140–4
belief systems and self-image 249
bilateral relationship *see* individual countries
bipolar structure 45
Blair, Denis 231
Blanchard, Jean-Marc F. 8–9
Blight, James 238–9
Blumenthal, Dan 72
Bonner, Robert 238
Bosworth, Stephen 119
Brzezinski, Zbigniew 45–6, 205
Buff, Joe 242n23
Burghardt, Raymond 92
Burton, Dan 90

Bush, George H.W.: China–US relationship history 30; economic relations 139; military-to-military relations 207, 209–11; secret dialogues 184–5

Bush, George W.: arms sales to Taiwan 102–3, 115, 117; China–US relationship and structural factors 14n10; China–US relationship history 32–3; cooperation 172; democracy and Taiwan 93; energy relations 160; EP-3 incident 231; foreign policy 34, 79; intellectual property rights (IPR) 34; military-to-military relations 209–11; self-image 249; trade policy 140–1

Cai Yingting 212, 222n61
Cairo declaration 95
"campaign contributions-space technology sale" controversy 208
Campbell, Kurt M. 75, 89, 93, 101, 195, 209
capacity building and energy security 162–3, 168–9
CAPSTONE 216, 223n76
Carter, Jimmy: cooperation 29; energy relations 159; military-to-military relations 205–6; secret dialogues 184; Taiwan 103, 104n3, 187
censorship 258–9
Cha, Victor 121–2
Chai Zemin 98
Chang Wanquan 212
changing balance of power *see* balance of power
Chen Bingde 78
Chen Guangcheng 194–5
Chen Shui-bian 33, 34, 95, 97–8, 210
Cheonan 73, 76, 120, 122–3
Chi Haotian 207–8
Chiang Ching-kuo 98
China: arms sales 99–102, 206; balance of power in Asia-Pacific Region (APR) 75–8, 252; banks 7, 52, 124; censorship 258–9; civil rights activists 194–5; civil war 26; core national interests 69–71, 79, 83n7, 114, 123, 240, 250, 252–3, 259, 261–2; crisis management 230, 241n3; currency policy 141, 144–5; cyber warfare 6; defense spending 56–7; dual leadership structure 47–9; economic growth 46, 49–55; economic leader in Asia-Pacific Region (APR) 2, 14n12; economic relations 143–7, 149; emerging leadership role 49–55; energy policy 167; energy security 157, 160–1; evolving policies in Asia-Pacific Region (APR) 69–71; foreign direct investment (FDI) 54, *54*, *55*; foreign policy and low profile *taoguang yanghui* policy 75–6; foreign reserves *51, 52, 55*; free trade agreements (FTAs) 52; G2 concept and global leadership 148–9; global financial crisis (2008) 25, 32, 140, 238; "going out" strategy and oil supply 158; gross domestic product (GDP) 49–51, 71; human rights 4, 6, 30–1, 139–40, 181, 183, 185; humiliations *(guo chi)* 45, 95, 106n44; industrial policy 7, 140, 143, 145–7; influence 46, 50; initiatives in East Asian energy regimes 158–9; intellectual property rights (IPR) 139, 141, 145–6; internet politics 258–9; maritime security 157, 160; media and youth 259–60; military build-up 216–17, 219; military relationships in Asia-Pacific Region (APR) 56–8, 68–9, 94; national security apparatus reforms 237–8; pluralization of voices 261; practical modernization 254; regional economic power 52, 54, *54*; self-image 248–9; sovereignty 68–71, 76–7, 82–3, 97, 123, 261; state–society relations 260; telecommunications standards 146; territorial integrity 95–6; trade 52–5; World Bank 30, 50; World Trade Organization (WTO) 33, 139, 141, 146–7
China build-up 34–5, 45–63, 99–103, 250–1
"China model" 21, 27, 254, 265n20
"China threat theory" *(zhongguo weixie lun)* 249
China–Japan relationship and territorial issues 95, 261–2
China–North Korea relationship 112–27, 193
China's Energy Conditions and Policies 163
China's Policies and Actions for Addressing Climate Change 163
China–South Korea relationship 73, 76–8, 114, 116, 120, 159, 161, 190, 257
China–Soviet relationship 26–7, 30
China–Taiwan relationship 4, 34, 45, 93–9, 106n44, 208
China–US 1982 Arms Sale Communiqué 4

China–US relationship 3-Cs principle 9, 58–61; anti-Americanism 233, 249, 259–60; arms control and disarmament 100–3; arms race and foreign policy 99–102; balance of power 3, 4, 12, 45–63, 252; competitive dynamics 5; conflict 1–9, 25–8; containment 76; contemporary relationship 25, 36–7, 167–70; convergence versus divergence and approaches to nuclear crisis 115–27; cooperation 1–3, 7–8; cooperation agreements 171; cooperation and shared issues re: Soviet Union 27–9; crisis management communications mechanisms 2, 3, 11, 25, 225–9, 232–5, 242n23; cultural differences 258–60; dialogue and implications 181–98; differences in approach to North Korean nuclear crisis 120–3; diplomacy and regional energy initiatives 165; diplomacy disputes and maritime security 77–8; dispute over US arms sales to Taiwan 96–9; disputes and diplomacy 115–27, 248; dual leadership structure 9, 45–63, 254; dyad 13; economic interdependence 254; economic relations cooperation 136–43; economic relations tensions 143–7; energy relations 1, 3, 5–6, 10, 157–73; environment 4, 7, 8; EP-3 incident compensation 234; evolution 255–8; forecasts 196–8; foreign policy strategy 59–8, 79–81, 82; future obstacles 3, 260–3; G2 concept and global leadership 2, 45, 148–9; global war on terror (GWOT) 25, 32, 35, 140, 238; hegemony 252; historical comparative perspective 1, 8–9; history 25–37; intellectual property rights (IPR) agreements 139; investments 6, 8, 33–4, 137, 166; leadership role 45, 55–8; "low politics" issues 4; military relations and territorial disputes 11, 76–8; military training 216, 223n76; military-to-military relations 204–20, 256; models 253–5; most favored nation (MFN) status 29, 138–40; mutual strategic trust 126–7; new relationship 250; North Korean nuclear crisis 115–27; nuclear weapons test data dispute 208; obstacles 248, 256–8, 266n37; One China Policy 33, 34; political issues versus economic relations 142–3; security strategy 140–1; shared interests 112, 118–19, 123–7, 265n30; solar panels dispute 166–7, 170, 171; structural factors 12, 14n10; surveillance and reconnaissance operations (SRO) 260; systemic differences 258–60; tariffs 141; territorial integrity 45, 95–6, 106n44; themes 11–12; tolerance of Taiwan 2, 94; trade disputes 2, 5, 137–47; trade imbalance 140–4; transition of power 45–63; US anti-China legislation 141, 145; US arms sales to Taiwan 9, 29–30, 33–4, 89–90, *91*, 91–104, 205–6, 210; US capacity for energy diplomacy 168–9; US economic power versus China *55*; US energy diplomacy capacity 168–9; US influence in Asia-Pacific Region (APR) 68–9; US leverage 80–1; US media independence 261, 266n38; US perception of China 249; US re-engagement in Asia-Pacific Region (APR) 191, 193, 195, 196; US strategy to Chinese build up 78–83, 94; USS *Kitty Hawk* encounter (2006) 210–11, 226–35

Chinese Communist Party National Security Committee 7

Chinese embassy bombing 31, 209, 225, 226, 256, 260

Chinese Energy Research Institute (ERI) 159

Chinese National Development and Reform Commission (NDRC) 160

Choe Ryong-hae 121

Christensen, Thomas 187

civil rights activists 194–5

clean energy 161–2, 166–7

climate change 7, 163, 169

Clinton, Bill: constructive engagement 185, 266n38; diplomacy North Korea 119; human rights 4, 30–1, 139–40, 188; military-to-military relations 207–9; "Three Noes" 31

Clinton, Hillary: capacity for energy diplomacy 168–9; cooperation 256; dialogue and tension 190–1; diplomacy 72, 77, 78, 92, 93, 102, 119; economic versus strategic track 190; soft power versus smart power 57; strategic bipolarity 80

Cold War 227, 238–9, 242n14

co-management approach *see* dual leadership structure

competition: conflict and confrontation 58–60; definition 158; dialogue and

Index 273

implications 183; divergence and dialogue 192–3; economic relations 143, 149; energy relations 165–7; energy security 171; military relations 215, 220
competitive dynamics 5
conflict: causes 2–3; versus cooperation 1–7, 12, 25–8, 36–7; crisis management 226–7; intellectual property rights (IPR) 31
Congressional China Caucus 189
Congressional dialogues 183, 187–9, 196, 208
constructive engagement 188–9, 195, 196, 266n38
constructivists 2
Container Security Initiative 238
containment policy 79–80
contemporary relationship 25, 36–7, 167–70
convergence versus divergence and approach to nuclear crisis 115–27
cooperation: causes 2–3, 11–12; versus competition 251–2; versus conflict 12, 260–3; definition 158; dialogue 186–91, 194–6, 250, 251; economic relations 7–8, 136–43; energy relations 157–62, 170–2; global financial crisis (2008) 147–9, 256; global war on terror (GWOT) 25, 32, 35, 140, 238; history (1972–1989) 28–30; intelligence sharing 91; joint military exercises 218, 219, 235–8; military relations 211, 218, 225–6; military-to-military exchange program 235–8; most favored nation (MFN) status 207; obstacles 256–8; shared threats 26–8; strategic discourse 79; strategic partnership 185; technology transfer 161, 162, 170–1; weapons of mass destruction (WMD) North Korea 32–3
Coordinating Committee for Multilateral Export Controls (COCOM) 206, 221n11
coordination and cooperation 48, 49, 58–60
core national interests 69–71, 79, 83n7, 114, 123, 240, 250, 252
counter-terrorism *see* global war on terror (GWOT)
Cox Report 208
crisis encounters: communications mechanisms 225–41; comparative analysis of EP-3 incident and USS *Kitty Hawk* encounter (2006) 226–35;

cooperation versus competition 251–2; historical background 226–7
crisis escalation 253
crisis management: Chinese view 241n3
crisis management communication mechanisms: Cold War 227, 242n14; EP-3 incident (2001) 3, 225, 226, 228–9; factors for change 235–8; high level dialogues 230; initial communication 229–32; overview 228–9; post-crisis behavior 235; reforms 239–41; resolution 232–4; security framework restructuring 238; USS *Kitty Hawk* encounter (2006) 226, 228–9, 242n23
crisis management structures 227
Cuban Missile Crisis 238–9, 242n14
Cui Tiankai 70, 195, 197–8
cultural differences 214–16, 219, 222n68, 248, 258–60
curator mentality 102, 107n80
Currency Exchange Rate Oversight Reform Act (2010) 141
currency policy 6, 25, 33–4, 141, 144–5
cyber warfare 6, 240–1

Dai Bingguo 190
Dalai Lama 6, 58, 78–9, 190, 256
decision-making 230, 258, 264n16
Defense Policy Consultative Talks (DPCT) 211
Democratic People's Republic of North Korea *see* North Korea (Democratic People's Republic of North Korea – DPRK)
democratization 93, 240, 255, 259, 261
Dempsey, Martin 212, 218
Deng Xiaoping 96, 97, 98, 159, 205, 252
denuclearization 10, 32–3, 112–22, 123, 127, 227, 257
developing countries 7, 52
dialog policy instruments 10–11, 12, 183, 262
dialogue: "26 specific outcomes" 190; accommodation 196–8; background 184–5; Congressional 183, 187–9; cooperation 194–6, 250, 251; dialog policy instruments "tool kit" 183; divergence and competition 183, 192–3; forecasts 183–4; foreign policy 189–93; high-level 92, 182–3, 186–7, 190–2, 197, 205–6, 211–13, 230, 236–7; implications 181–98; maritime cooperation 237–8; military relations

dialogue *continued*
  183, 225–41; military-to-military exchange program 257; motives 181–2; multilateral 72–5, 112–13, 208–9; role and engagement 191–8; scope in 2014 197–8; secret 182, 184–5; specialist participants 198n3, 200n49; tensions 186, 188, 190–1, 193
Diaoyu/Senkaku Islands 5, 25, 68, 70, 73, 261
disputes and diplomacy 115–27, 188, 248; *see also* maritime security; territorial issues
distrust: military relations 214–15, 253; mutual distrust 183, 219, 262; sources 262–3; *see also* mutual strategic trust
domestic politics 2–3, 10, 12, 138, 144, 196
Donilon, Tom 250
Dougherty, James 49
Du Ruiqing 249
dual leadership structure 45–63

East Asia Strategy Review 79
East Asia Summit (EAS) 164–5
East Asian energy initiatives 163
East Asian energy regimes 158–9
East Asian Summit 5
East Asian Summit Energy Cooperation Task Force 164–5
East China Sea (ECS) and territorial issues 5, 68, 70, 159, 193
economic cooperation: Asia-Pacific Region (APR) 61–3; senior dialogues 186–7; trade and investment policy 6, 8, 10, 33–4, 136–43
economic growth and transition of power 45–63
economic interdependence 254
economic relations: background 138–43; Congressional opinion 196; currency policy 141, 144–5; intellectual property rights (IPR) 139, 141, 145–6; versus political issues 142–3; tensions 143–7, 149; trade deficit 141, 143–4
economic stimulus 94, 103, 147
economic versus security dichotomy 46, 49
economic versus strategic track 190
emerging leadership role 49–55
energy diplomacy 167–73, 251
energy initiatives 159, 163, 169
energy regime complex 159, 164–5, 171
energy relations 1, 3, 5–6, 10, 157–71

energy security 157, 160–3, 166–8, 171–3, 251
EP-3 incident (2001) 3, 221n40, 225, 226–35, 256
European Union 48
exclusive economic zone (EEZ) 5, 76–7, 217, 229–30, 263

Fallon, William 228, 235, 236
Fan Changlong 250
Fang Fenghui 218
financial crisis (2008) *see* global financial crisis (2008)
First Solar Decathlon China 170
fishing bans 70
Five-Country Energy Ministerial 161, 168, 171
Fleischer, Ari 231
Flournoy, Michelle 211
Forbes, Randy 189
Ford, Gerald 29
foreign direct investment (FDI) 25, 52, 54, *54, 55*, 137, 139
foreign policy: belief systems and self-image 249; China and decision-making 264n18; China and evolving policies 69–71; China and low profile policy (*taoguang yanghui*) 75–6; China and new relationship 250; China and "three prongs of sovereignty" 261; US and Asia-Pacific Region (APR) 185; US Congressional opinion 196; US containment policy 76, 79–80; US dialogue and implications 184; US and North Korean nuclear crisis 115–27; US and soft power diplomacy versus smart power 57; US strategy to Chinese build-up 78–81, 102–3
foreign reserves *51, 52, 55*
free trade agreements (FTAs) 52, 141–2
frictions *see* tensions

G2 concept 45–6, 80, 148–9
Garrison, Jean 184
Gates, Robert 73, 75, 119, 183, 191, 237
Geithner, Timothy 190
Germany 47
global energy governance 172, 251
global financial crisis (2008) 35, 45, 46, 48, 51, 52, 62, 137, 142, 143, 147–9, 240
global leadership 148–9
Global Shale Gas Initiative 169
global war on terror (GWOT) 25, 32, 35, 140, 186, 238

"going out" strategy and oil supply 158
"good neighbor policy" (*mulin zhengce*) 69
Graham, Lindsey 141
gross domestic product (GDP): China 49–51, 71, 140; global military expenditures *55*; top 10 world economies *50*; US 140
Gulf of Aden 158, 218
Gutierrez, Carlos 141

Hagel, Chuck 183
Harding, Harry 13
He Yafei 253, 262
hedge and emerging power 79–81
hegemony: Chinese perception of US 75, 233, 249, 252, 253–4; offensive realists 266n37; regional hegemony 59, 79, 80–1, 83, 216, 217, 263
Helvey, David 93
high-level dialogue 92, 182–3, 186–7, 190–2, 197, 205–6, 211–13, 230, 236–7
historical perspective of China–US relationship 1, 8–9, 25–37
Hong Kong and Chinese human rights policy 6
Hong Kong Closer Economic Partnership Arrangement (CEPA) 52
Hormats, Robert 62
Hu Jintao 117, 157, 161, 168, 189, 190, 191, 204, 211, 265n33
human rights 4, 6, 30–1, 139–40, 181, 183, 185

ideology: 3-Cs principle 254; China model 21, 27, 265n20
imbalance of power *see* balance of power
Indonesia 73–4
industrial espionage 25
industrial policy 7, 140, 143, 145–7
influence: American influence in Asia-Pacific Region (APR) 5, 68–9, 72–5, 77, 78, 119; American perception of Chinese influence 46, **46**; perceived influence 48; soft power diplomacy versus smart power 57–8, 82
information sources 26
Inoyue, Daniel 189
intellectual property rights (IPR) 6, 31, 34, 139, 141, 145–6
International Atomic Energy Agency (IAEA) 115
International Energy Agency (IEA) 158

International Monetary Fund (IMF) 46
international relations theory 59, 100, 136, 260
international trade 52, *53*, 54–5, *55*
Internet politics 258–9
Iran 7–8

Japan 47, 73, 95, 141–2, 261–2
Jiang Zemin 4, 28, 31, 102, 117, 208–9, 266n38
Jing Yu 232
Joint Commission on Commerce and Trade (JCCT) 186
Joint Commission on Science and Technology 186
Joint Defense Conversion Commission 207
Joint Economic Committee of the US Treasury Department 186
joint military exercises 73, 218, 219, 237–8, 263

Kagan Robert 47
Kerry, John 197
Kim Jong-il 115, 117, 119
Kim Jong-un 115, 121
Kirk, Mark 189
Kirk, Ron 141
Kissinger, Henry 62, 95, 96, 184
Kitty Hawk see USS *Kitty Hawk* encounter (2006)
Korean War 27, 113

Lampton, David 230
Larsen, Rick 189
Lawrence Berkeley Laboratory 159
leadership structure *see* dual leadership structure
Leap Day Agreement 119–20
Lee Myung-bak 122
Lee Teng-Hui 31–2, 208
leverage 69, 80–1, 114, 120–1, 124, 126, 148
Li Jianguo 121
Li Yuanchao 121
Liang Guanglie 212
liberal theory 12
Lieberman, Joseph 231
Lieberthal, Kenneth 192, 255, 265n33
Limited Test Ban Treaty (1963) 242n14
linkage policy 31, 187–9
liquified natural gas (LNG) exports 170
Locke, Gary 97
"low politics" issues 4

Ma Ying-jeou 101, 103, 194, 211, 214
MacArthur, General Douglas 94
Malacca Strait 71, 157–8, 171
Mann, James 254–5, 259
Manzullo, Donald 188–9
Mao Zedong 28, 77, 113, 181
maritime security: military cooperation 218, 223n74, 235–8, 266n37; parallelism 158; sea lines of communication (SLOC) 157–8, 160, 166; territorial issues 5, 9, 68–9, 70–8, 82–3, 83n7, 159, 193; *see also* disputes and diplomacy
Market Access Memorandum of Understanding (MOU) 139
McCain, John 74
McNamara, Robert 238–9
Mead, Russell 81, 82
Mearsheimer, John 59, 253–4
media and Chinese youth 259–60
media independence 261, 266n38
Memorandum of Understanding (MOU) 169
military build-up 68, 102–3, 192
military capabilities 4, 34–5, 215, 217, 219
military cooperation: definition 204–5; high-level dialogue 183, 194, 205, 206; shared security cooperation 28–30
military exercises *see* joint military exercises
military expenditures 55
military imbalance 101
Military Maritime Consultative Agreement (MMCA) 205, 209, 212
military measures by US re: China build-up 191
military, political leadership and 45, 55–8
military student exchanges 218
military-to-military exchange program 234–7, 252, 257
military-to-military relations: competition 220; cooperation 211, 218; crisis encounters 225–41; cultural differences 214–15, 222n68; forecasts 219–20; high-level dialogue 213; history 205–12; joint exercises 218, 219; leadership role 55, 56, 56–8, 59, 72–5; mechanisms and policies 218; negative factors 212–15, 263; new dynamics and reciprocity 215–18, 223n74; new dynamics and transparency 215–16, 223n74; "new kind of military power relationship" 222n61; as "political football" 212–13; principles 212; purpose 204–5;

recommendations 218; strategies 218; tensions 11, 76–8, 206–7, 211–14, 218, 219; "three obstacles" 219, 223n77, 262–3
military training 216, 223n76, 263
Minxin Pei 230
missile crisis: Cold War 238–9, 242n14; Taiwan Strait 208, 213–14
mistrust *see* distrust
modernization versus ideology 149, 254
most favored nation (MFN) status 29, 30–1, 137–40, 207
mulin zhengce ("good neighbor policy") 69
Mullen, Michael 77–8, 157–8
multilateral dialogues 72–5, 112–13, 208–9
multilateral institutions 62, 251
multipolarity 50, 80–1
Mulvenon, James 230, 237
mutual strategic trust: cultural differences 214–15; military relations 197–8, 212, 216–17, 236–7; regional stability 126–7; trust building 194–6, 257–8
mutual suspicion 216–17, 219, 253

Nabors, Robert 93
Nathan, Andrew 249
National Defense Authorization Act (NDAA 2000) 208, 217, 218, 219, 223n77, 262
national defense university (NDU) 215–16, 263
national interests 259
National Security Council 237
National Security Strategy of the United States of America 140–1
National Unification Council 34
National Unification Guidelines 34
nationalism 264n18
natural security apparatus reforms 237–8, 252
navy-to-navy relationship *see* military-to-military exchange program
negative leadership principles 58–60
"new kind of military power relationship" 222n61, 250, 253
new regional order and shared interests 59–60
Nixon, Richard 1, 25, 28, 181, 184, 187
Normalization Communiqué (1979) 29
North Atlantic Treaty Organization (NATO) 91
North Korea (Democratic People's

Republic of North Korea - DPRK): bilateral cooperation 3, 7, 9–10, 25, 30, 32–3, 35; Chinese diplomacy 114–18, 120–5; destabilizing effects 124–5, 191; missile testing 193; nuclear crisis 112–18, 120–3; US diplomacy 4, 119–20, 211
nuclear brinkmanship 114–15
nuclear crisis 10, 32–3, 112–22, 123, 127, 227, 257
Nuclear Security Center of Excellence 8
nuclear tests 112–22, 242n14
Nye, Joseph 79

Obama, Barack: dialogue 13, 14n10, 78–9, 93, 189–93; economic policy 141–3; G2 concept 148; military-to-military relations 211–12, 225; North Korean nuclear crisis 119, 120, 123–4; re-engagement in Asia-Pacific Region (APR) 73–4, 195, 196; summit conferences 72, 77, 123–4, 212, 240, 250
obstacles *see* cultural differences
offensive realists 59, 253, 260, 262, 266n37; *see also* realist theory
oil resources 71, 157, 165, 251
O'Leary, Hazel 159–60
One China Policy 33, 34
online piracy 146
opinion *see* public opinion

Paal, Doug 230
Panetta, Leon 183
parallelism 158, 162–5, 172
Paulson, Henry 186
"peak oil theory" 165
People's Republic of China (PRC) *see* China
Perkinson, Michael 234, 236, 238, 241n1
permanent normal trade relations (PNTR) 139–40
Perry, William 207
Pfaltzgraff, Robert 49
Philippines 75
pivot *see* balance of power
PLAN Song class submarine *see* USS *Kitty Hawk* encounter (2006)
Politburo Standing Committee 230
political influence *see* influence
Powell, Colin 231, 233
power imbalance *see* balance of power
power transition theory 4, 45, 47–9, 59, 253–4

presidents *see* individual names
Proliferation Security Initiative (PSI) 114
public opinion 57, 100, 103, 118, 182, 185, 188, 196, 264n18
public–private partnerships 160, 169–70
Pye, Lucien 248, 256

Qi Jianguo 261–2
Qian Lihua 236
Qian Qichen 116

Rama, Ali 62
Reagan, Ronald 29, 35, 184, 206–7
realist theory 2, 12, 32, 45, 82, 122, 136–7, 227, 252; *see also* offensive realists
rebalance of power *see* balance of power
reciprocity 214–16, 223n74, 265n33
re-engagement in Asia-Pacific Region (APR) 191, 192–3, 195, 196
Regional Comprehensive Economic Partnership (RCEP) 5, 142
regional economic power 52, 54, *54*
regional energy initiatives 165
regional hegemony 80
regional security 123–7, 257
regionalism 62, 142
Republic of China (ROC) *see* Taiwan
Rim of the Pacific (RIMPAC) exercises 218
rising power versus superpower 2, 248, 260
Ros-Lehtinen, Ileana 90
Ross, Robert 249
Roughead, Gary 232
Rumsfeld, Donald 72–3, 74–5, 183, 209–10
Ryukyu kingdom 261

sanctions 6, 7–8, 13, 30, 112, 118, 122, 123, 126, 159
Saunders, Stephen 228
Schiffer, Michael 212
Schlesinger, James 159
Schumer, Charles 141
sea lines of communication (SLOC) 157–8, 160, 166
secret dialogues 182, 184–5
securitization of energy *see* energy security
security issues 4–5, 8–9, 12, 49, 89–104, 227, 238, 242n23
self-image 248–9
senior dialogues 92, 182–3, 186–7, 190–2, 197, 205–6, 211–13, 230, 236–7
shale gas technology 161, 165–6, 169–70

Shambaugh, David 193
Shanghai Communiqué (1972) 98, 226
Shanghai Cooperation Organization 56
shared threats 26–30, 36–7
Shen Guofang 117
shifting balance of power *see* balance of power
Sino-American relationship *see* China–US relationship
Sino-DPRK Treaty (1961) 124
Sino-Indian Border War (1962) 27
Sino-Soviet Treaty of Friendship, Alliance, and Mutual Assistance (1950) 26–7
Six-Party Talks (6PT) 7, 32–3, 35, 49, 59, 60, 112–13, 117, 211
Skelton, Ike 189, 237
Slocombe, Walter 208
Snowden, Edward 6, 240–1
Snyder, Scott 121
soft power diplomacy versus smart power 57–8, 82
solar energy panels 166–7, 170, 171
Solyndra 166
South China Sea (SCS): exclusive economic zone (EEZ) 5, 76–7; territorial disputes 25, 68, 70, 72–5, 83n7, 159, 193
South Korea 73, 76–8, 114, 116, 120, 159, 161, 190, 257
sovereignty and Chinese core national interests 69–71, 82–3, 261
Soviet Union 27–9, 106n45
Soviet–US relations: Cold War 238–9, 242n14; economic interdependence 254; MIG aircraft crisis 229, 242n30
stability 123–7, 158, 160
Stanton, William 93
State Planning Commission (SPC) 159, 174n18
state–society relations 260, 264n18
Steinberg, James 70
Stevens, Ted 189
Strategic and Economic Dialogue *see* US–China Strategic and Economic Dialogue (S&ED)
strategic bipolarity 80
strategic discourse 79–81
strategic mutual trust *see* mutual strategic trust
strategic petroleum reserves (SPRs) 161
strategic track versus economic track 190
strategic trust *see* mutual strategic trust
strategies for cooperation 147–9, 218, 257
structural factors 12, 14n10

submarine encounters *see* USS *Kitty Hawk* encounter (2006)
Sunnylands Obama–Xi Summit 123–4, 212, 240, 250
Suntech 166–7
superpower versus rising power 2, 248, 260
surveillance and reconnaissance operations (SRO) 217, 218, 225, 260, 263; *see also* EP-3 incident (2001); USS *Kitty Hawk* encounter (2006)
suspicion *see* mutual suspicion
Swaine, Michael 226–7
systemic differences in China–US relationship 258–60

Taiwan: arms sales 9, 29–30, 33, 89–90, 91, 91–104; elections 194, 210; foreign policy and China 93–6; model of democracy 93; non-NATO ally 91; Normalization Communiqué (1979) 29, 96; post-normalization period 92, 96; public opinion polls and support for unification with China 100–1; tensions within China–US relationship 28–30, 31, 33–4, 39n28, 94–9, 194, 205–6, 213–14, 219; US relationship 4, 27, 33–4, 89–94, 96; World Health Organization (WHO) 92
Taiwan Enabling Act 104n3
Taiwan Foundation for Democracy 104n1
Taiwan Policy Act (TPA) 99, 101–2
Taiwan Policy Review (1994) 91
Taiwan Relations Act (TRA) 29, 89, 93, 104n3, 187, 205–6
Taiwan Strait arms buildup perceptions 99–103
Taiwan Strait Crisis (1995/1996) 1, 25, 27, 31–2, 208
Tang Jiaxuan 116
tariffs 141, 145, 166–7
technology transfer 161, 162, 164, 170–1
telecommunications standards 146
Ten Year Framework (TYF) 169, 171, 172
tensions: Chinese embassy bombing 31, 209, 225, 256, 260; dialogue 186, 188, 190–1, 193; economic relations 143–7, 149; military relations 186, 206–8, 211–14, 219, 223n77, 260–3
territorial issues 69–78, 82–3, 95–6, 261–2; *see also* disputes and diplomacy; maritime security
terrorism *see* global war on terror (GWOT)
"the Islands" *see* Diaoyu/Senkaku Islands

"theory of China's energy responsibility" 168
Thompson, Fred 94–5
Thompson, James C. 102, 107n80
"Three Noes" 31, 39n28
"three obstacles to military relations" 217, 218, 219, 223n77, 262–3
Tiananmen crackdown (1989) 25, 30, 138, 139, 159, 181, 183, 185, 207
Tibet 6, 27
Tkacik, John 90
trade: foreign direct investment (FDI) 137; foreign reserves *51*, *55*; gross domestic product (GDP) 49–50, *50*, 51, *55*, 71, 140; intellectual property rights (IPR) protection 34; investment policy 6, 8, 30, 33–4
Trade and Investment Framework Agreement (TIFA) 92
trade deficit 33–4, 141, 143–4
trade disputes 2, 5, 6, 28–9, 137–47, 166–7, 171
trade imbalance 140–4
trade liberalization 149, 162, 193
trade sanctions *see* sanctions
trade surplus 166
transition of power 45–63
Trans-Pacific Partnership (TPP) 62, 92, 141–2, 170, 193
transparency 214–16, 223n74, 240–1, 258
Trina 166
trust building *see* mutual strategic trust

Unconventional Gas Technical Engagement Program (UGTEP) 169
United Kingdom 47, 106n44
United Nations Security Council (UNSC) 27, 30, 35, 112
United States: arms sales to Taiwan 93–4, 99–102; Congressional opinion of China 196, 208; debt *51*; decision-making and curator mentality 107n80; domestic politics 10, 144, 196; economic stimulus 94, 103, 147; energy security 162–3; exports 170; global financial crisis (2008) 45, 46, 48, 142; imports of solar panels 166–7; influence 72–5; military relationships 55, 56, *56*, 72–5, 76, 94; partisanship and foreign policy 188; power transition in history 47; re-engagement in Asia-Pacific Region (APR) 191, 192–3; security framework restructuring 238; security policy 89–94; self-image 248–9; *see also* China–US relationship
United States Agency for International Development (USAID) 163
United States Trade Representative (USTR) 141, 146
US–Asia-Pacific Comprehensive Energy Partnership (USACEP) 164–5
US-centric information sources 26
US–China Clean Energy Forum 172
US–China Clean Energy Research Center 8
US–China Congressional Working Group 189
US–China Defense Consultative Talks (DCTs) 209
US–China Energy Cooperation Act 162
US–China Energy Policy Dialogue 161
US–China Energy Summit 172
US–China Joint Commission on Commerce and Trade (JCCT) 141, 197
US–China Joint Communiqué (1982) 90, 94, 98
US–China Joint Statement on Energy Security Cooperation 169
US–China Oil and Gas Industry Forum (OGIF) 160, 161, 169–70
US–China relationship *see* China–US relationship
US–China Renewable Energy Partnership 172
US–China Strategic and Economic Dialogue (S&ED) 8, 49, 145, 161, 172, 181, 186–7, 190, 197, 240, 257
US–China Summit (2011) 191
US–China Ten Year Energy and Environment Cooperation Framework 161
US Department of Commerce 166, 206, 221n11
US Department of Defense (DOD) 91, 102, 183, 204, 206, 231, 234, 262
US Department of Energy (DOE) 159–62
US House of Representatives Inter-Parliamentary Exchange 188–9
US International Trade Commission 145
US National Security Agency 91
US Priority Watch List 145
US Senate US-China Inter-Parliamentary Exchange 189
US Treasury securities *51*
US–Japan defense treaty 5
US–Korea Free Trade Agreement (2011) 73

US–North Korea relationship 119–20
US–ROC Mutual Defense Treaty (1954) 96
USS *Impeccable* 225, 239
USS *Kitty Hawk* encounter (2006): comparative analysis of EP-3 incident 226–35; crisis management communications mechanisms 11, 210–11, 225–6, 232–5, 239, 242n23
US–Soviet relationship 205, 229, 242n30, 254
US–Taiwan relationship *see* Taiwan

Vietnam 27, 72–3, 74–5, 107n80

Wal-Mart 52
Wang Jianwei 198n1
Wang Jiarui 121
Wang Jisi 192, 262
Wang Qishan 190
Wang Wei 229, 230, 231, 233
weapons of mass destruction (WMD) 7, 9–10, 25, 30, 112–18, 238; *see also* nuclear crisis
Weinberger, Caspar 206
Wen Ho Lee 208
Wen Jiabao 77, 148
Wilder, Dennis 187

World Bank 30, 50
world economic activity and Asia-Pacific Region (APR) 46, **46**, *50*, *53*
World Health Organization (WHO) 92
World Trade Organization (WTO) 6, 31, 33, 34, 137–41, 146–7
Wu Xinbo 232
Wu Yi 186

Xi Jinping 13, 61, 97, 121, 123–4, 191, 237, 240, 250, 257–8, 265n33
Xia Liping 160
Xu Xiaojie 165

Yang, Dr. Andrew 91, 92
Yang Jiechi 93, 160, 197, 225, 229
Yang Yi 98
Yanlin, Tan 165–6
Yingli 166–7

Zhang Guobao 161
Zhang Jianxin 168
Zhang Zhijun 97
Zhou Enlai 96
Zhu Chenghu 219, 223n77
Zhu Feng 70
Zhu Rongji 138
Zoellick, Robert 149, 161